AMERICAN AND CATHOLIC

Books by Robert Leckie

American and Catholic
Warfare
Ordained
The Wars of America
Challenge for the Pacific
These Are My Heroes
With Fire and Sword
(edited with Quention Reynolds)
Strong Men Armed
Conflict
The March to Glory
Marines!
Lord, What a Family!
Helmet for My Pillow

For Younger Readers

The War in Korea
The Story of World War II
The Story of World War I
The Story of Football
The Battle for Iwo Jima
Great American Battles
Stormy Voyage
Keeper Play!
The Big Game

ROBERT LECKIE

American and Catholic

1970

DOUBLEDAY & COMPANY, INC.

GARDEN CITY, NEW YORK

Grateful acknowledgment is made to the following for their
permission to use copyrighted material:
America Press for material from *Religion and American Democracy* (America Press, 1949), pages 30–31.
Doubleday & Company, Inc., for an excerpt from *The Catholic Experience* by Andrew M. Greeley. Copyright © 1967
by Andrew M. Greeley. Used by permission of Doubleday
& Company, Inc.

To
Helen Regan O'Brien
1924–1970
She Had Five Children
She Lived,
She Laughed and She Loved
the Lord

Acknowledgments

My gratitude is expressed to the following persons who were of assistance to me in one way or another during the writing of this book:

John Cardinal Cody, Archbishop of Chicago.
Richard Cardinal Cushing, Archbishop of Boston.
Patrick Cardinal O'Boyle, Archbishop of Washington, D.C.
The late Joseph Cardinal Ritter, Archbishop of St. Louis.
Most Reverend Carl J. Alter, Archbishop of Cincinnati.
Most Reverend Philip M. Hannan, Archbishop of New Orleans.
Most Reverend Robert E. Lucey, Archbishop of San Antonio.
Most Reverend Henry J. O'Brien, Archbishop of Hartford.
Most Reverend Paul Schulte, Archbishop of Indianapolis.
Most Reverend Lawrence B. Casey, Bishop of Paterson.
Monsignor Joseph W. Baker, Director, Office for Ecumenical Affairs, Archdiocese of St. Louis.
Monsignor Henry C. Bezou, Pastor, Our Lady Star of the Sea, New Orleans.
Monsignor William J. Mullen, Secretary to the Archbishop, Archdiocese of Hartford.
Monsignor John M. Oesterreicher, Director of Research, Institute for Judeo-Christian Studies, Seton Hall University, South Orange, N.J.
Monsignor William J. Sherzer, Director, Sacred Heart Seminary, Archdiocese of Detroit.
Monsignor Cornelius B. Sweeney, Chancellor, Archdiocese of Indianapolis.

Reverend John T. Catoir, Presiding Judge, Diocesan Tribunal, Diocese of Paterson.

Reverend Bernard Doyon, O.M.I., Instructor in History, Oblate College of the Southwest, San Antonio.

Reverend William D. Driscoll, History Department, Seton Hall University.

Reverend Charles R. Meyer, Librarian, Feehan Memorial Library, St. Mary of the Lake Seminary, Mundelein, Ill.

Reverend Arthur A. Weiss, S.J., Theology Department, St. Peter's College, Jersey City, N.J.

Dr. Theodore Tuleja, History Department, St. Peter's College.

My editors, Charles W. Ferguson and Alex Liepa, and Mr. Liepa's assistant, Miss Maud Savage.

The staffs of the New York Public Library, the Johnson Memorial Library at St. Peter's and the Seton Hall University Library.

Finally—yet foremost—my wife, who typed this manuscript, as always, somewhere and somehow in between the manifold cares of being a mother.

Prologue

Nearly four thousand years ago a Semitic patriarch named Abraham led his family from Mesopotamia (modern Iraq) into Palestine, there to settle and to be chosen by the Lord as the founder of a great nation, which, walking before the Almighty and being perfect, would become His people. Thus was born the Jewish race with its unique faith in a single omnipotent God. Because of that faith, the Jews inevitably aroused the hostility of surrounding tribes who worshiped many gods and resented the intrusion of a Chosen People. But the descendants of Abraham multiplied, until, in the time of his grandson, Jacob, whom the Lord God renamed "Israel," a famine forced them into Egypt. There they fell into captivity. It was not until five hundred years after Abraham's covenant with the Lord that Moses was able to lead the Israelites back to Palestine. En route, while passing through Arabia, he gave them the moral code known as the Ten Commandments.

For the next thousand years the Jews dwelt in Palestine, clinging to their belief in one God and their own peculiar relation to Him, while composing those sacred writings which formed the early chapters of the dialogue between God and Israel known as the Old Testament. Meanwhile, they became divided by schism into the kingdoms of Juda and Israel. Neither kingdom, however, was strong enough to withstand the growing military might of neighboring Assyria and Babylon. Israel was destroyed by Assyria and Juda carried into a second captivity in Babylon.

Now, as military prowess began to unify the myriad kingdoms and principalities of the Near East, two great captains entered

Jewish history. The first, Cyrus the Great of Persia, freed the Jews from the Babylonian Captivity; the second, Alexander the Great of Greece, extended to their religion the protection of his arms. However, in the power struggle which erupted upon the death of Alexander, Palestine was conquered by the kings of Syria and then overrun by the rulers of Egypt. Still, the Jewish people kept their faith, in which there had gradually evolved a belief in a heavenly figure called the Messiah who was to restore them to earthly power and lead them to eternal salvation. Because the Jews had been so many places and known so many peoples, this faith was also influenced by the religious legends, traditions and practices of the then-civilized world. One more influence remained: that of Rome.

Toward the end of two thousand years of Jewish history the little Italian republic on the Tiber had emerged as the world's foremost military power. She had conquered Carthage, subjugated the city-states of Greece and made the Mediterranean a Roman lake. In the year 63 B.C., the Roman conqueror Pompey entered the Jewish capital city of Jerusalem. Eventually, the Promised Land became the Roman province of Judea, ruled by Herod, king by grace of Rome, under the watchful eye of a Roman proconsul named Pontius Pilate.

It was the fullness of time. The civilized world lay quiescent in the firm if sometimes brutal grasp of the Roman peace. And here, in this insignificant strip of land between the Mediterranean and the Dead Sea, during the reign of the Emperor Tiberius, a thirty-year-old carpenter named Jesus put himself at the head of twelve followers called the Apostles and presented himself to the people as the Messiah.

Jesus was a sensation. His many miracles were offered as proof that he was not only the Messiah but the very Son of God. "Before Abraham was, I am," he said, and for such seeming blasphemies the Jewish authorities had him arrested and brought before Pontius Pilate.

The Roman proconsul was a weak man. Although he found no evil in Jesus, he nevertheless feared to offend his accusers. He therefore bowed to their wish that Jesus be crucified, and on the eve of the great Jewish feast commemorating the flight from Egypt, Jesus died on the cross.

This, it would seem, was the end of still another of those false Messiahs common to Jewish history. But not so. Two days after Jesus died, his tomb was found empty. The guards whom the Jewish authorities had placed outside the tomb had no explanation. But the followers of Jesus did. They said that Jesus had risen from the dead, as He had promised; they claimed that no less than forty of their number had seen Him or spoken to Him before He ascended into heaven; and they joyfully announced that their leader was indeed the Son of God whom they now called Jesus the Christ, using the Greek word for Messiah. These followers, most of them Jews, came to be called Christians—and they were subjected to harsh persecution by their orthodox Jewish brethren.

Among the persecutors was a man named Saul, who later became one of the Christians, changing his name to Paul. Steeped in knowledge of the Jewish law and scriptures, familiar with both Roman and Greek culture, Paul was a formidable propagandist. He became the Christians' chief theorist, or theologian, and it was he who persuaded the Christians to admit gentiles as well as Jews to their faith. Through Paul's prodigious mission journeys, a good part of the Roman world became Christianized.

Meanwhile, the chief of the Christians had gone to Rome itself. He was a former fisherman whose name had been Simon, until Jesus Christ said to him: "Thou art Peter, rock, and upon this rock I will build my church." Peter, then, was the first of the leaders of the Christian Church who came to be called "Popes." In that same first century (Christians dated all events from the time of the birth of Jesus Christ) a writer named Ignatius of Antioch gave the Christian Church the name "Catholic," the Greek word for general or universal.

Throughout the first three centuries of the Christian era the Christian or Catholic Church was subjected to fearful persecution by the Roman authorities. The charges against the Christians were that they worshiped a common criminal who had been crucified in some outlandish province called Judea and that they denied the existence of the Roman gods. They were blamed for every misfortune. "Let the Tiber overflow its banks," it was said, "and the cry is raised: 'To the lions with the Christians!'" Still, the seeds of Christianity were truly the blood of its martyrs, and the new religion grew stronger.

Its message of eternal life for those who do God's bidding was especially attractive to slaves and all the other wretched unfortunates of the Roman underworld. Gradually, Christianity evolved a theology which was also appealing to intellectuals. It clung to the Jewish doctrines of an omnipotent God who created the world and made man in his image and likeness, that is, with an immortal soul; of Heaven, the abode of God and his angels, and of Hell, the domain of the Devil, the fallen angel Lucifer who had defied God; and of an Original Sin committed when the first man also defied God and thus brought upon himself and all his descendants the judgment of death and an inclination toward evil. What was new in the Christian message came from the accounts of the life of Jesus called the Gospels, and the writings of Paul. One new doctrine was the Trinity, that God was indeed one but was also in some mysterious way united in the three persons of God the Father, the Son (Jesus) and the Holy Spirit (the "comforter" of whom Jesus spoke). Another was the Incarnation which held that in order to redeem man from the effects of Original Sin, God had become man in the person of Jesus Christ. Jesus was thus true God and true man. He had been conceived by the Holy Spirit and born of a Virgin named Mary, and by his Resurrection from the dead he signified that all men would rise, either to share eternal glory with Jesus in Heaven or endure the endless fires of Hell. Judgment of them would be based on how well they had kept the Jewish moral code of the Ten Commandments, and Jesus's single commandment: "Love thy neighbor as thyself."

It was this Christian emphasis on love or charity that so impressed the Romans. Among these admirers was the all-powerful Emperor Constantine. In the year 313, Constantine issued his famous Edict of Milan which granted religious freedom to the Christians. Soon, from being a persecuted faith, Christianity found itself the official religion of the Roman Empire. Constantine, meanwhile, had moved his capital from Rome to the city of Constantinople (modern Istanbul). He asked the Pope to follow, but the Pope stayed in Rome. Eventually, the Popes came into conflict with the patriarchs of Constantinople. Among other differences, the patriarchs refused to acknowledge that the Pope was the supreme head of Christianity. So the branch of Christianity under the patriarch came to be called the Eastern Orthodox Church, and the one under the Pope became the Roman Catholic Church.

It was this Western Christianity or Roman Catholicism which made Western civilization. In her were joined Jewish morality and monotheism, Eastern mysticism, Greek thought, Roman order and her own special message of love. Energized by this belief in the God-Man who had sacrificed his life to redeem the world, the Church preserved learning, reformed morals, converted the barbarians and upheld the law. Out of her womb was born the society called Europe, the mother of America. All this, however, was not done easily. Catholicism did not, as is generally believed, have smooth sailing between the end of the third and the beginning of the sixteenth century. On the contrary, the Church had to battle endlessly against enemies who struck at her from within and without.

The first was the great heresy called Arianism for the Egyptian priest, Arius, who taught it. Arianism denied both the Trinity and the Incarnation. It was far too subtle, however, to state that Jesus Christ was only human, and not divine. Instead it rationalized his divinity by stating that he was a creature more perfect than others—a demigod, perhaps—but still a creature. Such a doctrine had a powerful appeal to men unable to swallow the proposition of the God-Man, and as a result Arianism shook and nearly shattered the Catholic Church. It was a faith-within-a-faith. It had its own organization, its own bishops and priests. It captured the imperial court. It was the faith of the Roman army (one of its bishops baptized the dying Constantine) and it did not disappear for three full centuries.

Next, in the 600s, came Mohammedanism. Here was an amalgam of Jewish and Christian beliefs given a special sexual and emotional cast that proved irresistible to the hot-blooded nomads of the Arabian Desert. Mohammedanism all but destroyed the Eastern Orthodox Church. It swept over Syria, most of Asia Minor, Egypt and North Africa, obliterating all those ancient citadels of Christianity associated with the names of Paul, Augustine and Athanasius. Because the Moslem crescent supplanted the Christian cross in the Holy Land, the Catholic Church organized the counterattacks called the Crusades, which, at first successful, finally degenerated into dishonorable failure. In Spain, the Catholic counterattack was so fiercely resisted that it was not until the eve of the Reformation that Mohammedanism was at last evicted. Meanwhile, the Moslem Turks had conquered Constantinople and there had laid the cornerstone for the Ottoman Empire, which lasted until World War I; and it was not until 1683 that the Moslem tide was turned to the ebb at the gates of Vienna.

Long before Mohammedanism sank into the long sleep from which it may now be awakening, the Catholic culture in Europe had shuddered under two pagan onslaughts from the north and east. First came the irruption of pirates from Scandinavia. Seeking plunder and rapine, they rowed up rivers and estuaries in their long boats to burn towns and sack monasteries. Wherever they sailed, anarchy followed, until at last they were undone by their own disorganization. Next came the slightly better organized Mongol hordes from Asia. Their mounted spearheads pierced the very heart of France, they overran the Hungarian plain and went pounding into Russia until, at last, the Great Khan died and they turned their horses homeward.

By the last half of the twelfth century, the Catholic Church was a highly organized institution. It had, in effect, made the old Roman civil service its own. It was strongly clerical, with a hierarchy stretching from the Pope downward through cardinals, bishops and abbots to simple priests and finally the laity. It had long ago formulated its dogmas in the Nicene Creed and the Apostles' Creed, it had certified the books of the Bible, it had evolved a central rite of worship called the Mass and had specified the divine "helps" by which men were to avail themselves of God's grace in order to obtain salvation. These were the seven sacraments: baptism, which made a man a Christian; penance, through which he confessed his sins to a priest and received forgiveness; Holy Eucharist, by which he received the body and blood of Jesus through bread and wine that the priest, imitating Jesus at the Last Supper, consecrated with the words, "This is my body, This is my blood"; confirmation, an anointing of oil confirming a Christian's faith; matrimony, which joined a man and woman in marriage; holy orders, which conferred priestly powers; and extreme unction, which anointed the dying. On the intellectual side the Church had invented the university and begun to erect its cathedrals. Augustine had already "baptized" Greek thought by adapting Plato to Christianity and in another millennium Thomas Aquinas would do the same to Aristotle. Meanwhile, the Church was firmly in alliance, if not in control of, the civil rulers. Against this all-powerful, all-pervasive Church, then, there came a powerful new heresy which struck not only at the soul of Catholicism but at the very heart of society.

This was Albigensianism, so called from the city of Albi in southern France. Actually, Albigensianism was a derivative of mankind's immemorial attempt to divide the world into good and evil, spirit and matter. Matter being evil, the body was bad and the worst sin was to reproduce. Therefore, the Perfect among the Albigensians did not marry, did not eat meat or animal products and fasted rigorously. However, the Perfect understood the frailty of human nature and therefore permitted a second class of faithful, called Believers, who needed only to reverence the Perfect and promise to join them sometime before death. Meanwhile, the Believers were permitted every vice, all of which would be forgiven when they joined the Perfect. Should they relapse, however, they would be irretrievably damned. To prevent this, they were frequently killed. Moreover, the Albigensians also denied the sacraments, the authority of the Church and the power of the state to punish crime. Such was the aberration which imperiled not only the Church but society as well, and it was only suppressed through the combination of a Crusade, the efforts of St. Dominic's new order of preachers and the establishment of what was to become the iniquitous institution of the Inquisition.

Now came the high point of medieval Catholicism: the thirteenth century, an intellectual flowering side by side with the sweeter growth of charity and concern for the downtrodden as exemplified in the person of St. Francis of Assisi. In this century, the Papacy reached the height of its temporal power. Under Pope Innocent III it at last overcame the emperors of the Holy Roman Empire, who had for centuries sought to dominate the

Church and make it a mere state agency, as the Eastern Empire
had done to Eastern Orthodoxy.

But Innocent's triumph was too glorious. The fruits of his victory were rotten with the seeds of papal decay. Now was bred
in the Church a spirit of "triumphalism," and in the Papacy a
hunger for temporal power. Moreover, the weakening of imperial
authority invited the encroachments of the rising nationalist kingdoms, and this contributed to a decline in papal authority. The
Pope became dependent upon France and the Papacy became
a French thing. In the fourteenth century, it moved from Rome
to the French city of Avignon, where it became a decadent instrument dependent upon curial taxation and a crass commer-
cialism ending in nepotism. It stayed in Avignon for seventy
years, a scandal to all Christendom, and when it came back home
to Rome, the "cure" of the Avignon sickness became worse than
the disease. This was the Great Schism of the West: two and
then three Popes claiming the Chair of St. Peter, and excommu-
nicating each other. Another forty years had to pass before, in
1417, a single Sovereign Pontiff ruled Catholicism again from
Rome.

By then, however, irreparable damage had been done. Christian men had lived for 110 years in an atmosphere of contempt
for the Papacy. Equally bad, the social structure of Europe had
been racked by the Black Death. Throughout the latter half of
the 1300s, the streets of cities stricken by the plague were strewn
with the blackened bodies of its victims. In some regions, as much
as two-thirds of the population perished. Body, soul and spirit,
the Catholic culture of Europe was truly in travail. All efforts
to reform the Papacy during the following fifteenth century were
of little use. This was the Renaissance Papacy, characterized
by a very real love of learning, especially of the arts; but for all
its Leonardos and Michelangelos and its soaring Gothic, its
beauty was only skin-deep.

There was still much good, much holiness, in the Church—
especially among the people and the various orders—but there
was also an increasing worldliness and a decline in morals. The
spirit of the Word of God was stultified by the letter of Canon
Law. Everywhere the cry was raised, "Reform!" It was heard
loudest from such men as John Hus in Bohemia or John Wy-

cliffe in England. Joining it were the voices of the humanists declaring that the Church had preserved society and learning, yes, but chiefly for the benefit of an elite. Concern for the welfare of the people grew, gathering momentum under the impetus of the new forces of democracy, nationalism and money power which had battened on the weakness of both imperial and papal authority. People now spoke more of freedom than authority.

Some attempts at reform were made by Church councils held throughout the 1400s. But the Papacy eventually backed away from the conciliar movement because it seemed an attempt to place the council above the Pope. Eventually, however, Pope Julius II was all but compelled to call an Ecumenical or World Council at Rome. It lasted from 1512 to 1517 and accomplished very little. Abuses continued to flourish within the Catholic Church, and on October 31, 1517, a German friar named Martin Luther detailed the Church's wrongs in ninety-five theses which he posted on the church door in Wittenberg.

Here was the first breath of the storm that wrecked Christendom. Here was the end of the Middle Ages and the beginning of the Reformation. Between the revolting Luther and Church authorities there was no middle ground. With all the immense vitality at his command, Luther not only strove sincerely for badly needed reforms, but he also advanced a theory which disagreed with the Church on principle. He put his own and thereafter every individual's interpretation of Scriptures above the Church and her tradition. There were other differences—and there would be more—but this was the parting point: private judgment against the authority which the Church claimed to have received from Christ. Seen in retrospect, it is hard to see how there could have been any reconciliation of such mutually contradictory opposites. Unfortunately, both sides misunderstood each other and in harsh, unbending language ascribed to each other the lowest of motives. As the gulf widened, the Reform movement launched by Luther gained the name of Protestantism, after German princes among Luther's followers protested an imperial decree restoring the Mass in those German states where it had been discontinued.

Protestantism spread quickly, but in different forms which again divided and then redivided. Basically, there were four

forms: Lutheranism; Calvinism, based on the theory of predestination taught by the Frenchman, John Calvin; Anglicanism or
Episcopalianism, an Anglicized form of Catholicism arising from
the Papacy's refusal to grant a divorce to King Henry VIII of
England; and the Baptist-Independents professing a radical fundamentalism with strong emphasis on the Bible. In one way or
another, the new sects picked and chose from the body of Catholic belief; some retained one or two of the sacraments, usually
baptism and Communion, others rejected all seven; some worshiped at formal rites using vestments, candles and various other
Catholic "sacramentals," others were content with bare walls,
hymns and a sermon—or even, as with the Quakers, silence. In
general, Protestantism was to reject the Mass; to deny the supremacy of the Papacy; to insist that the Reformation had restored Christianity to its purer, primitive form, while Catholicism
remained caught in a tangle of rank, ritual and doctrinal subtlety
chiefly of its own devising; and to lay down the three divisive
principles that (1) the Bible gave sufficient instruction about
God and salvation, (2) that man could be saved by faith alone,
and (3) that there existed a universal priesthood of all believing
Christians.

To this charge that the Reformers stayed inside the Church
while Catholicism fell out of it, the Catholics were to reply, in
effect, "We were here first." Catholicism described itself as the
original and only true form of Christianity without which there
could have been no Protestantism. Centuries later, G. K. Chesterton defined this position with the observation that it was hardly
correct to suggest that a violent storm had blown Windsor
Castle loose from some of its shingles.

Nevertheless, the gulf widened; and for Catholicism one fortunate effect of the Reformation was that its impact brought
about the Council of Trent (1545–1547). At Trent was begun
the Catholic reform. Its decrees reached into every phase of
Catholic life: the education of priests, the life of religious orders, preaching, pastoral organization, instruction of the young,
missions, art, culture, mysticism and the care of the sick and poor.
Out of Trent issued that host of preachers, scholars, missionaries,
mystics and organizers which, led by St. Ignatius Loyola and
the Jesuits whom he founded, was to launch the Catholic

Counter-Reformation. That, of course, was to be the long-term mistake of Trent. It had convened, not so much to renew or restore the Church, but to combat Protestantism. The Reformation was to be checked, lost territory was to be reconquered and new lands gained. Trent drew up a plan of campaign, and it was highly successful. Not only did the faithful "dig in," to hold what remained, but the spearheads of the Counter-Reformation swept through Germany and France and penetrated as far east as China and Japan. So successful were the Jesuit counterstrokes in Germany that the end result was the catastrophe of the Thirty Years' War.

This ghastly struggle began as a conflict between Germans, but it soon drew in most of the kingdoms of western Europe. It was particularly vicious because to religious issues were joined those motives of personal greed and political ambition which, in the end, became paramount. Thus, the great Swedish captain, Gustavus Adolphus, a devout Protestant, fought in the employ of Cardinal Richelieu of France as that Prince of the Church sought to weaken the power of the Catholic emperor. After the Thirty Years' War ended in 1648, the division of Christianity was fixed.

Northern Europe and England (excepting Ireland) was Protestant, and the south of Europe was Catholic. The Protestant powers tended toward individual freedom, parliaments and an aristocracy based on money power, the Catholic ones toward authority, monarchy and the old hierarchy of altar and throne. This was the situation coinciding roughly with the dawn of American history, if this is to be taken as the founding of the colony at Jamestown in 1607 and at Plymouth thirteen years later.

But a good century before American history began, twenty-five years before the Reformation, a Catholic named Christopher Columbus discovered the New World.

Chapter I

The history of the Catholic Church in America may be compared to the story of a man who finds himself a stranger in his own home. Here is the oldest institution in American annals, with a story which runs concurrent with the history of the New World and continues unbroken down to the present day; yet, here also is the Church which has spent most of those forty-six decades struggling to escape the stigma of "foreigner" while fighting to demonstrate her loyalty to those American ideals that spring from her very own teaching on the dignity of the individual and the equality of all. Thus, an alien in the very land which her sons were first to discover, explore and evangelize, the Church has also, in effect, been compelled to bring suit to establish title to her own intellectual patrimony.

This is not to suggest that the goods of the so-called American way of life all spring from Catholic culture, for the slightest acquaintance with American history would show the absurdity of such a claim. As Cardinal Newman said of English literature, so may it be said of American society: that it has in the main been Protestant. Nevertheless, its origins were Catholic.

Whichever European was here first, he was a Catholic. If it was the improbable St. Brendan, it need hardly be said that a seagoing Irish monk of the sixth century was an orthodox son of the Church. If it was Leif Ericsson, as seems likely, then Leif was also a Catholic—as were the Norsemen who accompanied him, as well as Bishop Eric of Greenland who followed in 1112. Christopher Columbus, of course, was a devout Catholic of an especially appealing sort: all irascible ego and full of faults, he never lost faith or despaired of forgiveness. Catholic also was the vain

Amerigo Vespucci, who never reached these shores, yet gave his name to all the Americas. So was Isabella, in whose service Columbus sailed, and all those simple sailors who sang each day to the Virgin; including the fleet's "interpreter," a converted Jew named Luis de Torres.

In Puritan New England the name Cabot was and still is a distinguished one; but the first Cabots, father and son, were Catholics from Italy who sailed in England's service and gave her kings their rather tenuous claim to American soil. A Dutch-employed Pole named John Skolnow is also said to have reached Labrador in 1367, a Frenchman named Jean Cousin is supposed to have been beached on Brazil a dozen years later; and though they have left no name for history to preserve, it is likely that Breton and Basque fishermen may have fished the Newfoundland banks, going ashore to dry their catch, or that any number of European seafarers may have been blown this way—never, of course, to return to tell about it. Whoever they were, one thing is certain: they were all Catholics, because the unity of Western Christendom had to await the advent of the sixteenth century before it, too, made shipwreck.

There were no priests with Columbus, but in 1493 the New World's first bishop came out to Haiti. Although a Spanish subject, Bernard Boyl was of Irish extraction, and it may be said that even in its infancy the American Church was already top-heavy with those Irish prelates who remain to this day both the inspiration and the irritation of her millions of adherents. Bishop Boyl's first church was consecrated on the Feast of the Epiphany, 1494. By then, the first Mass must have been said in the New World.

It was not until 1513, however, that the American mainland was reached. On Easter Sunday (Pascua Florida), Ponce de León came ashore on the vast peninsula he named Tierra Florida. That same year, Balboa crossed the isthmus to look upon the vast Pacific from his "peak in Darien." Now was begun that glorious period of discovery and exploration that is irrevocably associated with the names of Catholics. In the south, Ponce de León, who was *not* seeking the Fountain of Youth, returned to Florida in 1521 to take possession for Spain and was mortally wounded by Indians. Two years before, Alvárez de Pineda came upon the mouth of the Mississippi and named it the River of the Holy Ghost. In 1541, de Soto crossed the Mississippi to explore the Southwest, coming back in 1542 to die on the great river's banks and to be buried in her waters to prevent the Indians from mutilating his body. That same year, the seeds of the American Church were nourished by the blood of her first martyr: Father Juan de Padilla, murdered by Indians on the Kansas plain. And to the northeast, Vásquez de Ayllón visited the Cape Fear district in 1521, and in 1526 he settled on the Chesapeake. Eighty-one years before the first settlement of English Protestants was made at nearby Jamestown, Holy Mass was celebrated among Ayllón's six hundred settlers on the Chesapeake. Their colony did not last, however, and within another year it was abandoned.

Not so St. Augustine in Florida, the oldest settlement in North America, which Pedro Menéndez founded in 1565, and at which today the Mass is still celebrated and the sacraments administered. So also survived Santa Fe—the City of the Holy Faith— the oldest capital city in the United States. It was founded around 1605 by that very Juan de Oñate whose great gift to the United States was a Southwest populated by domesticated cattle and horses. Today's Texas longhorns are descended from the cattle Oñate turned loose, and his horses are the ancestors of the wild mustang.

Out across the southern rim of what is now the United States, from Florida to California, flowed the Spanish Catholic tide— rolling farther and farther south until by 1600 all of coastal South America and much of the interior had been conquered. They did not only conquer, these *conquistadores;* they did not only advance, these *adelantados;* they organized and civilized their vast new empire. They brought not only firearms and steel, but the high arts of Europe. More than that, they brought Christianity. True, the love of gold was never far from the Spaniard's heart, but closer still was the love of God and the Catholic Church. Columbus himself had taken thought of the peoples of what he believed would be India and "the manner in which may be undertaken their conversion to our Holy Faith. . . ." When Vásquez de Ayllón sailed to the Chesapeake his instructions from Charles V were: "Whereas our principle intent in the discovery of new lands is that the inhabitants and natives thereof who are without the knowledge of faith may be brought to understand the truths of our holy Catholic faith, and that they may come to the knowledge thereof and become Christians and be saved, this is the chief motive you are to bear and hold in this affair, and to this end it is proper that religious persons should accompany you."

Paramount though the religious motive might be, the friars had far from a free hand in the New World. They wished to convert and civilize the Indians whom the conquistadors often wished to exploit and enslave; and because of the extremely close union of the Spanish Church and state, there was almost unending conflict between the political and ecclesiastical arms of the empire. The friars, of course, were not always in the right. A priest who believes he has God on his side can often be a most unreasonable critic of an administrator, who is, after all, only trying to enrich his master, the king. Still, the friars were fired by a deep compassion for the Indians and it was because of the protests of Father Bartholmew de las Casas that Pope Paul III in 1537 declared: "The said Indians and all other people who may later be discovered by Christians, are by no means to be deprived of their liberty or the possession of property, even though they be outside the faith of Jesus Christ." If it is too much to suggest that this protest and admonition place a priest and a pope in the position of being the first advocates of racial justice in America, it is nevertheless true that it was chiefly because of the efforts of the Catholic Church that the Indians under Spanish rule were not destroyed and dispossessed.

On the contrary, here and in South America they were converted by the millions. Where possible, they were organized in peaceful pueblos by Jesuit and Franciscan missionaries, many of whom were gifted scholars who had sacrificed the comfort of the universities to come to the New World. These were the Emperor Charles's "religious persons," and they taught the Indian men to plant, build and tend cattle, while instructing the women in sewing, cooking, spinning and weaving. Theirs were the missions that the American historian Herbert Eugene Bolton described as "a force which made for the preservation of the Indians, as opposed to their destruction, so characteristic of the Anglo-American frontier." For two more centuries they continued in this way, until they were destroyed by a secularizing Mexican government and then left to the tender mercies of the Yankee settlers and gold miners who followed in the wake of American victory in the Mexican War.

All of their labors may seem to have been in vain, but to men dedicated to the God who died ignominiously on the cross and who celebrate martyred comrades with a Te Deum, success is measured with another yardstick. And of the temporal glory of the Spanish conquest, the historian Samuel Eliot Morison has said: "Our forebears in Virginia and New England, the pathfinders of the Great West, and the French pioneers of Canada, were indeed stout fellows; but their exploits scarcely compare with those of brown-robed Spanish friars and armored conquistadors who hacked their way through solid jungle, across endless plains, and over snowy passes of the Andes, to fulfill dreams of glory and conversion; and for whom reality proved even greater than the dream." Finally, the American nation which was born nearly three centuries after Spain discovered the New World, became the chief heir to the Spanish legacy. Americans of California and the Southwest are proud of a "mission" style of architecture as distinctive and as apposite as the white colonial of New England or the red brick of Virginia, and as the American Catholic historian John Tracy Ellis has observed: "This old Christian civilization of the borderlands endured far beyond the age of Spanish greatness, and when the Americans arrived in those areas in the mid-nineteenth century, it afforded a link entirely absent from the plains and valleys to the north, with which to bind the old with the new order. It was facts such as these that Herbert Ingram Priestly had in mind when he said, 'It is of prime importance to the life of America today that the first white men to settle on these western shores were Spaniards and Roman Catholics, representatives of a powerful nation that was the citadel of a united faith.'"

After the Spaniards came the French, and they also were Catholics. As early as 1524, King Francis I sent the Italian navigator Verrazano to explore the North Atlantic coast, and ten years later the doughty Jacques Cartier entered and named the St. Lawrence River, sailing up that mighty stream as far as present-day Montreal. More than the Spaniards, the French were the true explorers of North America. The limitations of sailing ships and horses had confined the Spaniards to the rim of the continent, but the unfettered French penetrated its interior. On foot following the forest trails or paddling along the silent primeval rivers in bobbing birchbark cockleshells, they traversed the lake-and-water chain linking the St. Lawrence to the Hudson; they broke out into the Great Lakes and into the Illinois country beyond; they reached the Rockies; they descended the Mississippi to its mouth, cleaving a continent in two. Their names are immemorial and commonplace: Cartier, Champlain, Joliet and Père Marquette, Duluth and La Salle and Hennepin, to name the most illustrious, and after them in a swelling, anonymous flood, came those curious, dedicated and energetic missionaries, those Capuchins, Recollects, diocesan clergy and especially those black-robed sons of Loyola of whom Bancroft has written: "Not a cape was turned, or a river entered, but a Jesuit led the way."

More than the Spanish again, the French seemed to understand that the key to America was not in its coasts, but in its mighty forests and fertile plains, in its intricate network of rivers. So they built a chain of forts and trading posts stretching from Quebec to New Orleans, and when they had done this, they seemed to have blocked the westward movement of the struggling little cluster of English colonies on the Atlantic seaboard and to have checked Spanish ambition in the east. And because they also understood the Indians, neither forcibly converting them like the Spanish or eventually attempting to exterminate them like the English, but treating them like brothers, it would have appeared that the destiny of America was to be French—and Catholic. It is possible that this French penchant for exploration and fortification, together with their more humane approach to the Indians, might have sprung from a basic economic difference among the three colonizing powers. The Spanish, seeking gold, wanted the labor of the Indians as much as their salvation; the English, wishing to settle, cared chiefly for Indian land and little for their souls; but the French, looking for wealth in furs, needed the Indian hunters as commercial partners and Indian warriors as allies—in a word, as equals.

Whatever the reason, on the political side the French set themselves to charm the savages; and on the spiritual, their missionaries proposed to convert them by adapting themselves to the
red man's primitive way of life. To do so meant a life of appalling
hardship and intellectual degradation for these polished products
of what was then the highest civilization of the age, and yet, they
accepted it willingly, even eagerly, so ardent was their desire to
serve and to suffer in the cause of Christ and his Virgin Mother.
They were a noble and dedicated band, these Black Robes, and
no one seems to have appreciated and understood them better
than the Protestant historian Francis Parkman. Although far from
being in sympathy with the objectives of Jesuits such as Père
Marquette, Parkman could nevertheless write of him:

He was a devout votary of the Virgin Mary, who, imaged to his mind
in shapes of the most transcendent loveliness with which the pencil of
human genius has ever informed the canvas, was to him the object of
an adoration not unmingled with a sentiment of chivalrous devotion.
The longings of a sensitive heart, divorced from earth, sought solace
in the skies. A subtile element of romance was blended with the fervor
of his worship,* and hung like an illumined cloud over the harsh and
hard realities of his daily lot. Kindled by the smile of his celestial mis-
tress, his gentle and noble nature knew no fear. For her he burned to
dare and to suffer, discover new lands and conquer new realms to her
sway.

Idealists and visionaries that they were, the Black Robes were
nevertheless practical men. They realized that the Indians they
sought to convert were among the most mulish and perverse
savages in the world. They were men of noble bearing and great
courage, true, whose oratory had a movingly simple dignity encountered nowhere else on the globe and whose language was,
as one astonished Jesuit father wrote, "richer than the French
in its complex shades of meaning"; but the Indian was nonetheless a savage, a dirty, crafty savage whose high qualities were
all but obscured by his brutal sexuality, his obscenity, his cruelty
and his nature-worshiping superstition which led him to believe
that he must do whatever his *manitou* or *oki* (spirit) had sug-

* Like many non-Catholic writers before and since, Parkman confused Catholic
"veneration" of Mary and the saints with the "worship" which is given to God
alone.

gested to him in his dreams. Jean de Brebeuf, whom Parkman called "the lion of the Huron missions," understood the Indians well, and it is from his famous "instruction" to aspiring missionaries that one learns most of what the Black Robes had to endure among the savages. He wrote:

The Fathers and Brethren whom God shall call to the Holy Mission of the Hurons ought to exercise careful foresight in regard to all the hardships, annoyances, and perils that must be encountered in making this journey, in order to be prepared betimes for all emergencies that may arise.

You must have sincere affection for the Savages,—looking upon them as ransomed by the blood of the son of God, and as our brethren with whom we are to pass the rest of our lives.

To conciliate the Savages, you must be careful never to make them wait for you in embarking.

You must provide yourself with a tinder box or with a burning mirror, or with both, to furnish them fire in the daytime to light their pipes, and in the evening when they have to encamp; these little services win their hearts.

You should try to eat their sagamité or salmagundi in the way they prepare it, although it may be dirty, half-cooked, and very tasteless. As to the other numerous things which may be unpleasant, they must be endured for the love of God, without saying anything or appearing to notice them.

It is well at first to take everything they offer, although you may not be able to eat it all; for, when one becomes somewhat accustomed to it, there is not too much.

You must try and eat at daybreak unless you can take your meal with you in the canoe; for the day is very long, if you have to pass it without eating. The Barbarians eat only at Sunrise and Sunset, when they are on their journeys.

You must be prompt in embarking and disembarking; and tuck up your gowns so that they will not get wet, and so that you will not carry either water or sand into the canoe. To be properly dressed, you must have your feet and legs bare; while crossing the rapids, you can wear your shoes, and in the long portages, even your leggings.

You must so conduct yourself as not to be at all troublesome to even one of these Barbarians.

It is not well to ask many questions, nor should you yield to your desire to learn the language and to make observations on the way; this may be carried too far. You must relieve those in your canoe of this annoyance, especially as you cannot profit much by it during the work. Silence is a good equipment at such a time.

You must bear with their imperfections without saying a word, yes, even without seeming to notice them. Even if it be necessary to criticise anything, it must be done modestly, and with words and signs which evince love and not aversion. In short, you must try to be, and to appear, always cheerful.

Each one should be provided with half a gross of awls, two or three dozen little knives, called jambettes (pocket-knives), a hundred fish-hooks, with some beads of plain and colored glass, with which to buy fish or other articles when the tribes meet each other, so as to feast the Savages; and it would be well to say to them in the beginning, "Here is something with which to buy fish." Each one will try, at the portages, to carry some little thing, according to his strength; however little one carries, it greatly pleases the Savages, if it be only a kettle.

You must not be ceremonious with the Savages, but accept the comforts they offer you, such as a good place in the cabin. The greatest conveniences are attended with very great inconvenience, and these ceremonies offend them.

Be careful not to annoy anyone in the canoe with your hat; it would be better to take your nightcap. There is no impropriety among the Savages.

Do not undertake anything unless you desire to continue it; for example, do not begin to paddle unless you are inclined to continue paddling. Take from the start the place in the canoe that you wish to keep; do not lend them your garments, unless you are willing to surrender them during the whole journey. It is easier to refuse at first than to ask them back, to change, or to desist afterwards.

Finally, understand that the Savages will retain the same opinion of you in their own country that they will have formed on the way; and one who has passed for an irritable and troublesome person will have considerable difficulty afterwards in removing this opinion. You have to do not only with those of your own canoe, but also (if it must be so stated) with all those of the country; you meet some to-day and others to-morrow, who do not fail to inquire, from those who brought you, what sort of man you are. It is almost incredible, how they observe and remember even the slightest fault. When you meet the Savages on the way, as you cannot yet greet them with kind words, at least show them a cheerful face, and thus prove that you endure gayly the fatigues of the voyage. You will thus have put to good use the hardships of the way, and already advanced considerably in gaining the affection of the Savages.

This is a lesson which is easy enough to learn, but very difficult to put into practice; for, leaving a highly civilized community, you fall into the hands of barbarous people who care little for your Philosophy or your Theology. All the fine qualities which might make you loved and respected in France are like pearls trampled under the feet of swine, or rather of mules, which utterly despise you when they see that you are not as good pack animals as they are. If you go naked, and carry the load of a horse upon your back, as they do, then you would be wise according to their doctrine, and would be recognized as a great man, otherwise not. Jesus Christ is our true greatness; it is He alone and His cross that should be sought in running after these people, for, if you strive for anything else, you will find naught but bodily and spiritual affliction. But having found Jesus Christ in His Cross, you have found the roses in the thorns, sweetness in bitterness, all in nothing.

As much as French manners must have recoiled from such brutality, or French stomachs turned over at such food (sagamité, a "mush" made of pounded Indian corn boiled with scraps of fish, was compared by Chaumonot to wallpaper paste), nothing so frustrated or depressed them as Indian indifference and duplicity in matters of faith. Because an oral rather than a written language had compelled them to develop good memories, the Indians easily memorized their catechism. Believing it, however, still less acting upon it, was quite a different thing. "If only they believed as easily as they are convinced!" wailed Isaac Jogues. Moreover, the Indians very quickly tired of theological discussions (which they seldom understood) and resented being instructed in moral principles. Once, when Brebeuf was preaching to a council on the obligation to obey God and the perils of offending Him, a chief called out angrily: "What sort of men are these? They are always saying the same thing, and repeating the same words a hundred times. They are never done with telling us about their *Oki,* and what he demands and what he forbids, and Paradise and Hell."

True enough, the French missionaries did make many converts; but in more cases than they cared to admit, an Indian embracing Christianity would consider his baptism to be no more than a spell to ward off disease or death. Moreover, it was not an easy thing for an Indian to give up either the pleasures of polygamy or the delights of torturing a captive. He had no reply to friends who warned him that he would go bald or become a bad shot as a result of renouncing the ways of his fathers, and too often, to the never-ending despair of the missionaries, he considered the Black Robes to be no more than a sophisticated counterpart of his own shaggy, capering medicine man; that is, another sorcerer who also made magic and muttered incantations. Because of this, the missionaries were frequently blamed for pestilence or crop failure; and the infuriated Indians sometimes would threaten to burn the Black Robes alive unless they removed their spell. Still, the fathers persevered, and they did have their triumphs. One of them was Kateri (Catherine) Tekatwitha, an ascetic and mystic girl who became know as "the Lily of the Mohawks," and whose cause for beatification is still at Rome. Kateri's mother had been a Christian Algonquin, although the child herself was unbaptized when, orphaned by the death of her parents, she went to live with her aunt and uncle in a Mohawk village. Apparently her relatives treated her roughly because of her seemingly obstinate refusal to marry, and thus, in the Iroquois tradition, add the hunting and fighting skills of a young brave to the family circle. Kateri, however, had always been shocked by the public sexuality of the crowded Iroquois huts—where as many as five families dwelt openly together—and she was also horrified by the Iroquois custom of publicly torturing captives. On the advice of a Jesuit, she escaped to a village of Christian Indians near La Prairie, and there, as a young maiden still in her late teens, she took a vow of virginity and lived a life of piety and devotion which ended with her death in 1680 at the age of twenty-four. Since then, miracles have been attributed to her, and both the American and Canadian Churches have petitioned Rome that she be beatified, that is, called "blessed." In the little church near Montreal where her bones are preserved, the people still sing the Mass responses in Iroquois, perhaps the first instance of a vernacular liturgy in Church history.

In the main, however, the conversions were among women and children; and once a boy grew to manhood, the chances were good that he would slide back into his father's habits of magic and devil worship. Worse, he, too, would probably become a cannibal. Although most of the histories taught in American

schools and colleges generally ignore or glide over Indian can-
nibalism, the fact is that some of them, especially the savages of
the northeastern forests, were man-eaters of a particularly disgusting voracity. "In a word," Father Vimont wrote of the Iroquois in *The Jesuit Relations*, "they ate men with as much appetite and more pleasure than hunters eat a boar or a stag."

Much as the missionaries loathed the practice and strove to
stop it, the Indians persisted in it—even after they were converted. At the Mission of St. Joseph in 1638, the Hurons there
tortured a hundred Iroquois captives to death and then slung
the cooking kettles to boil their bodies for a feast. When the
Jesuits protested, the Indians derisively tossed them a human
hand as an invitation to the banquet. Their horror increased by
the knowledge that the man who was being eaten had been
baptized before his death, the missionaries took the grisly taunt
and buried it at a solemn mass of requiem.

Such was a missionary's life among the "friendly" Hurons and
Algonquins, and yet, it was a veritable honeymoon in comparison to the treatment which the Black Robes were to receive at
the hands of the Iroquois—the Indian of Indians, and the most
cruel and ferocious of red men. By a dreadful stroke of irony,
no less a Frenchman than Samuel Champlain, the father of New
France, had kindled the hatred of the Iroquois against his
countrymen. In 1609, Champlain became the ally of the Hurons
and Algonquins in their war against the Five Nations, as the
Iroquois were also known; and when he killed an Iroquois chief
and wounded two others on the shores of the lovely lake that
bears his name, Champlain emplanted in the Iroquois heart a
horrid ache for revenge. When it was eventually taken, it was
frightful; and some of its chief victims were those Black Robes
for whom the Five Nations reserved a special enmity.

Encouraged in their hatred of the Jesuits by Dutch traders at
Fort Orange (now Albany), who instilled in them a superstitious
dread of the sign of the cross, the Iroquois became the scourge
of the French missions. Isaac Jogues, one of their first captives
in their opening forays, lived to describe their fiendish knives,
although he did not survive his second sojourn among them.
Another victim who survived was Father Joseph Bressani, an
Italian Jesuit born in Rome who volunteered for the Canadian

missions. In the spring of 1644 he set out on a mission to the Hurons, but his party was captured by Iroquois. Months later, his superior received a letter, which began:

"I do not know if your Paternity will recognize the handwriting of one whom you once knew so well. The letter is soiled and ill-written because the writer has only one finger of his right hand entire, and cannot prevent the blood from his wounds, which are still open, from staining the paper. His ink is gunpowder mixed with water, and his table is the earth."

Thereafter Bressani described an ordeal which seems to have been typical of Iroquois victims. It began with the quartering, roasting and eating of one of his Indian converts before his eyes. Turning to the priest himself, the Indians began the sport by slowly splitting his hand with a knife between the little and ring fingers. Then they beat him with sticks until he was covered with blood. Next, to amuse a crowd of four hundred Iroquois, he was placed atop a torture scaffold, where he was stripped naked and forced to sing. Perhaps here, also, although Bressani does not say so, the children burnt the soles of his feet through the crevices of the scaffold floor, as was customary. But the young Iroquois (they were Mohawks) did order him to dance, jabbing him with sharpened sticks and pulling hairs from his head and beard. "Sing!" ordered one, while another shouted: "Hold your tongue!" Whomever he disobeyed, of course, burned him with a firebrand. "I will eat one of your hands," one child would scream, and another, "I will eat one of your feet."

So it went for a full week. Every night, a chief went through the village crying: "Come, my children, come and caress our prisoners!" And the torture would recommence. Bressani would be stripped again, burned with live coals and hot stones, forced to walk on hot coals. Now a fingernail would be burned off, now a knuckle; now a thumb would be slowly severed—usually with a clam shell because it was more painful—now a fingertip would be crushed to the bone between human teeth. Never were the Iroquois extravagant with their torture. Always they reserved a little human endurance for another night, careful not to endanger the source of so much pleasure. At about two o'clock each morning, after the fun had turned boring, Bressani would be left on the ground, fastened to four stakes and covered with a bit of deer skin.

But there were other villages to be entertained, and soon Bressani was forced on an exhausting march of several days' duration to another Iroquois dwelling place. There, the catalogue of horrors was repeated, augmented by such novelties as hanging him by the feet with chains and spreading food for dogs on his naked, quivering flesh so that the hounds might gnaw on him as they ate. At last, Father Bressani was such a ruin that even the Iroquois were revolted by the sight of him. "I could not have believed," he wrote later to his superior, "that a man was so hard to kill."

At length, the Iroquois fed him, assuring him that they were only fattening him for the kill and the kettle. In solemn council, however, they decided to give him to an old woman who had lost a son. She, finding him useless, ransomed him to the Dutch at Fort Orange, those same Dutchmen whose merciful rescue of so many missionaries was in contrast to their anti-Catholic propaganda among the Iroquois. Eventually, although maimed and disfigured for life, Father Bressani recovered his health and made a successful missionary trip to the Hurons.

Few other Iroquois captives were so fortunate, although it must be said, in justice to these savages, that they did not regard their cruelty as wicked. Indeed, its opposite—pity—was a weakness in their eyes. Compassion was considered cowardice. To torture a prisoner in public was to teach the young to become inured to the sight of suffering and bloodshed, to make them stoical. It also gave the captive an opportunity to show by his own stoicism that he was a brave man. At times, a victim's fortitude might so excite Iroquois admiration that they would cease and confer upon him the highest honor: adoption into an Iroquois tribe. This was what happened, in effect, to Isaac Jogues; and this Jesuit saint was again unusual in that he was one of the few Iroquois prisoners ever to escape his captors. Once again it was the merciful Dutch who helped to smuggle him aboard one of their ships bound for France. There, the mangled missionary made his way to the Jesuit house at Rouen, and the Jesuits have preserved the story of his touching meeting with his superior.

"Did you know any of the Fathers there?" the superior asked this ragged wraith from America. "Did you know Father Isaac Jogues?"

"I knew him very well."

"We heard he had been captured by the Iroquois. Is he alive or dead?"

"He is alive. It is he who speaks to you."

And so the bells pealed joyfully in the Jesuit house that night, as they had often pealed before when other travelers from America reported that one of the fathers had won a martyr's crown; and when Isaac Jogues journeyed on to Rome, Pope Urban VIII granted him the rare privilege of saying Mass and consecrating the Host with mutilated hands. "It would be shameful," said Urban, "that a martyr of Christ should not be allowed to drink the Blood of Christ."

Like so many other Black Robes, the indomitable Jogues returned to the missions; and this time, when he fell captive to the Iroquois again, his renewed ordeal of torture did end with a tomahawk in the brain.

The stake and the scalping knife, these were the twin horrors that haunted the dreams of the missionaries. All of them expected it, all of them prepared themselves for it—and none was known to flinch from it. "We shall be taken," wrote Jerome Lalemant, "we shall be burned, we shall be massacred. But that is a trifle. One's bed is not always the best place to die in."

What men! Even the most timid among them, such as the gentle, sickly Charles Garnier, faced their torturers and executioners with a calm courage that amazed their afflictors, sometimes drawing their last, sobbing breath while crawling over the ground to baptize or comfort some other victim of Iroquois revenge. They would submit to anything but an insult to their Master. As Parkman said of Jogues, "a derisive word against his faith would change the lamb into the lion, and the lips that seemed so tame would speak in sharp, bold tones of menace and reproof."

Personal derision, however, meant nothing to the Black Robes. They knew that Christ had been mocked on the cross and they often welcomed it in their own agony. Unfortunately, the Iroquois were masters of the mocking taunt. A captive's unflinching courage, so far from exciting admiration, might provoke them to redoubled ingenuity at the torture stake, while calling forth a biting, bitter wit. In the village where Lalemant and Brebeuf met their end, suffering exquisite refinements of torment which need not be detailed here, a converted Huron who had been adopted by the Iroquois suggested pouring hot water on their heads, because they had poured so much cold water on the heads of others. It was done, and the crowd cried: "We baptize you that you may be happy in Heaven, for nobody can be saved without a good baptism." Enraged when Brebeuf would not flinch, the mob tore strips of flesh from his limbs, devouring them before his eyes while other renegade Hurons called: "You told us that the more one suffers on earth, the happier he is in Heaven. We wish to make you happy. We torment you because we love you, and you ought to thank us for it." In the end, Brebeuf's invincible calm drove them into a fury of torture, ending when the mob tore open his breast to drink that brave blood and a chief ripped out that indomitable heart and ate it. It was Brebeuf who had triumphed, and Parkman wrote his epitaph: "He came of a noble race, the same, it is said, from which sprang the English Earls of Arundel; but never had the mailed barons of his line confronted a fate so appalling, with so prodigious a constancy. To the last he refused to flinch, and 'his death was the astonishment of his murderers.'"

A quarter century after Brebeuf's death in 1649, Iroquois revenge was complete. The Hurons had been crushed, the Algonquins scattered and the dream of the Jesuits utterly destroyed. Coming out to New France, the Black Robes had dedicated themselves to nothing less than the conversion of a continent. They had dreamed of establishing a chain of Indian missions stretching toward the western ocean, of gathering the savages in peaceful villages and there teaching them agriculture and a Christian loathing of violence and bloodshed. It had been the Jesuits' ambition to enrich New France through the fur trade with converted Indians, to help make her so powerful that she would ultimately triumph in the inevitable showdown with the weaker English colonies to the south. But the Iroquois tomahawk had made a bloody nightmare of that dream. A century later, the hatred of European anticlericals seemed to have made an end of the Jesuits themselves. In 1773, one decade after

Britain, not France, had won colonial supremacy in America, Pope Clement XIV yielded to political pressure and ordered the suppression of the Society of Jesus.

Like the first missionaries—like St. Peter and St. Paul—the apostles to the Indians had fought the good fight, they had finished their course. A shining chapter in the glorious history of Christian missions had come to a close in blood and betrayal. Now, the Catholic Church in America was to enter upon a new apostolate. From converting Indians, it would turn to caring for immigrants.

Chapter II

For all its "firsts" in the New World, the Catholic Church in what is now the United States of America had a modest beginning indeed.

It was in every sense "a grain of mustard seed." It entered history much like Christianity itself; a tiny islet trembling in an angry sea of hostility. For even as the orthodox Jews of Jerusalem had persecuted and proscribed that dangerous new heresy of Christ's, so also did the English settlers of the Atlantic seaboard hate and harry this ancient, detestable and discredited creed.

It had indeed been discredited in the England which had been their home. To these grandchildren of the Reformation, nothing was more abhorrent than this "whore of Babylon," as they called the Catholic Church. They despised it with all the fervor which a convert to a new faith may direct against the old one he has abandoned. It was not even Catholicism, but "Popery" or "the Romish harlot." It was a religion full of iniquity and corruption, of idolatry and sacrilege, or whatever other foul epithet the antipapal propaganda of the day might wish to pin upon it. In the England they had known, in which the new faith and the "new men" it had made strove to make their rebellion an accomplished fact, no invective against the Church was too scurrilous to be kept out of print. Martin Luther himself, sharing the conviction that converts among the common people were to be won more with the club of contumely than the rapier of theological debate, had suggested that historians of the Papacy "can bring no higher or more acceptable praise offering to God than all they can say or write against this bloodthirsty, unclean, blasphemic whore of the devil." His recommendation, it appears, was followed. In 1559, a group of Protestant "scholars" published the first of those "histories" of the Church filled with such undying lies as the legend of Pope Joan and the thousands of baby skulls that are to be found, even today, underneath convent cellars.

It was on such fulminate of bigotry that the early English settlers had been suckled; and yet, in fairness to them, it must also be said that even more than they hated Catholicism as a rival and reprobate religion, they feared it as a foreign political power seeking to overthrow the English government. In this, they had good cause. Ever since Henry VIII had placed his country in the Protestant camp, the enemy powers of Catholic Spain and Catholic France had consistently plotted with the papal party in England. Obviously, not only those who had profited from Protestantism but those who sincerely believed in the new faith would surely suffer through any return of Catholicism. And there had been many attempts. The fathers and grandfathers of these American colonists had already trembled for their religion during the brief Catholic restoration under Mary Tudor (the wife of Philip of Spain), they had been infuriated by the excommunication of Elizabeth, they had been frightened again during the periods of French support for the Catholic rebels of Ireland and for Mary Queen of Scots and under the threat of the Spanish Armada. Papal plotting in England had also resulted in the infamous Gunpowder Plot by which the foolish and inept Guy Fawkes, seeking to advance the Catholic cause by blowing up King and Parliament, only succeeded in driving the anti-Catholic spirit indelibly deeper into the nation's heart.

In a word, No-Popery in England was a form of patriotism. Again, it was not "Catholicism" as such that was hated, but "Popery" or "Romanism"—a foreign, fawning, treacherous and decidedly "un-English" thing. A Catholic was usually *ipso facto* a traitor, and a priest always was. Catholics executed in England were never tried for professing their faith but rather on charges of treason. By extension, then, if Catholicism was foreign and anti-English, Protestantism was native and pro-English. From this carefully nourished habit of mind it followed that every blow struck against France and especially Spain was also a blow for Protestantism and against the Papacy. When the struggle for colonial dominion and supremacy of the seas began, the same spirit prevailed. Freebooters such as Drake and Hawkins not only enriched Queen Elizabeth when they robbed Spanish treasure ships or sacked Spanish settlements in the New World, they also served the Protestant cause. As the historian Louis Wright has said:

One particular issue the clergy kept alive. That was the danger to England from Catholic Spain. The Protestant clergy unanimously agreed that Spain must be thwarted in her colonial empire. From the reign of Elizabeth to the end of James's life, and later, the preachers waged an incessant and bitter war against Spain. . . . With the increase of Puritanism, the attack on Spain intensified, and English Puritans on two continents continued an ideological war against Spain. . . . The preservation of the Protestant faith and the English realm depended upon clipping the wings of the Spanish eagle.

They were golden wings, of course, and thus the motives of material gain and national honor were joined to the appeal of religion. Where the new faith had celebrated its martyrs who had ennobled themselves at the stake, it now saluted the new saint who could serve his religion by enriching himself and his king. Such a "call," of course, is merely irresistible. But this is not to say that the Catholics who came to the New World from Spain and France (and the handful from England as well) were not also motivated by dreams of financial gain. Nor does it suggest, granted the mutual intolerance of the age, that an America wholly French or Spanish would not have proscribed Protestantism. However, it does help to explain the ferocious animosity characteristic of what has been called the "Protestant Crusade" in America, and why that hostility should have endured here for nearly four centuries.

By the time the first permanent English settlement was founded at Jamestown in 1607, English Catholicism had been utterly crushed. Elizabeth's Act of Supremacy in 1559 had guaranteed the establishment of English Protestantism, and in the half century intervening between that historic milestone and the Jamestown founding, Roman Catholics had been completely excluded from English public life. To exist at all, the faith had to go underground, where it remained for nearly three dark centuries.

Strangely enough, very few Catholics seem to have sought sanctuary in the New World. It is true that there were Catholics with Sir Humphrey Gilbert when he led England's first—and unsuccessful—colonizing expedition onto the bleak and wintry shores of Newfoundland in 1583; and in 1605 the Catholic lord, Sir Thomas Arundel, met with similar failure. In the main, however, the Catholics stayed home. Catholic overseas colonies—if they would have been permitted at all—were considered too likely to deplete the already dwindling ranks of Catholics at home, they were too uncertain to risk limited Catholic wealth on them, and the opportunity to convert Indians which had so fired French and Spanish imagination had little appeal to people struggling to keep their own faith. So it was the Protestants who colonized English America. Many of them were also fleeing religious persecution, albeit of a milder form imposed by fellow Protestants, but they nevertheless brought with them the post-Reformation Englishman's ingrained, inherited hatred of Catholicism. From the Puritans of Massachusetts Bay to the Anglicans of Virginia, they also disfranchised Catholics and put the ancient creed to the ban.

As appears to be true of all kinds of prejudice, the antipapal spirit was highest where there were no "papists." Priests were threatened with imprisonment or death by Pilgrim Fathers who had probably never seen a chalice or a chasuble. Although not a single Catholic appeared in Massachusetts Bay during the first twenty years of its existence, that did not deter the colony from passing an antipriest law in 1647. In 1629, when the Catholic Sir George Calvert sailed to Virginia seeking a haven for his coreligionists, he was quickly informed that there was no place for Romanists in the Old Dominion.

Doubtless this unpleasant confrontation helped to deepen Calvert's conviction that he must found his own colony. It could not, of course, be purely Catholic. Having been a Protestant himself, Calvert understood the hostility of his former brethren. He had been secretary to Sir Robert Cecil, the chief minister of King James I, and with his father, William, the coauthor of that shrewd and devastating policy by which Romanism was vanquished, not by a bloody pogrom which might sow English soil with the seeds of too many martyrs, but by a deliberate and careful program of financial impoverishment and political and social ostracism. More than a century later, Edmund Burke was to write of a similar system applied in Ireland: "You abhorred it, as I did, for its vicious perfection. For I must do it justice; it was a complete system, full of coherence and consistency, well digested and well composed in all its parts. It was a machine of wise and elaborate contrivance, and as well fitted for the oppression, impoverishment, and degradation of a people, and the debasement, in them, of human nature itself as ever proceeded from the perverted ingenuity of man." George Calvert also began to perceive the injustice in the system, even as he rose rapidly in power and in favor with the king. By 1624, he had become convinced of the truth of Catholic doctrine and announced his conversion to it. By that single courageous act, Calvert slammed the door shut on his own career. Resigning his position as one of the king's secretaries of state, as well as his seat in Parliament, Calvert was prepared to join his coreligionists in impotence and poverty; but to the king's great credit, he retained his former secretary as a member of his Privy Council and raised him to the peerage as Baron of Baltimore.

Almost at once, the new lord began searching for a New World refuge for his new brethren. He had long been interested in colonizing ventures, having been a member of both the Virginia and New England Companies, and having, in 1620, acquired a grant of land in Newfoundland for a colony which he called Avalon. Here, he made his first attempt to introduce religious freedom. Ironically, his colony was resented by the Catholic French, who regarded Calvert as an intruder, as well as by his Protestant countrymen, who objected to his toleration of Popery. Worse than these difficulties was the iron northern winter, and Calvert abandoned Avalon, sailing south in search of milder lands in which to found his colony. It was then, in 1629, that he reached Jamestown, and came up against the hostility of the colonists there. Returning to England, Calvert continued to press King Charles I for a grant of land in which he might establish a sanctuary for persecuted Catholics. In 1632, Charles granted him a huge territory along the Chesapeake to be called Maryland in honor of the king's wife, Queen Henrietta Maria. Two months later, however, the first Baron Baltimore was dead.

Now the grant devolved upon Calvert's oldest son and heir, Cecilius Calvert. At twenty-seven, the second Baron Baltimore found himself proprietor of the most independent colony in America. All the others in existence, and those which were to follow, were ruled by governors appointed by the Crown, but Maryland was to have a governor appointed by the Proprietor, who in his turn was answerable to the Crown. Thus, authority had been placed one extra step away from the ultimate source.

Probably, this was no accident. As a secretary of state, the first Baron Baltimore had had wide experience drawing up charters. His own colony, obviously, was going to need one which would evade the Penal Code against Catholics. To have the Proprietor appoint the colonial governor would help, and Cecilius Calvert did name his brother, Leonard, also a Catholic, to that post. Maryland's charter was also very vague about such things as the freedoms to be granted to Catholics, specifying only that in this matter the colony was to adhere to "the ecclesiastical laws of England," whatever they were. To spell out anything, of course, would only have been to alarm a Puritan Parliament already suspicious of King Charles's well-known "Anglo-Catholicism." Although the second Baron Baltimore was not distinguished by the high-minded integrity which characterized his father, he was also a loyal Catholic, and so he, too, did all in his power to thwart exportation of the Penal Code to Maryland.

One of his first steps was to press his father's invitation to the Society of Jesus to interest itself in the colony. Accordingly, the Jesuits assigned two priests, Fathers Andrew White and John Altham, and one lay brother, Thomas Gervase, to the expedition. They had to join as gentlemen adventurers, like everyone else, inasmuch as there could be no question of government support of Catholic priests. The Protestants in the party were free to choose their own ministers.

Although the free exercise of religion, as well as conversion of the pagan Indians, was never far from Cecilius Calvert's mind as he worked to organize his expedition, the fact was that the second Baron Baltimore was an extremely hardheaded man, a cautious, careful driver of bargains. Having no wish to repeat his father's financial failure at Avalon, he invested very little actual cash in his venture beyond purchase of two ships, the *Ark* and the *Dove*. Gentlemen adventurers to Maryland came at their own expense, and they also paid the expenses of their servants and indentured men. In repayment, they were given additional land. That was how the colony worked: rent for land, and the more settlers the more rents for Baron Baltimore.

Cecilius Calvert had plenty of land: from 10,000,000 to 12,000,000 acres. To his brother, Governor Leonard Calvert, and then members of his family, relatives and friends, he conveyed manors of about 6,000 acres each. Next were some sixty families holding manors of from 1,000 to 3,000 acres apiece. These first few groups supplied the members of the governor's council. The last and most numerous group was the freeholders holding tenements of from less than 100 to 1,000 acres in size. From their ranks were to come the representatives whom the deputy governor would summon to discuss colonial affairs. After them, of course, were the servants and indentured men with no political or social standing, although the indentures could become freeholders once they had discharged an obligation of about five years' service.

Thus, the structure of early Maryland, and to organize it Cecilius Calvert had a much easier task than to bring it into being. Throughout 1633 he was harassed by enemies (his father had made no friends when he blocked Jamestown's expansion southward) seeking to strip him of certain charter rights, by Admiralty demands to inspect his ships and by insidious whispers to the Star Chamber about his intentions to ship Papists aboard the *Ark* and the *Dove*. In fact, both ships were called back to London after they sailed; but they were finally cleared in November of 1633. How his Catholic passengers avoided taking the Oath of Supremacy, by which they would have had to repudiate the Pope and forswear their faith, is not exactly known. It is believed that they either hid themselves aboard ship or came aboard farther down the Channel. At any rate, they were far from being in the majority among the two hundred to three hundred passengers who braved the bleak North Atlantic in that memorable wintry voyage, a fact suggested by Father White's report of a fever epidemic in which "about twelve died, among whom were two Catholics." Catholics were not only out-numbered but also out of standing. Ten days before the ships sailed, Baron Baltimore handed his brother instructions enjoining the Catholics aboard the *Ark* and the *Dove* to be careful "that they suffer no scandal or offence be given to any of the Protestants," and that they hold their own services "as privately as may be," remembering "to be silent upon all occasions of discourse concerning matters of Religion." Baltimore not only sought "unity and peace amongst all the passengers on Shipp-board," but ashore as well, and thus he also gave orders that upon landing the Catholics should immediately make a public oath of allegiance to the king, that when a messenger was sent to Virginia he should be "such a one as is conformable to the Church of England," and that throughout their governance of Maryland "the said Governor and Commissioners [who were all Catholic] treate the Protestants with as much mildness and favor as Justice will permit."

In these famous instructions, then, Cecilius Calvert wrote the blueprint for religious freedom in America. His father had conceived of a colony in which Protestants and Catholics might live side by side in amity, each respecting the rights of the other, and he himself had put it into execution. True as it undoubtedly is that the Calverts were motivated by expediency, that they desperately desired to obtain religious freedom for their persecuted brethren, and that there is no reason to believe that they would have offered it had the Catholic party, rather than the Protestant, been in power, the fact remains that the Maryland colony was tolerant at a time when all others were intolerant, and in this it was unique. As John Tracy Ellis has observed: "Two years before Roger Williams fled the Puritan wrath of Massachusetts Bay to establish religious tolerance in Rhode Island, Baltimore had laid the groundwork for such a policy in Maryland."

That policy was put into effect when, after an arduous four-month voyage, the colonists landed on St. Clement's Island on March 25, 1634. While the Protestants held religious services of their own, the Catholics gathered for their first Mass in the New World, after which, according to Father White: ". . . we took upon our shoulders a great cross, which we had hewn out of a tree, and advancing in order to the appointed place, with the assistance of the Governor and his associates and the other Catholics, we erected a trophy to Christ the Saviour, humbly reciting, on our bended knees, the Litanies of the Sacred Cross with great emotion."

Next, Governor Calvert sought out the neighboring Indians, purchasing about thirty miles of territory from them, including the village which became St. Mary's City, the capital of the new colony. With that, it appeared that the colony's dual mission of providing a haven for religious freedom while ministering to the Indians had been successfully begun, and that Maryland was now embarked upon a peaceful career. This was true enough between the colonists of rival faiths and between them and the Indians, but between the Jesuits and the Lord Proprietor back in England there came to be anything but peace.

Quite understandably, the Jesuits had been zealous in their attempts to convert the Indians, and the red men, in gratitude, had conveyed to them certain lands. Angered at what he considered to be an invasion of his proprietary rights, Baltimore informed the Jesuits that they could neither accept lands nor evangelize the savages without his permission. Naturally enough, the Jesuits resented what they considered to be the Proprietor's interference with their mission in America. Although the quarrel was chiefly over jurisdictional and property rights, the Jesuits were also annoyed by Baltimore's unbending insistence that they pay him quitrents as well as an assessment to build a fort, that their servants discharge a military obligation and that they themselves stand answerable to civil law in temporal matters. In a word, the Jesuits did not like being treated like everyone else. Actually, it would have been impossible for Baltimore to grant them either special status or liberty of action in Maryland. To do so would be to alarm the surrounding Protestant colonies. On his side, however, Calvert was a bit too distrustful of the Jesuits and too jealous of his own prerogatives, and when he sent over secular priests to take over the Jesuits' responsibilities he merely fanned the flames of their resentment. Then, when the secular priests promptly sided with the Jesuits, Calvert lost his proprietary temper.

Naturally, such mutual misunderstanding only served to deepen the dispute until it was finally appealed to Rome. There, the Jesuit General decided in favor of Baron Baltimore, ordering the Jesuits in Maryland to resign all claims to Indian land and to submit to the will of the Proprietor. "I should be sorry indeed," he observed, "to see the first fruits which are so beautifully developing in the Lord, nipped in their growth by the frost of cupidity."

Maryland, meanwhile, appeared to be prospering. The woods were full of game and timber for manorial houses, while the bay was full of fish and ships arriving with goods to exchange for the tobacco which, introduced from neighboring Virginia, had become the colony's staple and its currency. With tobacco, unfortunately, had come the Negro slaves used to work Maryland's expanding plantations. Catholics as well as Protestants, the Jesuit fathers included, depended on slave labor, which rapidly became the colony's economic base. Like the colonies around her, Maryland did not look upon slavery as an evil. Otherwise, she was still trying to be different, still trying to be true to her high ideal of religious freedom. Actually, the Catholics, who held all the top offices from governor on down, bent over backwards to carry out Calvert's admonition to "treate the Protestants with as much mildness and favor as Justice will permit." In 1638, when William Lewis, an overseer at the Jesuit plantation at Saint Inigoes, reprimanded two of his Protestant servants for deliberately reading an anti-Catholic book aloud in his presence, he was quickly brought to trial and convicted of violating the injunction against religious disputes. Here, everyone but the plaintiffs were Catholic, but the sentence was approved by everyone, including Lewis's Jesuit employers. Nor did anyone protest when Lewis was given the stiff fine of five hundred pounds of tobacco. Three years later another Catholic, Thomas Gerard, was convicted of having taken the books and key from the Protestant chapel. Compelled to restore these stolen articles, he was also ordered to pay a fine of five hundred pounds of tobacco toward the support of the first Protestant minister to make use of the chapel.

Again and again, the Catholics in Maryland dissembled before their Protestant brethren. True, the Catholics were in a minority, however dominant, and to abuse their power would have been suicidal. Yet, if their policy was self-serving, it was at the least wise and prudent.

Not nearly as discreet was their benevolent attitude toward the victims of prejudice in the neighboring colonies. To placate Maryland's Protestants was one thing, but to make the colony a haven for Protestants fleeing Protestant persecution elsewhere was quite another. Yet, in 1643, when Samuel Gorton and his followers sought to escape Puritan hostility in Massachusetts Bay, Governor Calvert invited them to Maryland. He did the same to a group of Puritans in Virginia who had brought three of their ministers with them from New England, by that act so inflaming Anglican ire that the Virginia Assembly passed a law against any minister who did not conform to the doctrines of the Church of England. In 1649, a group of three hundred Puritans migrated to Maryland to take up residence along the Severn near present-day Annapolis. By then, however, Governor Calvert's imprudent policy of introducing a Trojan horse into his colony had come an inevitable cropper, and Leonard Calvert was himself dead.

In England at this time the Puritan party had grown both in power and intolerance, so much so that in 1641–1642 eleven Catholic priests were put to death. In August of 1642, civil war erupted between the Puritans and King Charles I, and the Puritan anti-Catholic spirit was quickly reflected in the colonies. One William Claiborne of Virginia, although not a Puritan himself, immediately availed himself of Puritan support in Maryland to settle an old grievance against the Calverts. Claiborne had a claim to Kent Island, now part of the new colony of Maryland, and it was an old and defensible claim indeed. Unfortunately, Claiborne used it as a stick with which to beat the Maryland Catholics. Allying himself with a Puritan pirate named Captain Richard Ingle, he invaded Maryland, compelling Governor Calvert to flee to Virginia and bringing the manorial estates of the Catholics under attack.

From the autumn of 1644 to December, 1646, Claiborne and his Puritans were in complete command in Maryland. In 1645, they seized Fathers White and Copley, put them in chains and shipped them to England to be tried for having entered that country against the law. That they should even have been put on trial was travesty enough, but fortunately the English did accept the Jesuits' plea that they had come against their will, acquitting them and banishing them to the Low Countries. In the meantime, friendly Indian converts helped two other Jesuit priests, Roger Rigbie and John Cooper, to escape to Virginia, where the miserable life they were forced to lead finally killed them a year later.

Now Leonard Calvert fought back. Putting himself at the head of a small army in Virginia, the ousted governor in turn evicted Claiborne and his Puritans and resumed power. The effort, however, was apparently too much for Leonard Calvert, and he died on June 9, 1647. In the following year, his brother decided to placate the Protestants by appointing a Protestant, William Stone, as the second governor, and making three of his five new councilors Protestants. With this, the Jesuits returned to Maryland.

By then, however, it had become most difficult for a Catholic to practice his religion openly in the colony. The Protestants were growing in number, either because of the deceased Calvert's misguided policy of hospitality, or because most of the indentured servants who came over were Protestants who immediately augmented the ranks of non-Catholic freeholders the moment their term of service expired. Moreover, the civil war in England was going badly against King Charles, and Puritan success in England only increased Puritan intolerance in America. When Charles was beheaded in January, 1649 and the Puritan Commonwealth was born, the future for Maryland's frightened little band of Papists appeared forbidding indeed.

At this juncture, to guard against a civil war of religion in his own colony, Baltimore drew up his famous Act of Toleration. On April 21, 1649, Governor Stone introduced it to a mixed assembly in which the Protestants held a slight majority, and it was passed. In part, it declared ". . . that nœ person or psons whatsoever within this Province . . . professing to believe in Jesus Christ, shall from henceforth bee any waies troubled, Molested or discountenanced for or in respect of his or her religion nor in the free exercise thereof. . . ."

The free exercise thereof. . . . It was a phrase that was to go ringing through American history, to be echoed a century and a half later in the First Amendment to the Constitution, the keystone of civil and religious liberty in the United States. True enough, by limiting itself to persons "professing to believe in

Jesus Christ," the Toleration Act appeared to exclude Jews and unbelievers. In fact, however, Jews were not molested in Maryland. Doctor Jacob Lumbrozo, a Jew, lived there at this time and even served as a juryman. And if it is argued, once again, that Baltimore was only trying to protect Catholics against Puritan persecution, the fact is that he did draw up the first formal enactment of this kind and that it was passed at his request by a mixed assembly. There again, the colony of Maryland ruled by a Catholic proprietor was unique.

Calvert's toleration, however, was by its very nature no match for Puritan intolerance. In 1651, with Oliver Cromwell swiftly rising to power in England, the old enemy William Claiborne and Richard Bennet, one of the Puritans to whom Leonard Calvert had granted sanctuary, were named by Cromwell to investigate the allegiance of American colonies. With this as their warrant, they put themselves at the head of a small force of Puritans, invaded Maryland, summoned an assembly from which all Catholics were excluded and repealed the Toleration Act. Now it was Governor Stone who fought back, but his forces were defeated in 1655 at the Battle of the Severn. Although Claiborne had promised quarter to those who surrendered, four of Stone's followers, three of whom were Catholics, were hung—and the priests of Maryland fled again for Virginia, this time taking refuge "in a mean hut, sunk in the ground like a cistern or a tomb."

With the Puritans again in complete control, it appeared that the Catholic and Calvert causes were doomed. Cecilius Calvert, however, had no scruples about making a deal with the fiercely anti-Catholic Oliver Cromwell. A year later, he was confirmed in his privileges. Another Protestant, Josias Fendall, was named Governor of Maryland. But then the colony's affairs turned another somersault: the Assembly which declared itself free of the Proprietor also ousted Fendall, who had been anti-Proprietor himself. Next, in 1658, the death of Cromwell gave the wheel of political fortune another brisk spin which ended in 1660 when King Charles II, son of the beheaded king, ascended the English throne and restored Baltimore's proprietary rights. Immediately, Cecilius Calvert installed his own son, Charles, as governor and instructed him to reinstate the Act of Toleration.

Obviously, religious freedom in Maryland—which is to say the Catholic cause—now depended on the religious convictions of whoever held power in England. Like his father, the new Stuart king was a tolerant man, and as long as he reigned and as long as Charles Calvert continued as Governor of Maryland and then, after his father died in 1675, as the Proprietor, no one in the colony was to suffer for his faith. Unfortunately, however, the third Lord Baltimore was a bit too autocratic for the liberty-loving colonials. Tolerant though he was in religion, he was most unbending in insisting upon his rights, including complete review of the courts and absolute veto over legislation. Although he was the first Lord Baltimore to live in Maryland, he seems to have been insensitive to the spirit of independence which even then was an identifiable American characteristic. The merest hint of democratic sentiment among the settlers brought his lordly stick of authority swinging down hard, and he did not hesitate to beat down opposition by limiting the suffrage or the size of the Assembly itself. Naturally enough, Maryland's largely Protestant population resented their high-handed Catholic Governor, and there were many complaints about being taxed for the benefit of a favored few of a rival and detested faith. Intrigues against Baltimore were hatched by malcontents and denunciatory letters went across the sea to London. Finally, in 1684, Baltimore took ship for England to answer the charges, and also to settle a boundary dispute with Pennsylvania.

That same year Charles II died professing the Catholic faith, and in 1685 his Catholic brother, James II, ascended the throne. Under James, a Catholic bishop named John Leyburn came to London. He was the first Catholic bishop in England for 60 years and the first to function openly in 130 years. It was he who had authority over Catholics in the colonies, and with his arrival it appeared that the ancient faith might also come out into the open. But James II sat on the throne only briefly, fleeing to France in 1688 after his defeat in what the English called the Glorious Revolution. A year later, Parliament proclaimed James's Protestant son-in-law and daughter, William of Orange and the Princess Mary, as the rightful rulers of England. With that, the British crown became a Protestant prerogative, and the period of toleration in Maryland came to a close.

In 1691, King William annulled Baltimore's charter and ordered Maryland to become a royal colony. Among the first acts of the Assembly there was to establish the Church of England as the official religion and to compel every citizen—Puritan as well as Catholic—to pay an annual tax of forty pounds of tobacco to support it. And so, the attempt at religious freedom failed. Under the Barons Baltimore, there had not been a single act of Catholic violence against Protestants, but now the Penal Age had come to this former haven for the persecuted.

Faithfully reflecting the laws of England, which forbade Catholics the right to bear arms, to vote, to argue law, to inherit or own land or even to ride a horse worth more than five pounds, and which made all priests liable to life imprisonment, Maryland also put her Catholics to the ban. They were forbidden to hold public services, denied priests, fined for educating their children as Catholics or for importing Catholic servants, excluded from office, forbidden to vote, denied parental rights, for a time afflicted with double taxation, and finally, after the capital had been transferred from Catholic St. Mary's City to Protestant Annapolis, their old chapel at St. Mary's was demolished to efface the last visible vestiges of Catholicism from the Maryland earth.

Yet, in 1708, the very midnight of the Penal Age in America, a census showed that of Maryland's 34,000 residents—including 4,600 slaves—nearly 3,000 were Catholics. Three decades earlier, they had numbered only 1,670 out of 20,000 settlers. As though to prophesy the history of Catholicism in the United States, Maryland's Catholics had not only kept the faith in the face of persecution, they had also increased and multiplied.

Chapter III

If the grain of mustard seed was continuing to sprout in Maryland, even without the sunlight of religious freedom, it had fallen on barren ground indeed elsewhere in English America.

Virginia and later the Carolinas and Georgia, of course, had flatly excluded Papists from their territory. During the colonial period, few Catholics sought to emigrate to the South. In the North, however, there was a fair-sized influx of Irish, especially during the harsh persecution of the Cromwellian regime in Ireland. Most of these refugees arrived as indentured servants or temporary slaves, and because their faith was also proscribed in New England, they had little or no opportunity to practice it. Moreover, there were no priests to say Mass or to administer the sacraments. Their only alternatives were to conform to the Puritan Protestantism of the region or to go underground, and it appears that most of them chose apostasy, being lost to the Church forever.

They did not entirely escape persecution, however. The famous preacher Cotton Mather has left a record of one Goody Glover, "one of the wild Irish," who was executed as a witch in 1688. According to Mather, she "profest herself a Roman Catholick and could recite her Paternoster in Latin very readily." Perhaps the stern saints of Salem considered familiarity with Latin as evidence of demonic seizure, and poor old Goody's prayer a kind of magical incantation. At any rate, the gallows from which Goody Glover bade her importunate neighbors good-bye must have seemed sufficiently discouraging for any further open confessions of Catholicism in the northernmost colonies.

Catholics might, however, go south to Rhode Island, where

Roger Williams had founded a colony with complete religious freedom. But it would not have been wise, inasmuch as the truculent Williams also hated Popery. He had, it is true, been the first Protestant to preach toleration, but any Catholics aware of his denunciations of "the Romish wolf" bloated on "huge bowls of the blood of the saints," would have been pardoned if they doubted Roger Williams's sincerity. Whatever the reason, during Williams's lifetime there is no record of Catholics availing themselves of his toleration in the way Protestants took advantage of Calvert's.

New York was only a trifle less biased than the northern colonies. The Dutch who settled New Netherland were strict Calvinists who prohibited public worship by anyone other than a member of the Dutch Reformed Church. They were also, as has been seen, possessed of an intensely human ambivalence toward Catholics themselves, encouraging the Iroquois in their bloody enmity toward the Black Robes of New France, yet ransoming or rescuing some of the priests who did fall into their clutches. After 1664, however, the colony became English, named New York after its Proprietor, James, Duke of York, brother of Charles II and later the unfortunate King James II. Two years after James became a Catholic in 1672, he named Major Edmund Andros as governor and instructed him to permit ". . . all persons of what Religion soever, quietly to inhabit within ye precincts of yor jurisdiccon, wthout giveing ym any disturbance or disquiet whatsoever, for or by reason of their differeing opinions in matter of Religion."

The heavy-handed Andros, however, one of the most unpopular governors in American history, ran into open hostility whenever he attempted to name Catholics to official posts, and the anti-Catholic bias was still prevalent when the second governor, Colonel Thomas Dongan, an Irish-born Catholic, arrived in New York in 1683. Under Governor Dongan's direction, the first legislative assembly in New York's history passed a Charter of Liberties and Privileges providing ". . . THAT Noe person or persons, which profess faith in God by Jesus Christ, shall at any time, be any ways molested, punished, disquieted, or called in question for any difference in opinion or matter of religious concernment."

Once again, under Catholic auspices, a broad grant of religious freedom had been made in America. If it was extended only to Christians, the fact is that it is very doubtful if New York's almost wholly Protestant population would have allowed it to embrace Jews and others. Actually, when the Jews in New York City did petition Dongan for the right to trade there and practice their religion, the governor recommended their appeal to the mayor, only to have it refused. Before Dongan did leave office, however, a synagogue was actually erected in New York, two Jews appeared on the rolls of freemen for 1687–1688 and Jews generally were granted the right to engage in wholesale trade. Dongan also welcomed the Huguenots (French Calvinists) who came to New York to escape the persecution of his fellow Catholic, King Louis XIV of France.

Once again, however, tolerance in America depended on tolerance in the mother country. The Glorious Revolution which deposed the Catholic James II and put the Protestant William of Orange in his place ended religious freedom in New York as quickly as it had foreclosed it in Maryland. When news of the revolt reached New York in 1689, a German-born soldier named Jacob Leisler put himself at the head of an anti-Catholic mob, expelled Lieutenant Governor Francis Nicholson from office, abolished the franchise for all Catholics, ordered the arrest of anyone suspected of Popery, and organized a manhunt for Governor Dongan, who only luckily escaped to England. In the meantime, the Jesuit priests in New York fled, abandoning the little chapel and school they had opened, most of them leaving the country, although Father Henry Harrison did steal back from his Maryland hide-out to minister to the proscribed Catholics of the colony.

Although the usurper Leisler was himself executed on a conviction of treason, the bigotry and persecution which he had resurrected in New York was to endure through the American Revolution and on to 1806. With the arrival in 1697 of Richard Coote, Earl of Bellomont, as Governor of New York, Massachusetts and New Hampshire, the few remaining Catholics in the colony along the Hudson realized that the night of the Penal Age was closing around them. If there had been any doubts of whether or not Bellomont shared the anti-Catholic bias of his father, another Richard Coote notorious for his savagery against Catholics in Ireland, he quickly dispelled them by the speed with which he induced New York to impose the death penalty on priests. In fact, it may be said that Bellomont probably cleared the colony of Catholics.

In defense of the English settlers, it must be made clear that much of their hostility sprang from that deep, ingrained conviction that Catholicism was a foreign, anti-English and treacherous thing. Whether or not this fear was baseless is beside the point: the conviction was a psychological fact, and they acted out of it. To these people, it might very well have been that Catholic toleration was no more than a "Popish plot," a smoke screen under cover of which more and more Catholics, that is, potential traitors, would be smuggled into English America. Certainly, the settlers felt uneasy about being caught between two Catholic fires: Spain to the south in Florida, and a most powerful France to the north in Canada. Again and again, parties of French and Indians had scourged the borders of New York and New England. The massacres at Schenectady (1690) and Deerfield (1704) were very fresh in the English memory, and many of the colonists of New York and New England firmly believed that priests were responsible for such atrocities. No fear of Catholics, then, was too irrational; no charge against them was too wild to be doubted. And in such an atmosphere of fear and hatred, it is no wonder that, when no Papist priest could be found to satisfy the frenzy of the mob, one had to be invented or at least trumped up.

This was what happened in New York City in 1741. Because of the partial burning of a chapel in the fort, attributed to some captive Spanish-Catholic Negroes, it was rumored that the Negroes planned to massacre the city's white population. At that moment, a message arrived from Governor Oglethorpe of Georgia warning of Spanish priest-spies who were planning to burn the chief English cities of the north. Looking around for the hidden priests, the frenzied New Yorkers discovered an Anglican minister named John Ury. Although innocent, Ury was suspected because he was a nonjuring clergyman, that is, one who would not take the oath of allegiance to King William, an attitude which was not uncommon among Protestant ministers, particularly Scots Presbyterians. Charged, nevertheless, with being a priest as well as the leader of the Negro "conspiracy," Ury went on trial with the captive black men. All were convicted. Ury was hung, while the Negro "conspirators" were either hung or burned to death. A few years later, an Anglican minister celebrated this triumph over the wiles of Rome by writing: "There is not in New York the least face of popery."

Little trace of Popery was to be found in neighboring New Jersey, either, or in Swedish-founded Delaware farther to the south. These two colonies have very little Catholic history, only entering it as a sometime haven for Catholics fleeing persecution in New York or Maryland, or as an avenue for Catholic migration to tolerant Pennsylvania.

Like Maryland, Pennsylvania was founded by a Proprietor who had felt the whip of religious bigotry. Having been imprisoned more than once for his ardor in the Quaker cause, William Penn well understood the need for toleration, not only for himself and his coreligionists, but for all other Christians as well. Thus, in 1682, when he drew up his Frame of Government for the colony of Pennsylvania, he declared:

That all persons living in this province, who confess the Almighty and eternal God, to be the Creator, Upholder and Ruler of the world; and that hold themselves obliged in conscience to live peacably and justly in civil society, shall, in no ways be molested or prejudiced for their religious persuasion or practice, in matters of faith and worship, nor shall they be compelled at any time, to frequent or maintain any religious worship, place of ministry whatever.

Penn did not thus franchise Catholics out of any fondness for Popery. In fact, he detested the old faith. He did, however, share the conviction of his friend, James, Duke of York, that the consequences of religious intolerance were far more to be feared than the danger of a rival faith flourishing in an atmosphere of religious freedom. To his great credit, he took this stance in the face of the inevitable opposition of Puritanism and Anglicanism, the twin terrors of English Protestantism which had already used his own Quaker brethren so badly. Moreover, Penn and the tolerant Quakers went so far as to pass a law permitting anyone who professed Christianity to hold office. This, however, was a bit too much for Penn's enemies to swallow, and in 1705 the mother country compelled the Assembly to pass a new office-holding law which excluded Catholics.

Nevertheless, Catholics were seldom molested in Pennsylvania. English, Irish and German, they continued to migrate west of the Delaware, and by 1707 the staunchly anti-Catholic population on the New Jersey side of the river buzzed with rumors of "the Popish Mass at Philadelphia." In truth, it was being said openly, and by 1720 the Catholics of that city had a spiritual leader in the person of Joseph Greaton, another Jesuit priest, and in 1733 a layman named John Dixon conveyed to Father Greaton the deed for a lot on Walnut Street. Here was erected St. Joseph's Chapel, the second Catholic edifice to appear in America since the now-vanished chapel at St. Mary's City in Maryland. Testimony to the existence of public Catholic worship in Philadelphia was given eight years later by another Jesuit, Father Henry Neale, who reported to his Provincial: "We have at present all liberty imaginable in the exercise of our business, and are not only esteemed, but reverenced, as I may say, by the better sort of people."

Doubtless Father Neale's report was made wearing rose-colored glasses; but it is undoubtedly true that the German Catholics who came to Pennsylvania, like their Protestant countrymen from the Palatinate, were warmly welcomed because of their skilled craftsmanship and their solid respectability. Soon there were so many Germans in the colony, concentrating around Philadelphia, Goshenhoppen (near present-day Bally), Conewago and Lancaster, that two German-speaking Jesuits, Fathers Theodore Schneider and William Wappeler, were sent over from the old country to take care of them. Eventually, they outnumbered the English and Irish—949 to 416 in the year 1757—and the fact that they insisted upon having fellow Germans as spiritual leaders was a faint adumbration of the Irish-versus-German controversy which was to rock the young Church a century later.

Even so, a Catholic population of 1,365 out of a Pennsylvania total estimated at between 200,000 and 300,000 would not seem very encouraging to the Office of Propagation, under which the infant Church still operated. Certainly, it should not have frightened Pennsylvania's Protestants. But it did. Pennsylvanians who could still believe that William Penn had died a Jesuit had no difficulty perceiving popish plotters everywhere. In 1744, at the time of King George's War, when England was arrayed against the Bourbons of France and Spain, Governor Lewis Morris of New Jersey had warned Governor George Clinton of New York of Catholic "traitors" in their colonies, and added: "Pennsylvania is in much like condition and I fear our enemies know it too well. They have there a popish chapel and numbers of Irish and Germans that are Papists and I am told that should the French appear and 1500 to 2000 men, they would in that Province soon get ten or twelve thousands together, which would in that case, be not a little dangerous to these and neighboring colonies."

Pennsylvania, however, did not look wildly around for a scapegoat, as New York had done with the unfortunate John Ury three years before, and this self-restraint was probably due in great part to the influence of the Quakers there. Moreover, when the French and Indian War erupted a decade later, Pennsylvania was kindlier than most other colonies to its allotment of Acadians, those French Catholics of Nova Scotia whom the British, suspecting them of sympathizing with the French enemy, had torn from their homes and distributed along the Atlantic seaboard. Generally, the miserable Acadians were treated with coldness and hostility in English America, but from the Quakers of Pennsylvania they received nothing but kindness. Once again, when the French and their Indian allies defeated General Braddock near present-day Pittsburgh in 1755, the Catholics of Pennsylvania could have expected a bloody witch-hunt. But none was forthcoming. True, a Philadelphia mob threatened to burn down St. Joseph's Chapel in reprisal for the atrocities visited upon Braddock's men by "priest-led" savages, and Catholics were asked some unpleasant questions and called uncomplimentary names during an alarm caused by circulation of false charges that a treasonable correspondence with the French was being carried on by "an ingenious Jesuit in Philadelphia." In the main, however, the abhorred Papists were harmed only in their pride or their personal feelings, not in their persons or property.

Actually, by 1763 there were two popish churches in Philadelphia, after the erection of St. Mary's Church on Fourth Street.

By that time also, Great Britain had emerged triumphant in her duel with France for colonial supremacy. Supreme on the sea and master of the American continent, she now turned to ruling both Canada and the colonies with policies which were to have grave consequences both for America and the American Church.

Chapter IV

Although there was now a small Catholic community in Pennsylvania, what may be called the Catholic "main body," or at least those colonists to whom the American Church may trace her origin, continued to reside in Maryland.

Life for these people was hard indeed. Much like the Negroes of the post-Reconstruction South, they were everybody's whipping boy, vilified from every side in small talk, in public documents, on the pulpit and in every form of print extant. Novels, plays, pamphlets, ballads, tracts and newspapers, all combined to pour a flood of invective upon the bowed and silent heads of the Catholics of Maryland, and there was hardly a child who could not skip or play hopscotch to such chants as:

> Abhor that arrant whore of Rome
> And all her blasphemies
> And drink not of her cursed cup,
> Obey not her decrees.

Nevertheless, Maryland's Catholics persevered, even after a new Protestant dynasty, the Hanoverians of Germany, ascended the British throne. But then, in 1713, Benedict Leonard Calvert, the fourth Baron Baltimore, renounced the Faith and embraced Anglicanism in an effort to recover his family's proprietary rights in the colonies. It was a futile gesture, inasmuch as he died two years later, but it convinced many of Maryland's leading Catholics that their cause was finished, and they followed Calvert out of the Church. More defections came after King George I invested the dead man's son, Charles, with all the first Baron Baltimore's original rights in Maryland, thus compelling the colony's Catholics to live under a Protestant Proprietor; and there were more defections after the Stuart attempt to regain power was finally crushed in 1745.

Defeated and deprived of civil rights, the Maryland Catholics, like so many other oppressed minorities, turned to making money. All of their thwarted energies and efforts could now be channeled into a field in which no barriers had been erected against them, and as a result none of them suffered economic hardship and quite a few amassed considerable private fortunes. Outstanding among these wealthy Maryland Catholics were the Carrolls, a family founded by Charles Carroll, a fiery and fearless lawyer who came to Maryland from England as Calvert's attorney general in 1688. His term of office was brief, however, and yet, after he became a casualty of the Glorious Revolution, he proved to be a capable businessman. The fortune he founded in land and tobacco was passed along to his sons, who in turn expanded their share and bequeathed it to their own numerous progeny. One of Carroll's sons was Charles Carroll of Annapolis, and his son was Charles Carroll of Carrollton. Charles Carroll, the attorney general and founder of the family, was a courageous man who again and again challenged the Protestant Establishment during the early part of the century. Of him it has been written: ". . . in spite of the tremendous odds against him he usually managed to make fools, single-handed, of the entire House or the entire Governor's Council. He was a magnificent fighter because he never knew when he was beaten."

The Jesuits also prospered, because they also owned plantations. Thus, they were able to purchase land on which they established missions or schools. Education, of course, was always close to the hearts of the scholarly sons of Saint Ignatius. As early as 1634, when they landed in Maryland, they had envisioned setting up an institution of higher learning in the New World, as their French colleagues had done with Quebec College in New France. None of their grandiose schemes became reality, however, although Brother Ralph Crouch did found an academy at Newtown in 1639, two years after the founding of Harvard College. Newtown lasted until 1707, when it was legislated out of existence by "An Act to Prevent the Growth of Popery." After that, Catholic children received their elementary education from itinerant Irish schoolmasters, usually going abroad for further study. Much as it was against the law to educate children abroad as Catholics, Maryland's wealthy faithful could afford to pay the fine. What was wanted after 1707, however, was a place for elementary studies, and in 1745 the Jesuits established Bohemia Manor on a tract of land near the Pennsylvania border. To this clandestine or at least illegal academy came the sons of rich Catholics, many of whom would go on to European institutions such as St. Omer in France. Among the young gentlemen who were to take this academic road were two distant cousins named John and Charles Carroll.

Charles Carroll of Carrollton, of course, was the grandson of the attorney general of that name who had distinguished himself in Catholic causes during the early 1700s. In 1748, Charles Carroll was at St. Omer in France with his friend and cousin "Jacky" Carroll. A few years later, he departed for England to pursue his studies there, before returning to Maryland. At home, Charles Carroll built steadily on the fortune begun by his grandfather and continued by his father until, on the eve of the Revolution, he was probably the richest man in America. Although such wealthy Maryland Catholics had been slowly recovering the social status denied them since the Glorious Revolution, they were still excluded from political life. Among other disabilities, Catholics were still taxed to pay the salaries of ministers of the Church of England, and when a dispute over these payments arose between the Assembly and Governor Robert Eden, Charles Carroll boldly joined the popular assault upon the Crown's power to tax at all.

Actually, he led that attack, for in January of 1773 a series of letters on the subject between adversaries signing themselves "First Citizen" and "Second Citizen" appeared in the Maryland *Gazette*. Very soon it became known that "First Citizen" was Charles Carroll of Carrollton and that his opponent, who later changed his pen name to "Antillon," was Daniel Dulany, a leading Maryland lawyer with royalist sympathies and a reputation for invincibility in debate. To the surprise and delight of the popular antiroyalists, Carroll proved Dulany's superior, and instead of chastising this Roman Catholic upstart for his impertinence in speaking out on public issues, they applauded him instead. Dulany, meanwhile, lost his temper, and in an effort to discredit his opponent, he appealed to religious prejudice, writing:

Who is he? He has no share in the legislature, as a member of any branch; he is incapable of being a member; he is disabled from giving a vote in the choice of representatives, by the laws and constitution of the country, *on account* of his principles, which are *distrusted* by those laws. He is disabled, by an express resolve, from interfering in the election of members, on the *same account*. He is not a protestant.

Overjoyed that Antillon had taken such a false step, Carroll boldly replied:

What my speculative notions on religion may be, this is neither the place nor time to declare; my political principles ought only to be questioned on the present occasion; surely they are constitutional, and have met, I hope, with the approbation of my countrymen; if so Antillon's aspersions will give me no uneasiness. He asks, who is this Citizen? A man, Antillon, of an independent fortune, one deeply interested in the prosperity of his country: a friend to liberty, a settled enemy to lawless prerogative. . . .

With this and a second reply to Dulany's insinuations, Carroll demolished the royalist position, and in the end his letters were chiefly responsible for the popular party's landslide victory in the Maryland election of 1773. Now the Catholic Carroll was fairly launched on a public career. Moreover, he had compelled his Protestant colleagues to respect his faith, a changed attitude which was demonstrated when, as the pot of revolutionary fervor came to a boil in the colonies, he was named to the Maryland Committee of Correspondence. Carroll was also asked to be a delegate to the First Continental Congress gathering in Philadelphia the following year. With the political shrewdness he was to display again and again, he refused on the ground that his religion might alienate other delegates and thus cripple him as a representative of Maryland. Instead, he chose to attend the Philadelphia meeting as an unofficial observer. There, he was surprised to encounter what can only be described as a diminution of the typical colonist's ordinarily implacable hatred toward Rome. Perhaps this was because, Parliament now being the enemy, there was little hostility to be spared for the Catholics; or it might have been that the colonists already realized, as Benjamin Franklin was to quip later, that if they did not all hang together they would all hang separately, or even that they dimly perceived that opposition to Great Britain might *ipso facto* mean friendship with Catholic France. Whatever the reason, the faith which Charles Carroll had pleaded as a political impediment was now held so little in abhorrence that that crusty anti-Catholic, John Adams, did not hesitate to join George Washington in attending a Catholic service at St. Mary's Church. His impressions of that event have been recorded in a letter to his wife, and they are at once entertaining and full of insights into a New England Congregationalist's horror of popish mumbo-jumbo. Adams wrote:

This afternoon, led by curiosity and good company, I strolled away to mother church, or rather grandmother church. I mean the Romish chapel. I heard a good, short moral essay upon the duty of parents to their children, founded in justice and charity, to take care of their interests, temporal and spiritual. This afternoon's entertainment was to me most awful and affecting; the poor wretches fingering their beads, chanting Latin, not a word of which they understood; their pater nosters and ave Marias; their holy water; their crossing themselves perpetually; their bowing to the name of Jesus, whenever they hear it; their bowings, kneelings and genuflections before the altar. The dress of the priest was rich white lace. His pulpit was velvet and gold. The altar-piece was very rich, little images and crucifixes about; wax candles lighted up. But how shall I describe the picture of our Saviour in a frame of marble over the altar, at full length, upon the cross in the agonies, and the blood dropping and streaming from his wounds! The music, consisting of an organ and a choir of singers, went all the afternoon except sermon time, and the assembly chanted most sweetly and exquisitely.

Here is everything which can lay hold of the eye, ear, and imagination—everything which can charm and bewitch the simple and ignorant. I wonder how Luther ever broke the spell. Adieu.

Even more remarkable than Adams's presence in "a Romish chapel" is the fact that he entered it at a time when news of Parliament's passage of the Quebec Act had set the anti-Catholic hounds baying throughout the colonies again. This piece of legislation had not only confirmed the French in the free exercise of their religion and the practice of their native law, it had also granted the Quebec government those lands in the west which the English colonies claimed. Now, the colonists fancied themselves surrounded by French-speaking Catholics, the old enemy of former years, and their rage was so unbounded that on October 21, 1774, the Continental Congress addressed a letter to the British people admonishing them for tolerating in America a religion which "has deluged your island in blood, and dispersed impiety, bigotry, persecution, murder and rebellion through every part of the world."

Once again, it was popular to quote Samuel Adams, who had said six years earlier: "I did verily believe, as I do still, that much more is to be dreaded from the growth of popery in America, than from the Stamp Act or any other acts destructive of civil rights. . . ." Once again, the popular press picked up the old anti-Catholic cudgels, and one journal went so far as to predict: "We may live to see our churches converted into mass houses and our lands plundered by tythes for the support of the Popish clergy. The Inquisition may erect her standard in Pennsylvania and the city of Philadelphia may yet experience the carnage of St. Bartholomew's Day." Others, misrepresenting the truth of the Quebec Act, insisted that it actually established Romanism as an official religion, and warned:

> If Gallic Papists have a right
> To worship their own way
> Then farewell to the liberties
> Of poor America.

Ministers, of course, were in full voice once more, but so also were John Adams, apparently recovered from his momentary lapse into tolerance, Patrick Henry, Richard Henry Lee, the inevitable Samuel Adams, and none other than Washington's protégé and confidante, Alexander Hamilton, who thundered: "If [Parliament] had any regard to the freedom and happiness of mankind they would not have done it. If they had been friends to the Protestant cause, they would never have provided such a nursery for its greatest enemy . . . They may as well establish Popery in New York and the other colonies as they did in Canada!"

More than the Stamp Act, perhaps more than any other act by Parliament or any British minister, the Quebec Act was a direct cause of the American Revolution. It so inflamed colonial hatred of the mother country that even that staunch and solid Protestant, King George III, was accused of being a Jesuit in disguise, and his statues, from which the rebels later were to melt so many serviceable bullets, were adorned with mocking rosaries. Meanwhile, patriots such as Paul Revere did a brisk business in scurrilous engravings which depicted His Majesty and his Ministers clothed in the livery of the Pope of Rome. To the Catholics of colonial America—who actually represented no more than 1 per cent of the total population of three million persons—it appeared that it was time to pull tight the shutters again, and it was this furor of anti-Catholic sentiment that rose about the ears of Father John Carroll when he returned to his native Maryland in 1774.

After his famous cousin Charles left St. Omer, John Carroll continued studies which led him into the Society of Jesus in 1762. He was ordained seven years later at the Jesuit seminary in Belgium, remaining on the Continent to teach in the schools which the Society maintained there for the education of the sons of well-to-do English and American Catholics. Four years after that, the blow fell: Pope Clement XIV suppressed the Society of Jesus.

Suppression of the Jesuits came as a particularly stunning blow to American Catholicism. Since 1634, when Jesuits landed with the first Maryland settlers, the fortunes of the Church in the English Colonies had been almost exclusively in the hands of the Society. From that date until the suppression 139 years later, more than 140 of its members had served at one time or another in English America. They had come to love both their mission and their communicants, and when the suppression raised a jurisdictional question, they were most reluctant to return to Europe.

Under terms of the bull of suppression, bishops all over the world were to take possession of Jesuit properties in the name of the Holy See, and to arrange for the transfer of the Jesuits themselves to the status of secular priests. As far as the American Jesuits were concerned, this obligation fell on Bishop Richard

Challoner of London. Loathe to accept it, Challoner appointed Father John Lewis, the Society's American provincial, as his vicar-general and instructed him to oversee dismantling the Jesuit organization in the English colonies. Apparently, Lewis had no wish to replace these ex-Jesuits, and so, they were permitted to remain where they were, that is, in Pennsylvania and Maryland, the two colonies which tolerated priests.

As far as the American ex-Jesuit, Father John Carroll, was concerned, he was offered a chaplaincy in England. But he refused, returning home instead in the late spring of 1774. At the age of thirty-nine, it appeared that his career was a wreck, and he retired to live in seclusion at his mother's home in Rock Creek. He still possessed his priestly faculties, however, that is, the permission to preach and administer the sacraments, and he used them to minister quietly to Catholic families in the neighborhood.

Although shocked by the enmity which passage of the Quebec Act had unleashed against his faith, Father Carroll nevertheless sided with the Patriots in their dispute with England. He proudly followed the career of his famous cousin, Charles, sympathizing with his republican convictions and becoming so independence-minded himself that he refused his obedience to Father John Lewis, acting as Bishop Challoner's vicar-general. By this act, like so many of his fellow priests in America, he made it clear that he had no wish to submit to ecclesiastical authority based in England. Nevertheless, John Carroll was far from enthusiastic when his cousin Charles approached him with the astounding invitation to help win the Catholics of Canada to the Patriot cause.

After its first outburst against the Quebec Act, Congress had had second thoughts about Canada. On the very same day that it had excoriated King George for tolerating in America a religion which "has deluged your island in blood," they addressed a quite dissimilar letter to the people of Quebec, inviting them to join the fight against tyranny and declaring:

We are too well acquainted with the liberality of sentiment distinguishing your nation, to imagine, that difference of religion will prejudice you against a hearty amity with us. You know, that the transcendent nature of freedome elevates those, who unite in her cause, above all such low-minded infirmities.

The Canadians, however, were also "too well acquainted" with the true religious sentiments of the Protestants to the south, and they angrily spurned the overtures of what they called "the perfidious Congress." Moreover, Bishop Briand of Quebec deeply distrusted the Americans, and forbade any of his flock to join them under pain of excommunication. Thus, Canada remained loyal to the British crown, and in 1775 Congress, despairing of diplomacy, authorized a two-pronged military assault on Montreal and Quebec under Richard Montgomery and Benedict Arnold. Although this expedition ultimately ended in failure, Congress flip-flopped back to diplomacy again. Already aware that the traditional American hatred of Catholicism was going to have to be muted during the war against England, it authorized a diplomatic mission to Canada charged with impressing upon the Canadians its new-found tolerance of Popery. Benjamin Franklin was the obvious choice to lead the embassy, along with Samuel Chase, known to have Catholic friends, and the Catholic Charles Carroll. A few weeks later the British-born General Charles Lee wrote to his friend, John Hancock: "I should think that if some Jesuit or Religieuse of any other Order (he must be a man of liberal sentiments, enlarged mind and a manifest friend of Civil Liberty) could be found out and sent to Canada, he would be worth battalions to us." The same idea had occurred to John Adams, who wrote to a friend: "We have empowered the Committee to take with them, another gentleman of Maryland, a Mr. John Carroll, a Roman Catholic priest, and a Jesuit, a gentleman of learning and Abilities." Obviously, when John Adams could swallow his hatred of priests, and especially Jesuits, to the extent that he could praise one, Catholicism was once again in good odor in Philadelphia.

Thus, Charles Carroll approached his cousin, who promptly informed Congress of his doubts about being of any service. First, he said, he had no experience in diplomacy; second, he was reluctant to compromise his priestly office. "I have observed," he remarked with customary frankness and acumen, "that when ministers of religion leave the duties of their profession to take a busy part in political matters, they generally fall into contempt, and sometimes even bring discredit to the cause in whose service they are engaged."

Nevertheless, Father Carroll accompanied the mission, which ended in complete failure. The invasion of Canada itself, the presence around Quebec of the remnants of Montgomery's and Arnold's forces and the firm opposition of Bishop Briand were enough to convince most Canadians that the Americans did not sincerely wish to respect their religion.

Just before the mission departed, Benjamin Franklin became quite ill, and Father Carroll joined him at St. John's while Charles Carroll and Samuel Chase continued on to Philadelphia. This chance association between the ex-Jesuit and the mandarin of American diplomacy was to have great consequences seven years later. Doctor Franklin certainly never forgot Father Carroll, writing: "I find I grow daily more feeble, and I think I could hardly have got along so far, but for Mr. Carroll's friendly assistance and tender Care of me."

So Father John Carroll returned to comparative obscurity in Maryland, while the war against the Crown continued and the Catholics of the colonies made up their minds which side to take. Obviously, neutrality was out of the question. At that moment, neither Parliament nor Congress appeared disposed to refranchise the Romanists. True, the Crown had been tolerant toward the Catholics of Canada, and recently there had been Catholics in New York, Delaware and even Maryland who had been hounded out of their homes by the Patriots. On this score, the mother country appeared less to be feared—if one could forget her record prior to the Quebec Act. Apparently, not many Catholics could, and the religious question apparently had little influence on their ultimate decision. Like their fellow Americans, they resented the increased taxes of the mother country; and even though they could not vote or hold office, they felt attracted to representative government. Thus, the overwhelming majority of the Catholics in America sided with the Patriots.

There were some Catholic Tories, of course, but not very many. In all, three units of Catholic Tories were raised during the war, including one recruited by Lord Rawdon in New York, which, although Irish, was far from being completely Catholic.

However, it now seems quite certain that in proportion the number of Catholics serving the Patriot cause was at least equal to that of the Protestants, and that the record left by Catholic Tories was nothing in comparison to that of the Catholics who broke with the Crown.

Charles Carroll was by far the most famous. After his return from the Canadian fiasco, he was elected to the Continental Congress and was one of the signers of the Declaration of Independence. No man in the colonies had more to lose than this rich American, and yet, Carroll seems to have felt that he had the most to gain. As he was to write later: "I had in view not only our independence of England, but the toleration of all sects professing the Christian religion." Throughout the war Carroll shuttled back and forth between Baltimore and Philadelphia, serving in both the Maryland Senate and as a member of the Board of War. In the latter capacity, he was of great service to his friend George Washington, helping to thwart the infamous Conway Cabal, a conspiracy to replace Washington with either General Horatio Gates or General Charles Lee as commander of the Continental Army.

Among other Catholics, the Irish-born John ("Fighting Jack") Barry is now rightfully regarded as the founder of the American navy; another Irishman, Stephen Moylan, joined Washington's staff as mustermaster general, rising to the rank of brigadier general, the highest held by a Catholic during the war; Daniel Carroll served as a member of Congress from Maryland and Thomas FitzSimons sat as a representative from Pennsylvania; Captains Roger Kean and John Walsh served with distinction; a volunteer fighting unit was raised by George Meade of Philadelphia; and when George Rogers Clark led his expedition to the West, his success was in great part due to the help given him by Father Pierre Gibault, an ex-Jesuit trained in the seminary at Quebec. Another French priest who dared the wrath of the anti-American Bishop Briand, Father Louis Eustace Lotbiniere, joined the American invasion of Canada and ultimately became the first Catholic chaplain to be enrolled in the armed services of the United States. The record of European Catholics such as Lafayette, Pulaski, Kosciusko and others, to say nothing of the

French army and fleet under Catholics such as Rochambeau and d'Estaing, are too well known to be repeated here.

How many Catholics or what proportion of them served as junior officers or in the ranks probably will never be known. If one is to judge from the rolls of the Pennsylvania Line, however, it would appear to be a considerable number. No less than 300 Irish Catholics marched at one time or another with that famous outfit, and when it is remembered that the Irish were outnumbered among Pennsylvania Catholics by both the Germans and the English, it would seem fair to conclude, even allowing for the ordinary Irishman's fondness for a fight, that as many as 600 Catholics from this province saw military service. If this is true, the figure is staggering, if only because a Continental "line" regiment numbered only 728 men. Even if the Pennsylvanians were replaced three times over, as seems doubtful, the Catholics would have accounted for 30 per cent of their number.

Here is more than sufficient evidence to refute the uncharitable claims of anti-Catholic historians such as Bancroft, who accused the Catholics of being Tories and deserters, or those others who seem curiously capable of dismissing every Irish name as "Scotch-Irish" or "Ulster Scots" from the Protestant North of Ireland. On the other hand, as Theodore Maynard has pointed out, to insist that every Irishman on the Patriot side was a Catholic is to ignore the ineluctable fact that most of the Irish Catholics who came to New England during the earlier decades had been lost to the Church.

Maynard adduces the striking example of General John Sullivan of New Hampshire. General Sullivan's grandfather was Major Philip O'Sullivan, a Catholic who fought at the siege of Limerick. But his father was an Irish schoolmaster who migrated to New England and lost his faith. His sons included not only the famous general, but three other Revolutionary officers as well, a governor of New Hampshire, a governor of Massachusetts and a judge; and his grandsons numbered a governor of Maine, a United States senator from New Hampshire, an attorney general of that state and another judge. All, of course, were Protestants; and if there was one characteristic shared by this illustrious progeny standing only a few score years away from the ancient creed, it was their virulent hatred of Rome. Thus, if it is true that there were many Irish in the Revolutionary armed forces, it is not true to say that they were all Catholics. To be safe on this question of Catholic service to the Revolution, to avoid the dangers of overstatement always inherent in explorations of this kind, it is probably best to quote the meticulously fair and sober Father John Carroll, who said: "Their blood flowed as freely, in proportion to their numbers, to cement the fabric of independence as that of their fellow citizens. They concurred with perhaps greater unanimity than any other body of men in recommending and promoting that government from whose influence America anticipates all the blessings of justice, peace, plenty, good order, and civil and religious liberty."

Appreciation of Catholic services rose higher after the alliance with France in 1778. Three years earlier, George Washington had wisely perceived the political folly of continuing to make mock of Popery, banning his army's attempt to celebrate Guy Fawkes Day at Cambridge with a stern command against "that ridiculous and childish custom of burning the Effigy of the pope," but in 1778, with powerful France now an ally, to offer public or official insult to Catholicism would be impolitic indeed. After Spain declared war on England a year later, and contributed a million dollars to the Patriot cause, it became unthinkable.

The first French minister to America, Conrad Alexandre Gérard, became one of the most popular members of Philadelphia society. In 1779 he sent out invitations to a Te Deum in St. Mary's Church celebrating the third anniversary of American independence, and two years later to another one sung to commemorate the Franco-American victory at Yorktown, and on both occasions members of Congress found it expedient to attend. They were also present in St. Joseph's Church in 1780 for a requiem mass for the Spanish agent, Juan de Miralles, much to the outrage of Benedict Arnold. Later attempting to justify his treason, Arnold spoke of having seen "your mean and profligate Congress at Mass for the soul of a Roman Catholic in purgatory and participating in the rites of a Church against whose anti-Christian corruption your pious ancestors would bear witness with their blood."

Perhaps inevitably, as the fear of Rome waned among the Patriots, it waxed hotter among the Tories. While the French fleet was on its way to America, the Tory *Rivington's Royal*

Gazette warned that the ships were carrying "tons of holy water, and casks of consecrated oil, reliques, beads, crucifixes, rosaries, consecrated wafers, and Mass books, as well as bales of indulgences." No propagandist can fail to admire that masterful "bales of indulgences," and yet, the paper's description of the instruments of torture to be employed by the Inquisition which was to be set up in cis-Atlantic was equally compelling. Samuel Adams, of course, was taking instructions with an eye toward trying on a Roman collar, presumably with the intention of joining William Penn and King George III on the Jesuitical deathbed.

In a reverse way, these quaint or comical forebodings do testify to the genuine fear of French power felt in the Loyalist camp, and the fact is, much as high school history books continue to minimize it, the alliance with Catholic France was decisive in the American victory. Once it was won, the American Catholics rejoiced in the realization that they had helped to win not only political independence but religious freedom as well. Their patriotism in the war, the French influence and a growing awareness of the impossibility of establishing any one of the numerous Christian sects of America as an official religion had made it clear to all fair and thoughtful minds that only complete religious liberty would do for the new republic.

One by one, led by Pennsylvania and Maryland in 1776 and with Massachusetts the last in line in 1833, the states did away with their old anti-Catholic laws or disestablished this or that official religion. To the joy of all Catholics, the First Amendment to the Constitution stated: "Congress shall make no law respecting an establishment of religion, or prohibiting the free exercise thereof." Here was the Maryland phrase, the concept of the Catholic Calvert, given its fullest and most complete expression. No wonder then, that Daniel Carroll of Maryland and Thomas Fitz-Simons of Pennsylvania, both delegates to the Constitutional Convention, should favor this principle so heartily and campaign for its adoption so strenuously. No wonder either that the Roman Catholics of America should write to George Washington to congratulate him on his election as the first President of the United States, and to say: "Whilst our country preserves her freedom and independence, we shall have a well founded title to claim from her justice equal rights of citizenship, as the price of our blood spilt under your eyes . . ."

In reply, Washington spoke of his hope that as men grew more liberal, they would be more inclined to grant equal rights to all, and that he hoped to see America lead the world in this attitude. "And I presume that your fellow-citizens will not forget the patriotic part which you took in the accomplishment of their Revolution, and the establishment of their government; nor the important assistance which they received from a nation in which the Roman Catholic religion is professed."

Though inadvertently perhaps, the Catholics of America had won their religious freedom. For the first time in the history of mankind, a proscribed faith had been recognized at the expense of no other creed. That was the novelty of the First Amendment, of the American way. No other Church, then, had so much to be thankful for, so deep an interest in seeing this American way spread and prosper.

Chapter V

True ecclesiastical rule for the English-speaking Church in America was some time in coming. As John Tracy Ellis has observed, its very origins are lost in obscurity, and this is probably because Catholicism, like the faith in the mother country, had been for so long a clandestine creed.

Apparently, the missionaries who came here received their faculties from the bishops from whose diocesan ports they sailed for the New World. Between 1631 and 1685, however, there was no Catholic bishop in England, and so, acting upon another procedure whereby missionaries received faculties from the superiors of their various orders, the first Jesuits who came to Maryland obtained them from the Jesuit General. In 1696, Pope Innocent XII sought to regularize this practice by issuing a brief ordering missionaries to apply for faculties to the vicars apostolic, that is, titular bishops representing the Holy See itself, in whose jurisdiction they lived. For the missionaries in the English colonies, this meant the Vicar Apostolic of the London District, a fact confirmed by the Sacred Congregation for Propaganda in 1756.

Propaganda was the direct ecclesiastical ruler of the Catholic Church in English America. It was and is the arm of the Holy See which oversees mission activity all over the world, and the Catholic Church in the United States was to remain a mission church until 1908, when it finally ceased to be under Propaganda and became, like the mature churches of Europe, answerable directly to the Holy See. It was to Propaganda then, that Richard Challoner appealed after he became Bishop and Vicar Apostolic of London in 1758. Challoner wanted clarification of his responsibility to the outlawed Church in the colonies. But Propaganda moved slowly, not only because this is the normal ecclesiastical pace and style, but also because by then it was aware of the potential vastness of the problem. Bishop Challoner, however, sincerely concerned that Catholics in the colonies were going to their death without being confirmed, continued to press the Sacred Congregation on the subject of a resident bishop there. To his surprise and dismay, when the Catholics in America learned of his intentions, they immediately moved to block them.

Already laboring under the disabilities of the Penal Age, the Catholic settlers were far from eager to have the millstone of a bishop hung around their neck. Even the Anglican Church had discreetly shelved its own plans to introduce episcopal rule in America, once it understood how such a move would infuriate the Congregationalists of New England. If the established Church of England dared not send a bishop across the sea, then how much more imprudent would it be for a disfranchised church to attempt it. For this and other reasons, in 1765 a group of about 250 prominent laymen forwarded a petition to the English Jesuit provincial protesting against a bishop for America, and in that same year Charles Carroll of Annapolis, father of the signer of the Declaration of Independence, wrote to Bishop Challoner: ". . . such a step, I am afraid, will create great troubles here, and give a handle to our enemies to endeavor at the total suppression of the exercise of our religion, and otherways most grievously to molest us."

Unconvinced, suspicious that the Jesuits, who feared appointment of an anti-Jesuit bishop, were behind the protests, Bishop Challoner still importuned Rome for the appointment, finally suggesting that perhaps Bishop Briand of Quebec might confirm the Americans. Propaganda agreed, and in 1773 it requested Briand to do so. Before going south, Briand asked the Jesuits in Philadelphia what they thought of his visiting them, and Father Ferdinand Farmer replied that "it would create great disturbances, with the danger of depriving us of the paltry privileges we are now enjoying," and declared: "For it is incredible how hateful to non-Catholics in all parts of America is the very name of Bishop, even to such as should be members of the Church which is called Anglican."

Briand was convinced, and he informed the Holy See that it

would be unwise for him to enter the American colonies. A few months later the uproar which succeeded passage of the Quebec Act confirmed the wisdom of his decision. And with that, there were no more attempts to provide episcopal government in the English colonies until after the Revolution.

Life for the handful of ex-Jesuit priests in the colonies continued to be almost entirely unregulated. It was also extremely hard. "Our journeys are very long," Father James Mosely wrote to his priest brother in England, "and our rides constant and extensive. I often ride about three hundred miles a week, and never a week but I ride one hundred and fifty to two hundred. In our way of living we ride as much by night as by day; in all weathers, in heats, colds, rain, frost, and snow. You must not imagine that our chapels lie as yours do . . . They are in great forests, some miles away from any house of hospitality. Swamps, runs, miry holes, lost in the night, etc.—this, as yet, and ever will in this country, attend us. Between three and four hundred miles was my last Christmas fare on one horse."

To the hardships of travel were added the ordeal of extreme poverty. Although the ex-Jesuits had managed to hold onto property which their predecessors had obtained in the capacity of gentlemen adventurers, their personal possessions were scanty, and they were very often reduced to being their own farmers, butchers and bakers. Their numbers also were dwindling, for as Father Mosley was to write: "We are all growing old, we are very weak handed, few come from England to help us."

Thus, as the war came to a close, it became obvious that some form of government was needed, and in 1782, Father John Carroll proposed his Plan of Organization. Although an ex-Jesuit himself, Carroll had always felt that his colleagues were deluded in dreaming of the day when their Society would be restored. He also thought that their lack of organization made it difficult for them to deal practically with the problems of Catholics in the colonies, and that the time had come to settle the problem of the properties which they held.

Accordingly, on June 27, 1783, six priest deputies met at Whitemarsh plantation midway between Georgetown and Annapolis, and there they divided the mission field into three districts—Northern, Middle and Southern—and asked the priests of each district to meet to appoint two deputies who would attend a second meeting. At this second Whitemarsh gathering, on November 6, 1783, they formed what they called the Select Body of the Clergy, bound by a constitution providing rules of government and individual conduct, and disposition of their property. Other priests were to be admitted to this Select Body, if they agreed to adhere to its provisions. Thus, the Whitemarsh meetings provided a rule of life which the ex-Jesuits in America were to follow until their Society was restored in 1806, while also preserving property rights which it also would claim then.

More important was the decision to name a committee to petition the Holy See for a regular form of ecclesiastical government. Once again, the American priests were careful to warn against the dangers of introducing a bishop into the United States, reiterating their fears that the fiercely independent Americans would consider such an appointment as interference in their own affairs by a "foreign" power. Instead, they suggested that Rome grant Father Lewis, their superior in England, certain episcopal powers such as administering the Sacrament of Confirmation, blessing chalices and altar stones and imparting priestly faculties. When a reply was received from Rome, the American priests were astonished to hear that Pope Pius VI had appointed Father Carroll as superior of the American missions. To their deep chagrin, the fathers also learned that the Apostolic Nuncio to France had opened negotiations with Benjamin Franklin, the American Minister to France, concerning the future government of the American Church.

Naturally enough, rumors grew and flew. There was talk that a French bishop would rule Catholics in the United States. John Carroll was deeply distressed to see the American clergy ignored on a matter in which it was so intimately concerned. Every fear of non-Catholic Americans over the "foreign" nature of the Church seemed vindicated, and Carroll said he would protest directly to Franklin, except that, being under consideration for promotion himself, his action might be misconstrued.

What had happened, of course, was simply that Rome had been groping in the dark. For the first time in its long history, the Holy See had been asked to provide ecclesiastical government for a tiny group of Catholics living in an overwhelmingly

Protestant country which had just presented the world with "a new order of things." There was simply no precedent. To attempt to deal with the Vicar Apostolic in London was out of the question, if only because these former English subjects had, in fact, "de-Englished" themselves. Even for the American priests to have asked that an Englishman, Father Lewis, continue as their superior must have seemed perplexing to Rome. Moreover, the American priests were all ex-Jesuits, and the Society through which Propaganda might have dealt with them had been out of existence for a decade. No wonder then that Leonardo Cardinal Antonelli, prefect of Propaganda, should have turned to France, the ally of America and the eldest daughter of the Church, in his efforts to clarify the situation.

Actually, even before Father Carroll and his fellow priest-deputies assembled at Whitemarsh, Antonelli had ordered the Apostolic Nuncio at Versailles, Archbishop Joseph Doria Pamfili, to gather whatever information he could concerning the Catholic situation in the United States, and to consult with France on the kind of ecclesiastical organization that could be set up there. This was the time of the negotiation of the peace treaty which ended the Revolutionary War, and Archbishop Pamfili was also ordered to ask the French government to insert a clause in the treaty granting religious liberty to the Catholics of America. France, however, declined this request. The French had been cooling toward their American allies lately, chiefly because of the Americans' refusal to let France call the peace tune and their failure to repay French loans, and they refused to attempt to influence the new government in Philadelphia. As it turned out, of course, the Americans were to attend to the problems of religious liberty themselves, and in far more comprehensive style. Rebuffed here, Archbishop Pamfili now turned to his other assignment: the problem of ecclesiastical rule.

As is customary in such matters, he approached an official representative of the nation involved; in this case, Benjamin Franklin, the American Minister to France. Pamfili told Franklin that Propaganda wished to establish a vicar apostolic with episcopal powers in one of the American cities and that it favored an American citizen for the appointment. Enthusiastic, Franklin forwarded the request to Congress, and that body in truth did suggest that Rome must now deal with "a new order of things" when it replied: "Resolved: That Doctor Franklin be desired to notify the Apostolic Nuncio at Versailles, that Congress will always be pleased to testify their respect to his sovereign and state; but that the subject of his application to Doctor Franklin being purely spiritual is without the jurisdiction and powers of Congress, who have no authority to permit or refuse it, these powers being reserved to the several states individually."

Never before had the ancient Church encountered a government which refused to claim a power which many still exercise, the privilege of being consulted in high ecclesiastical appointment. So the distracted nuncio went back to Benjamin Franklin, who this time suggested that if no suitable American could be found, he saw no difficulty in the naming of "a French ecclesiastic who would remain in France and, through the medium of a suffragan residing in America, would conduct the spiritual affairs of Catholics in those states. . . ." So it was Doctor Franklin, the man whom Father Carroll had nursed with "tender care," who had unwittingly infuriated his old associate of the mission to Canada. Not only did he want a foreign bishop, but absentee rule as well. And for some inexplicable reason, Franklin seems to have regarded the future of the Church in the United States as somehow bound to the destiny of France. Thus, he could also suggest that the French bishop who would rule it would do so in concert with the nuncio to France and the American minister there; and he coolly proposed that the King of France confiscate the revenues of four English Benedictine monasteries then in France to finance the infant Church. Propaganda, however, politely declined to rob Peter to pay Paul, and persisted in its conviction that the American bishop should reside in the United States, and that he be a citizen of the new republic—if one worthy of the office could be found.

Obviously, Propaganda was convinced that the Church in the United States had all but vanished, leaving no vestiges upon which to build—until the Whitemarsh petition arrived from across the sea. At once, the situation became clearer. Messages of inquiry went out from Rome. It was learned that Father Lewis was too old to take up the duties of mission superior and that Father John Carroll was a priest of high moral character and ability. When Franklin learned that his former associate was being considered for superior he expressed his approval with such enthusiasm that, in the end, Father Carroll was named as a prefect apostolic, rather than a simple superior, with the promise of being made a bishop. In his letter of appointment, Cardinal Antonelli leaves no doubt of Franklin's influence, when he wrote to Carroll: ". . . you, Reverend Sir, have given conspicuous proof of piety and zeal, and it is known that your appointment will please and gratify many citizens of the republic, particularly Mr. Franklin, the eminent person who represents the same republic at the court of the Most Christian King . . ."

Typically, Father Carroll was reluctant to accept the office, if only because he understood the cares that would come with it. Finally, however, he yielded to friends who warned that his failure to accept might mean a foreign prelate for America, and he sent his formal acceptance to Propaganda in January of 1785. Before that, again characteristically, Father Carroll called another meeting of the Select Body of the Clergy at Whitemarsh, where it was declared that a prefect apostolic would suffice for American needs, and that no bishop was needed. In blunt language, the American clergy said: "That if one be sent, it is decided by the majority of the chapter, that he shall not be entitled to any support from the present estates of the clergy." Carroll himself, with great prescience, wrote to a friend: "You well know that in our free and jealous government, where Catholics are admitted into all public Councils equally with the professors of any other Religion, it never will be suffered that their ecclesiastical Superior (be he Bishop or Prefect-Apostolic) receive his appointment from a foreign State, and only hold it at the discretion of a foreign tribunal or congregation . . . for the consequences sooner or later would certainly be that some malicious or jealous-minded person, would raise a spirit against us, and under pretence of rescuing the State from foreign influence and dependence, strip us perhaps of our common civil rights."

There is no doubt that Carroll and his fellow ex-Jesuits distrusted Propaganda. Cardinal Antonelli was known to be an enemy of the Jesuits and his Congregation had distinguished itself for the zeal with which it had been seizing former Jesuit property throughout Europe. Any bishop appointed by Antonelli, they reasoned, would certainly be no friend of theirs. As Doctor Peter Guilday has observed: "Episcopal authority could mean only one thing to the beaten remnants of the Jesuit Society— confiscation of all they possessed, and with the confiscation the fall of the missions and the end of their own maintenance." Doubtless these misgivings became known to Propaganda, and they probably helped to delay the promised bishop's miter for another five years. In the meantime, Father John Carroll plunged into his duties as Prefect-Apostolic.

One of Carroll's first acts was to report to Rome on the condition of Catholicism in the United States. It was not a very encouraging report. In the year 1785, out of a total American population of more than 3,000,000 people only about 25,000 were Catholics. Serving this tiny fraction of the populace were twenty-four priests, of whom two were more than seventy years old, three others were near that age, others were in very bad health and one whom Carroll had recently approved was reported to be acting in an unpriestly way. Speaking of the laity, Carroll reported:

In Maryland a few of the leading more wealthy families still profess the Catholic faith introduced at the very foundation of the province by their ancestors. The greater part of them are planters and in Pennsylvania almost all are farmers, except the merchants and mechanics living in Philadelphia. As for piety, they are for the most part sufficiently assiduous in the exercises of religion and in frequenting the sacraments, but they lack that fervor, which frequent appeals to the sentiment of piety usually produce, as many congregations hear the word of God only once a month, and sometimes only once in two months. We are reduced to this by want of priests, by the distance of congregations from each other and by difficulty of travelling. This refers to Catholics born here, for the condition of the Catholics who in great numbers are flowing in here from different countries of Europe, is very different. For while there are few of our native Catholics who do not approach the sacraments of Penance and the Holy Eucharist, at least once a year, especially in Easter time, you can scarcely find any among the newcomers who discharge this duty of religion, and there is reason to fear that the example will be very pernicious especially in commercial towns.

Obviously, American Catholicism did not seem to have a promising future, and Father Carroll's report reflects his deep concern for its chief problem of "leakage." By then, the country contained an estimated quarter-million lapsed Catholics, ordinary people who, unlike the wealthy planters of Maryland and farmers of Pennsylvania, had found it exceedingly difficult to practice their religion. With the shortage of priests continuing, and the immigrant tide rising daily, many more were to be lost irrevocably. Even today, the presence of so many Protestant Irish in the South testifies to the mass defection of their ancestors. They lost their faith, wrote Father Carroll, not only because they found no place to practice it or found hostility to the public profession of it too much to bear, but also because of "unavoidable intercourse with non-Catholics." This produced moral laxness, or at least a relaxing of comparatively stricter Catholic morality, and what the prefect apostolic considered a greater danger: mixed marriages. Again and again, Carroll was to complain of this problem and his helplessness against it. In 1798 he wrote to a friend in England: "Here our Catholics are so mixed with Protestants in all the intercourse of civil society and business public and private, that abuse of intermarriage is almost universal and it surpasses my ability to devise an effectual bar against it. No general prohibition can be exacted without reducing many of the faithful to live in a state of celibacy." In other words, if one Catholic family was set down in a community of, say, thirty Protestant families, where would the Catholic children find partners? And if they accepted reality and chose them from among the Protestants, would it be very likely that the offspring of the dominant majority would embrace an abhorred minority faith? If one is to judge from so distinguished a Catholic as Charles Carroll of Carrollton, here is the answer: all of Carroll's children married non-Catholics; and apparently none of his grandchildren were raised as Catholics. Another outstanding Catholic, Dominick Lynch of New York, one of the pillars of the Church who signed the letter to Washington, fathered a family of thirteen children, but within a few generations almost all of his descendants were lost to the faith.

Leakage, one of the continuing problems of the Church in America, was confined not only to the laity. Even before Carroll became Prefect-Apostolic he had to deal with the problem of clerical apostasy. The priest was another ex-Jesuit, Maryland-born Father Charles Wharton, who had been chaplain to the Catholics of Worcester, England, before returning to America in 1783. A year later Wharton published his *Letter to the Roman Catholics of the City of Worcester*, a polished and apparently erudite refutation of the Catholic religion. In it, Wharton claimed that he had been unable to find intellectual freedom inside the bosom of the Church. Because of the dignified style, and because of the appeal to freedom, an almost sacred shibboleth in those days, Wharton's letter shook the tiny American Church. It had to be answered, and Father John Carroll was asked to write the reply. He did, but only after much difficulty caused by Wharton's garbling of his supposed quotations from St. John Chrysostom, one of the Fathers of the Church. Obliged to track down the true source from Philadelphia to Annapolis, Carroll discovered that it was not Chrysostom at all but a discredited work written two centuries after his death, and that the passages quoted were inimical not only to Catholicism but Protestantism as well. Writing his reply with matching dignity, Father Carroll was able to set uneasy Catholic minds at rest by supplying facts with which to defend their faith, but he failed in his appeal to Wharton to return to the fold and remember his vow of chastity. Joining the Protestant Episcopal Church, Wharton became twice married, thus becoming the prototype of those apostate priests, who, even today, perhaps especially today, abandon their faith with the explanation: "The Church is corrupt, the Papacy is dishonest, and therefore I'm getting married in the morning."

Wharton, however, was perhaps a genteel problem in comparison to the tempestuous priests who came under Father Carroll's authority as Prefect-Apostolic. Like the immigrants with whom they arrived in the land of the free, they had exaggerated notions of what freedom was, particularly in matters of ecclesiastical jurisdiction. Some of them were at the least eccentric, like Father Claude de la Poterie, a former chaplain under Rochambeau, whom Carroll appointed as the first pastor of Catholics in Boston. After Poterie had informed his flock of "credentials" which consisted in part of "a patent of Count Palatine, which His Holiness grants as Sovereign in his Dominions, to those he thinks worthy of that dignity," the Prefect-Apostolic decided that the new pastor was "a sad rascal" and suspended him. As though to confirm Carroll's judgment, the embittered Poterie next published an attack upon the ex-Jesuits in general and Carroll in particular, accusing the Prefect-Apostolic of attempting a surreptitious "resurrection" of the suppressed Society in the United States. Sending a copy of his diatribe to Propaganda, Poterie demanded that he be appointed Prefect- or Vicar-Apostolic of New England. Its suspicions aroused, Propaganda investigated Poterie's past life, and when it found it disgraceful, ordered him out of the country. Unfortunately, his successor, Father Louis Rousellot, was no improvement and he too had to be suspended.

At about this time an intemperate Irish secular priest named Patrick Smyth pushed the thorns on Carroll's brow down just a little deeper. Father Smyth landed in America in 1787 and was sent to work among the ex-Jesuits in Frederick, Maryland. Fancying himself slighted because of his Irish blood, his resentment apparently nourished by a fondness for drink, Smyth sailed back to Ireland, where he published a vicious diatribe accusing the ex-Jesuits of living in idle opulence on the labor of mistreated slaves while seculars such as himself were left to do all the hard work. Because Smyth's attack coincided with Poterie's equally false charges that Carroll was attempting to resurrect the Jesuits, it proved to be damaging; and because it was circulated in Ireland, where Carroll hoped to recruit most of the laborers for the American vineyard, it was even devastating. So Father Carroll wrote a reply which he asked the bishops of Ireland to publish. They advised against it, promising instead to make the truth known quietly, and thus deprive Smyth of the kind of polemical heat in which his lies might flourish. One passage of Father Carroll's rejoinder, however, deserves to be quoted, if only because of its description of how the priests in Maryland did treat their slaves. He wrote:

The few [priests] to whom this management [of a plantation] is committed, treat their negroes with great mildness and are attentive to guard them from the evils of hunger and nakedness; they work less and are much better fed, lodged and clothed, than labouring men in almost any part of Europe; the instances are rare indeed, and almost unknown, of corporal punishment being inflicted on any of them who

are come to the age of manhood; and a priest's negro is almost pro-
verbial for one, who is allowed to act without control.

Much as Carroll might have exonerated himself in the eyes
of the Irish hierarchy, and also in Rome, where a copy of Smyth's
attack had been received, he was unable to infect them with any
of his own enthusiasm for the American missions. The only
priests whom the Irish bishops were willing to let go were the
ones they wanted to see gone; and so, the American Church
continued to be plagued by a shortage of priests. West of the
Alleghenies, there were almost no clergymen. In his first report
to Propaganda, Carroll had said, "This tract of country contains,
I hear, many Catholics, formerly Canadians, who speak French,
and I fear that they are destitute of priests." The only one resident there was Pierre Gibault, the doughty ex-Jesuit who had
defied Bishop Briand and marched with George Rogers Clark.
For a while Carroll sent two more priests to join him, one as his
vicar general, but Gibault resented both as intruders encroaching
on the rights of the Diocese of Quebec. With this, Carroll entered a jurisdictional dispute with Bishop Hubert, the successor
of Briand. Although this region now belonged to the United
States, Hubert insisted that he was still responsible for it; and he
did hold onto Detroit until the British flag was finally lowered
there in 1796. To solve the problem, both he and Carroll agreed
to submit the dispute to Propaganda; and in the meantime, the
Spanish lured all three priests in the area across the Mississippi
by promising them a fixed salary—thus leaving this huge area
completely bereft of spiritual ministration.

Similar difficulties existed south of the Ohio River, in present
Kentucky and Tennessee. Catholics had joined the westward
expansion movement and had asked Carroll to supply them with
a priest. When he did so, these carefree frontiersmen decided
that they did not really care for any form of restraint, and their
frustrated pastor quickly abandoned them. Clearly, the air of
freedom was exhilarating, much to the exasperation of the dis-
traught Prefect-Apostolic. Again and again, Father Carroll found
himself compelled to confront freewheeling clerics who seemed
to equate the independence of the new republic with independ-

ence from ecclesiastical authority. Worse, the laity also challenged his control.

What has been called "trusteeism," a lay-clerical jurisdictional dispute peculiar to American Catholicism, seems to have begun, understandably enough, among the turbulent Irish of New York City. Probably through contact with Protestantism, and certainly assisted by the encouragement of non-Catholics who were delighted to discomfit the ancient creed, the lay faithful there came to the conclusion that they had the right to hire and fire their pastors and that the Prefect-Apostolic had no right to interfere with them.

In 1784, after the New York legislature had repealed the state's antipriest laws, the Catholics there sent to Ireland at their own expense for a clergyman. The man who came over was Charles Maurice Whelan, a Franciscan who had served as a chaplain with the French fleet during the Revolution and been captured by the British at Jamaica. He arrived before Father Carroll was made Prefect-Apostolic, and without faculties, but he nevertheless began to administer the sacraments. After Carroll received the power to impart faculties, he granted them to Whelan, albeit reluctantly, his misgivings over the friar's disregard for procedure being overcome by his anxiety to provide New York with a priest. Next, the same faithful who had sent for Whelan on their own incorporated themselves as the "Trustees of the Roman Catholic Church in the City of New York," bought land and began building a church.

Soon the congregation of St. Peter's, as it was to be called, became disenchanted with Father Whelan. Although a pious man, he was a blunt one who did not look with equanimity on any vice, even drink. Moreover, he was a poor preacher who fell far short of the standards of Irish eloquence. So Father Whelan was persuaded to send to Ireland for the instrument of his own destruction: a fellow friar and a preacher of renown, Father Andrew Nugent. Immediately, the two friars fell out and the congregation divided into rival camps. Eventually, Nugent gained the support of the trustees, Whelan was ousted and Father Carroll was asked to confirm Nugent in his place. Evidently, the trustees thought that, like many of the Protestant churches around them, they possessed the right to appoint to the pastoral office. Carroll tried to explain to them that they did not, that this episcopal power was held by himself alone, also pointing out that there was as yet no office of parish priest in the United States. Finding his efforts unavailing, in October, 1787, Carroll went to New York to take personal charge of the situation.

While he was in the sacristy vesting for Mass, Father Nugent went into the pulpit to denounce him. Carroll suspended him on the spot, but Nugent said Mass in defiance of his authority. Now the trustees sided with Father Carroll and locked the church doors in an effort to keep the Nugent faction out. To the horror of the Prefect-Apostolic, Nugent's aroused followers broke down the door and not only prevented Carroll from saying Mass but forced him to take refuge in the home of the Spanish minister.

Because New York was then the capital of the United States, the event was given wide publicity, causing great embarrassment among the Catholics. Many of the Protestant onlookers who had followed the wild-eyed Nugentites into the church were delighted to interpret the clash as a collision between the spirit of American democracy and popish autocracy. Scandalized, Father Carroll attempted to say Mass the following Sunday, and was again put to flight by the Nugent faction. Finding no other recourse, he took the case to court, where the trustees were upheld and Nugent was himself ousted. With that, Carroll placed William O'Brien, an Irish Dominican, in charge of St. Peter's.

Trusteeism, however, was far from dead. Too many factors in American society tended to give it a long and flourishing life. First, Catholics in America had lived so long without episcopal rule that they had no idea of what the Church's ecclesiastical government was like. Second, the Protestants around them placed strong emphasis on lay administration, and the civil laws of the various states favored lay ownership of ecclesiastical property. Seeing how their Protestant neighbors organized their churches and appointed or removed their own pastors, it was probably inevitable that some Catholics should wish to do the same. Thus, when the Prefect-Apostolic returned from his unpleasant experiences in New York, he can hardly have been surprised to find that the normally peaceable Germans in Philadelphia were demanding a church of their own.

From the beginning the Germans at St. Mary's Church had resented being ministered to by English-speaking priests, and had complained that they were being shorted in such things as pew allotments and cemetery space. To mollify them, the pastor at St. Mary's had invited Father Lawrence Graessl of Bavaria to come to Philadelphia. Unknown to Carroll, the Germans had themselves advertised for priests in German newspapers. Two brothers, the Franciscan priests John and Peter Heilbron, answered the appeal and came to the United States, landing in Philadelphia in October, 1787, the same month in which Father Graessl arrived. Immediately, the Heilbrons won over most of the Germans at St. Mary's Church, inflaming their already considerable desire for a church organized on nationalist lines. Next, in 1788, the Germans bought a lot and asked Carroll for permission to build Holy Trinity Church. It was then that the Prefect-Apostolic, having only just emerged from the New York fiasco, decided to grant their request rather than provoke a repetition of the scandals of trusteeism in Philadelphia.

In fact, though, his decision only guaranteed such unrest. The trustees preferred the Heilbron brothers to Father Graessl, and they elected Father John Heilbron as their pastor, asking the Prefect-Apostolic to approve their choice. He refused. Even so, Father Heilbron presided at dedication ceremonies for Holy Trinity Church, and in the ensuing squabble between the Heilbron–trustee faction and Father Carroll supporting Father Graessl, the parish went into a nationalist schism for a few years. Meanwhile, the dispute boiled over to engulf those volatile Irish spirits at St. Mary's, where three rebellious Irish-born priests joined the lay trustees in open war against ecclesiastical authority. Although the Heilbrons made their submission to Carroll in 1790, a full generation was to pass before the Church in Philadelphia was free of trustee troubles.

In the meantime, all these obstinate priests and misguided trustees had convinced John Carroll that the time had now come for a bishop in America. Too many clerics and lay committees had scoffed openly at the limited powers of a prefect-apostolic. The visible authority of a miter and a crozier, and behind that the ultimate episcopal thunderbolt of excommunication, was now required to govern the American Church. Moreover, Protestant opposition to any form of episcopal authority appeared to be softening. In 1787, the Archbishop of Canterbury in England had consecrated bishops for Pennsylvania and New York in what is now called the Episcopalian Church. If the Protestant Episcopal Church could have bishops without stirring up a storm, why not the Catholic Church?

Accordingly, in March of 1788 a petition was sent to Rome requesting the Holy Father to appoint a bishop as soon as possible and to allow the American clergy to elect him from their midst. With surprising speed, Pope Pius VI gave his assent to the American requests, and Cardinal Antonelli wrote to Father Carroll: "By you, therefore, it is first to be examined in what city this episcopal see ought to be erected. . . . This having been done, his Holiness as a special favour and for this first time, permits the priests who at the present time duly exercise the ministry of the Catholic religion and have care of souls to elect as bishop a person eminent in piety, prudence, and zeal for the faith, from the said clergy, and present him to the Apostolic See to obtain confirmation."

On May 18, 1789, the clergy gathered at Whitemarsh again to make unanimous selection of Baltimore as the site for an episcopal see and to elect John Carroll as bishop by a vote of 24 to 2. Again moving rapidly, Pius VI confirmed the choices in the bull *Ex hac apostolicae* issued the following November, which constituted the entire United States as the diocese of Baltimore in direct dependence upon the Holy See. In his letter forwarding the official documents to Carroll, Cardinal Antonelli made it clear that permission for American priests to elect their own bishop had been granted *for this time only,* and that in the future the bishops themselves would nominate prelates for appointment by the Pope, as was customary.

Nevertheless, at the very inception of a government for the American Church, the American way had prevailed. Equally significant, the new Church had been born in the same year in which George Washington took his oath as the first President of the United States. Both infant church and young republic had been through the stormy and formative decade of the eighties together, and the one was now putting out like a rowboat from the Bark of Peter, the other setting sail for destiny in the magnificent vessel of its new Constitution. Both were in the hands of splendid captains, and in fact, Washington and Carroll were so similar in character that they might have come from the same mold. Neither was very profound or clever, and yet each had a deep reverence for their native land and the American style. In his inaugural address, Washington could speak movingly of a "reverence for the characteristic rights of freedom," and John Carroll before his consecration also could salute the new day of civil and religious liberty with the remark: ". . . America may come to exhibit a proof to the world, that general and equal toleration, by giving a free circulation to fair argument, is the most effectual method to bring all denominations of Christians to a unity of faith."

In August of 1790, John Carroll was consecrated the first Catholic bishop of the United States. The ceremony took place in Lulworth Castle in Dorsetshire, England. Carroll's old friend, Father Charles Plowden, preached the sermon. Praising the American Revolution, Plowden declared that its "earliest and most precious fruit" had been the freeing of the Catholic Church there from the bondage of a hundred years.

Now, having kept the faith, the American Church would turn to spreading it.

Chapter VI

In the year 1790 when John Carroll was consecrated as the first Catholic bishop in the United States of America, he found himself at the head of what may be called a Church Suffered.

With a membership of only 35,000 souls out of a total population of 3,929,214, the Church was still a tiny minority—and still a suspect one. True, five of the thirteen states had by then granted equal rights to Catholics, and the remaining eight were to do likewise during the next four decades, but when the Protestant Establishment thought of a Catholic equal it was usually a Carroll or a member of one of the old, wealthy, English-stock Maryland families such as the Brookes, Neales or Taneys.

These people could be trusted, so completely, in fact, that in 1792 Charles Carroll was considered as the Federalist candidate for President. Having already refused the presidency of the Continental Congress in 1778, believing, as always, that he could perform his best service in his native Maryland, Carroll was nonetheless considered as a Federalist candidate in 1792. George Washington was neither enamored of the job nor popular with everyone in his party, and the Federalists, fearing that he might not run, were alarmed at the prospect of a campaign against Thomas Jefferson. According to Alexander Hamilton, it was suggested to him that Carroll might be the kind of candidate who could command national support against Jefferson. At least, Hamilton has written that if Washington did not run, he would have thrown his support to Carroll. However interesting it may be to speculate that the second President of the United States might then have been a Catholic, it is probable that Carroll, who had by then retired from national politics, would have declined this honor as well. The point here, however, is that the old-line Catholic families of Maryland were socially acceptable. But they were the exception. The rule, the true Catholics in the eyes of the Protestant Establishment, were the humble English workingmen, German-speaking farmers and mechanics or Irish laborers and servants, with here and there a scattering of those high-living French émigrés whom Carroll himself had found "a scandal to religion." To these people the Establishment extended neither civil trust nor social equality, but only sufferance; and so, when Carroll took charge of his enormous diocese of Baltimore he was exclusively concerned with the care of souls and with little or no thought of Catholic participation in or contributions to American public life.

In a word, the new bishop sought to establish discipline, and to this end he convoked a synod that met at Baltimore in November, 1791. At this first convocation of the American Church, attended by only twenty-two priests, a total of twenty-four decrees were formulated. In the main, they dealt with the administration of the sacraments, although some were pointedly shaped toward safeguarding the faith of this Catholic island adrift in a Protestant sea. To this end, mixed marriage was sternly discouraged, but if it could not be prevented, then the non-Catholic partner was to be compelled to promise that all children issuing from the union were to be educated in the Catholic faith. Here, then, at the outset of the Church's history in the United States, was that intransigent position on the education of children which many modern non-Catholics, and Catholics as well, find so irritating. Far from being the arrogant and aggressive prescription of a proselytizing, all-powerful Church, however, it was in reality only the self-defensive stance of a tiny minority at bay. This first synod also passed a decree on Lenten fasting, and its severity is to be noted. Only liquids were allowed in the morning, and meat, milk and eggs were banned from all meals except those taken on most Sundays and Saturdays, when they might be had once a day. This, for poor, struggling laymen compelled to earn their bread in the sweat of their brow and for priests who spent most of their time in the saddle!

Priests, of course, or rather the shortage of them, were Bishop Carroll's first, indeed his enduring problem. Vocations among

American Catholic boys were scarce, if only because few of the wealthier youths of English stock were attracted to the hard life of a missionary, and the sons of illiterate immigrants apparently were not yet considered as candidates for the priesthood. Carroll would still have to look to Europe, and at first it appeared that he would get little help there. English Catholicism was still struggling to free itself from the shackles of the Penal Laws and had few priests to spare; Ireland appeared to have too many of the wrong kind, that is, those clerical free lances who crossed the ocean hoping to make their fortune, ecclesiastical or otherwise; and the German priests were frequently either incapacitated by their inability to speak English or too susceptible to trusteeism. France, of course, was at that time entering the ordeal of the Revolution and the Church there was preoccupied defending her own life.

To Carroll, the answer to his problem appeared to be the new college which he planned to establish on former Jesuit property at Georgetown. Here, he planned to train native-born young Americans for the priesthood, and while he was in England awaiting consecration as bishop, he received so many donations for Georgetown from English friends that he was convinced that the project would succeed. But then, to his surprise, the very excesses of the French Revolution offered him a solution of a different kind entirely.

Although the Reign of Terror and the guillotine had not yet made their appearance in France, the Revolution's hatred of the Church was already apparent, so much so that in Paris the Sulpician fathers who specialized in the training of priests feared the extinction of their society. Looking around for a refuge, they thought of the United States and sent an emissary to Father Carroll while he was in England awaiting consecration. To the American bishop-elect's astonishment, the Sulpicians not only offered to open a seminary in his country, complete with a faculty and several English-speaking students as the nucleus of a student body, but also promised to pay their passage and all expenses connected with acquiring property and erecting a building. Delighted and grateful, Carroll accepted, even though, as he said: "I feel great sorrow in the reflection, that we owe such a benefit to the distressed state of Religion in France."

In the autumn of 1791, Father Francis Charles Nagot opened St. Mary's Seminary at Baltimore. With him were three other Sulpician instructors and five seminarians, and in the following year, six more instructors and two seminarians came to St. Mary's. Here was the foundation stone of the American Church. "All our hopes are founded on the Seminary of Baltimore," Bishop Carroll wrote to the Holy See. Two years later, he ordained his first priest, Father Stephen Badin, a Frenchman who had arrived in the United States in minor orders and who went west to become the apostle to Kentucky. The second priest was ordained in 1795. He was a Russian nobleman and a convert, the famous Prince Demetrius Augustine Gallitzin. Choosing to be known henceforth as "Mr. Smith," Gallitzin also went west, to Loretto, Pennsylvania, where he was the constant astonishment of the humble Catholic folk, dressing like a peasant and acting like an aristocrat, teaching his parishioners fencing and meanwhile losing a fortune in his attempt to found a model Catholic community complete with tannery, flour mill and sawmill.

Slowly, gradually, the little trickle of priests issuing from St. Mary's turned into a rivulet, but then the rise of Napoleon and his subsequent Concordat with the Holy See threatened to dry it up entirely. With seminaries once again legal in France, the Sulpician superior general, Father J. A. Emery, planned to recall his priests from Baltimore. Fortunately, however, he broached his plan to Pope Pius VII, who dissuaded him with the remark: "My son, let this seminary subsist, let it—it will bear fruit in time. To recall the directors in order to employ them in France, in other houses, would be stripping St. Paul to clothe St. Peter." So St. Mary's Seminary stayed, continuing to bear fruit in the Pope's prophetic words, until, by 1829, fifty-two priests had been ordained, of whom twenty-one were native-born Americans, thirteen were Irish or English and eighteen were French or German. In fact, St. Mary's gained so much prestige in Maryland that the state granted it the charter of a university, and so it continued until 1852, when the Sulpicians finally closed their doors in deference to the new college opened then by the Jesuits.

In the meantime, Bishop Carroll's dreams of a Catholic college at Georgetown had also been realized. In 1791, a few weeks after St. Mary's Seminary was founded, Georgetown also opened its doors. This forerunner of what is today a great university was then hardly more than an academy, as might be judged from a broadside which promised to prepare students for "Study of the higher Sciences in the University of this or those of the neighboring States." Nevertheless, if Brother Crouch's short-lived school at Newtown in 1639 be dismissed, Georgetown stands as the first Catholic school in the United States. Moreover, it was begun with a spirit of toleration which was so far typical of American Catholicism, for it was expressly stated: "Agreeably to the liberal Principle of our Constitution, the Seminary will be open to Students of Every religious Profession. They, who, in this respect, differ from the Superintendent of the Academy, will be at Liberty to frequent the places of Worship and Instruction appointed by their Parents; but with Respect to their moral Conduct, all must be subject to general and uniform Discipline."

Set down in the unhealthy swamp that was now dignified with the title of District of Columbia, Georgetown had little to commend it but a magnificent view of the Potomac. Nevertheless, like the ramshackle, mud-mired national capital around it, Georgetown persevered; especially after 1806, when the Society of Jesus was restored in the United States and the successors of the old Jesuits of Maryland stepped forward to reclaim their patrimony and to take charge of the school. Two years later, a second school was founded at Mount St. Mary's College in Emmitsburg, Maryland—and in the following year the dynamic Elizabeth Bayley Seton founded the first Catholic school for girls in the same little hamlet.

The passionate, gay and charmingly frank woman who has entered Church history as Mother Seton was probably Catholicism's most distinguished recruit thus far from the ranks of the Protestant Establishment. Born in 1774, a relative of the Roosevelts, at the age of twenty she married the well-to-do New York merchant William Seton. While living with him in Italy, she came under the influence of the Felicchi brothers of Leghorn, business associates of her husband and devout Catholics. Thus, after Seton died in 1803, leaving his widow with five children and very little money, she left Episcopalianism for Catholicism. Disowned by her relatives, she opened a school in New York to support herself and her family. From there she moved to Baltimore and on again to Emmitsburg, where she founded the Sisters of Charity, the first native religious community for women in the United States.

In a sense, Mother Seton was the foundress of the Catholic parochial school in America. There had been such schools before her, but these were conducted by lay teachers for a fee. Elizabeth Seton's first school, however, was the prototype of that parochial school so peculiar to American Catholicism: one which is completely free and which is conducted, in the main, by religious orders of women. "Had I been a man," Mother Seton would say, "the whole world would not be enough for me. I would tread in the footsteps of St. Francis Xavier." Apparently, however, her native land was wide enough, and her gift to it remains the huge company of teaching sisters which she founded.

Meanwhile, branches of some of the older religious orders and societies had also come to the United States, most of them arriving as refugees from the French Revolution. In 1790, the Carmelite nuns established themselves at Port Tobacco in Maryland; in 1793 the Poor Clares arrived, later merging with the new native-born Visitandine nuns; the Augustinians came in 1797; the Trappist monks located in Kentucky in 1805, only to have their monastery destroyed by fire, after which they drifted across the country, returning to France after the downfall of Napoleon; and in 1805 the Maryland-born Dominican, Father Edward Fenwick, laid the foundations for his order in this country. The oldest order of all—the Benedictines—was also represented in the ill-fated Ohio colonizing scheme known as the Gallipolis Project.

Early in the Church's history, land companies were active in promoting the sale of large tracts among Catholics overseas. During the French Revolution, the Scioto Company decided to found Gallipolis in present Ohio for Catholics seeking to escape the French Revolution. The first of these colonists arrived at their destination in early 1791, only to find that they had been swindled and that their claims, for which many of them had paid a second time, had no legal standing. Disheartened, they settled elsewhere, many of them moving into the Northwest Territory which a recent decision of Propaganda had removed from the jurisdiction of the Diocese of Quebec and placed in Carroll's care.

Here, in Vincennes, the Illinois country and Detroit, the lands above the Ohio, there was a growing number of Catholics, most of them French-speaking and completely devoid of priests—until the French Revolution again came to the aid of American Catholicism.

Among the French refugee priests whom Bishop Carroll was able to send to the Old Northwest were Father Benedict Joseph Flaget, the future bishop of Bardstown in Kentucky, and Father Gabriel Richard, the apostle of Michigan and the first and only Catholic priest to be elected to Congress. There were many more like them—gallant, self-sacrificing men who had exchanged a life of cultivation and ease for the rude hardships of pioneer life— and there is no doubt that without them the young Church in America would have had a different history indeed. The East also owed its debt to the refugee priests, Boston most of all. Here, in 1792, Father Francis Matignon, "a priest of experience, having taught theology in the College of Navarre, with experience among English-speaking Catholics, came to devote his learning, his ability, his eloquence, as well as his deep piety and wide charity to the little flock of Catholics in New England." After Father Matignon came his pupil and peer, Father John Cheverus, who became the first Bishop of Boston.

French priests also proved useful to Bishop Carroll when his already extensive administrative problems were increased by the purchase of the Louisiana Territory from Napoleon in 1803. For a time, some Spanish Franciscans claimed this huge diocese, but in 1805, Propaganda made Carroll its administrator. After nearly seven years of futile attempts to induce priests to take over as his vicar-general in New Orleans, he finally persuaded Father William Du Bourg, the president of St. Mary's University, to go there.

Such snowballing duties, however, had already convinced the aging Bishop of Baltimore that his enormous diocese was just too big to be governed efficiently. He had already asked and been granted a bishop coadjutor—at first the beloved Bavarian priest Father Lawrence Graessl, who died before he could receive the miter; and then Father Leonard Neale, the President of Georgetown—and he next petitioned Pope Pius VII to divide the diocese. To his surprise, Propaganda replied that Baltimore was indeed too big and that an extra diocese would hardly suffice for its needs. Instead, Propaganda proposed an American province, in effect, with Baltimore raised to the rank of an archdiocese served by four or five suffragan sees. Consulting with the priests of his diocese, Bishop Carroll notified Rome of his selection of Boston, New York, Philadelphia and Bardstown in Kentucky, with responsibility for the Northwest, as suffragan sees; and in 1808, Pius VII issued two briefs which elevated Baltimore to the rank of an archdiocese and created the four new dioceses.

With that, the new Archbishop of Baltimore was well content. Within less than three decades, the infant Church in the young republic had grown to a population of seventy thousand Catholics served by seventy priests and eighty churches. The foundations had been laid for the training of priests and nuns, for Catholic education and for the growth of piety as exemplified by the establishment of religious monasteries and convents. Perhaps just as important, the American Church at that point in its history was enjoying a period of "good feelings" with its Protestant neighbors.

John Carroll himself had remarked of this warming attitude when he visited Boston in 1791, and the *Herald of Freedom* had bestowed encomiums upon him, declaring: "Boston would congratulate the hour of this Gentleman's return, and will remember with gratitude and pleasure, his visit to the State." In fact, the reception given to the Catholic bishop had been so effusive as to lead him to write: "It is wonderful to tell what great civilities have been done to me in this town, where, a few years ago, a Popish priest was thought to be the greatest monster in the creation. Many here, even of their principal people, have acknowledged to me that they would have crossed to the opposite side of the street rather than meet a Roman Catholic some time ago." In fact, puritanical Boston, where even to this day the phrase "R.C." carries a singularly Bostonian accent of deprecation, had so far warmed to Catholicism that when Fathers Matignon and Cheverus began collecting funds to build a church, the Protestants contributed almost as much as the Catholics. George

Washington and John Adams also subscribed to Catholic building funds, and it was during the administration of the priest-hating John Adams that Congress named John Sartori as the first American consul to the Papal States, a post which was continued until the collapse of the Papacy's temporal power in 1870.

Perhaps the most famous incident illustrative of American good will was the trial of Father Anthony Kohlmann, the Administrator of the Diocese of New York. Kohlmann had returned some stolen property and when the suspected thieves were arrested he was called upon to tell what he knew about them. He refused on the ground that whatever knowledge he possessed had come to him in the confessional, and he could not break the seal of secrecy. "If I did," he said, "I should render myself liable to eternal damnation." The court upheld him, and De Witt Clinton, who presided at the trial, handed down the landmark ruling that has since respected the secrecy of the confessional as inviolate.

Even more remarkable was the case in which the Pennsylvania assemblyman Miers Fisher attacked a proposed lottery as being "like the Papal indulgences, forgiving and permitting sins to raise money." Challenged by the prominent Catholic, Matthew Carey, Fisher apologized. He said he had meant no offense and might have been misinformed on the subject, after which he asked for a book which might help to dispel a prejudice arising from his habit of reading only anti-Catholic literature. Such frankness was not only disarming but heartwarming to Catholics who had heretofore known little other than snarls and sneers. Ironically enough, however, while the Church found herself at peace with former enemies outside her walls, within them she was again beset by her own children misled by what has been called "trusteemania."

Chapter VII

The problem of trusteeism which was to mortify the American Church like a bloody hairshirt until well into the middle of the 1800s was fundamentally a problem of lay as opposed to clerical control over the appointment of pastors.

Ironically, in its essence, this difficulty of the "foreign" Catholic Church was a purely American phenomenon, and it is possible that it might not have arisen had John Carroll been other than the good American that he was. Although Carroll believed that the law of God superseded the rule of nations, that a man must put conscience before country, he was also a deep admirer of the new American spirit of independence. To encourage it among the Catholics whose souls were in his care, he permitted the introduction of the trustee system in his see.

Normally, the Catholic Church's method of holding property is to place it in the hands of the bishop, always with the understanding that he is to make provisions for the orderly transfer of all he so possesses to his successor. Indeed, one of the first duties of a new ordinary is to meet with his diocesan consultors to sign the last will and testament which they have prepared to that end, after which, if the consultors have a sense of humor, he may be taken into the cathedral basement to be shown his predecessor's tomb as well as the open niche designed to receive his own remains. In other words, the ordinaries come and go, but the see remains; it is the office, not the man, which actually possesses both power and property.

When the American Church began in Maryland, property was held by the individual Jesuits in their capacity as gentlemen adventurers. After the Society was suppressed, this and other prop-

erty acquired in Pennsylvania was secured for the American
Church by the institution of the Select Body of the Clergy. Following the Revolution, this property became insufficient for the
needs of a growing Church; and so, it devolved upon the laity to
provide for the sustenance of priests and the erection and maintenance of churches and schools. Because of this, Carroll considered it only fair that laymen should also be entrusted with
the administration of both funds and property. Thus was born
the trustee system whereby each congregation was incorporated
under the laws of the various states and managed by elected
lay trustees.

Theoretically, it was a good system. It relieved a priest's mind
of temporal cares and allowed him to concentrate upon his spiritual ministry. If he also had to attend to distant missions, it
enabled him to be away from his parish for long periods of time.
As Archbishop John Hughes of New York was to say years later:
"Regarded *a priori*, no system could appear to be less objectionable, or more likely, both to secure advantages to those congregations, and at the same time to recommend the Catholic religion
to the liberal consideration of the Protestant sentiment of the
country." Unfortunately, like all tidy systems, trusteeism foun-
dered on the rock of human nature.

Frequently, the trustees were less than they should have been.
Some were arrant meddlers seeking either prestige or profit.
Many were not even churchgoers. Worse, these ambitious men
joined forces with rebellious clergymen who had axes of their
own to grind. Sometimes fractious priests would encourage the
trustees to defy the bishop on the ground of the old European
custom of the "right of patronage." The argument here was simply that, having provided the "living" at this or that parish, they
had the right to name the priests who would occupy it. What the
trustees did not or would not understand was that Bishop Carroll
had permitted the introduction of the trustee system as a means
of protecting church property adaptable both to the spirit and
laws of America, but always *under ecclesiastical control.* Only a
bishop could create a parish or appoint a pastor. Unfortunately,
there were boards of trustees claiming that they could do both.

Trusteeism also embraced a growing spirit of nationalism
among German Catholics, a schism which spread from Philadel-

phia to Carroll's own episcopal city of Baltimore in 1797. There, a priest named Caesar Reuter turned the Germans against their bishop. Opening the independent parish of St. John, Reuter induced the trustees to bar Bishop Carroll on the ground that he had no jurisdiction over German Catholics in the United States. With great reluctance, Carroll went into the civil courts and won a lawsuit that compelled the trustees to return the church to his jurisdiction. Meanwhile, Holy Trinity in Philadelphia erupted again.

This once-turbulent parish had been peaceful after Father John Heilbron made his submission to Carroll in 1790, so much so that the bishop permitted him to go to Spain on a begging tour. While in Europe, Heilbron strayed into Revolutionary France and lost his life to the Reign of Terror. His successor at Holy Trinity was his brother Peter, who unwisely took in the unruly Father John Goetz of Austria as his assistant. In gratitude, Father Goetz persuaded the trustees to depose Heilbron in his own favor, after which, joined in his defiance of Bishop Carroll by another obstreperous clergyman named William Elling, he appealed to Rome for a German bishop for the German Catholics of America. When this maneuver failed, Father Goetz disappeared. Like so many of these wayward priests who were to sail in and out of the history of the early Church, he just upped and vanished; and in 1802 Father Elling and the parish he had helped to disturb became reconciled to Carroll's authority.

For the next five years, the American Church was relatively free of trustee troubles, until the cathedral parish of St. Mary's in Philadelphia boiled over once more. This time, the disturbance was caused while the new Bishop of Philadelphia, Michael Egan, had gone on tour of his extensive diocese, which included Pennsylvania, Delaware and western New Jersey. In his absence, St. Mary's was administered by the eloquent and brilliant Irish Dominican, William Vincent Harold. With him was his uncle, Father James Harold, a secular who had participated in Irish insurrections against Britain, been captured and escaped from imprisonment at Botany Bay. Naturally enough, the overwhelmingly Irish congregation of St. Mary's gave a warm reception to this grizzled martyr to Irish independence. Soon, however, his quarrelsome nature wore out his welcome, and the trustees objected to supporting him. At once, Father William Vincent came to his uncle's side, just as Bishop Egan returned from his visitation tour. Worn out by his travels, the bishop requested the Harolds to do all the preaching in St. Mary's, providing the older Father Harold with the opportunity to mount the pulpit and excoriate the trustees for their niggardliness. Scandalized, Bishop Egan proposed to transfer the old man, whereupon his nephew came to his uncle's side, and the trustees, with that impartial perversity which is both the delight and despair of the Irish temperament, promptly joined forces with the Harolds in opposition to the bishop. Now, the Harolds conspired to gain a bishop's miter for the junior partner, offering his undoubted brilliance and zeal as proof of his worthiness, and advancing the complaint that too many ecclesiastical plums were going to Frenchmen. Thwarted in this gambit, both Harolds packed their bags and sailed back whence they had come. Now the trustees were infuriated. Suddenly recalling the older priest's services to Erin and the younger one's lost eloquence, they turned on the ailing old bishop and blamed him for hounding the Harolds across the sea. So ended an episode which might have been comical, had it not exposed the Church to ridicule and scandalized so many earnest souls, and had not the intransigence of the trustees caused Bishop Egan so much anguish that he died in 1814, only four years after his consecration, "a martyr to trusteemania."

The death of Egan, however, was far from being the end of trustee troubles in the tempestuous Diocese of Philadelphia. Now an "Irish" party in Ireland and an "American" party in the United States proposed rival candidates for the vacant see, and to the consternation of Carroll the Irish party won. Henry Conwell, Vicar-General of Armagh in Ireland, was named by Rome as the second bishop of Philadelphia. He was seventy-four years old and approaching senility; yet, the Catholics of Philadelphia prepared for his coming with great joy. Unfortunately, many of the trustees of St. Mary's Cathedral parish, still sulking over the loss of Harold, had other plans—and they deputed the unscrupulous Father William Hogan to preach the welcoming sermon.

Hogan had been in the city only a few months, having come from his native Ireland with his ecclèsiastical free lance unsheathed. At once, he became a favorite with the women. Father

Hogan was extremely handsome, perhaps even beautiful, with his peaches-and-cream complexion and striking blond head. Although "deficient in the most common branches of an English education," his golden voice and splendid presence in the pulpit apparently more than compensated for what he lacked in learning. Young mothers all but swooned when Father Hogan approached them in their pew to chat and perhaps pat the heads of their children. Their husbands, naturally enough, experienced different sensations, but even though Hogan had numerous non-admirers who distrusted him as an ambitious fop, the fractious trustees of St. Mary's found him a willing tool for their purposes. Thus, when Bishop Conwell arrived in St. Mary's to take possession of his see, Father Hogan "welcomed" him with an abusive sermon, which he repeated so often that the aging Conwell was finally obliged to suspend his faculties.

This, of course, merely enraged the trustees, who elected Hogan as pastor of St. Mary's and barred Bishop Conwell from his own cathedral. Next, they published and circulated a letter among all Catholics of the United States, inviting them to join their independent Church. In this, they were abetted by two so-called "experts" in canon law. Both were Spanish priests. One was a free-lance Franciscan named Rico, who styled himself as "Vicar General to the Armies of Spain," while running a cigar store to earn his living; and the other was one Miers, a fugitive from the Inquisition in Mexico. Such were the "brains" of the Hogan Schism, as it came to be called; and yet, the "body" of his followers was hardly less bizarre. Among the cranks and malcontents who formed the bulk of Father Hogan's supporters was one "Crazy Norah," a gaunt, obviously unbalanced woman who wore an immense stovepipe hat and prowled about Philadelphia swinging a couple of shabby carpetbags stuffed with novels and bills for collection. This was Crazy Norah's profession, bill-collecting. Her technique was unique. If the debtor refused to pay his bill, she stationed herself opposite his dwelling place. There, surrounded by a crowd of children, she would chant the Litany of the Saints, in which she had included her grandmother, and if the debtor, either embarrassed by her presence or frightened by what might have seemed a kind of ecclesiastical curse, changed his mind and gave her the desired money, she would immediately deduct her commission before turning the remainder over to the creditor. Crazy Norah has been immortalized in a verse that goes:

> To young and old
> Abroad she wails.
> "Keep tight your hold
> On God's coat-tails!"

With such "characters" at their backs, Father Hogan and the trustees redoubled their attacks upon Bishop Conwell, until, in 1821, he pronounced public excommunication on Hogan. When the schismatic priest persisted in his defiance, Pope Pius VII approved his excommunication and expressly denied the right of patronage to the trustees of any parish.

Later on, His Holiness clarified the Church's position on the holding of ecclesiastical property. The trustee system was to be tolerated where it already existed, provided it was hedged about by legal safeguards, but no new parishes were to be created unless the property rights were turned over to the ordinary. With this, the Hogan Schism began to lose momentum. Father Hogan drifted out of the Church, toying with the idea of offering himself to the Protestant Episcopal Diocese of New York, but deciding instead to marry a wealthy twenty-year-old widow, and after her death another well-to-do widow. Meanwhile, he practiced law, became violently anti-Catholic and finally died in apostasy in 1842.

In the meantime, the trustees at St. Mary's decided to try subtlety on the aging Bishop Conwell, suggesting that he sign an agreement by which any dispute over an appointment would be resolved by a special committee, half-lay, half-clerical. For the sake of peace, Conwell signed, but if he congratulated himself on his acumen, he was brought up short by a roar from Rome. Declaring the contract null and void, Propaganda stripped the senile old man of his jurisdiction and ordered him to report to the Holy City for an accounting. This Conwell did, but then got into trouble again by inexplicably violating Propaganda's prohibition against leaving Rome. Now his brother bishops in the United States came to his side, pleading that he be allowed to end his days in Philadelphia, then under the administrator of the coadjutor bishop, Francis Patrick Kenrick. The request was granted, and although the never-say-die trustees thereupon attempted to enlist this weak-minded old man in their intrigues against Kenrick, they were not successful. In 1842, Conwell died, Kenrick became the bona fide Bishop of Philadelphia, and trusteeism there began to die its own natural death.

By then, of course, Archbishop John Carroll of Baltimore had also breathed his last.

If any man can be regarded as the Father of the American Church, it is John Carroll of Maryland. Bearer of a respected American name, ordained in that Society which had planted the faith on the shores of the Chesapeake, he took charge of the infant Church as naturally and firmly as a man bringing order to his own household. To the handful of ex-Jesuits demoralized by the suppression of their order he brought inspiration and direction, while guiding the Church herself out of the night of the Penal Age and into the sunlight of religious freedom. John Carroll organized the American Church. Under him, its diverse and disparate elements were unified, and by his establishment of a seminary and schools, its future was assured.

Although his administrative ability was indeed great, coming at a time when it was most needed, his insights into the American character may have been even of more value to the Church. He realized that in the matter of religion the genius of the new American political system was the separation of church and state. His writings and his speeches are full of encomiums, not on behalf of toleration, for that presumes an established church, but for complete religious freedom. It may be that, like the Calverts before him, this attitude was born of expediency: that Catholicism had more to gain from religious freedom than any other American creed. True enough, but so also did the Founding Fathers of the United States have the most to gain from independence.

So it was John Carroll who gave the American Church, this congeries of European races forever in conflict over tastes and customs, yet joined together in the unity of the One Faith, its peculiar American stamp. Most astonishing, he also foresaw its future. "To dissipate prejudice," he said in 1785, "time will be our best aid, as also will divine Providence and the experience of our fellow citizens in our devotion to our country and its independence."

In many ways, John Carroll resembles the Fathers of the Ancient Church. Like them, he was impeccably moral, orthodox in belief, diligent and devout, patient and prudent—and some of the challenges he faced were similar to those met by Ambrose or Augustine. It is, of course, fatuous to suggest that he merits the title of "Father," if only because he did not live in antiquity. Yet, he was at least a "Founder." And if his more famous cousin can enter American history as "First Citizen," then John Carroll can well claim the epitaph of "First Catholic."

Upon the death of Archbishop Carroll on December 3, 1815, he was immediately succeeded by Leonard Neale, his coadjutor with the right of succession. At once, a fresh storm of trustee controversy burst upon Archbishop Neale's aging head and he lived only until June 18, 1817. His successor was the French Sulpician, Ambrose Maréchal, who had twice before refused the miter. Consecrated in December of 1818, Archbishop Maréchal remained at the head of the American Province for ten tempestuous years. It was Maréchal who had to endure the most tumultuous years of the Hogan Schism in Philadelphia, as well as the trustee troubles which also disturbed every other diocese in the American Province but Bardstown and Boston. In these two places alone the bishops held the property in their own names. Ironically enough, the most insolent and insubordinate claims of all were to issue from the Baltimore archbishop's own outposts in Virginia and South Carolina. And it seems hard to deny that it was Maréchal's own character, his stern inflexibility and his unconcealed attachment to the cause of French influence in the American Church, which so helped to inflame the Irish-French conflict within the Catholic community that some Irish trustees in the South moved from demanding the right to install pastors to claiming the prerogative of electing their own bishops.

It was perhaps inevitable that the American Church should experience a dispute based on racial differences, if only because the Church here was so truly catholic. In every other country, the Church was either German or French or English as the nationality might be. In the United States, however, it was exactly as America was becoming: a melting pot.

As John Tracy Ellis has observed: "An Irish Lutheran, a German Episcopalian, a French Methodist, a Swiss Baptist, and an English Mennonite might then have been thought something of an oddity, but no one thought it strange to see men of all five nationalities occupying neighboring pews in a Catholic church of New York, Philadelphia or Baltimore."

Indeed, the question of how best to turn all these immigrants into good Americans was to be the Church's most pressing and persistent problem, just as her success in doing so was to become her most distinguished service to the United States. No other church was compelled to receive so many foreign-born into her bosom, and it is again an irony to realize that just because she did Americanize this army of immigrants, counseling them in her rectories or instructing them in her schools, she seemed to justify the charge of being an "alien" faith of doubtful loyalty. In this, she was like the man of good will whose efforts to help black men improve themselves are rewarded with the epithet of "nigger-lover." Moreover, this thankless mission, which she certainly did not seek but only accepted because it came to her, not only strained her human and financial resources to the breaking point, it also threatened to destroy her very unity.

This was because so many races under one roof were bound to come into conflict. In the beginning, briefly, the dispute had been between the Irish and the Germans; but then, after the French Revolution, it became an Irish-French struggle. Although many French priests had fled anticlerical France to the United States, they were not followed by a proportionate number of French laymen. Instead, the increase in the American laity came chiefly from Ireland. Very soon, the Irish came to resent being ruled by French priests and, later on, by French bishops. By the time the Frenchman Maréchal succeeded to the archepiscopal see of Baltimore, there was a French bishop in Bardstown, in Boston and in Louisiana, and in 1826, another Frenchman, Jean Dubois, was Bishop of New York. Thus, of the six American miters, five were worn by Frenchmen. Moreover, the seminary was in the hands of French priests. Obviously, or at least obviously to many Irishmen, the American hierarchy was well on its way toward becoming a French thing. It was this conviction which was at the back of the Harolds affair in Philadelphia. Indeed, the younger Harold had partly based his claim to a miter on the complaint of a Frenchified Church, and he had written to Propaganda: "Subjects [for the priesthood] alone are wanted. They are not to be found in the United States, and a French clergy will never look for them in Ireland where they abound."

Doubtless the Sulpician fathers at St. Mary's Seminary had an understandable preference for French candidates for the priesthood, carefully screening non-French recruits for any incipient pro-Irish sympathies. Perhaps their most outstanding success was the Englishman James Whitfield, a protégé of Maréchal's who became the fourth Archbishop of Baltimore. Like Maréchal, Whitfield disliked the Irish, and he wrote to a French bishop on the subject of a new bishop for Cincinnati: "If possibly a good choice can be made, let an American born be recommended and (between us in strict confidence) I do really think we should guard against having more Irish Bishops . . ." From the other camp, an Irish-born bishop with the improbable name of John England had this to say about the French:

I am daily more convinced that the genius of this nation and the administration of the French are not easily reconciled. Besides this, one of the strongest topics of prejudice against our religion is that it is a foreign Religion, and it is not American, that it is the religion of strangers, of aliens . . . The French can never become Americans. Their language, manners, love of *la belle France*, their dress, air, carriage, notions, and mode of speaking of their religion, all, all are foreign. An American then says, "It might be very good, but 'tis a foreign aristocracy." . . . The French clergy are generally good men and love Religion, but they make the Catholic religion thus appear to be exotic, and cannot understand why it should be made to appear assimilated to American principles.

It was just this foreign, aristocratic quality which the English-speaking, democratic Irish resented in the French clergy. Moreover, because of their undoubted chauvinism, the French priests were a little careless about learning to speak English, thereby enraging the eloquent Irish. Writing of Bishop Dubois in 1829, Father John Power said: "[He] is thirty-six years in America, and when he attempts to give common instructions, thirty-six out of three thousand cannot understand a word of what he says. Hundreds leave the Church and go into the Rum Shops while he is speaking." For their part, the French clergy considered the Irish altogether too fond of drink and dissent, and they could not quite conceal their disdain for "*la canaille Irlandaise*," most of whom, thanks to the efficiency of the English Penal Laws in Ireland, arrived in this country illiterate. Rabble or not, the Irish were not docile, and if the sometimes tactless Archbishop Maréchal had understood their bellicose nature he might have prevented the rebellions that broke out in Richmond and Charleston.

Unfortunately, Maréchal persisted in his custom of sending French priests to these predominantly Irish congregations. Both Norfolk and Richmond rebelled. They ousted the Frenchmen, after which they conspired to have a priest from Ireland go to Holland, where he would be consecrated by a Jansenist bishop and come to America as the first presiding bishop of a projected Independent Catholic Church of America. Here was schism, unabashed and unadulterated, and when Rome learned of the conspiracy she became seriously alarmed. However, with a wise forbearance which might have proved useful during the Reformation, she did not pick up the customary cudgels. Instead, Propaganda decided that it would be prudent to create two new dioceses—one of Virginia, with a see at Richmond; another of South Carolina, North Carolina and Georgia, with a see at Charleston—and to staff them with bishops from Ireland. Thus, in July of 1820, John England was made Bishop of Charleston and Patrick Kelly named Bishop of Richmond.

A victory, it would seem, had been gained by the rebellious Irish trustees of the South. Unfortunately, in Richmond they celebrated their triumph by turning against Bishop Kelly, so harassing him that he resigned his see after about a year, whereupon it reverted to the jurisdiction of Archbishop Maréchal of Baltimore. In Charleston, however, the American Church had cause for rejoicing, for in Bishop John England it had acquired the one man capable of solving the trustee problem.

In the history of the Catholic Church in the United States there are some men who loom larger than life, and John England of Ireland is one of them. Born in County Cork in 1786, he was a priest by the time he was twenty-two, and in the decade during which he served his native diocese he demonstrated an originality of approach and a talent for organization which, fired by a whirlwind energy and a passionate heart, were both the delight of the downtrodden Catholic peasantry and the dismay of the conservative clergy. So great was Ireland's capacity for work that at one time he was a Sunday preacher at the diocesan cathedral, rector of the diocesan seminary (where he taught philosophy and theology), secretary to the board of examiners of candidates for holy orders, secretary to the Fever Hospital, chaplain of the city prisons, chaplain of the Magdalene Asylum and chaplain of the convent of nuns, as well as diocesan superintendent of schools and editor of a newspaper. Concurrently, John England was a fiery Irish patriot who had no qualms in battling against the right of the British Crown to appoint Irish bishops. He was also a friend of the great Daniel O'Connell, openly joining forces with him as a leader of Irish nationalism.

Inevitably, the British became interested in this political firebrand in a clerical collar, and the Bishop of Cork, though sympathetic to England's ideals, discreetly appointed him pastor of Brandon, a village situated a comfortable distance from the inflammable patriot city. Even at Brandon, England continued to alarm the conservative Irish hierarchy, who feared that this talented priest might soon be elevated into their own ranks, where he could be a more effective "troublemaker." Thus, it was with no visible reluctance that the bishops of Ireland allowed John England to become the Bishop of Charleston, so many thousand miles across the sea. On the twenty-eighth of December, 1820, the sailing ship *Thomas* anchored in Charleston harbor with the thirty-four-year-old prelate and his younger sister aboard.

At once, Bishop John England attacked the Charleston trustee problem, not so much destroying the tiger of trusteeism but rather pulling its teeth. Realizing that what the rebellious trustees really sought was prestige, he set about devising a system whereby they could "cooperate but not dominate." This was the Charleston Constitution, providing for a Convocation of the Clergy and a House of Representatives for the Laity. It was purely a consultative body, with power only to recommend to the bishop, whose own decision was final and binding. But by this device not only status-seeking laymen but contentious clergymen as well could slake their thirst for distinction. Property, meanwhile, was to be held by the ordinary, and all powers of appointment were vested in him. To legalize his system, England formed a diocesan corporation which was approved by the three states of his diocese. It was this corporation which held the property, and no new churches were dedicated until they were turned over to it. With this, he brought peace to congregations which only a short time earlier had been plotting to set up the Independent Catholic Church of America.

Not everyone in the American Church, Archbishop Maréchal least among them, approved of England's solution, especially when it was observed that his Constitution was based upon the government of the Church of England. However, it was typical of the daring and unorthodox England that he should not be frightened by the charge of either "heresy" or "innovation" while moving to meet an emergency. Thus, becoming convinced of the dangers of the French influence in the Church, he decided to open his own seminary, where he himself taught. He also taught in the school for Negro children which he set up, politely ignoring Southern prejudices, and for which he formed an order of nuns. Devoted to the ideal of education, he established a book society and a library in his diocese, as well as the famous *United States Catholic Miscellany*.

The *Miscellany* was the first real Catholic weekly newspaper in the United States, the mother of hundreds more to follow, and England may thus be regarded as the father of American Catholic journalism. He was a born journalist, and also a natural controversialist. Assisted by his sister Joanna, who sank her small fortune in the *Miscellany*, he used the magazine to reply to the attacks of the nativists. Much as posterity has remembered him for his bold exposition of Catholic compatibility with the American way, it is not as a journalist but as a speaker that his own time honored him.

His was not only a golden but an iron tongue. In the fashion of the day, he could preach for hours, riding horseback up and down his vast diocese, frequently borrowing a courthouse or even a church from friendly Protestants, and doing his utmost to dispel the incredible misconceptions which the South held about his faith. A man of great charm and earnestness, as well as zest and an enormously varied store of information, he was in great demand as a speaker outside his own diocese and was even invited to address Congress. On that occasion, January 8, 1826, in the presence of President John Quincy Adams, he discoursed at length on the doctrines of Catholicism, and as he later wrote to William Gaston, a Catholic layman who became an associate justice of the North Carolina Supreme Court: "When I was done I certainly felt a very extraordinary gratification at the intense attention with which I was heard, & that every face seemed to say 'go on.' But I thought two hours enough for them & for me,—I made the sign of the cross . . ."

To Bishop England's pleased surprise, many of his listeners emulated him in crossing themselves. Unfortunately, his gratification at this symbol of good will was not to last. The "era of good feelings" was coming to an end, and Bishop England's appearance before the President and Congress may be regarded as the high point of that period. Now, under the impact of what has been called "the Catholic invasion," the reaction known as "the Protestant Crusade" was about to begin.

Chapter VIII

The year 1820, when Rome created the two sees of Richmond and Charleston and decided to fill them with Irish bishops, marks the end of French predominance in the American Church and the beginning of that Irish influence which continues to the present day.

French power, of course, did not immediately evaporate. In fact, it was nine years later that Jean Dubois became the first Bishop of New York. But the Irish had gained a foothold and they were tenacious of it. By 1830, four of the ten bishops in America were Irish-born or native Americans of Irish ancestry. Inexorably, as the tide of Irish immigration to the United States rose to a flood, as the English and French laity continued to stay at home and the end of the Napoleonic Wars shut off the flow of French priests to these shores, the bulk of the candidates for the priesthood came to be recruited from among the sons of the immigrant Irish and the American Church came to resemble what the Gaelophobic Evelyn Waugh has caustically described as "an Irish tribal cult." Probably, it was fortunate that the Irish rather than some other European race should have taken charge. If it had been the English, then the Church would have prospered at a circumspect and unalarming pace more or less in proportion to its tiny beginnings in Maryland, becoming, in the end, the genteel faith of a handful of bluebloods discreetly worshiping the Crucified Christ in quaint little private chapels at the end of the paddock. If it had been the Germans, it is possible that their intense attachment to their own language and customs might have served the divisive concept of America as a "New Europe" in which transplanted races from the Old World might escape certain disabilities such as obligatory military service while continuing to live in the old way in "Little Germanys" or "Little Austrias" established across the face of the continent. Finally, if it had been the French—the only other sizable ethnic group in the American Church of the time—they might have justified every charge of a foreign and aristocratic creed inimical to the American way of life.

But the Irish, they thought of themselves as American the moment their feet touched American soil. Hitting the docks with swinging caps and cries of "Hooray for Ginril Jackson!" their Americanism was perhaps a little bit too instantaneous for many of the old-stock Yankees. Yet, it was deep and sincere. Moreover, the Irish did have the splendid advantage of speaking the language, their love of freedom made them eminently adaptable to the spirit of American independence and because they had kept the faith in face of a shrewd and systematic persecution they were inured to the kind of hostility which they were to encounter on these shores. Thus, by one of those huge ironies which make such a fascinating mosaic of the history of mankind, the conquering English had conferred upon the unconquerable Irish exactly the right language and habits of mind by which they were to make their abhorred religion flourish across the seas.

England's penal laws had also sharpened the ordinary Irishman's loyalty to his priest. It has been said, "When nothing is left to a people but its religion, priests become its leaders." In Ireland, the Penal Laws stripped the Catholics of all but their religion, with that result. According to Tocqueville: "There is an unbelievable unity among the Irish clergy and Catholic population. The reason for that is not only that the clergy are paid by the people, but also because all the upper classes are Protestants and enemies. The clergy, rebuffed by high society, has turned its attention to the lower classes . . . [a] state of affairs altogether peculiar to Ireland." To this the Irishman added loyalty to home and family, always under the benevolent despotism of the parish priest as tribal chief.

Thus, the Irish gave to the American Church its middle-class mystique based on family life, as well as its structure of parishes organized on a territorial basis. They also built the Church. The wages that they earned digging the nation's canals and building its railroads were ever at the service of their faith, and: "The result is that there are everywhere Catholic Churches, convents, schools and colleges." The conservative, authoritarian stamp peculiar to the American Church may also be traced to the Irish. For one thing, they had no anticlerical traditions like the French or Germans. For another, their very lack of learning made them unusually passive in the presence of their educated clergy. Without a large body of articulate laymen in the Church, there was practically no one to challenge the growing autocratic power of the Irish hierarchy. The rule of thumb appeared to be that it was the laity's duty to pay and pray, leaving all else to the clergy. And the trustee scare, once it had passed, only served to intensify the bishops' distrust of laymen. In brief, it may be said that the Irish endowed the American Church with the very siege mentality which had been their own in the Old Country, together with the manpower and ammunition (i.e., funds) to withstand assault; and this, it can be added, was indeed fortunate, if only because the old-stock Protestants were preparing to go over to the attack. Between 1820 and 1865 no less than 1,900,000 Irish immigrants arrived in America, swelling the enrollment of the Catholic Church from 250,000 to nearly 3,000,000 members—and arousing the long-dormant American antipathy toward Popery.

Actually, the period of good feelings was only one of false security. Nativism, that is, the dislike of things foreign, and especially the Catholic Church, had never really vanished from American life. In spirit, nativism was perhaps best defined by Congressman Uriah Tracy of Connecticut, who, traveling through Pennsylvania in 1800, wrote home: "I have seen many, very many, Irishmen, and with a very few exceptions, they are United Irishmen, Free Masons, and the most God-provoking Democrats on this side of Hell." What he meant, of course, was that he had seen quite a few "foreigners"—political refugees from the Old World, Irishmen fleeing the unsuccessful Rebellion of 1798—in fine, people to be distrusted. Nor is there anything particularly perplexing about his making Masons of so many Catholic Irish, for one of the characteristics of the nativist was the uninstructed ignorance which could lead him to equate this secret, oath-taking, ritualistic order with its archenemy and diametric opposite, Roman Catholicism. It was this nativism which in good part inspired the Alien and Sedition Acts of 1798. At that time, fear of a war with France had sharpened nativist animosity toward aliens, and the Federalists, chafing under the criticism of Republican writers who were also refugees from Europe, took this opportunity to pass a series of laws which, while aimed at silencing or deporting aliens, would also have the effect of suppressing the Republican opposition.

By then, Irish immigrants had formed the American Society of United Irishmen to aid their countrymen struggling against British oppression, and so alarming London that it protested to the pro-British Federalists. Thus, the abhorred Acts were aimed as much at the united Irishmen as at a possible threat from France, and as Professor Ray Allen Billington, the historian of nativism, has observed: "It was no accident that Mathew Lyon, an Irish Catholic, was first to suffer under the Sedition act, nor that the alien riots in Philadelphia were staged just outside a Catholic church."

Nativism subsided during the War of 1812, in which the Irish joyfully seized the opportunity to square accounts with Old Mother England, and in which other Catholics such as Thomas Macdonough, victor in the critical naval Battle of Lake Champlain, distinguished themselves. But then, the need for manpower to work the new manufacturing plants spawned by the war, to build the canals and roads and railways by which the West was being settled and the frontier pushed farther back opened the immigrant floodgates.

Paradoxically, this inundation of cheap labor so badly needed to work an expanding economy threatened to lower the American standard of living. Moreover, there was no doubt that some European countries were using America as a dumping ground for their own undesirables. Some German states offered pardons to petty criminals if they would leave the country, which is to say if they would go to America. England promised bounties to paupers who emigrated, ostensibly to her colonies, but most of those who went to Canada eventually worked their way south to the United States. Many of these Old World rejects became public charges in the United States. In 1835, of 10,089 paupers in the almshouses of New York, Philadelphia, Boston and Baltimore, 5,303 were foreign-born. Of 105,000 paupers in the entire country, more than half were immigrants, and the estimated annual bill for their support was put at four million dollars. Thus, forced to compete with cheap foreign labor, compelled to pay for the support of foreign shiftless, it is no wonder that the native Americans rebelled. Unfortunately, when the nativists took up the cry "America for Americans," they really meant "America for Protestants," if only because most of their resentment was directed against the Catholic Irish.

Even though the half century which witnessed the arrival of nearly two million Irish also saw the influx of nearly as many Germans, these people, whether Catholic or Protestant, usually took themselves off quietly to the Midwest, where they settled in foreign colonies which, in a word, gave trouble to no one. But the rambunctious, pugnacious Irish! They came into the country as though it were their own, a legacy from St. Brendan, as it were, and they reacted to discrimination with a customary lack of docility. Often they were drunk and disorderly, and when they were not fighting the nativists they were fighting each other. It was region against region, "the Far-Ups" of the north against the "Far-Doons" of the south; or county against county, Kerry against Cork. Frequently these fist-and-spade battles along the railroad rights-of-way or the banks of the new canals erupted because some of the workmen were convinced that the foremen, displaying the preference for "one of ours" which was to facilitate the Irish stranglehold on the American episcopacy, had hired only hands from his own county. Naturally enough, the native Americans were shocked by these battle royals and donnybrooks, especially if the Irish ire happened to be directed outward against the Establishment. Thus, the press could carry indignant lamentations such as the following:

On the 29th and 30th ult. it was known that a contractor on the 3rd division of the Baltimore and Ohio railroad . . . had absconded, leaving his laborers unpaid, and that they (as too often happens in Ireland, the country which, in general, they had recently left) had taken the law into their own hands, were wantonly destroying the property of the company, because their employer had wronged them! They were between 200 and 300 strong, and, with pick axes, hammers and sledges, made a most furious attack on the rails, sills, etc., and whatever else they could destroy. The sheriff of the county, and his posse, were resisted by these ignorant and wicked men. . . .

Nativist sensitivities were also outraged by the numerous Irish "shantytowns" which sprang up on the fringes of the great Eastern cities. Here, the newcomers lived in dirt, disorder and drunkenness, or at least, so the nativists and many other Americans thought. They did not notice or chose to ignore the great majority of the newcomers, who lived together in peace and quiet. Actually, it might also be said that it was not the Irish who were the cause of the disquiet but the New World itself. Although it is true that they brought with them a deep contempt for English law, and were therefore too prone to equate American liberty with license, they also discovered in America that habit of violence which persists to this day. Moreover, according to a contemporary physician, Dr. Thomas M. Nichols:

The great mass of the Irish people of the class that emigrates to America live in Ireland chiefly on potatoes, oatmeal, buttermilk— on a simple and almost entirely vegetable diet. They have not the means, if they have the inclination, to drink much whiskey, or use much tobacco. They land in America with clear, rosy complexions, bright eyes, good teeth, and good health generally. They are as strong as horses. They find themselves in a land of good wages, cheap provisions, cheap whiskey and tobacco. Flesh meat they have been accustomed to consider a luxury of the rich, and they go in for it accordingly. They eat meat three times a day, rudely cooked, and in large quantities. Whiskey, of an execrable quality, is plentiful and cheap; so is tobacco, and they drink, smoke, and chew abundantly.

With justice, then, the indignant Irish could and did tell their critics that they were only doing what Americans did. There is no doubt that the ordinary American of that day, the one the newcomers were imitating, was an unlovely person indeed. His ideal was no longer the refined and cultivated gentleman of the Virginia Dynasty, but the apotheosis of Jacksonian democracy, "Old Hickory" himself, a man who could dismiss an accomplished diplomat with the sneer: "He is fit only to write a book and scarcely that." Narrow, nationalist and swaggering, scornful of silk or subtlety while convinced of the innate superiority of everything that was American, he liked to describe himself as "a ring-tailed roarer, half-horse and half-alligator," who lived on "whiskey and bear's meat salted in a hailstorm, peppered with buckshot, and broiled in a flash of forked lightning." With such roisterers as exemplars, it was small wonder that the Irishman's shanty should only be, after all, a replica of the ring-tailed roarer's shack. Moreover, the Irish did have the excuse of a poverty induced by self-sacrifice. Many of them, especially the single girls who came over to work as servants, saved all that they could to send to "the folks back home." Unfortunately, this habit of sending money out of the country also contributed to the wrath of the nativist. Nevertheless, for all the resentment which their coming provoked, if the Irish had not been Catholic it is likely that their very energy and adaptability, their natural aptitude for politics, would have enabled them to melt very quickly into the American mass. Unfortunately, they were Papists, and, to paraphrase Shakespeare, "'Tis but thy faith that is my enemy."

Their coming had given a despised religion, latterly ignored or tolerated, a sudden and unprecedented growth, one that became alarmingly evident when the First Provincial Council of Baltimore convened in 1829. Called at the insistence of John England, a democrat of deep conviction, it was to have allayed the fears of the nativists by exhibiting to them the "Americanism" of the Church. Instead, the sight of red-robed bishops assembled in all their glory angered the simplicity-loving Americans, and some of the decrees warning Catholics against "corrupt translations of the Bible" or urging the construction of Catholic schools to save children from Protestant "perversion" seemed only more infuriating proof of the arrant arrogance of this alien creed. Coincidentally, John England founded his *Miscellany*, and this, together with the subsequent appearance of other Romish periodicals, was taken as the beginnings of Catholic "aggression." Finally, the trustee scandals, fought out in the open and ending with the vindication of ecclesiastical authority, seemed rather to be the triumph of tyranny over the cause of "freedom." All of these considerations, then, coming concurrently and thus with a sudden and crushingly cumulative effect, served to remind the Protestants that the old enemy was not dead or even sleeping, but alive and vigorous and *growing!* Meanwhile, as Professor Billington observed in his book *The Protestant Crusade:*

More important in preparing the American mind for the crusade against Catholicism which was to come were the new tendencies becoming apparent in religion. About 1826 the term "New Measures" began to come into use to designate the means being employed by the churches. The New Measures represented a swing away from the liberalism and Deism which had followed the Revolution toward a rigid fundamentalism which rivaled the stern religion of the Puritans of colonial New England. This new revivalism was introduced by the Reverend Charles G. Finney, whose efforts and success in western New York soon began to attract national attention. As its influence spread, preaching throughout the land became bolder and more denunciatory, the practice of praying for individuals by name was begun, converts were pleaded with and led to the anxious seat, females were encouraged to speak and pray at public meetings, revivals were held everywhere, and religious newspapers devoted regular space to ecstatic descriptions of the thousands who were finding their way to the truth. The whole country was under the influence of a wave of religious excitement; Protestantism suddenly became a thing to be venerated and protected, while Catholicism, as an antagonistic system, was proportionately resented. Those who attacked it became crusaders in the popular mind and were assured of a large following.

With the emotional ground thus prepared for the Protestant Crusade, the first clash came between the American Bible Society and the Catholic Church. In this skirmish, the Church successfully defeated the Society's attempt to distribute free copies of the King James (i.e., Protestant) version of the Bible among poor Catholics. At once, this quite defensible maneuver was interpreted as an attack upon the Bible itself, and as the old charges of suppressing the Word of God were raised against the Catholics, the Protestant churches began to interest themselves in the Crusade. No-Popery sermons began to be preached, and soon, as it became apparent that the faithful needed instruction in the dangers of Romanism, anti-Catholic papers were founded.

Unfortunately, at about this time the Catholic Emancipation bill was under debate in England. As eventually enacted, it restored civil rights denied to Catholics since 1688, a prospect which seemed so dreadful to some Englishmen that they dusted off and refurbished all the old horror stories about the ancient Whore of Babylon. Many of these books and pamphlets came across the sea to America, to be emulated by American anti-Catholic writers. By 1827 there were thirty religious newspapers engaged in vilifying the Catholic Church, and by 1829, the anti-Catholic journalism of the day had invaded even the secular press, leading the prelates of the Baltimore Provincial Council to exclaim: "Not only do they assail us and our institutions in a style of vituperation and offense, misrepresent our tenets, vilify our practices, repeat the hundred-times refuted calumnies of the days of angry and bitter contention in other lands, but they have even denounced you and us as enemies to the liberties of the republic, and have openly proclaimed the fancied necessity of obstructing our progress, and of using their best efforts to extirpate our religion."

A year later, as though to demonstrate the futility of the appeal to reason or decency in the face of religious passion, the first openly anti-Catholic weekly, *The Protestant*, was launched. Its purpose was made clear in its announcement that it would publish:

Narratives displaying the rise and progress of the Papacy; its spirit and character in former periods; its modern pretensions; and its present enterprising efforts to recover and extend its unholy dominion, especially on the western continent. Biographical notices of Martyrs, Reformers and Popish Persecutors. Essays describing the doctrines, discipline, and ceremonies of the Romish Hierarchy; and its desolating influence upon individual advancement, domestic comfort, and national prosperity. Illustrations of Sacred Prophecy relative to the Mystical Babylon. A faithful expose of the moral and religious conditions of Lower Canada, as debased by the prevalence of Roman supremacy.

Not all Protestants sympathized with the intemperate invective of *The Protestant*, if only because some of them thought that to persecute Popery would be to propagate it, and even as the moderates refused to give it their support, its columns were discredited by a young Philadelphia priest named John Hughes. Composing a carefully absurd anti-Catholic article, Father Hughes sent it to *The Protestant* under the pseudonym "Cranmer." It was printed, together with editorial encomiums for the unknown Cranmer and appeals for more of the same. Father Hughes obliged, again and again, always increasing the quotient of the ridiculous. Eventually, after *The Protestant* was fairly hooked, he exposed his own hoax in the *Catholic Truth Teller*. Embarrassed but unabashed, *The Protestant* continued to flail away at Popery until a decline in popularity compelled transfer of ownership to a less rabid group of anti-Catholics. These gentlemen announced that they would not attack Popery by mere invective or contumely but "by *solid arguments*, by *documents* and *facts*." Accordingly, they changed the paper's name to *The Reformation Advocate*, and when this fared no better than *The Protestant* they changed it again, this time to the monthly *Protestant Magazine*. Here is its anti-Catholic manifesto:

Deeply convinced of the dangerous tendency of this anti-christian system; of its soul-corrupting, soul-destroying influence; dreading the danger to which our country, if indifferent to its increase in political influence, is exposed; and influenced by a love of country, and by an ardent desire to promote the interests of immortal souls, we have entered upon this work, resolved, as far as in us lies, to defend the great truths of the gospel opposed by popery, and to exhibit those doctrines and practices of Roman Catholics which are contrary to the interests of mankind.

To the satisfaction of the editors, the *Protestant Magazine* not only proved popular but so profitable that in 1834 a rival anti-Catholic magazine threatened to enter the field. Apparently unwilling to accept assistance in God's work of exposing the evils of Popery, the *Protestant Magazine* blocked the appearance of its would-be competitor, meanwhile founding a new weekly newspaper called *The Anti-Romanist*. Nevertheless, the vineyard was too obviously heavy with fruit. Willy-nilly, no matter how selflessly the *Protestant Magazine* strove to bear the burden alone, other laborers flocked to the harvest; and soon, even the secular or merely pro-Protestant press began to carry articles such as *Priestcraft Unmasked* or *Priestcraft Exposed*.

Successful in the press, the crusade now turned to the public podium, the New York Protestant Association being the first to organize public meetings aimed at unfolding "the true character of Popery." They were an overnight success, becoming popular across the country. Admissions were charged, of course, and attendance mounted—especially after Catholics began to appear to listen to their priests attempt to defend their religion. Once this unforeseen landfall became apparent, priests were invited to appear on the platform. However, some Catholics considered this courtesy as hardly different from an invitation to attend their own auto-da-fé; and thus, in New York in March of 1834, a debate in Broadway Hall was interrupted when a large mob of Catholic Irish broke down the doors, after which, expressing their distaste for the evening's theme, "Is Popery Compatible with Civil Liberty?" they gave vigorous answer to this loaded question by chasing the speakers from the hall and generally "cleaning the place out."

This and other attacks had the effect of creating sympathy for the Protestant Crusade and giving it a unifying thrust. Anti-Catholic meetings and sermons spread from the East to the Midwest, and the specialty of the No-Popery speaker was brought into being to satisfy growing demands. Meanwhile, many nativists, sincerely convinced of the dangers of Popery, began to arrange for debates between Protestant and Catholic champions, hoping that "if the American people can be induced to look the monster in the face, and observe his hideous features, they would turn from it with horror and disgust." By the end of the 1830s, however, it began to become evident that these windy and often acrimonious contests were beginning to have the opposite effect. The mob, of course, reacted with predictable hysteria; but thoughtful Protestants were beginning to learn that the Catholic position was entirely defensible. Thus, free-and-equal debate had not ended in the anticipated Protestant victory, no matter how bitterly nativist apologists might complain that the Catholics were not bound by the same regard for truth as the Protestants, and so, unwillingly in some quarters, but nevertheless inexorably, the crusade shifted its tactics downward.

Propaganda replaced persuasion, and theological disputation was replaced by pornographic accusation. In the tradition of the "scholarship" launched in Reformation Germany in 1559, it was now thought wiser to concentrate upon the immorality of the Whore of Babylon, and to do so in a way which would make Catholic reply or rebuttal difficult. Consequently, scurrilous and spicy books and pamphlets began to appear. At first, they were imports from England with titles such as *Female Convents: Secrets of Nunneries Disclosed* or *Jesuit Juggling: Forty Popish Frauds Detected and Disclosed.* They were immensely popular, but even more delightful were the "true confession" books which followed. Supposedly written by ex-priests and ex-nuns, but usually by native Americans who, more often than not, were Protestant ministers, they described Catholicism as basically a system in which lecherous priests preyed on unsuspecting nuns or the innocent girls whom they lured into their confessionals. Every rectory, it appeared, was linked to a convent by a secret tunnel, and beneath the basement floor of every convent was a cemetery of baby skeletons. All efforts to refute these salacious monstrosities were, of course, futile, if only because the truth in pursuit of falsehood is always like the sound of an explosion trying to catch up with the flash. Moreover, the public palate has ever been susceptible to spice, and any effort to shut off this delicious flood of filth was not likely to be successful. And so, while smearing the name of Catholicism and vilifying virtuous women, the crusade's cloacal attack also had the unhappy consequence of raising the false but widespread fear that the immoral "convent system" was the device by which Protestantism was to be undermined and Popery made triumphant.

With convents now the target, one of the most illustrious—the Ursuline Convent at Charlestown, Massachusetts—was singled out for special hostility. Evidently, the Ursuline school for girls on Mount Benedict had been too successful, attracting many daughters of the wealthy in the Boston area. Most of these girls were Unitarians, a fact which angered lower-class Congregationalists, and which also had the effect of joining class jealousies to religious hatreds. Thus, nothing less preposterous than a Catholic-Unitarian plot was alleged, and one indignant editor warned: "Atheists and Infidels will be always ready to sympathize with Catholics, to unite with them in crushing Protestantism preparatory to the subversion of Christianity." Resentment of the Ursuline Convent grew. Wild tales about nuns' activities flew about the area, all of which appeared to be given credence when a book, *Six Months in a Convent,* was published by a dismissed and dull-witted postulant at Mount Benedict named Rebecca

Reed. Although Professor Billington maintains that Miss Reed's hints at the most awful crimes were adequately refuted at the time, they were, of course, believed. Worse, they prepared the public to believe the worst when an actual nun named Elizabeth Harrison really did "escape" from Mount Benedict. According to Billington:

Overwork and long hours of teaching had undermined Miss Harrison's health to such an extent that she had become mentally deranged. In this condition, she left the convent on the night of July 28, 1834, ran to the home of a neighboring brick manufacturer, Edward Cutter, and demanded refuge. Cutter took her to her brother in Cambridge, where reason returned, and Miss Harrison, realizing what she had done, immediately asked that Bishop Fenwick be sent for. He visited her the next day and readily granted her request to be allowed to return to the convent.

By then, unfortunately, the harm had been done. Boston was in a turmoil. Three straight days of anti-Catholic preaching had inflamed the people. Even the Reverend Lyman Beecher, perhaps the most famous Protestant minister of his time, and today probably more celebrated as the father of the author of *Uncle Tom's Cabin*, had mounted the pulpit to inveigh against the convent. Now it was charged that Miss Harrison had been forced to return to the convent against her will. Fire bells rang. Signal fires were lighted. A mob formed. Carrying banners and shouting "No Popery" or "Down with the Cross," the crowd poured into Charlestown and climbed Mount Benedict. There the marchers were met by the Mother Superior, who appealed to them to disperse. Failing here, she unwisely turned to threats: "The Bishop has twenty thousand Irishmen at his command in Boston." Perhaps. But at the moment, they were in Boston—and the infuriated marchers' reply was to break open the convent doors while the Ursulines hurried their sixty terrified students out the back door and into the night. Then, while fire companies stood by unmoving, they set fire to the convent and burned it to the ground.

During the next few days, the American nation professed to be shocked and outraged by the burning of the Ursuline Convent. Everywhere, public officials and the press—religious as well as secular—denounced this wanton assault upon private property and terrorizing of helpless women and children. Even Lyman Beecher, like Henry II turning on the men who had rid him of Thomas à Becket, condemned the mob for having taken his exhortation to "action" against Popery a bit too literally. Indignation meetings were held in Boston, and loud cries were heard for the arrest and trial of the convent-burners, as well as state restitution to the Ursulines for their losses. In the end, of course, nothing of the kind happened. The first man brought to trial for the crime was speedily acquitted to the thunderous applause of the courtroom. Acclaimed as a public hero, he was so showered with gifts that, unable to thank all his admirers personally, he had to insert a card of gratitude in the newspapers. And the Ursulines, so far from being recompensed, which one nativist editor described as a "lunatic" proposal, were so hounded and abused that pupils feared to attend the school that they reopened and they were forced to move to Canada. Obviously, the mass of the people, at least, had been more pleased than horrified by the burning of the convent.

Actually, having had a taste of riot and arson for which they had paid nothing, the lower elements among the New England nativists hungered for more—and mob attacks on Catholic churches there became so frequent that many congregations posted regular armed patrols to guard their property, and insurance companies refused to write policies on Catholic churches that were not constructed of nonflammable materials. In the end, more than the protection of a law which had given such short shrift to the Ursulines, it was the Irishman's willingness to fight in defense of his church property that discouraged New England nativism from making a burned and bloody reality of its "crusade" against Popery. Meanwhile, the convent burning had the disastrous effect of elevating the crusade to national status. Mob rioting against Catholic convents became so prevalent that it extended into the South, where John England hesitated to let a company of nuns establish a school in Charleston lest it inflame the populace, and the success scored by the falsehoods of Rebecca Reed inspired an entire new series of propaganda works intended to blacken the name of American nuns.

Intended also to make money—for the financial possibilities of

Miss Reed's *Six Months in a Convent* had not been ignored by
the shrewd Yankees of the north. Published in 1835 by a group
of enterprising Bostonians, it became what today would be described as a "runaway best seller," breaking all records for
popularity both in the United States and England. Astonishingly
enough, a golden flood was issuing from the cloaca—and so, a
week after the convent was burned, two new anti-Catholic
papers were founded. One of these, the *American Protestant
Vindicator*, was edited by the famous nativist preacher, the
Reverend W. C. Brownlee, who announced in his first issue:

With the deliberate conviction that Popery ought always to be
loathed and execrated, not only by all Christians, but also by every
patriot and philanthropist; we shall endeavor to unfold its detestable
impieties, corruptions and mischiefs. But we engage in this momentous
controversy with a deep conviction that there is an important dis-
sonance between the heinous crime and the bewitched transgressors.
We shall condemn the monstrous progeny of Babylon the Great without measure: but we shall not forget that the vast majority of the
Papists are blindfolded sinners; and we shall ever draw a broad line of
distinction between Roman Priests, the arch servant of the Dragon,
and the Beast who from the most hateful and inordinately sensual
motives are perversely deceitful leaders; and the misguided mortals,
their wretchedly deluded votaries whom they hurry into the bottom-
less pit of everlasting perdition.

Brownlee's paper was outstandingly successful, not only because of the stream of invective which he poured on the heads
of his Catholic fellow citizens, hoping to convert them, as he
said, "in the spirit of love and meekness," but also because of the
team of lecturers which he shrewdly sent around the country
to appeal for subscriptions. By 1840, he had six speakers constantly on the road denouncing Rome, and the practice was
quickly adopted by other anti-Catholic publications. By that
time also, numerous "agencies" and "societies" had been formed
for the express purpose of either instructing Protestants in the
abominations of Popery or of "converting the Papists to Christianity." The most famous of these was the Protestant Reformation Society, which adopted the *American Protestant Vindicator*
as its official organ. However, if these mission societies were
actually serious about converting the poor Papists to "Christi-

anity," the choice of the openly abusive *Vindicator* as the means
of persuasion appears rather like going courting with a club. Obviously, then, their object was rather to inflame the native
Protestant American against his Catholic neighbor; and it was
also, again, to make money. The showpiece of this kind of publishing—the veritable golden goose swimming gladly out of the
golden cloaca—was the *Awful Disclosures* of Maria Monk.

Published in 1836, the book was a stunning success. By comparison, *Six Months in a Convent* was a study of crime in a
kindergarten. Nothing like it had been published, before or since,
and it is not only still being reprinted today, ostensibly as a
pornographic curiosity, but actually to satisfy the same appetites
of prurience and hate, it is still being believed. In brief, Maria
Monk "disclosed" that she had been brought up as a Protestant
near Montreal. Entering the Hotel Dieu convent there to be
educated, she became a Catholic and decided to become a nun.
But then she had second thoughts, left the convent and married
—only to return and take the veil. Now, to her "utter astonishment and horror" she found herself ordered by her Mother
Superior to sleep with priests, just like the other nuns of the
Hotel Dieu. Children born from these unions, she said, were immediately baptized and strangled. Allegedly quoting the Mother
Superior, she wrote: "This secured their everlasting happiness,
for the baptism purified them from all sinfulness, and being sent
out of the world before they had time to do anything wrong, they
were at once admitted into heaven. How happy, she exclaimed,
are those who secure immortal happiness in such little beings!
Their little souls would thank those who kill their bodies, if they
had it in their power!"

Nuns who did not obey the order to submit to the priests,
Maria wrote, were executed on the spot. Their bodies were
thrown into a large hole in the basement, not too far from the
familiar secret passageway to the priest house. Terrified, Maria
said, she fell from grace. Eventually, not to say inevitably, she
found herself with child, the father being one "Father Phelan."
And so, rather than acquiesce in the final horror of infanticide,
Maria Monk bravely threw her cloak over her shoulder, rushed
outside the Hotel Dieu—and told all. Thus, the *Awful Disclosures
of the Hotel Dieu Nunnery of Montreal* as written by Maria

Monk. But now, from Professor Billington, a Protestant whose splendid impartiality is a credit to both himself and his faith, a somewhat different version:

The account of Maria Monk's life given by her mother differed greatly from that contained in the *Awful Disclosures*. The mother, a Protestant living near Montreal, testified that her daughter had never been in the Hotel Dieu convent and that the whole tale was the product of a brain injured in infancy when the child had run a slate pencil into her head. Maria Monk, the mother insisted, had been a wild girl who was constantly in trouble and had of necessity been confined in a Catholic Magdalen asylum in Montreal. Even there she had erred and had been aided in her escape by a former lover, who was really the father of the child born in New York.

In all probability, the mother's story was substantially correct. It is likely, too, that the man who aided her escape to the United States was the Reverend William K. Hoyt, long active among Canadian Catholics as president of the Canadian Benevolent Association. He undoubtedly took her to New York where he arranged with several other unscrupulous clergymen, among whom were the Reverend J. J. Slocum, the Reverend Arthur Tappan, the Reverend George Bourne, and Theodore Dwight, to employ her as a dupe for their own mercenary schemes. Later Slocum admitted that Maria Monk and Hoyt called upon him to write the story of her life and that he had done so, although he insisted that the account was substantially that dictated by Maria Monk. Subsequent legal proceedings growing from the publication of the *Awful Disclosures* indicated that Slocum actually had been responsible for most of the writing of the book, but that Hoyt, Bourne, and others had given suggestions and taken the largest share of the profits. It is probable that the editors of the *American Protestant Vindicator* were also interested, for just before the *Awful Disclosures* appeared they devoted an unusually large amount of space to articles dealing with the alleged immorality of convent life and even hinted that there was an escaped nun in the city who was soon to write her memoirs.

The manuscript of the book was offered first to Harper Brothers. This publishing house, although tempted by the prospect of large profits, was unwilling to risk its reputation by printing so scurrilous an attack on Catholicism. An agreement was eventually arranged through which two employees of the firm, Howe and Bates, set up a dummy publishing house under their own names and the book finally appeared in January, 1836.

Publication of the book produced an angry outcry from Catholics who had heretofore maintained an attitude of injured silence, and then, into the crossfire of charge and countercharge, there stepped a rival claimant to the fame and fortune which had befallen Maria Monk. She said her name was Sister Saint Frances Patrick. She, too, had been in the infamous Hotel Dieu, she said, and she had come to confirm what Maria Monk had written. Actually, this transparent fraud, backed by the publisher of a nativist paper, had come to get "a piece of the action," and when she and Maria tearfully embraced at a public meeting, many Protestants found it was a bit too much and an impartial Protestant committee was chosen to investigate Maria and to inspect the Hotel Dieu. With this, it came out that Maria had been a delinquent confined to a Catholic reformatory. It was from this institution that she escaped, and the child born to her in New York was fathered by a lover, not by the fictitious "Father Phelan." Moreover, after two Protestant ministers and later the nativist editor Colonel Stone went over the Hotel Dieu floor by floor, they came back to report that the convent did not in any way resemble the building described by Maria. Stung, the nativists replied that the Hotel Dieu had been restructured to deceive the ministers. Colonel Stone, they said, was either in the pay of the Jesuits or "Stone-blind."

In the end, Maria Monk produced another illegitimate child, and when her backers sought to exculpate her with the explanation that this event had been "arranged by the Jesuits," she repaid them rather badly by getting herself arrested and convicted for picking the pocket of a man in a New York bawdyhouse. As a fitting postscript to the entire affair, "Sister" Saint Frances Patrick again seconded Maria by producing her own illegitimate child.

Nevertheless, the drive to discredit Catholic nuns and convents was a long time dying, and as late as 1855 Massachusetts had an official "Nunnery Committee" empowered to report on religious institutions in the commonwealth. In that year, this august body singled out a harmless school at Roxbury for investigation. Although there were supposed to be only seven members on the committee, no less than twenty men went eagerly nosing through the grounds, tearing open closet doors, frighten-

ing the children and treating the nuns with little respect.
Finding nothing, the committee and friends sat down to a cham-
pagne dinner, followed by a few more drinks at Lowell. Quite
properly, the committee forwarded a bill for its expenses to the
state, whereupon some objections were raised to the item relating
to the services of "Mrs. Patterson," a lady whose profession was
very well known. As the Boston *Pilot* observed, at least one
member of the committee had investigated "nuns of the type
who got him intoxicated and stole $71 from him."

Although nativism had been successful in arousing many
Americans against the menace of Popery, a large part of the
populace remained indifferent to its appeal. Laborers and
workingmen generally could not care less about the alleged immorality of Catholicism. They did care, however, about the competition of immigrants willing to work for less pay. Therefore, to
gain the allegiance of this large body of Americans, nativist
propaganda began to sound the tocsin over the evil alliance between foreigners and the Catholic Church.

It was charged that the Pope and the Catholic monarchs of
Europe were plotting to seize control of the Mississippi Valley.
Here, in this vast, fertile and strategic region, Catholicism and
Protestantism were to meet again in a struggle for world
supremacy. Here was to be fought out a New Reformation. Here,
even now, nativist propaganda warned, Catholic settlers from
Europe had begun to infiltrate in great numbers, gathering in
expectation of the day when they would rise in armed revolt,
seize power and invite into their midst the Pope of Rome who
would make the area his headquarters for his campaign to bring
the entire American continent, and later the world, under his
dominion.

At first, Protestant propaganda made this charge against American Catholicism alone, if only because its well-known "foreign"
character seemed to substantiate it. But then, becoming aware of
two European missionary societies which sent funds to the American Church, it fastened on them as the agents of the papal plot.
One of these was the Society for the Propagation of the Faith,
established in France in 1822 as a result of the appeal of Bishop
Du Bourg of Louisiana and the inspiration of a pious young

Frenchwoman. Its members met once weekly to pray and meditate and to contribute a penny to Catholic missions. Although the society operated on a world-wide scale, much of its assistance went to the United States, where its contributions were very helpful—especially, of course, in the West. The other was the Leopold Association, founded in Austria in 1828 in response to pleas from Bishop Edward Fenwick of Cincinnati. Because the Leopold Association concentrated on the young American Church, and again because its funds were going chiefly to the West, it became the special target of the Protestant Crusade.

Foremost among the nativists warning that "all America west of the Alleghenies will eventually be a Catholic country," was Samuel F. B. Morse, the inventor of the telegraph. That distinguished contribution to mankind, however, came later in Morse's career—after he had become famous as an artist and anti-Catholic propagandist. Although his father was a New England minister with nativist sympathies, Morse himself appears to have been indifferent to the problem of Catholicism. Actually, as an artist, he was attracted to the beauty of the Church, an admiration which drew him to Rome during the Holy Year of 1830. There, as he watched a papal procession: "I was standing close to the side of the house when, in an instant, without the slightest notice, my hat was struck off to the distance of several yards by a soldier, or rather by a poltroon in a soldier's costume, and this courteous manoeuvre was performed with his gun and bayonet, accompanied with curses and taunts and the expression of a demon on his countenance."

What had happened was that Morse had neglected to uncover at the appearance of the Pope. Unhappily, however, the overzealous guard's violent reminder of what Romans do in Rome was to have severe consequences for his coreligionists across the sea. He had made a bitter enemy of Catholicism, and upon Morse's return to the States he seized upon the Leopold Association as the stick to beat the Church with. Believing that his own European tour had made him an authority on the papal plot, in 1834 he published a series of twelve letters entitled "A Foreign Conspiracy against the Liberties of the United States." Printed in book form a year later, *Foreign Conspiracy* was so well received that Morse wrote another series of letters exposing Rome's alleged designs on the West, exclaiming: "Up! Up! I beseech you. Awake! To your posts! Let the tocsin sound from Maine to Louisiana. Fly to protect the vulnerable places of your Constitution and Laws. Place your guards; you will need them, and quickly too.—And first, shut your gates."

The gates, of course, were the wide-open immigration laws which allowed a foreign flood to break over the Alleghenies and wash into the West. As yet, no serious attempt to alter them was under consideration. But the propaganda of Samuel F. B. Morse, ably seconded by the Reverend Lyman Beecher, who also perceived a Romish conspiracy to win the West, succeeded in drawing attention to foreign immigrants. All who were Catholic were looked upon as papal serfs; even Protestant foreigners were sometimes castigated as Jesuits in disguise and all among them who were paupers or criminals were advanced as proof of Rome's insidious scheme to weaken and undermine America. Thus, the attempt to associate Catholicism with immigration was successful, and nativism was able to recruit the support of large numbers of heretofore indifferent laborers and working-class people. Now it remained to gain the minds of Catholic children.

No-Popery had always maintained that Catholicism was an enemy of the Bible. It was falsely charged that Catholic laity were forbidden to read Holy Writ for fear that they would discover the true Word of God and become convinced of the error of their own religion. Indeed, the opening skirmish of the Protestant Crusade had been the American Bible Society's attempt to circulate free copies of the Protestant Bible among Catholic poor people. When the Church successfully repelled this intrusion, she was represented as an enemy of Scripture, not of just a different and disapproved version of it. This conflict, however, had been forgotten in the crusade's steadily escalating war upon Popery, and it might have remained so had not the American Bible Society in 1839 pledged itself to have the Protestant Bible read in every public school classroom in the nation. Immediately, this objective received the enthusiastic endorsement of American

Protestantism generally, meanwhile provoking the vehement opposition of the Catholic hierarchy.

Once the battle was joined, it began to rage nationwide, but it was in New York City that the Protestant-Catholic confrontation took on its most dramatic form. Here, the schools were under the control of the Public School Society, a predominantly Protestant association. Under the Society's virtual monopoly of the school system, the Protestant Bible was read in all classes, and the prayers, hymn-singing and religious instruction were all in accord with general Protestant belief. Moreover, the school's textbooks were often blatantly anti-Catholic. Histories described the Church as "the man of sin, mystery of iniquity, son of perdition," and Catholic children were obliged to read attacks on their faith such as this fancied rebuke from William Penn to Hernando Cortez: "Though what thou sayest should be true, it does not come well from thy mouth. A Papist talk of reason! Go to the Inquisition and tell them of reason and the great laws of nature. They will broil thee as thy soldiers broiled Guatimozin. Why dost thou turn pale? Is it the name of the Inquisition or of Guatimozin? Tremble and shake when thou thinkest that every murder the inquisitors have committed, every torture they have inflicted on the innocent Indians, is originally owing to thee."

Some Catholics might have smiled at the irony of Americans, even then engaged in exterminating their own Indians, railing at Spaniards for an annihilation which never occurred. Most of them, however, were infuriated when their children came home with such anti-Catholic textbooks in their hands. And none was more provoked than John Hughes, the second Bishop of New York, who led the fight against the Public School Society with the rallying cry: "We are unwilling to pay taxes for the purpose of destroying our religion in the minds of our children."

Bishop Hughes was the same man who had worked the "Cranmer" hoax on *The Protestant*. He was a vigorous, belligerent, tireless man, powerful in oratory and joyful in combat. Born in Ireland, he came to America with his parents and began his training for the priesthood at Mount St. Mary's in Emmitsburg. Because his own education at the time was limited, Hughes was not actually accepted as a student but rather as an overseer of slaves permitted the loan of books. The combination was just right for this rawboned peasant youth. Living in a one-room shack overlooking the vegetable garden, he could study at his window while calling instructions to the slaves, thus exchanging his knowledge of gardening for the more ardently desired understanding of Latin. Admitted finally to regular classes, he displayed great diligence and dedication, as well as a fondness for debate and authority, qualities which, not always desirable in a candidate for the priesthood, were to prove of great value in New York's battle over classroom Bible reading.

Probably, John Hughes loved controversy a little too lustily. In print or in the pulpit, he was a fierce and angry man, and much as he might remain invincible in debate, it is doubtful if his furious oratory ever made a friend of any foe, or worse, actually ever changed anyone's mind. When, as a young priest in Philadelphia, he brought off his "Cranmer" hoax, he justified what seems to have been an indiscreet and perhaps even mischievous act with the bitter words: "I was satisfied that no enlightened man would believe a line published in *The Protestant,* and that no modest woman who had read it once by accident would ever read it again by design. I wanted to ascertain whether or not conscience had anything to do with the columns of *The Protestant.* I found it did not. I found that from the moment I spoke against Catholics and adopted the signature of a coward, I might write anything, however false, nay the falser the better . . ." Obviously, he was not a meek man, as he demonstrated when Bishop Francis Kenrick nominated him to become the first Bishop of Pittsburgh, and then, at the urging of John England, changed his mind. At once Hughes demanded an explanation, which even the equally belligerent John England was eager to furnish, rather than make an enemy of Hughes. Nor is it too much to suggest that the mild and gentle Kenrick was not unhappy to see the tempestuous Hughes—who was at best a mediocre administrator —become auxiliary to Bishop Dubois of New York. There, Hughes did not scruple to write a letter to Rome insisting that he was not trying to take over Dubois' diocese, but which, by the simple process of detailing the aging and inept bishop's defects, had exactly that effect.

Unscrupulous as this course may appear, the fact is that Hughes believed that under Dubois the faithful were not being properly led, and because the spiritual welfare of the Catholics in his charge was always Hughes's paramount concern, he was unafraid to take any legitimate action which would also mean that the Church would be defended and Catholics protected. Thus, always eager to defend the faith, Hughes was constantly in controversy; and two days after he became Bishop of New York, he called a meeting at which he announced his plans to petition the Common Council asking that Catholics be given a share of school money and accusing the Public School Society of sectarian instruction. When the petition was presented, it provoked a storm of outrage from the Protestants, and the Common Council decided to hold a public meeting on the subject. On October 29, 1840, the debate began with Bishop Hughes standing alone for the Catholics. He spoke for three hours, clearly although sometimes hotly outlining the Catholic position. Briefly, this was that because of the few parochial schools in the city, Catholic children were obliged to attend public schools where their religion was attacked and the Protestant Bible was read, with the result that most of them stayed away and received no education whatever. In this, he was to be supported by Governor Seward of New York, who believed that the children of immigrants could not become good citizens unless they were educated.

The Protestant reply took two whole days, inasmuch as an army of oratorical talent had been recruited from the ranks of the clergy and the legal profession. Catholics were attacked as idolators, murderers and enemies of the Word of God, and one minister thundered: "I do say that if the fearful dilemma were forced upon me, of becoming an infidel or a Roman catholic, according to the entire system of Popery, with all its idolatry, superstition, and violent opposition to the Holy Bible, *I would rather be an infidel than a papist.*"

Obviously, when one party to an argument appeals thus to hatred and prejudice rather than to reason, it feels quite confident of the outcome, and the preacher who preferred heathenism to the oldest form of Christianity was upheld the following January when the Common Council by a vote of 14 to 1 rejected the Catholic claim.

Thus rebuffed, the undaunted Bishop Hughes entered the

political arena, and for the next two years New York politics was heavily weighted with the religious issue. Bishop Hughes— "Dagger John" or "Cross John" as the Protestants called him both from his temperament and his custom of putting a cross above his signature, as many Catholic bishops do—was not one to retreat, and the vituperation directed at him by the secular Protestant press only served to stiffen his determination. In the end, he entered a Catholic ticket in the city elections of November, 1841, with the result that the fiercely anti-Catholic Whigs scored a sweep. This, of course, was exactly what Dagger John had intended. The Democrats, who had refused to support his appeals, at once realized that the Catholic defection had cost them an easy victory, and they made haste to lure their departed brethren back into the fold. In April, 1842, the Democratic-controlled state legislature passed the Maclay Bill which included New York City in the state educational system and forbade sectarian teaching in schools receiving state funds. This broke the power of the Public School Society, but it also denied funds to religious schools. Thus, Bishop Hughes had both won and lost.

Actually, the belligerent bishop may have lost more than he gained, if only because of the public storm blown up by passage of the Maclay Bill. It appeared that the worst fears of a papal plot had been realized. "The dark hour is at hand," the New York *Observer* lamented. "People must only trust in God to be saved from the beast." That night, street mobs attacked passing Irishmen and Bishop Hughes's windows were stoned. Moreover, because there never has been a law capable of dispelling prejudice, the reply of New York City's Protestants—and the nation as well —to the ban on "sectarian" instruction was merely to snort that "the Bible is not a sectarian book."

To Dagger John's dismay, the Protestant Bible remained firmly entrenched in New York City's public schools, and his only recourse was to concentrate all of his energy on construction of more parochial schools—thus increasing the financial burdens born by his mainly working-class flock. His attempt to exclude the Protestant Bible from the city's public schools—misrepresented as it was as an attack upon Holy Scripture—had only given the nativists more ammunition in their crusade to arouse the nation to the dangers of Romanism. And the anti-Catholic fires were literally fanned brighter in 1842 when an overzealous priest in the Lake Champlain area of New York State gathered up copies of Protestant Bibles distributed among his parishioners by Bible societies, and publicly burned them. No greater insult could have been offered American Protestantism. The "Champlain Bible burning," as it was called, was compared to the Gunpowder Plot in England, and one editor hoped that it would "kindle a flame that shall consume the last vestige of Popery in this land of ours."

Beyond doubt, no matter how justly the priest may have resented distribution of an unauthorized Bible in his parish, no matter how logically Bishop Hughes's own *Freeman's Journal* might defend this "praiseworthy act," the fact remains that it was a blunder.

Apparently, American Catholics of that era could not comprehend the American Protestant's devotion to the Bible. It was sacred to him. It was *the* Book, not only the center of his faith but very often the central authority of his life. It is possible that he did not believe that there was any other version. After all, he had been taught to believe that Catholicism was against the Word of God, that Catholics were forbidden to read the Bible. To speak of a Catholic version, let alone to suggest that the Church considered herself to be the sole, divinely appointed custodian of Holy Writ, would only have deepened his conviction of the deceitful nature of Popery, if it did not also infuriate him. Nationalist as the ordinary American of that age might have been, he was perhaps even more intensely Protestant, and to have burned the flag would have seemed an act less blasphemous than to have burned the Bible. Moreover, if the modern public school is secular and even antireligious, the public school of that day had a religious base—indeed a religious origin—and it was *de facto* Protestant. Thus, any Catholic attempt to drive the Protestant Bible from the public school was judged an attack upon religion. Therefore, Bishop John Hughes's campaign had truly boomeranged, and the school controversy followed by the Bible-burning incident now had the effect of arousing those middle-class but high-minded Protestants who had up until this point held aloof from the drive against Catholicism. Yet, much as Dagger John's booming belligerence may have enrolled still more Americans beneath the banners of the Protestant Crusade, another Bible-reading dispute in Philadelphia was to prove that the response of Christian forbearance would lead— not to peace and understanding—but to open warfare.

Francis Patrick Kenrick, a mild-mannered, scholarly priest who abhorred violence, was the Bishop of Philadelphia. In 1842, inspired by Bishop Hughes's campaign in New York, Kenrick wrote to the Philadelphia school authorities complaining that the Protestant Bible was being read to Catholic children and that Protestant religious exercises were being made part of their instruction. Kenrick requested that the Catholic children be allowed to use their own version of the Bible and that they be excused from the Protestant services. Although his request did not appear unusual to the school board, it outraged the city's Protestant ministers, and a week after it was made, ninety-four of them met to form the famous American Protestant Association. In its constitution, the A.P.A. expressly stated that it believed "the system of Popery to be, in its principles and tendency, subversive of civil and religious liberty," and dedicated itself to oppose it.

The first real opportunity came in the following January, when the school board granted Bishop Kenrick's request. Throughout that year and into the summer of 1844, the A.P.A. did all in its power to stir up resentment against the Catholics of the city, always maintaining that Bishop Kenrick's motive was to "banish the Bible from our public institutions." Unlike the fiery Hughes, Kenrick did not defend himself against the attacks, nor did he prepare his flock to protect themselves and their churches against the violence which the A.P.A.'s agents were working so assiduously to provoke.

Thus, in May, when several thousand nativists deliberately staged an anti-Catholic meeting in a heavily Irish section, one of them was killed by shots which could have come from the mob itself or from an Irish firehouse. Whichever side fired, it provoked the inevitable rioting. For three days Philadelphia was given over to arson and bloodshed. Whole rows of Irish homes were burned to the ground. Priests and nuns trembled for their lives.

St. Michael's Church went up in flames, along with an adjoining seminary. At St. Augustine's Church, the mayor attempted to save the edifice by standing on the steps and telling the crowd there were no arms inside. That, of course, merely assured the rioters that they could attack in perfect safety, and St. Augustine's also was set on fire. Naturally enough, the Irish did not submit tamely to the onslaught. They fought back. But they were not only outnumbered, they were also unorganized and unarmed—and when Bishop Kenrick issued a typically pacific proclamation deploring Catholic participation in the disorders, the nativists tore the placards down and made them into cockade hats to identify themselves. Meanwhile, native Americans or Protestant Irish in the besieged areas made haste to protect person and property by fastening large signs saying "Native American" to their doors. Two months later, when the nativists attempted to turn Independence Day into a memorial service for their own members killed in the rioting, violence erupted again. This time the nativists brought two cannon from ships at the wharves and attempted to shoot down the doors of St. Philip Neri Church, where the militia held one of their number captive. Fortunately, the wet powder would not ignite, and the rioters contented themselves with battering the doors down and freeing their comrade.

In the end, thirteen citizens were killed in the Philadelphia rioting, fifty were wounded, two Catholic churches and a seminary were destroyed and others were damaged, while an untold number of homes of Catholic Irish were burned to the ground. Once again, as in Boston after the burning of the Ursuline Convent, the nativists professed to be shocked. But those who deplored the outrages in public, spoke quite differently of them in private; and the grand jury empowered to investigate the disorders blamed it on "the efforts of a portion of the community to exclude the Bible from the public schools," meanwhile indicting for murder several Irishmen who had tried to defend their homes.

Once the news of the disorders reached St. Louis with its heavily Catholic German population, there were riots there. It was alleged that the cadavers used in the medical school conducted by the Jesuits were actually the corpses of Protestant men and women cruelly tortured to death by "the American Inquisition."

The news from Philadelphia also moved New York's nativists to the attack. A mass meeting was held to denounce Popery and to appropriate rewards for "Irish rioters," a measure which seems to suggest that someone, at least, expected a riot. When a second mass meeting of *all* the citizens of New York was scheduled for Central Park, Bishop John Hughes entered the conflict. His first move was to ask the legal authorities if state law could compel the city to recompense Catholics for any damage done to their churches by mobs. When he received No for an answer, he stationed armed patrols of a thousand to two thousand men around all the churches and paid a call on Mayor James Harper, a nativist and also the clandestine publisher of Maria Monk, to inform him that if the city would not protect the Catholics' churches, they would do so themselves.

"So you are afraid for your churches," Harper taunted.

"No," Hughes replied. "I am afraid for yours." With pointed emphasis he added: "If any Catholic church is burned here, New York will be a Moscow."

The Bishop made his point, and the nativists, alarmed by his warlike preparations, postponed the Central Park mass meeting. Thus, by his firmness, Hughes prevented a repetition of the Philadelphia riots in New York. But he—and his fellow bishops as well—remained defeated on the issue of Bible reading. The Protestant Bible stayed in the public school and the public school stayed Protestant. And it is to this setback that the development of the enormous American parochial school system—unique in the Catholic world—can be traced.

In the meantime, the Philadelphia and other riots had the happy effect of discrediting the nativists. The political party which they had begun—the American Republicans—fell apart on the defection of large numbers of native Americans who did not wish to be associated with bloodshed and destruction. No-Popery entered into a desuetude hastened by the distraction of the Mexican War.

Chapter IX

As in the Revolution and the War of 1812, Catholics served in the Mexican War in at least representative numbers. Two of them, James Shields and Bennet Riley, both brigadier generals, fought with distinction, while the young Lieutenant John Paul Jones O'Brien helped to save the day at Buena Vista for Zachary Taylor.

President Polk appointed two Jesuits to serve as chaplains to the invading army, and also asked Bishop Hughes of New York to "disabuse the minds of the Catholic priests and people of Mexico in regard to what they erroneously supposed to be the hostile design of the government and people of the United States upon the religion and church property of Mexico." Actually, this conviction was not quite so "erroneous," if American intentions were to be judged by attempts to recruit volunteers with promises of "plenty of whiskey, golden Jesuses, and pretty Mexican girls." At any rate, the proposal raised such a storm of nativist protest that Hughes prudently refused.

Although sleeping, nativism had its momentary waking starts of No-Popery. Thus, while the overwhelming majority of Catholics were loyal to their government in a war against a Catholic country, and one which many Protestant ministers denounced as criminal and unjust, offering to serve with the Mexican army rather than under the Stars and Stripes, all the nativists seemed to see was the isolated although spectacular exception of the "St. Patrick's Battalion." This was a unit of mainly Irish deserters which turned out to be the finest fighting force Mexico had in the field. The men had been recruited from General Taylor's little army on the Rio Grande. At the time, 47 per cent of the regulars in the American Army were foreigners, of whom 24 per cent were Irish. Guessing that they were also Catholic, the Mexican authorities played upon their religious sympathies, offering them bounties of land and an escape from the undeniable brutalities visited upon them by their officers. St. Patrick's Battalion —or *los San Patricios*—fought to the last bullet in a fortified convent at Mexico City. After the survivors were captured, most of them were sentenced to be hung, while those who had deserted prior to the outbreak of hostilities were to be branded on the forehead with a D. Execution of the sentence, however, was withheld until the moment the American flag should fly above Chapultepec. With singular obtuseness, the gallows was erected directly in front of a Catholic church, and when the tiny speck of red, white and blue could be seen waving over the Mexican strongpoint, the men were executed in celebration of the victory. The deserters, meanwhile, were branded with hot irons, their leader being branded twice because the first D was burnt on upside down. Quite naturally, many Mexicans were horrified by what they judged to be the deliberate desecration of a church by a form of execution which they regarded as a profanation of the crucified Christ. To the nativists, however, the only point in the entire episode was that the desertion of this band of Irish mercenaries was proof positive of the "disloyalty" of all Catholics, and they used it as ammunition once the end of the war brought a revival of No-Popery.

The end of the war also brought a tremendous challenge to the American Church. The lands ceded in the Treaty of Guadalupe Hidalgo had made the United States a huge continental power stretching from sea to sea. The territorial acquisitions resulting from the Mexican War had been stupendous, including the modern states of California, Nevada, Utah, Arizona, New Mexico, Texas and parts of Wyoming and Colorado. There is no other land grab in history which matches it. In fact, all other comparable expansions through military power have since been dissipated. With only a few small exceptions, all great empires except the Russian have now receded to within their own natural boundaries. But American imperialism, augmented by the Gadsden Purchase and the compromise with Great Britain which led to annexation of the Oregon Territory, has remained successful.

Because of it, the struggling young Church was compelled to make a coterminous expansion of its own.

When American Catholicism pushed westward into former Mexican territory it came upon the ruins of what had once been the glories of Spanish Catholicism. For centuries before the birth of the American Church, these lands had been the vineyards in which Spanish missionaries labored. The black-robed Jesuits came first, but then, after Charles III banished the sons of St. Ignatius from Spain and all Spanish possessions, the brown-robed Franciscans took charge.

California had been the special triumph of the great Spanish Franciscan, Junípero Serra. Born on Mallorca in the Balearics on November 24, 1713, Serra was the son of devout peasant farmers. Early in life he came under the influence of the Franciscans, and after he was ordained in that order he became a professor in philosophy at the Lullian University conducted by the friars. However, much as he delighted in the subtlety of the mind of the English theologian, Duns Scotus—his special field—Serra cared amazingly little for academic honors. He yearned, rather, for the missions and around 1748 he was sent to Mexico. Shortly after his arrival, he was bitten in the foot by a snake, and because he had not considered the bite worthy of medical attention, the foot festered and thereafter Junípero Serra walked with a pronounced limp. Nevertheless, he worked with great success for nearly twenty years among the Pame Indians of Mexico. Then, in 1767, King Charles III of Spain expelled the Jesuits from all his dominions, and when the Franciscans took over the Jesuit missions in California, Serra went with them.

With his fellow friars, this indomitable cripple built a chain of mission stations from San Diego to Sonoma, a stretch of six hundred miles. The Franciscans' objective was nothing less than the conversion and civilization of the California Indians, perhaps the slowest and most primitive of all the aborigines of America. Although it was years before they could gain as much as one convert among these simple savages, once they had made an inroad their progress was astonishing.

Convinced that the chief obstacle in their path was not the red man's alleged stupidity but rather the cupidity of the white man, the friars devised a system by which the Indians could be taught all the advantages of civilization while being kept free of its contaminations. Each mission station, therefore, was a kind of incubator.

It usually consisted of a village attached to the mission quadrangle. Those who did not live in the village lived in the quadrangle, where there was a dormitory for girls and another for young men. The quadrangle also contained the workshops in which all the crafts and skills were taught. Discipline was strict, although the punishment was meted out by the Indian chiefs themselves. All the lands and buildings also belonged to the Indians, the Franciscans being nothing more than the administrators, as well as the commanders of small guards of a half-dozen soldiers attached to each station. It was all quite paternal, of course, very authoritarian, but granting the nature of the people they were trying to civilize, any other approach would have been highly impractical. Moreover, the paternalism was considered an intermediate step toward full independence.

Unfortunately, the California missions were too successful. By the time Mexico shook herself free of Spain, there were twenty-one missions in which 35,000 peaceful Indians lived in possession of nearly 400,000 head of cattle, over 300,000 hogs, sheep and goats, and 62,000 horses, together with a complex of farms yielding 120,000 bushels of grain annually along with all the other produce of orchards, vineyards, wine presses, gardens, looms, shops and forges. So much wealth was bound to excite considerable covetousness, and thus, under the charming euphemism of "secularization," it was in fact confiscated. Salaried commissioners appointed by the governor managed to speed the work of robbing the Indians, and the Franciscans who sought to defend them were ejected, chiefly, it must be noted, because they were Spaniards who refused to renounce their allegiance to the Spanish crown. In their place went Mexican secular priests, many of whom were lazy and cared nothing for the Indians. Thus, when California became a part of the United States, nothing was left of the work of Junípero Serra and a hundred and fifty other Franciscans but a string of place names like a ghostly litany of vanished missions—San Luis Rey, Santa Clara, San Juan Capistrano,

San Luis Obispo—and moldering white ruins which became the inspiration for the "mission" style of architecture.

Dissolution and decay had also overtaken the missions in the Southwest. In 1630, the Franciscan superior in New Mexico could report that there were thirty-five thousand Christian Indians living in ninety pueblos attached to twenty-five missions, but by the time this territory passed to the United States, all this had vanished. So, too, had the monument of missionary organization built by the Jesuit Father Eusebio Kino (or Kuhn). An accomplished mathematician in his native Tyrol, Father Kino had nevertheless decided to come to Mexico to work among the primitive Indians. In 1687, at the age of forty-three, he was assigned to Pimería Alta, an area which included what is now southern Arizona.

On his way north, Father Kino learned that some Spanish officials were mistreating the Indians, forcing them to work in the mines before they could be baptized and thus freed for a time from this dreadful labor. Kino at once requested that the natives should not be forced to work in the mines for five years after their baptism, and that those converted Indians who did work there voluntarily be paid a fair wage. Fortunately, a royal edict had just arrived from Spain to the effect that no Indian should be taken to the mines for twenty years after his conversion, and thus, Kino's appeal received a quick and favorable reply.

Armed with this order, always guided by his conviction that an abused and resentful Indian could not possibly open his soul to the white man's religion, Kino began his remarkable career. Within twenty-four years he and his Jesuit colleagues had converted thirty thousand Indians. Kino alone could report: "I have solemnized more than four thousand baptisms, and I could have baptized ten or twelve thousand Indians more if the lack of father laborers had not rendered it impossible for us to catechize them and instruct them in advance . . ." To convert so many red men, Father Kino had to undertake the most arduous journeys. In all, he made some forty expeditions of from 90 to 720 miles, always carefully writing down what he saw or mapping the ground over which he passed on horseback or on mules. His *Favores Celestiales*, as he called it, remains the best historical source for his time and place, and his maps were for many years relied upon by European geographers. Moreover, Kino was also a successful rancher. He taught many Indian tribes stock raising and established at least twenty different ranches. "He was easily the cattle king of his day and region," wrote the historian Herbert Eugene Bolton.

Nevertheless, Father Kino's labors also ended in failure—or at least failure as it is measured in worldly terms. His string of mission stations was finally unraveled under the pressure of recurrent Indian mutinies, the attacks of the Apaches, the fact that the Jesuits unwisely trained up no native priesthood, the unstable character of the Indians themselves, the decline of Spanish power, and finally, in 1767, the sharpest stroke of all, the edict of Charles III banishing the Jesuits from his possessions.

Thus, when the Americans took possession of the Southwest, nothing was left but Indians living once again in primitive savagery. Yet, how much there *was* left! As Bolton has observed, these missionary labors of Spanish priests were "a force which made for the preservation of the Indians, as opposed to their destruction, so characteristic of the Anglo-American frontier."

It was mostly these Indians, the pagan descendants of Christian red men, to whom the American Church addressed herself when she entered the new territories. In Texas, of course, there was already a vicariate apostolic at Galveston under John Odin, and it became a bishopric after the war. In New Mexico and Arizona there was nothing, until John Baptist Lamy arrived to begin a career immortalized in Willa Cather's novel, *Death Comes for the Archbishop.*

Lamy was one of those French priests to whom the early Church owes such an enormous debt. He had worked in the dioceses of Louisville and Cincinnati before he was made Vicar-Apostolic of New Mexico in 1850, charged with the mission of winning the affection of Spanish Catholics resentful of the American intrusion and of regaining the allegiance of Indian tribes lost to the faith. With his great tact, charm, diligence, and above all, his gentle sense of humor, he was able to do both. Because he was a Latin, the Spanish in his huge vicariate readily opened their ranches to him, even allowing him the run of the kitchen where he would prepare roast lamb to suit his French tastes. To the Indians, Lamy was always a "big priest," and he rode untold thousands of miles to join them at their campfires, to eat dog's flesh with them without a grimace or a murmur, sitting out under the stars with them, talking gravely of God and the soul. John Baptist Lamy was the friend of everyone, including Lew Wallace and Kit Carson. Even the lazy priests whose indolence he had to overcome with gentle firmness came to love him. Fifteen years after he arrived, Lamy could report to Propaganda that there were a hundred thousand Catholics in New Mexico alone, with another eight thousand in Arizona and Colorado. Moreover, he had built forty-five churches and repaired eighteen more. Ten years later, his vicariate had become the province of Santa Fe and John Baptist Lamy was its first archbishop.

By then, the American Church had begun to divide and subdivide into provinces like the original one at Baltimore, that is, an archdiocese surrounded by a cluster of suffragan dioceses. This was what was done in California, after the Dominican Father José Sadoc Alemany, the first ordinary of that state with a see at Monterey, pleaded that administration of his enormous diocese was complicated by the fact that it was inhabited by two radically different kinds of Catholics. To the south were the earlier settlers, usually Spanish, and the lapsed Indians; while to the north were the "Forty-Niners," the prospectors and entrepreneurs of the Gold Rush, a rambunctious and sometimes unsavory breed of Catholic indeed, but Catholics nonetheless. In response to Alemany's plea, Propaganda in 1853 divided California into the northern province or archdiocese of San Francisco, with Alemany as its first archbishop, and the southern diocese of Monterey as a suffragan see under Bishop Thaddeus Amat.

A similar solution was adopted in the huge new Oregon Territory, where Father Francis Blanchet became Archbishop of Oregon City with a suffragan see at Walla Walla, Washington. Unfortunately, an Indian massacre ended Walla Walla's brief history as a Catholic see, and it was eventually suppressed.

Thus, step by careful step, a solid and durable ecclesiastical structure was erected in the trail of American military conquest, and as such old eastern cities as Philadelphia, New York and Boston became provinces in their own right, similar status was conferred on former frontier outposts such as St. Louis and, later, Chicago.

Meanwhile, as Propaganda went carefully about the business of organizing a continental Church, the American bishops had begun to gather in those councils which were to unify it.

Among John England's many contributions to the American Church was his insistence that the Archbishop of Baltimore convene a provincial council, that is, a gathering of all the bishops of the province at which the archbishop himself would preside.

John Carroll had called no council because he had not had the time; Leonard Neale did not live long enough to call one; and the autocratic Archbishop Maréchal had not the inclination. Maréchal appears to have believed that the province could function smoothly enough under the supervision of the archbishop. When matters of common concern arose, the bishops could consult with one another by correspondence.

For a time, the bishops agreed—until they observed that their archbishop took no steps to propose native-born candidates for vacant sees, with the result that Rome continued to fill them with Europeans. With unconscious irony, John England, a European himself, proposed the need of provincial councils to discuss such matters. He even appealed to Rome on the matter. But Maréchal, who distrusted England's democratic convictions, consistently refused. And so, it was not until 1828, one year after Maréchal's death, that the English-born Archbishop James Whitfield convoked the First Provincial Council of Baltimore. It was from this gathering and its successors that the American Church gained its uniformity of practice.

Meeting together, the bishops learned to know each other and to exchange information on common problems. They prevailed upon Rome not to exclude them in the naming of new bishops or in selecting the area of a new diocese. Gradually, throughout the 1830s, these new sees began to spring up across America: Detroit, Vincennes, Nashville, Natchez, Dubuque, Pittsburgh . . . Wherever the American pioneers ventured, a Catholic see was erected in their trail—if one of the old Spanish ones was not already there to receive them. Meanwhile, as the Church expanded westward with the nation, it was being compelled to meet its unique mission of caring for the foreign-born. Whether in Cincinnati or St. Louis or any of the other Western sees where German Catholics were concentrated in great numbers, or in Boston or New York and the other big Eastern cities which attracted almost all of the Irish, the Church had to solve the problem of how to make good American citizens of all these foreign-born without depriving them of those unique customs and characteristics which would also enrich America. To do so, whether consciously or not, the councils evolved a fourfold response based upon education, charity, press and clergy.

Since its inception, the American Church had always suffered from a shortage of priests, especially native-born Americans. Now, with the number of dioceses, as well as missions to the Indians, steadily increasing, it became evident that the Church could no longer depend on Europe but must begin large-scale training of its own. Again and again, the councils recommended that each diocese erect its own seminary. Toward the end of the thirties, there were eleven of them in the country with 148 students.

Often, these makeshift seminaries were institutions in name only, being located in the episcopal "palace," itself sometimes no more than a rude shack. In some sees, the bishop was his seminary's only instructor, and his students in turn taught in the local college or school. Nevertheless, they did train young men to be priests, and if the education of these newly ordained ministers was sometimes no more elegant than the seminary that produced them, their ardor was almost irresistible. Again and again visitors to America remarked on "the morality of the Catholic clergy in this country." One English Protestant traveler, Thomas Hamilton, exclaimed in 1833: "I am not a Catholic, but I cannot suffer prejudice of any sort to prevent my doing justice to a body of Christian ministers, whose zeal can be animated by no hope of worldly reward, and whose humble lives are passed in diffusing the influence of divine truth, and communicating to the meanest and most despised of mankind the blessed comforts of religion."

On the dusty crossroads of lonely frontier towns or the littered pavements of crowded industrial cities, the first person that an immigrant Catholic usually met was one of these parish priests. He was his counselor as well as his confessor, and often the two services were intertwined. Moreover, the interior of a Catholic church with its familiar statuary and sacramentals and its centuries-old liturgy was frequently about the only place in which an immigrant could feel at home. Should he be too slow or too set in his ways to receive instruction in a new language or to become assimilated to a new way of life, then his children, at least, could be indoctrinated in the educational system which the expanding Church was establishing across the country.

Although it was far too early in the Church's history to set itself the ambitious goal of every Catholic child in a Catholic school, the decade of the 1830s nevertheless did set the trend toward a Catholic educational system. Schools were ever the desire of the bishops. By the end of the period, there were fifteen colleges for young men, twenty-seven religious institutions and thirty-eight academies for young women and two hundred parochial schools, half of the latter being located west of the Alleghenies.

It was in these schools that immigrant children might mingle with the offspring of native-born Americans and thus become adapted to American ways. It may even be said that the parochial grade school was perhaps more American than the public school, if only because it was open to all who attended the Catholic Church—regardless of class or color—and even to children of other creeds. This, of course, was no more intentional than the accidental fact that organization of the public school on a neighborhood basis tended to result in a *de facto* segregation based on the neighborhood's economic or racial character. Nevertheless, it was a fact. It was also true that the parochial school was actually a copy of the public school, and that it may never have come into existence if the public school had not possessed such a strong Protestant and frequently anti-Catholic cast. Its reason for being was nothing other than the Catholic objection to the Protestant Bible and Protestant instruction in the public schools, and it differed from this institution only in its use of the Catholic Bible and its classes in Catholic beliefs. Some schools, it is true, were taught by non-English-speaking teachers; but even in these, some English was taught, so that there is no record of immigrant children being graduated from a parochial school without knowledge of the language of their new homeland.

Institutions of higher learning were also founded during the organizational period, the most famous of them, and the one that still has a special place in the hearts of most Americans, being the University of Notre Dame. Again reflecting the strong French influence in the Catholicism of the day, the University of Notre Dame du Lac—"Our Lady of the Lake"—was in its inception and formative years the work of French priests. Just before Celestine de la Hailandiere became the second Bishop of Vincennes, he visited France to obtain priests and teachers for the diocesan schools. Among them was Father Edward Sorin, a priest of the Congregation of the Holy Cross. In 1842 he and six brothers settled on a magnificent piece of land—the gift of Father Stephen Badin, the first priest ordained by John Carroll—and the following year he opened the school. "This college will be one of the most powerful means of doing good in this country," Father Sorin predicted in a letter to his superior-general, and so it has become, even if its intellectual greatness is eclipsed by the celebrity of its football team; and it may very well be that the final triumph of Catholic Gael over Catholic Gall was consummated when this magnificent gift of French culture came to be known as the home of "the Fighting Irish."

A third means of binding the allegiance of Catholic immigrants to the American Church was the institution of charity. If he were sick or aging, the newcomer could find a place of care in Catholic hospitals or of comfort in Catholic old-age homes, and those who suffered economic hardship could place their children in Catholic orphanages. Catholic charity—apart from the efforts of the early missionaries—may be said to have begun in Philadelphia in 1814, when three Sisters of Charity opened St. Joseph's Orphanage, the first of 317 such asylums in the United States. Fourteen years later in St. Louis, the same order opened the first of 931 American Catholic hospitals, and it was in that same city that the first American chapter of the French Society of St. Vincent de Paul was organized to assist the Catholic poor.

Although these institutions were primarily established by Catholics to help their less fortunate brethren, they were by no means exclusive. Then, as now, they were open to all Americans, and the first official record of this non-discriminating attitude came during the cholera epidemic of 1832. One of the greatest scourges in the history of American medicine, the outbreak of Asiatic cholera struck particularly heavy blows at the Catholic community. Among its victims were Gabriel Richard, the French Sulpician who was the first vice-president of the University of

Michigan and the only Catholic priest to serve as a member of Congress, and Bishop Fenwick of Cincinnati. Cholera was particularly devastating in the South. When it reached Baltimore the Sisters of Charity there organized an emergency hospital in the archbishop's residence. Their unselfish devotion was described by Mayor William Stewart as "the purest system of unostentatious Charity that could have been devised." Baltimore, of course, was only one of many cities in which Catholic charity came to the aid of all.

The Catholic press, the fourth means by which the immigrant might be bound to his faith, was originally founded as a means of replying to the attacks of the nativists. John England's *Miscellany* was the first newspaper, of course, and in the two decades following its establishment in 1822 there were twenty more periodicals for English-speaking Catholics and one for Germans. Gradually, these newspapers became perhaps the chief means through which a bishop might communicate with his flock, although eventually the Church was to employ virtually every form of printed publication—with heavy emphasis on pamphlets—in its continuing effort to enlighten the faithful.

It was also through the agency of this steadily expanding Catholic press that the Church was able to reach the minds of Protestant Americans, and to begin to make converts among them.

Chapter X

Without riches or prestige, the earlier Church seldom attracted non-Catholics. When conversions did occur, they were usually the result of a mixed marriage in which the non-Catholic partner, for one reason or another, adopted the religion of his or her spouse. Conversions of the intellectual sort, in which a reflective, inquiring mind addresses itself to the truth or falsehood of Catholicism's unique claims, were very rare indeed, if only because the intellectualism of the day was hardly more than a mirror reflecting the mind of Europe. Thus, even educated Americans could not escape the legacies of anti-Catholic England, and they were steeped in a literature permeated with horror and hatred of Popery. For the Church to be considered at all, it had to await a truly American intellectual flowering together with a relaxation of prejudice in the Mother Country.

Both of these events occurred almost simultaneously, at roughly about the beginning of the fourth decade of the nineteenth century, when Catholic Emancipation freed the English Church of the penal bonds hung on her in 1688, thus preparing the way for the Oxford Movement led by such Anglican clerics as John Henry Newman. Hoping to bring about a reconciliation of Anglicanism and Catholicism, Newman's investigations actually brought him inside the bosom of the Church, and his writings thereafter began to exert a great influence on members of the Anglican communion.

In the United States, where a truly native American culture had begun to bud, a young Episcopalian clergyman named Pierce Connolly traveled a similar road, and four years after he was married, he and his wife Cornelia became Catholics. Unfortunately, Connolly's conversion did not survive the ill winds of fortune. Rather it was his wife, Cornelia Peacock Connolly, who remained true to her new faith, and her story is a poignant compound of tragedy, humiliation and unswerving fidelity.

After the birth of their second son, John, the Connollys suffered financial losses which made it necessary for Pierce to take a teaching job at the Jesuit College in Grand Coteau, Louisiana. There, their second daughter was born, only to die a few weeks later. There also, Mrs. Connolly was out walking with the children one day when three-year-old John ran on ahead of her, stumbled—and fell into a kettle of boiling maple juice, where he was fatally burned. And there, her husband came to her and said: "Cornelia, I want to be a priest." Aghast, she replied: "A priest, Pierce, but you can't—you are married." Connolly replied that if Cornelia would agree to go into a convent, he could be ordained. Mrs. Connolly was stunned. She was then pregnant with her third son. Grief-stricken, she went to see a young priest who later would become Cardinal McCloskey, the first American prince of the Church, and told him: "Is it necessary for Pierce to make this sacrifice and to sacrifice me? I love my husband. I love my darling children. Why must I give them up?" Father McCloskey counseled her to wait and pray. In the end, Cornelia Connolly submitted to her husband's desire. After the birth of her last child, she went into a convent. Her husband became ordained and her children were put in private schools.

Soon Cornelia Connolly was invited to England by Cardinal Wiseman to educate Catholic girls. She became Mother Connolly, author of a rule for a new religious community to be called "The Society of the Holy Child Jesus." She had her own convent. One day when she was thirty-seven, Father Pierce Connolly came to see her. He was bored. His hopes of gaining ecclesiastical preferment had been dashed by the death of the Pope who had been interested in him. Now he was only a private chaplain to the Earl of Shrewsbury. Now he wished to tell Mother Connolly how to run her community. But he was told instead that his visit was improper, that Mother Connolly would not see him and that he must go away and not return. Enraged, Father Connolly departed, took his children to Italy with him, where he put them in school while journeying to Rome in an attempt to change the Rule of his wife's society, posing as the founder. Unsuccessful, he returned to England where he again attempted to see Mother Connolly. Rebuffed once more, he departed vowing vengeance.

Eventually, Pierce Connolly went into the civil courts in an attempt to recover his conjugal rights. The verdict was in his favor, but the Privy Council overruled it. Now Connolly flung himself out of the Church, took his children out of school to put them in a home and returned to the Episcopal communion, where he became rector of a church in Florence. Mother Connolly's cup of anguish was overflowing. Both her children and her husband were outside the religion into which he had led them all. She had taken the veil to gratify his ambition, and he had left her with nothing but her vows. To these she also remained faithful. Her calmness and gentleness were household words among the sisters of her religious community. Only once was she known to lose them. Her oldest son had died at twenty of yellow fever, still outside the Church, and when the sisters came to comfort her, she turned away from them bitterly and sobbed: "None of you can understand the feelings of a mother." Meanwhile, her society grew. She had schools in England, the United States and France. In 1879, at the age of seventy-three, she breathed her last. Her life had been a model of courage and steadfastness.

Of quite different character—more like a Jerome than a Monica—was a second nineteenth-century convert to American Catholicism: the writer and social reformer Orestes Brownson. Here was an irascible and somber man indeed. Born in the little village of Stockbridge, Vermont, in 1803, as a child he was given to a lonely, elderly couple to raise. As a result, Brownson said, "I had no childhood." His only friends were the books in his foster parents' collection of gloomy Congregational theological works, and it was on these that he fed his childish imagination, growing up contemplating heaven and hell, election and damnation. At eighteen, already tall and imposing, with his jet black hair combed straight back from his noble forehead, his gray eyes flashing black when he was excited, he joined the Presbyterian Church. But the doctrine of predestination, which Brownson described as one that "foreordained the wicked to sin necessarily so that God might damn them justly," appalled him. Worse, when he objected to it to clergymen, they advised him not to think about it. To a man of Brownson's undeceived intelligence, such self-deceit was contemptible—and in 1823 he left the Presbyterian Church.

There followed a period of two years during which he taught school, came down with malaria and continued his self-administered education. Brownson was happiest with a book in his hands. He seemed to enjoy being with other people only insofar as he might reveal to them the truths that he had learned through reading and meditation. Now his reading introduced him to Universalism. Here was a creed which was the exact opposite of Calvinism. It denied evil altogether and it was a pleasant if bland refuge for Protestants repelled by grimmer creeds preaching the "total depravity" of mankind. In 1825, Brownson became a Universalist minister.

Inevitably, however, his penetrating mind became dissatisfied with what seemed to him to be a facile faith, one which dissolved Christianity into a few vague generalities. Three years later, he left Universalism. Disillusioned, Brownson interested himself in social reform. Rather, he plunged into it, for this most serious of men took nothing lightly. For two years he preached and wrote socialism, completely abandoning belief in divine revelation, concerning himself exclusively with attacking the injustice of the new industrialism. He had become an agnostic, a humanist. But to a man of his temperament, faith in man was not enough. He had to have faith in a higher being, in God. Brownson was not only a passionate seeker of the truth, he also sought to save his own soul. He was Thompson's Hound of Heaven, ceaselessly chasing his Savior down the labyrinthine way of his own tortured mind. "I have . . . a witness within," he wrote, "and having this witness, I can find its testimony corroborated by the whole of external nature."

Returning to Christianity, Brownson preached for a while as an independent minister, until the writings of William Ellery Channing attracted him to Unitarianism. He found: "Unitarian discourses are most practical; their lessons inculcate charity, a refined moral feeling, and universal benevolence." Applying for the Unitarian pulpit in Walpole, New Hampshire, he was accepted there. There also he immersed himself in the study of philosophy and theology, taught himself French, learned some

German, and made frequent trips to Boston, where he met all the leading Unitarians.

In 1834, Brownson became pastor of the Unitarian Church in Canton, Massachusetts. George Ripley, the celebrated literary critic and social reformer, preached the installation sermon. It was at Canton that Brownson became famous. Tall and slender in his swallowtail coat and loose black trousers, an immaculate white handkerchief ever knotted at his throat, his intense voice vibrant and his eyes burning with the fervor of his convictions, he was an impressive figure and his sermons were well attended. Gradually, Brownson evolved his vision of the "Church of the Future," a new synthesis combing the spirituality of Catholicism and the humanitarianism of a Protestantism which he already professed to find a vitiated chaos of conflicting sects.

It was at Canton one summer that Brownson was asked to examine a Harvard sophomore who wanted to teach in the town school. "The two sat up talking till midnight," Channing recalled later, "and Mr. Brownson informed the school committee that Mr. Thoreau was examined, and would do, and would board with him." Thoreau stayed with Brownson for six weeks. "They were an era in my life," he wrote to Brownson, "the morning of a new *Lebenstag*."

As Brownson's reputation as a thinker of unusual clarity and penetration began to spread, his circle of friends among New England intellectuals grew wider. In 1836 he met with Ripley, Ralph Waldo Emerson, Bronson Alcott and others to form the famous Transcendentalist Club. He became one of its leading members, and the second meeting was at his home. He also came to be known as perhaps the most contentious member. Brownson did not "discuss" problems of the day, he discoursed on them. His style was to shout and to pound the table, to fix his opponent —or at least the person with whom he disagreed—with his flashing eyes and proceed to demolish his position with a bombardment of facts fired from the iron barrel of his logical mind. "No one loves to break a lance with him," his protégé Isaac Hecker remarked, "because he cuts such ungentlemanly gashes." And Emerson complained: "Brownson will never stop and listen, neither in conversation, but what is more, not in solitude."

Many of the Unitarians or Transcendentalists found Brownson's unremitting attacks on the injustice of the new industrialism quite disturbing. Channing, for instance, could say to a group of underpaid coal miners: "Your true strength lies in growing intelligence, uprightness, self-respect, trust in God, and trust in one another." But as early as 1840, Brownson declared: "Wages is a cunning device of the devil, for the benefit of tender consciences, who would retain all the advantages of the slave system, without the expense, trouble, and odium of being slave holders." Such remarks, whether spoken from the pulpit or written in his own *Boston Quarterly Review*, shocked and outraged those "tender consciences" he despised so utterly. But no man saw so clearly or so soon that capitalism was a method by which the rich get richer and the poor get poorer. Like Hilaire Belloc a century after him, he realized that "permanent employment" was a euphemism for a new kind of industrial servitude.

By then, Orestes Brownson also was beginning to realize that Unitarianism was hardly more than a dechristianized form of humanitarianism. To him, it was a kind of ethical society in which Jesus Christ was portrayed as no more than "a very exemplary sort of man, a very zealous and able reformer, whom we should do well to respect and to remember along with Plato, Alfred, Luther and Swedenborg." To Brownson, however, Jesus Christ was divine, he was the God-Man, the mediator between God and man, the Redeemer. Once his mind had returned to the Incarnation—the basic proposal of Christianity—and had become convinced again of its truth, he relaxed. "I can preach now," he said, "not merely make discursions on ethics and metaphysics . . ." Convinced of Original Sin and the need for a Redeemer, he turned toward Catholic theology. He read Newman. As his biographer Arthur M. Schlesinger has observed: "Brownson's faith grew so powerful that he finally rushed to the Christian epic of sin and redemption, deeply grounded in the experience of the ages and magnificently realized in Catholic theology."

Brownson's thinking was taking him further and further away from his Transcendentalist friends. He seldom visited Brook Farm, the community venture which they had founded to work out a way of life. Although he was still fond of Ripley and Emerson and the others personally, he did not approve of their ideas. Scrupulously honest, he did not wish his name to be associated with the place famous for their theories.

Yet, he drew back from taking the final step. To have moved from one Protestant sect to another, even to agnosticism and back again, had been easy. It was, as Father John O'Brien has observed, like moving from one room to another in the same building. But Catholicism! That was a different house entirely. From what he had been taught to think of it, it could be the abode of the Devil. "To the Protestant mind," he wrote later, "this old Catholic Church is veiled in mystery, and leaves ample room to the imagination to people it with all manner of monsters, chimeras, and hydras dire . . . To enter it seemed to me like taking a leap in the dark; and it is not strange that I recoiled, and set my wits to work to find out, if possible, some middle ground, on which I could be faithful to my Catholic tendencies without uniting myself with the present Roman Catholic Church . . ." Like Newman, like so many other converts from a creed with a tradition of No-Popery, he was trying to find a middle way. But there was none, as he discovered when he went to Bishop John Fitzpatrick of Boston for instructions in Catholicism. In October, 1844, he was received into the Church.

Some of his friends smiled when they heard of his latest conversion. He would think his way out of Catholicism soon, they declared. Others said good riddance to this difficult, truculent man, and Thurlow Weed remarked: "He'll wreck whatever he anchors to, and I hope it's the Roman Catholic Church." The gentle Doctor Channing thought otherwise. "All his changes have not been fluctuating but steps in ethical progress." And in England, John Henry Newman considered Brownson's conversion an event of the greatest importance for the English-speaking Church.

There is no doubt that Orestes Brownson was one of the most powerful and original minds in American Catholic intellectual history. Schlesinger has judged his essay on "The Laboring Classes" to be "perhaps the best study of the workings of society written by an American before the Civil War." Newman invited him to occupy a chair—any chair—at the University of Dublin he was planning to found; this, from Dr. Newman of Oxford, the greatest Catholic theologian to write in English, from a future cardinal, to the rude Vermonter with but one year of formal education. Nevertheless he has been forgotten, neglected even in Catholic institutions of higher learning, while lesser men are still remembered and read.

Had Orestes Brownson remained a Transcendentalist, it is likely that he would still be a living force in American thought, quoted and consulted like Emerson and Thoreau and the others who were his friends. But he chose to embrace a despised and alien creed, taking a step which many considered to be an insult, a slap in the face to all that was cultivated and refined in the Protestant American tradition. Certainly he alienated them when he went over to the attack upon everything that they revered. Even before his conversion, he had turned upon the religious liberalism of New England with this bellowing repudiation:

We have demolished hell; scouted the devil; laughed at the fall; reduced the Son of God, first, to a promising Hebrew youth, who was a successful mesmeriser, and, finally, to a mythic personage, created by the creeds and fancies of men; we have, moreover, successively disrobed God himself of His justice, His truth, His sovereignty, His paternity, His providence, at last of His personality, and resolved Him into a blind force, or a mere fate or irresistible necessity. And in all this we have been guilty of no heresy . . . have been, in fact, good, true, faithful, enlightened, liberal Christians, the reformers of the church and the restorers of primitive Christianity!

Thus chastised, the fathers of American liberalism were that much more offended by Brownson's truculent attempts to drag them off to Rome. Thoreau and Ripley sidestepped his freeswinging net, although he did manage to convert Ripley's wife, Sophia. And no one at Brook Farm applauded when the promising young Isaac Hecker actually preceded Brownson, his spiritual father, into the Church.

Isaac Hecker was born in New York City on December 18, 1819, the youngest son of Prussian immigrants to America. His mother was a devout Methodist, and she imparted her religious fervor to her son. Sensitive, introspective, mystic, Isaac Hecker was one of those unusual men who believe almost from the first moment of reflection that God has brought them into the world to perform a special mission. Because the failure of his father's brass foundry compelled him to go to work at the age of thirteen, first with a newspaper, then in another foundry and finally in the bakery founded by his brothers, he became concerned with the problems of the workingmen with whom he associated. To correct social injustice, he decided, would be his life's work.

Throwing himself into the movement for social reform, Hecker joined a radical political group called the Equal Rights party, participated in park protest meetings, became an agitator for workers' rights and attended lectures on the subject. One night at the age of twenty-one, he heard a lecture by Orestes Brownson. He was deeply moved. With his brothers, he became a disciple of the tall, roughhewn sage from Vermont. In 1842, while delivering another series of lectures in New York, Brownson stayed for three weeks in the Hecker home. Isaac was enchanted. Night after night he sat in the family kitchen listening to Brownson expand on his talks, spinning out his own profoundly original theories on the problems of the day. Because Brownson was convinced that a new religious synthesis such as his Church of the Future was the answer, he impressed the young baker with the need to deepen himself in philosophy and theology. Knowing German, he began to read the theories of German thinkers, becoming so deeply immersed that he would find himself "kneading at the dough-trough with Kant's *Critique of Pure Reason* fastened upon the wall."

Gradually, however, the mystical side of Hecker's nature gained the ascendancy over the philosophical. He lost interest in "issues," in his work, in everything but musing over the question: "What does God desire of me?" Soon, he was living in an ethereal, visionary world. Constantly dreaming, he dreamed one night of "a beautiful, angelic being, and myself standing alongside of her, feeling a most heavenly pure joy." From this "visitation" he concluded that he should not marry, and soon he had expanded this into a conviction that he must leave all—family, friends, work— to be able to consecrate himself to Christ. At this point, his family became concerned. Brownson was called upon for assistance and he advised the too-introspective young man to go to live at Brook Farm, the center he had helped to found for high-minded people who wished to live simply and in an intellectual atmosphere.

At Brook Farm, young Hecker befriended men such as Emerson and Channing. He studied French under Sophia Ripley and listened to her husband's lectures on Kant. He was so serious, so intent upon acquiring knowledge, and yet so obviously unsure of where he was going, that he was called "Ernest the Seeker." Eventually, however, he discovered that neither Brook Farm nor Fruitlands, an even more austere New England aesthetic sanctuary, could satisfy his restless quest. He went back to Brownson, who was at that time following the Oxford Movement in England. Brownson interested him in the Catholic Church. On Easter Sunday, 1842, he went to Mass at the church in West Roxbury. Immediately, he fell under the Church's spell. Ritual, statuary, music and sermon, all seemed to suggest to him that he had found his spiritual home at last.

Still, he hesitated. He returned home to live, and deliberately began to investigate all the Protestant faiths, going from one to another: Episcopal, Congregational, Baptist, Methodist. None had the same attraction for him as the Catholic, and yet, he wrote: "I am not prepared to enter the Roman Catholic Church at present. The Roman Catholic Church is not national with us, hence it does not meet our wants, nor does it fully understand and sympathize with the experience and disposition of our people. It is principally made up of adopted and foreign individuals."

Here, with an unconscious irony that is simply staggering, Hecker reveals how deeply the No-Popery virus had infected his own thought. Here he was, the son of Prussian immigrants, of people whose heavy German accent made them more identifiably foreign than any tempestuous Celt just off the boat from Wexford or from Cobh, and here he was looking down his nose at a Church of "adopted and foreign individuals." Evidently, in the America of his day, to be completely American one must also be Protestant, or at least not Catholic. Nevertheless, out of this unconscious conviction, this inherent No-Popery, was to rise Hecker's true lifework: the "Americanization" of the American Church.

Unlike Brownson, the earnest young seeker did not procrastinate. Once he had discussed his spiritual dilemma with John McCloskey, auxiliary bishop of New York and the same man who had counseled Cornelia Connolly, he decided to become a Catholic. Brook Farm was horrified. Thoreau was upset that first his teacher, Brownson, and next his young friend, Hecker, should be taking the road to Rome. He told Emerson, who tried to dissuade

Hecker one day when the two were visiting Bronson Alcott and Charles Lane. Each time Emerson approached the subject, Hecker gently steered the conversation in another direction. But Emerson was not to be put off.

"Mr. Hecker," he said finally, "I suppose it was the art, the architecture, and so on in the Catholic Church which led you to her?"

"No," Hecker replied, "but it was what caused all that."

On August 2, 1844, he was received into the Church by Bishop McCloskey in old St. Patrick's Cathedral. Immediately, Isaac Hecker wanted to become a priest. But he had to wait the prescribed two years following his conversion, and it was not until September, 1845, that he arrived in Belgium to begin his studies at the Redemptorist seminary there. Hecker had chosen the Redemptorists, who specialized in mission work, because he was still fired with belief in his mission to convert America. On October 23, 1849, a few months short of his thirtieth birthday, he was ordained a priest. After a year in England as a parish priest and private chaplain, he returned to the United States.

Here, he plunged into mission activity in the company of four other Redemptorists, all English-speaking converts like himself. At the time, most of the Redemptorist "mission" activity in America, that is, preaching intended to renew the faith of lapsed or lukewarm Catholics, was done by German-speaking missionaries among the Germans. Hecker and his band, however, preached to the English-speaking faithful, and frequently to non-Catholics of the old stock. Hecker himself became an eloquent preacher. Tall, pale, with a commanding head and a ruddy brown forked beard, he made a splendid figure in the pulpit. His style was deliberately unemotional. He depended on his enormous knowledge and clear understanding of Catholic history and doctrine to answer questions shot at him from listeners who were not always sympathetic to his faith. From 1851 to 1857, Hecker and his fellow convert-priests preached eighty-six missions from New York to Florida and as far west as Cincinnati. They became convinced of the need for foundation of a special house for English-speaking missionaries, either in New York City or Newark, New Jersey. In this they had the support of John Hughes, now an archbishop, and Bishop Bayley of Newark. However, Father

Hecker's Redemptorist superiors both in this country and Rome disagreed. Hecker and his friends were dismayed. How could they continue their work among non-Catholics, the mission closest to their heart?

So they agreed that Hecker should go to Rome to lay their cause before the general of their congregation. They did this, knowing full well that it was against the rules of their order for anyone to go to Rome without the previous permission of the general. Thus, when Father Hecker arrived in the Eternal City, he was expelled from the Redemptorists. Hecker was broken-hearted. "I have lost the home of my heart," he said in despair; but then, his appeals to Propaganda for reinstatement in the Redemptorists resulted in an entirely unexpected but happy solution. Pope Pius IX dispensed Hecker and his four companions from their vows as Redemptorists and authorized them to form their own order of missionaries.

Jubilant, Hecker came home to organize and become the first superior of the Missionary Society of St. Paul the Apostle, commonly known as the Paulist Fathers, the first strictly American congregation in the United States. The choice of the Apostle to the Gentiles as patron was significant, for the Paulists were to aim at nothing less than the conversion of their country. Father Hecker and his fellow convert-priests were convinced that America was the land of the future for the Catholic Church. "So far as it is compatible with piety and faith," Hecker said, "I am for accepting the American civilization with its usages and customs." He believed that Americans were a new people. Industrious and prosperous, they had espoused the new democracy and made their country a sanctuary for the downtrodden and the oppressed, an achievement which he believed could not have been possible without the blessings of God. Thus, it was the will of God that America should become Catholic, and the chief obstacles to this conversion, as Hecker saw it, were the native American's mistaken belief that the Church was a "foreign" institution inimical to the American way of life, as well as all those other misconceptions which arose either out of involuntary ignorance or the deliberately misleading propaganda of No-Popery. Rid the Protestant mind of these hobgoblins, Hecker believed, show America that the principles of the Church, so far from being hostile to American democracy, were in the fullest accord with it, if they were not also its source, and the Paulist mission would be accomplished. "The controlling thought of my mind for many years," Hecker wrote later, "has been that a body of free men who love God with all their might, and yet know how to cling together, could conquer this modern world of ours."

To achieve this lofty ambition, the Paulists had a modest start indeed, beginning their career in the home of Hecker's brother George, also a convert to Catholicism, and with funds provided by him. Eventually, with what was to become the customary Paulist skill at fund-raising, enough money was acquired to buy land at what is now the corner of Fifty-ninth Street and Columbus Avenue in New York City, where the Paulist mother house was built and St. Paul's Church, one of the largest in Christendom. Here also Hecker located the Paulist Press which he founded to publish his own *Catholic World*, an intellectual and influential magazine still in existence, and the literally hundreds of millions of pamphlets and paperback books which have since become an indispensable part of the Paulist apostolate to America.

That apostolate, once it was begun, was to be a great boon to an American Church struggling to prove that, so far from being the home of the ignorant and the uninstructed, it was the repository of the intellectual and artistic treasures of the ages. The conversion of Brownson and Hecker gave the lie to such charges as the one made in 1876 by Octavius Frothingham when he said that "Romanism had no hold on the thinking people of Boston. None besides the Irish laboring and menial classes were Catholics, and their religion was regarded as the lowest form of ceremonial superstition." Nathaniel Hawthorne certainly came under the spell of this "ceremonial superstition," and his daughter, Rose, like Ethan Allen's daughter, died a Catholic nun. Even Emerson, who did not love the Church, had this to say of a Mass he attended in Baltimore: "There is the way religion should be—the priest and the people are nothing and the fact is everything." Isaac Hecker himself very nearly converted Thoreau, one of the finest flowerings of New England intellectualism, and he always regretted that the solitary of Walden Pond had not embraced the faith which could have made a modern St. Francis of him. Nor was the Church's appeal confined to New England. Even before

Hecker founded his society, Levi Silliman Ives, the Episcopal Bishop of North Carolina, was received into the Church, the first Protestant bishop to become a Catholic since the Reformation. Thus, by mid-century the Church had already begun to exert an attraction among the non-Catholic elite. The ability to gain converts which was to become another outstanding characteristic of the American Church was already evident. The grain of mustard seed had sprouted into a sapling, and now the yeast of the faith was at work leavening the American lump. Nevertheless, the Catholic Church in America was still fundamentally the church of the immigrants; and even as it made inroads in the ranks of the Protestant Establishment, it was suffering once more under the attack of renascent anti-Romanism.

Chapter XI

Because of the distraction of the Mexican War, and the sectional discord which succeeded it, the Protestant Crusade had been neglected. Too busy fighting the war, and then too busy arguing over whether or not the huge territories acquired from it were to be organized on the basis of slavery or freedom, Americans had no time to listen to the dire warnings of nativists and anti-Catholics. But then the Compromise of 1850 put the slavery issue on the shelf for four years, during which time nativism and No-Popery regained their popularity, reaching a pitch of virulent hatred which remains unrivaled in American history.

Immigration was the chief reason for this animosity. The fifties were the decade of the Irish invasion and the Teutonic flood. In ten years, the Catholic population rose from 1,606,000 to 3,103,000. Almost 1,000,000 immigrants largely accounted for this doubling of the membership of the despised Church, and of these 602,000 came from Ireland, 245,000 from Germany, 58,000 from France and the remainder from other European countries.

Most of the Irish immigrants were refugees from the dreadful famine of 1845–1848. After centuries of English rule, Ireland had become a land of poverty and oppression. English law in the service of English industry had crushed Irish factories out of existence, and a system of rapacious absentee landlordism with its merciless rack rents left the population dependent upon a precarious potato crop. When this failed in 1845, and when the potatoes that were available were sold to pay the rents, starvation stalked the land for three gaunt and devastating years. Much has been written about the Great Famine, about starved and delirious human beings falling down faint and writhing to die where they fell; of the countryside strewn with corpses, their mouths stained green with grass and their flesh torn and mangled by starving dogs; or of cemeteries which were actually only open carcass pits where the hinged coffins arrived in steady streams to disgorge their loads of dead; but the net result was that at the end of the forties and throughout the fifties those who sought to escape starvation and those who had survived it fled a land in which the mere struggle for existence was becoming a hopeless battle. Most of these fugitives came to the United States. When they arrived, seeming to join forces with a rising stream of German immigrants fleeing the unsuccessful revolutions of 1848, they appeared to give credence to the Protestant charge that the Pope was plotting to make England and the United States into sanctuaries for a European Catholicism apparently in the final stages of decline. Protestant Americans seem to have misread the anticlericalism of France, Italy, Germany and other Catholic areas as a sign of a "new Reformation." Actually, it sprang more from the secularizing spirit of the new liberalism. Whatever the source, however, the attacks on the Church in Europe appeared to be succeeding, and thus, these incursions of Catholic foreign-born were taken as proof that the Papacy was preparing to shift its base.

These were the fears of No-Popery. They were not, at least not originally, the fears of the nativists, who carried on a separate campaign against the immigrant. Only later, under the banner of Know-Nothingism, did nativism and No-Popery join forces. In the beginning, native Americans were outraged by the presence of a growing number of foreigners, whom they resented for their turbulence, their drunkenness, their political activity and their willingness to work for lower wages.

There is no doubt that many of the immigrants, especially the Irish, were quarrelsome. The Irish fought the native-born, the Germans and each other. One group of canal workers posted a warning against any "damned Yankees" working on their job with the threat to "send them to hell with powder and ball."

Insobriety is another matter, and it does not appear that the immigrants drank more than the native-born, if the amazingly cheap and abundant American whisky was not more the cause of their intemperance than any bad habits brought over from the old country. Nevertheless, the Catholic Church was linked to the iniquitous traffic in drink. "They bring the grog shops like the frogs of Egypt upon us," a nativist writer complained, and Protestant temperance societies insisted that their cause could not succeed unless the immigration gates were slammed shut. Actually, the Catholic Church was waging its own war against drink. In 1849, the Irish temperance apostle Father Theobald Mathew visited the United States and for two years campaigned across the country persuading an astonishing number of Catholics to "take the pledge." Moreover, the First Plenary Council of Baltimore urged priests not to administer the sacraments to saloon-keepers who sold liquor on Sundays or kept disorderly houses. True enough, the Church did not condemn drink as such as evil, like some of the Protestant faiths. She could not because Catholic theology considers nothing that God has made as intrinsically evil. It is the abuse of a thing, not the thing itself, that is sinful. Such a balanced viewpoint, however, was derided as only so much more "Jesuitical" casuistry, and willy-nilly the Church found herself denounced as the home of drunken rioters.

She was also accused of complicity in the growing political power of the foreign-born. At first, the immigrants were merely the tools of native-born politicians, who met the newcomers at the docks, had them fraudulently naturalized by the judges they controlled and then marched them off to the polls to vote as they were told. Soon, however, foreign-born politicians began to appreciate the power of the ballot box and they organized their people to challenge the hitherto unrivaled supremacy of the native stock. Because the American political parties were fairly evenly matched, the foreign-born also held the balance of power. Whichever side they took automatically became the stronger, and even where they were outnumbered by the natives, the immigrants could exercise control. Naturally enough, the parties wooed the foreign vote, paying for it with political plums for the leaders and minor offices for the ward bosses. Thus, in the election of 1852, the immigrant vote helped to elect a Democrat, Franklin Pierce, and when he named the Catholic James Campbell as his postmaster general and chose other foreign-born Democrats for diplomatic posts, the Whigs bitterly complained that he was paying off an election debt and that the foreign-born were controlling

American politics. Inevitably, the solidarity of the immigrant vote created the impression of an organized mass responsive to a single voice, and that that voice was the Catholic Church. As Billington has observed: "Nativists who thought that priests bartered the political power of their parishioners for favors and protection for Catholicism were afraid that this unholy alliance would spell the doom of both Protestantism and democracy . . ."

On the fourth nativist complaint, at least—that immigrant labor was lowering the standard of living—the Catholic Church escaped the charge of connivance. Nativist workingmen blamed all immigrants regardless of their religion as the cause of an economic crisis which was actually the result of inflation, rather than the foreign-born's alleged willingness to work for less. To protect themselves, they formed various workingmen's societies such as the Order of United Americans which carried on propaganda aimed at shutting off immigration. Although they were not anti-Catholic in origin or purpose, the members of these organizations —usually secret societies with elaborate rituals, handclasps and passwords—were perfectly willing to believe anything wicked about the foreign-born, and thus they were easily recruited for No-Popery when the Know-Nothings brought the separate campaigns against Church and immigrant into coalescence.

In the meantime, the Church had been under an increasingly virulent and scurrilous literary attack. As early as 1835, one native writer had complained: "The abuse of the Catholics . . . is a regular trade, and the compilation of anti-Catholic books . . . has become a part of the regular industry of the country, as much as the making of nutmegs, or the construction of clocks." By the late forties and early fifties the anti-Catholic book had become one of the most lucrative staples of American publishing. Lurid and spicy narratives of the Maria Monk genre were especially popular. Usually they were based on the theme of a pure Protestant girl spirited away to a priestly prison, there to repel all manner of unclean advances until rescued by her Protestant lover. One of these books sold forty thousand copies in its first week of publication, and went through five editions in a single year. Even in today's America—fourteen times larger in population, much more literate and possessed of far more sophisticated means of advertisement and distribution—such sales would be regarded as stupendous. Apparently the theme of the designing and depraved priest was irresistible. Again and again, anti-Catholic writers returned to it, attacking the confessional as the device by which innocent virgins were lured to their shame by crafty, lecherous clergymen. For some reason, the Protestant mind seemed to resent the celibacy of the Catholic priesthood, and took particular delight in unmasking it as the hypocritic pretense of a band of depraved libertines. Perhaps this was because married ministers regarded the continence of Catholic priests and nuns as an implied rebuke. Obviously, they did not understand the difference between denunciation of sex as evil—a doctrine repeatedly condemned by the Church—and renunciation of it as a distraction from one's consecration to God or an impediment to one's work among men. So they repeatedly impugned the purity of priests and nuns in an apparent effort to show that the real reason for Catholic celibacy was to create a smoke screen concealing a deeper depravity.

Another popular form of anti-Catholic literature was the novel relating how the Protestant hero thwarted the Catholic villain's plot to capture the United States for the Pope. They had titles such as *The Female Jesuit; or, the Spy in the Family.* One of these, *Beatrice, or, the Unknown Relatives,* came out in 1853 with its publisher confidently boasting that it would outsell *Uncle Tom's Cabin.* So-called "history" was also pressed into service. Seemingly scholarly works rewrote the past to portray Catholic missionaries as oppressors of the American Indians. Almanacs and gift books also drove home the anti-Catholic message, and thus, weather forecasts and the editor's "best bits" and "favorite passages" were intermixed with invective aimed at every practice or doctrine of Roman Catholicism. The Church was castigated as "The Man of Sin" or "The Whore of Babylon" or "The Son of Perdition." A special enmity seemed to be reserved for the institution of the Papacy as a historical fraud and the sacrament of the Holy Eucharist (Communion) as an idolatrous absurdity. Nowhere in this torrent of vituperation was there the slightest hint of sympathy or compassion for the Catholic citizens of America. Their religion was simply evil incarnate, and the general estimate of it seems to have been expressed by the writer who said:

We regard the Pope as an imposter; and the Mother Church as the mother of abominations. We don't believe in the close-shaven, white-cravated, black-coated priesthood, who profess to "mortify the flesh" by eschewing matrimony and violating nature. We don't believe in the mummeries of prayers in unknown tongues; nor in the impious assumption of the power to forgive sins—to send the soul of a murderer to heaven, or to curse the soul of a good man down to the other place. We don't believe in Nunneries, where beauty that was made to bloom and beam on the world is immured and immolated, not to say prostituted.

Such was the published creed of American No-Popery, and if it was certainly not held by all non-Catholic Americans, it was at least the open profession of the leaders and the majority of the memberships of all the Protestant communions. There was nothing Catholics could do to change this hateful concept of their faith. Indeed, they were not only adjudged guilty beforehand, but guilty without the slightest chance of proving their innocence. Unfortunately, at the time, the Catholic hierarchy's shift from an attitude of quiet discretion to one of boldness and even arrogance seemed to suggest that some of these charges were true.

Because of the flow of immigrants into the Church, many Catholics began to believe that their faith would soon become the dominant one in America. Consequently, they dropped their earlier timidity and adopted a more aggressive attitude. New churches once quietly opened were now dedicated with the ritual and display which Protestants despised as idolatrous and decadent. Attacks on Protestantism delivered by converts such as Orestes Brownson in his *Quarterly Review* were emulated by priests and the editors of Catholic periodicals. Their theme was simply that an enervated and effete Protestantism would collapse "when it is fairly set, face to face, with Catholic truth."

All this seemed proof of Catholic arrogance. Much as it may be argued that the American Catholics were only, like their Protestant fellow citizens, exercising the right of free worship and free speech guaranteed by the First Amendment, the fact is that they could have acted a little less flamboyantly and spoken a bit more softly. They were, after all, a despised minority; and they were dealing, not with a decadent and despairing society such as the Rome which the early Christian minority converted, but with a vital and growing people intensely proud of their religion and the form of government which they believed it had produced. No man has ever been converted by epithets and sneers, and thus, to taunt such a majority was a mistake of the first magnitude. Yet, this policy of aggression was openly pursued, and it was perhaps inevitable that the most truculent of these attacks was delivered by the bellicose Archbishop of New York. In a speech delivered in November, 1850, Hughes boldly acknowledged the Church's desire to convert America, with the words:

There is no secret about this. The object we hope to accomplish in time, is to convert all Pagan nations, and all Protestant nations, even England with her proud Parliament and imperial sovereign. There is no secrecy in all this. It is the commission of God to his church, and not a human project . . . Protestantism pretends to have discovered a great secret. Protestantism startles our eastern borders occasionally on the intention of the Pope with regard to the Valley of the Mississippi, and dreams that it has made a wonderful discovery. Not at all. Everybody should know it. Everybody should know that we have for our mission to convert the world—including the inhabitants of the United States,— the people of the cities, and the people of the country, the officers of the navy and the marines, commanders of the army, the Legislatures, the Senate, the Cabinet, the President, and all!

Actually, there should have been nothing shocking in this. All high religions with a sense of mission seek to convert not just a few countries but the world itself. Judaism, Islam, the Protestant form of Christianity, all have sought it. So have all higher political systems. Moreover, Hughes said he wished to "convert" his country, not to enslave or subdue it. Nevertheless, this sincere but ill-considered statement could not have been more badly timed. Protestants were enraged, even those who had considered No-Popery propaganda to be the raving of unbalanced minds. Here, out of the mouth of its spiritual leader, the Romish Church stood condemned! It was true! The Pope did have designs on the Mississippi Valley. And so, the archbishop's remarks were given wide circulation.

So too were Catholic attacks on reading of the Protestant Bible in the public schools and Catholic demands for public funds for their schools. This campaign, probably conceived by Hughes, was launched in 1852. It was an echo of Hughes's unsuccessful drive of a decade ago, but this time it had the support of many Catholics, lay and clerical, who had been too timid to follow him then. The result, however, was the same. Protestantism formed a solid phalanx of reaction. Legislatures swamped with Catholic petitions for these changes were compelled to deny them. Catholic children who refused to read the Protestant Bible were expelled from public schools or whipped. In the end, reading of the Protestant Bible in the public schools of America was upheld. A ruling of the Supreme Court of Maine, adhered to by the rest of the nation, said that to do otherwise would yield to "sectarian interference in the selection of books."

With the disappearance of this grievance, however, the reappearance of the old Catholic problem of trusteeism furnished the leaders of the Protestant Crusade with another, trustier stick to beat the Church with.

Once again, John Hughes was at the center of the storm. His adversaries were the trustees of the Church of St. Louis in Buffalo, and their nativist and Protestant sympathizers. Once before, the trustees had refused to surrender church property to the custody of the bishop, but the firmness of Hughes had compelled them to obey. Resentful, they went into schism again after Buffalo had been made a diocese in its own right in 1846, appealing to the New York State law of 1784 requiring that lay trustees should control all church property within the state. Three years later, still adamant, their church was put under an interdict. From the standpoint of civil law, however, both Bishop Timon of Buffalo and his metropolitan, Archbishop Hughes, were powerless to move against them; and so, Hughes resolved upon having the law of 1784 removed from the statute books. In 1852 he secured introduction of the Taber Bill which would allow ecclesiastical authorities to hold church property. This, he reasoned, would cut the legal ground out from under the rebellious St. Louis Church trustees and also solve the trustee problem in New York for good and all.

But it was not to be. Enraged Protestantism, again interpreting the trustee controversy as a contest between American democracy and papal autocracy, warned that passage of the Taber Bill would be tantamount to "selling out to the Pope." As Hughes might have expected, it was defeated. As he also might have anticipated, it was to have even more disastrous repercussions. In 1854, having defied the interdict against St. Louis Church, the still-rebellious trustees were formally excommunicated. Their reply was to appeal to the State Legislature, claiming that they had been subjected to the pain of excommunication only because they had obeyed a state law, and requesting strict enforcement of the law of 1784.

Here was No-Popery's opportunity, and in 1855 the legislature passed the Putnam Bill ordering lay ownership of all Church property and actually making ecclesiastical ownership illegal. Fortunately, the state's officials wisely declined to enforce the measure, but it remained on the statute books until 1863. In the meanwhile, in other states the legislatures were passing similar measures, or rebellious trustees, encouraged by Protestants and nativists, were successfully defying their bishops. By then it appeared that the American Church's system of holding property was on the verge of being destroyed, and the Church itself was the object of an open, organized anti-Catholic fury which once again seems to have been in great part due to her own folly.

In 1851, while nativism and No-Popery were escalating their separate wars against the immigrant and the Church, Louis Kossuth visited the United States. Kossuth was a Hungarian patriot whose unsuccessful revolts against Austria in 1848–1849 had made him popular in this country. He came here at the invitation of the Senate and in an American warship. Before his arrival, however, Archbishop Hughes and other Catholics unwisely made the cause of Catholic Austria their own. Hughes called Kossuth a "humbug," Orestes Brownson said he was "one of the most dangerous characters now living" and Hughes's newspaper the *Freeman's Journal* described Kossuth and his fellow revolutionaries as "vipers too pestiferous and disgusting to be longer endured in society." No-Popery rejoiced at these egregious blunders. Kossuth was now a symbol of Protestantism as well as liberty, and his reception in New York—tumultuous with cannon salutes and such wild cheering from a crowd of 200,000 people that no one could hear Kossuth's speech—even outdid the welcome for Lafayette. Accurately gauging the religious climate, Kossuth made several anti-Catholic speeches, and his progress toward Washington was a triumphal procession. Kossuth's popularity, however, quickly waned after he switched from No-Popery to a direct appeal for American recognition of his Hungarian Republic, as well as direct intervention against both Austria and her Russian ally. Apparently, American fears of foreign entanglement were still stronger than any desire to chastise or embarrass Catholicism.

In the following year, however, the Pope himself handed No-Popery another anti-Catholic *cause célèbre*. This was the block of marble which Pius IX sent here to be placed in the Washington Monument with an inscription declaring his friendship for the American people and his esteem for George Washington. Protests arose immediately. Some Protestants proposed to contribute their own block of marble inscribed with scurrilous antipapal sentiments, a two-year squabble ensued, and in the end, a mob one night took the Pope's stone and threw it into the Potomac. Unfortunately, right in the middle of this controversy—in 1853—Archbishop Gaetano Bedini arrived in the United States for an ill-timed visit which aroused a new storm of anti-Catholicism.

Bedini's coming was directly related to trusteeism. En route to Brazil as the new papal nuncio to that country, he stopped off here to settle trustee troubles in Philadelphia and Buffalo, and to report on the condition of Catholic immigrants in this country. Few missions could have been better calculated to arouse Protestant wrath. Trusteeism could have been so much more discreetly left to the American hierarchy to settle in its own way and its own time—as eventually happened during the distraction of the Civil War—and to send a red-robed papal nuncio to settle a controversy which was passionately believed to be a clash between American civil liberty and the popish plot to conquer America seems to have been a blunder of the first order. Even before Bedini arrived, the nativist press was telling Protestants: "He is here to find the best way of riveting Italian chains upon us which will bind us as slaves to the throne of the most fierce tyranny the earth knows." Moreover, because it was known that Bedini had been papal representative at Bologna when Austria helped the Vatican to suppress the Young Italian rebellion there, it was falsely charged that he had connived in the execution of the patriot priest Ugo Bassi and other revolutionaries. Bedini was denounced as "the Bloody Butcher of Bologna," a phrase coined by the former Italian priest and revolutionary Alessandro Gavazzi.

Gavazzi had been deliberately brought to America by a No-Popery society, and he proved to be an incendiary par excellence. Tall, with long black hair and burning eyes, a fiery cross emblazoned on his black monk's robe, given to emotional gestures and excited exclamations uttered in broken English, he had a powerful effect upon his audiences. "No Popery!" he would cry. "No! No! Popery cannot be reformed. Therefore I go by myself and not protest at all. *Destruction to Popery!* No Protestantism. No protestations. Nothing but annihilation! Therefore I do not call myself a Protestant. *I am a Destroyer!*" And so, all unsuspecting the tumult that awaited him, "the advance agent of the Inquisition" landed in America, delivered Pius IX's official letter of friendship to the newly inaugurated President Pierce, settled the trustee disputes in favor of the clergy (as the anti-Catholic press had confidently predicted) and began a tour of Catholic dioceses.

It was not a tour, however, but a journey into outrage, indignity and bodily danger. Wherever the archbishop went, Gavazzi followed him—spewing out his denunciations of "the Gallows Bird Bedini." In Boston, huge crowds burned Bedini's effigy on the Common and threatened to assault the bishop's residence where he was staying; in Baltimore his effigy was again burned and bullets were fired into Bedini's room; in Wheeling, West Virginia, his bodyguard of Irishmen only just fought off a mob that intended to assassinate him; in Pittsburgh they could not prevent him from being manhandled; and in Cincinnati an attempt to lynch the papal nuncio provoked a riot in which one man was killed and sixteen were injured. Other cities provided similar welcomes, and the final expression of hostility came in New York, where an angry mob gathered at the dock to assault Bedini before he could board ship. Splendidly calm and courageous throughout his ordeal, the archbishop at last consented to being smuggled aboard a tugboat to escape harm.

Unhappily, the departure of the nuncio could not quell the hurricane of anti-Catholic feeling which his arrival had provoked. The campaign carried against him and his coreligionists in America had succeeded in drawing the lower classes into the

No-Popery crusade, and the rioting which had fallen into disfavor after the bloody clashes of 1844 was now back in fashion. Across the country Catholics had to defend themselves and their churches against angry mobs. At least two priests were severely beaten while carrying the viaticum to the dying, and in Maine one was tarred and feathered and ridden out of town on a rail. In many areas of America priests found it unsafe to venture outside at night, convents had to be barricaded, churches were blown up or burned down and work on the construction of new ones was forcibly halted.

To nourish this hostility, and to feed on it for financial gain, an entire new class of itinerant No-Popery preachers on the model of Alessandro Gavazzi had arisen. They went from city to city fomenting hatred, and the authorities were often powerless to control them or the people whom they inflamed. Frequently, a mob would rush from the street corner or common on which they had been harangued and go directly to the local Catholic church, either to burn it to the ground, to desecrate its altars or merely break its windows and tear down its cross. To attempt to restrain these rabble-rousers was only to court physical violence from the mob, and in Pittsburgh, where one Joseph Barker had at last been jailed by authorities exasperated by his anti-Catholic diatribes, the people were so enraged that they overwhelmingly elected him mayor while he was still in prison. Eventually, probably inevitably, there was bloodshed and death. In St. Louis during the election of 1854 an anti-Catholic riot resulted in the death of ten men, and a year later the Bloody Monday violence in Louisville, Kentucky, took the lives of twenty more. With these two events, the Protestant Crusade had reached its culmination in the emergence of the political party known as the Know-Nothing.

The Know-Nothings probably sprang from the Order of the Star-Spangled Banner, formed in 1849 by Charles Allen of New York. This was the period when the immigrant flood was cresting, and so-called "patriotic" secret societies were numerous. Allen's order was one of them. It did not enter politics directly, its members being content with supporting candidates from the established parties who were known to have nativist sympathies. Nor was it very effectual, never having more than thirty members until after April, 1852, when a prominent dry-goods merchant named James Barker took control. Barker was an organizing genius and a shrewd psychologist. Placing deliberate emphasis on secrecy and a feigned atmosphere of danger, he brought a thrill of excitement to the dull lives of the ordinary people he drew to his banner. Within four months he had one thousand members and was able to make the Order's influence felt in the municipal elections of 1852. Because of the Order's strict secrecy, however, its existence was not known yet, and the press mistakenly guessed that the mysterious nativist force was the workingmen's Order of United Americans.

Meanwhile, the elections of 1852 which put a Democrat, Pierce, in the White House had convinced the Whigs and the nativists of the danger of the foreign-born vote. Here was the opportunity for the Order of the Star-Spangled Banner to expand, and within another year it had organized itself on a national basis. Two degrees of membership were available. To be eligible for the first degree, a candidate had to be born in the United States, be a Protestant and not be married to a Catholic. He also had to answer "Yes" to the question: "Are you willing to use your influence and vote only for native-born American citizens for all offices of honor, trust or profit in the gift of the people, the exclusion of all foreigners and Roman Catholics in particular, and without regard to party predilections." Next, he had to pledge his allegiance to the American Party, as it came to be called, and to renounce all other political loyalties.

Admitted to the lodge, the new member was now introduced to all its delightful mysteries. He was told that notice of meetings would be given through distribution of heart-shaped pieces of white paper. If "danger" threatened, the hearts would be red. He was told how to make the Order's cry of distress, to be used only in times of danger, and he was taught the sign of recognition, the handshake grip, the passwords and the challenges. Secrecy, of course, was imperative, and if any member should be found speaking indiscreetly, another member was to silence him by drawing his thumb and forefinger across his eyes. To all questions from strangers, the members were to reply: "I know nothing." From this custom, of course, Know-Nothingism got its name.

Those who attained the Order's second degree could hold office and represent it as its nominee in regular political elections. They had to promise "that, if it may be done legally, you will, when elected or appointed to any official station conferring on you the power to do so, remove all foreigners, aliens, or Roman Catholics from office or place, and that you will in no case appoint such to any office or place in your gift."

Although Know-Nothingism appeared to oppose both the foreigner and the Catholic, it was actually aimed at Popery. Foreign-born Protestants were accepted as members. It was this common enmity which was chiefly responsible for the Know-Nothings' amazing unity. North and South, its members differed on every issue which then divided the country, but they were together in their hatred of the Catholic Church. As Billington says: "The Know-Nothing party was really a No-Popery party, despite all the gloss and fine phrases in its pronouncements."

Driven by this animus, the Know-Nothings in 1854 began to move to incredible success. They went to the polls instructed to write in the names of their candidates, and whole tickets not even on the ballot were swept into office. Seventy-five Know-Nothings were sent to Congress, and in Massachusetts, the scene of the party's most spectacular triumph, the governor and all state officers were Know-Nothings, the state Senate was solidly so and the state House of Representatives was composed of 1 Whig, 1 Free-Soiler and 376 Know-Nothings. The party also carried Delaware, and in the following year added Rhode Island, Connecticut, Maryland and Kentucky, and was in virtual control of New York, Pennsylvania, Virginia, Georgia, Mississippi, Alabama and California, while holding the balance of power in many other states. Where they found it necessary, the Know-Nothings used violence to keep rival voters away from the polls. In Maryland, ruffians armed themselves with shoemaker's awls, from which they took the name of Plug-Uglies. Know-Nothingism spawned a devil's brood of these election "clubs," all bearing bloodcurdling names such as Black Snakes, Tigers and Blood Tubs, while the embattled Democrats responded in kind with Bloody Eights, Calithumpers, Peelers and Pluckers. It was in clashes between them that lives were lost in St. Louis and Louisville. Such tactics horrified most

responsible Americans, and in 1855 the former Whig Congressman Abraham Lincoln wrote to a friend:

I am not a Know-Nothing; that is certain. How could I be? How can
any one who abhors the oppression of Negroes be in favor of degrad-
ing classes of white people? Our progress in degeneracy appears to
me to be pretty rapid. As a nation we began by declaring that "all men
are created equal." We now practically read it "all men are created
equal, except Negroes." When the Know-Nothings get control, it will
read, "all men are created equal, except Negroes and foreigners and
Catholics." When it comes to this, I shall prefer emigrating to some
country where they make no pretense of loving liberty—to Russia for
instance, where despotism can be taken pure and without the base
alloy of hypocrisy.

Such protests, unfortunately, were few and infrequent, and the
Know-Nothings carried their campaign against Popery straight
into the halls of Congress. In the House, however, a tirade against
the Pope's designs on America did have the happy effect of provoking a reply which may still stand as perhaps the clearest and
most complete declaration of a Catholic on the question of his
allegiance to his country. It was made by J. R. Chandler of Pennsylvania, who said: ". . . if, by any providence, the Bishop of
Rome should become possessed of armies and a fleet, and, in a
spirit of conquest, or any other spirit, should invade the territory
of the United States, or assail the rights of our country, he would
find no more earnest antagonists than the Roman Catholics. And
for myself, if not here in this hall to vote supplies for a defending
army, or if too old to take part in the active service, I should, if
alive, be at least in my chamber, or at the foot of the altar, implor-
ing God for the safety of my country and the defeat of its invad-
ers." To this, however, the Know-Nothing members responded
with their customary contumely.

In the meanwhile, with the approach of the 1856 presidential
elections, the Know-Nothings were confidently boasting that they
would win the White House. In truth, they appeared unstoppable
—until their success made most Americans aware that they were
confronting what was described as "a horrid conspiracy against
decency, the rights of man, and the principle of human brother-
hood." Their secrecy and their malevolent hatred were repulsive,
and once it became clear that they had nothing to offer except

bigotry, their followers deserted them in droves. Finally, the sectional spirit which was to divide the nation itself proved even too strong for the common anti-Catholicism which they had hitherto shared, North or South. Know-Nothingism was wrecked at last on the rock of the slavery issue. Soundly defeated in 1856, it sank into rapid decline and finally vanished with the advent of the Civil War.

With that conflict also the Protestant Crusade came to an end.

Chapter XII

During the bitter national debate on slavery which preceded the Civil War, Catholics were as divided in their convictions as their fellow citizens, and like them again, their positions seemed to have depended on whether they were Southerners or Northerners.

Catholic teaching on slavery was that it was a social evil but not necessarily a moral one. It was not contrary either to the divine or the natural law. In other words, slavery was not incompatible with a moral life or an impediment to salvation. Actually, the Church considered the master more likely to sin through the abuse of his power, and so, strong emphasis was placed on a master's obligation to treat his slaves with justice and charity. Slaveholders were also encouraged to free their bondmen whenever circumstances would permit them to improve their lives. Finally, the Church had repeatedly condemned the slave trade, the most recent pronouncement against it having been made in 1839 by Pope Gregory XVI.

Most of the Church's doctrine on slavery was relevant to the classical concept of bondage. Slavery was considered preferable to the destruction of society, to a return to primitive man's practice of slaughtering, sacrificing or eating his captives. Obviously, when men came to realize that slave labor could be useful, and consequently spared the lives of their prisoners, a great humanitarian advance had been made. Civilization based on slavery was, of course, far from being just. Having herself been born in the slave-based Roman Empire, having by her moral influence mitigated the hateful institution by bringing it through the intermediate stage of serfdom, the Church was well aware of the evils of the practice. Aware also of the evils of slave rebellions, she counseled against violence, looking instead toward a gradual and peaceful emancipation. American slavery, however, differed from this classical concept in that it was based, or at least defended, on the grounds that the black man was the white man's natural inferior and thus ought to be his slave. On this question, the Church made no specific pronouncement; although Pope Paul III's bull prohibiting the enslavement of the American Indians seems to suggest that she could not condone dividing the human race into men and sub-men. So she contented herself with denouncing the slave trade, an infamous traffic which was, after all, the virtual monopoly of men who called themselves Protestants.

Nevertheless, the Church's position was ambiguous at best and evasive at the worst. It angered those American intellectuals who looked upon slavery as a manifest injustice. With unconscious irony, the same persons who had worked so hard to exclude Catholics from public life or office, now demanded that they and their Church come out openly against slavery. Unfortunately, the Church had entered the murk of the American Catholic mental ghetto. No-Popery and Know-Nothingism had introverted American Catholics, driven them in upon themselves. Hurt and bewildered by decades of ceaseless insult to their faith, angered by endless attacks upon their loyalty to their country or their capacity to hold office, they had developed a distinct social inferiority complex. Because they did not feel that they really "belonged" to this society, they did not feel responsible for its ills. Moreover, these mainly working-class people were still too busy aspiring to the "good life" themselves to spare the time to correct injustice to the oppressed elsewhere. Nor did they have the self-confidence of the old-stock Yankees, who could expect an audience for their radical views. This was the explanation—although never the justification—for the American Church's signal failure to speak out against the injustice of slavery.

In fairness to her, the abominable institution was not of her devising, or of her sons, and she had made repeated attempts to ameliorate the lives of black bondmen. In 1835, Bishop John England opened a school for free Negroes in Charleston, only to abandon it under the pressure of a South still trembling from the shock of Nat Turner's Rebellion. In 1844, Bishop Peter Kenrick of St. Louis started a school for both free and slave Negroes, but two years later a midnight mob threatened the sisters who conducted it; and so, as the Mother Superior reported: "The day after our adventure the Mayor of St. Louis advised Bishop Kenrick to close that school for a time and he did so." Because of this antipathy, even more so because of the shortage of priests peculiar to the South, Catholic efforts to educate Negro children rarely succeeded.

Even though black chattel slavery may not have been of Catholic origin, there were Catholic slaveholders. Not many, of course, if only because most Catholics were of the poorer classes living in the North, but enough to suggest that Catholics did not regard slaveholding as being incompatible with Christian charity. From the beginning in Maryland, the Jesuit fathers held slaves. Archbishop Hughes had been an overseer of slaves in his student days, when some of the fathers of young men at Mount St. Mary's used to pay for their tuition by loaning slaves to the school. Most of the French Catholics in Louisiana held slaves.

Where they could, quite a few Catholics freed their bondmen. Archbishop Carroll directed that his "black servant Charles" be freed one year after his death, and his cousin Charles Carroll of Carrollton frequently manumitted slaves, freeing thirty of them at one time in 1817 and stating in his will that he hoped that none of his grandchildren would hold slaves. Charles Carroll was also a supporter of the American Colonization Society which was organized in 1817 to settle freed slaves in Liberia, serving as its second president. Roger Brooke Taney, the Chief Justice of the U. S. Supreme Court whose Dred Scott decision did so much to bring on the Civil War, also manumitted all his slaves, providing pensions for them when they reached old age. Other lesser-known Catholics did the same, perhaps the most outstanding among them being an Irish soldier of fortune named Michael Morris Healy.

While a soldier in the British Army stationed in Nova Scotia, Healy deserted and made his way to Georgia. There he became a plantation owner with as many as forty slaves. Against all the state's laws on miscegenation, he secretly married a sixteen-year-old mulatto slave girl. She bore him ten children, three of whom became Catholic priests. One of the priests, Patrick, rose to the rank of president of Georgetown University; and another, James Augustine Healy, became the Bishop of Portland, Maine—the first colored man born in slavery to wear a miter.

Most educated Catholics in the South, like their Protestant fellow citizens of intelligence and good will, deplored the "peculiar institution" but practically despaired of eliminating it. True, as early as 1831, Justice William Gaston of North Carolina daringly urged the students of the University of North Carolina to work for the elimination of slavery, but in the main Southern Catholics seldom swam against the tide. Bishop England expressed their attitude when he wrote: "I have been asked by many, a question which I may as well answer at once, viz: Whether I am friendly to the existence or continuation of slavery? I am not—but I also see the impossibility of abolishing it here. When it can or ought to be abolished, is a question for the legislature and not for me." While on the Maryland bench, Roger Brooke Taney had said: "A hard necessity indeed compels us to endure the evil of slavery for a time. It was imposed upon us by another nation while we were yet in a state of colonial vassalage. It cannot be easily or suddenly removed, yet while it continues it is a blot on our national character; and every lover of real freedom confidently hopes that it will be effectually, though it must be gradually, wiped away, and earnestly looks for the means by which this necessary object may be best attained." Yet, as the nation's chief judge, Taney also held that Negroes "had for more than a century before been regarded as beings of an inferior order" and "that they had no rights which the white man was bound to respect." In this, Taney was only advancing an opinion which he held to be "fixed and universal in the civilized portion of the white race." He was interpreting the Constitution, and not making moral judgments. Privately, of course, Taney abhorred the institution and had freed his own slaves.

In the North, Catholics were generally against slavery, although theirs was a moderate view compared to the rule-or-ruin attitude of the Abolitionists. Northern Catholics preferred to see a gradual emancipation with some form of compensation for the slaveholder's loss of his "property," rather than the abrupt abolition which actually did have the effect of bankrupting the South.

Compensated emancipation was what Lincoln had envisioned, until the venomous vehemence of the Abolitionists stilled the voices of moderation in both camps. Outright abolition claimed the allegiance of few if any Catholics, if only because so many Abolitionists had only lately been Know-Nothings. Massachusetts, the Know-Nothing state par excellence and the headquarters of No-Popery, was also the center of the Abolition movement. A hate-mongering press only lately stuffed with the profits of anti-Catholic literature was now busily pumping anti-slavery publications into the exasperated South. The Irish especially detested the Abolitionists, some of whom wished to enfranchise the Negro while disfranchising the Irishman. And the Irish also hated the Negroes, whom they mistakenly blamed for their own low pay.

Although the Catholics of both sections frequently differed in public, and such newspapers as the *Freeman's Journal* of New York and the *Catholic Mirror* of Baltimore carried on a sharp exchange, the Catholic Church in America was never sundered over slavery in the way that the Protestant creeds had begun to divide as early as 1845.* Catholic organization was proof against the slavery issue. To the very eve of the war, bishops from both sections continued to meet in Church councils, the Ninth Provincial Council being held as late as May of 1858. At this gathering, the bishops' pastoral letter declared that the laity "should be free on all questions of polity and social order, within the limits of the doctrine and law of Christ." This hands-off attitude was maintained throughout the war on both sides of the Mason-Dixon Line.

Thus, in New York, where Archbishop Hughes had come forth as an ardent Unionist, the editor of his *Freeman's Journal*, James A. McMasters, was a bitter and outspoken critic of President Lincoln. In June, 1861, McMasters published an editorial which declared:

Let those heed it who, one year ago, scoffed when we said that the election of Lincoln would cause civil war! We say, now, that if there be not conservatism enough in the country to stop and to rebuke the course of Lincoln and his Cabinet, we will have a bloody revolution

* Although the Methodist Episcopal Church divided in 1844, the M.E. South was not formed until 1845.

and anarchy, resulting in a military despotism, with a different man from Lincoln at its head. We speak what we see and know. Our Conscience forces us to speak, whether it please or offend.

For this and similar sentiments publication of the *Freeman's Journal* was suspended and McMasters was arrested and imprisoned in Fort Lafayette for nearly six weeks. Similarly in Baltimore, the mild and scholarly Archbishop Francis Kenrick disagreed with secession, but he did not restrain the fiery and secessionist editor of his *Catholic Mirror*, Courtney Jenkins.

When the war did come, the Catholics of both sections went off to the colors with great enthusiasm. In the North, there were a half-dozen Catholic admirals and at least twenty generals, among them the flamboyant Philip Sheridan, of whom Grant said that "he had no superior as a general, either living or dead, and perhaps not an equal," as well as William Rosecrans. Great numbers of Catholic Irish served in the Federal Army, and they came to be regarded as the best of soldiers. German-speaking regiments recruited from the Midwest were also heavily Catholic. In the South, meanwhile, although there were not quite so many Catholics in the ranks, there were distinguished commanders of the caliber of Pierre Beauregard or James Longstreet, and Admiral Rafael Semmes of the famous Confederate cruiser *Alabama*.

Even though Americans were now at each other's throats, the Catholic Church continued to display an amazing unity. In October, 1861, Archbishop Hughes of New York and Bishop Patrick Lynch of Charleston exchanged correspondence on the subject of the causes of the war, each prelate defending his section's position. Lynch charged that the election of Lincoln was proof of Black Republican determination to subjugate the South, claiming that the North should recognize the independence of the seceded states. Hughes replied that Lincoln's election was attributable to division among the Democrats, and argued that no state had the right to secede. Despite their basic disagreement, both churchmen carried on their debate in the most civil language, an attitude which was in marked contrast to the acrimonious disputes of the Protestant ministers of both sections.

Hughes and Lynch were also diplomatic rivals, President

Lincoln and Secretary of State Seward having commissioned the New York prelate to go to France to persuade Napoleon III to adopt a neutral position, the Confederacy sending Lynch to Rome to gain recognition from the Vatican. Hughes spent the better part of a year in Europe, making a favorable impression on the Emperor and Empress. How much his visit had to do with France's refusal to recognize the Confederacy, however, cannot be said. Lynch, meanwhile, failed in his mission to the Vatican. Pope Pius IX received him, but only as a bishop. Lynch also visited Ireland in an attempt to block Northern recruiting activity there, and in this he was more successful.

Irish combativeness, once deplored in the North as the vice of turbulence, was now prized as the soldierly virtue of valor, and now the very persons who had worked to have the immigration gates slammed shut on the Sons of Erin were at work recruiting them under the pretext of offering them employment. Whole boatloads of Irish were being brought into Northern ports, and when the promised jobs were not forthcoming, it was suggested that they might find employment in the Federal Army. To counteract this campaign, Bishop Lynch and the Jesuit Father John Bannon toured the Emerald Isle "educating" the Irish.

They told them of how the nativists and Know-Nothings had mistreated their countrymen before the war, and also emphasized Northern outrages against Catholics in the South. It was true that some Federal commanders in Virginia, Georgia and South Carolina had ordered the destruction of Catholic churches or rectories, or commandeered them for military storehouses rather than other more convenient buildings, sometimes stabling their horses in them. Also, in the Border States orders were issued that practically subjected the clergy to the civil power, and in Mississippi, the Bishop of Natchez had been expelled from his see city for nearly three weeks because he refused to allow the local commander to dictate the prayers to be said for civil officials. Harping on these insults to the blood or the faith of the Irish, Bishop Lynch and his associates were able to cripple Federal recruiting activity. They even persuaded some Irishmen to enlist in the Confederate cause.

With so many Catholic Irish, to say nothing of Catholics of other blood, serving in the armies of both sections, it is surprising that there were only seventy Catholic chaplains, forty in the North and thirty in the South. One reason for this discrepancy probably was the practice of allowing regiments to elect their own chaplains. Except for those units formed on strict racial lines, Catholics were generally in the minority and were thus deprived of the service of priests. Another reason was the continuing shortage of priests, and a third, probably more compelling cause was simple neglect on the part of Church authorities. Nevertheless, the Catholic chaplains distinguished themselves. Accustomed to the quasi-military discipline of the priesthood, they were eminently adaptable to military life in the field. Three of them—Lawrence McMahon, Francis Xavier Leray and John Ireland—lived to wear a miter. Ireland was probably the most famous, becoming, as Archbishop of St. Paul, a towering figure of American Church history. He volunteered for the Fifth Minnesota, helping to turn the tide at Corinth by rushing ammunition to his hard-pressed comrades with the cry: "Here are your cartridges, boys, don't spare them!" There were also priests without chaplain's rank who attended the troops. Among them was James Gibbons, who became the great cardinal of Baltimore, and Abram Ryan, the poet who gave the South such stirring verses as "Conquered Banner" and "The Sword of Robert E. Lee." Ryan risked the smallpox epidemic in Gratiot Prison when no other minister would go there.

Catholic nuns were equally brave and compassionate, and also more numerous. Nearly eight hundred sisters cared for the sick and wounded, and it is likely that these gentle and heroic women made a deep impression upon the predominantly Protestant soldiery of the Civil War. They organized and staffed their own hospitals which they often improvised from warehouses or schools. Often, they did the work of physicians or chaplains, on the one hand trying to save lives, on the other comforting the dying. Of the Catholic nuns who volunteered as nurses, President Lincoln said: "Of all the forms of charity and benevolence seen in the crowded wards of the hospitals, those of some Catholic sisters were among the most efficient." And the monument "Nuns of the Battlefield" erected in Washington stands as a public salute to their sacrifices.

Side by side with this record of Catholic service there also stands the disgrace of the draft riots of 1863. Indubitably, the wild and bloody protests against conscription in Northern cities were not exclusively the work of Catholics. These outbursts had, in fact, been provoked by the inflammatory editorials of anti-administration newspapers and encouraged by such dignitaries as Franklin Pierce and Governor Horatio Seymour of New York. Nevertheless, the rioters were in the main Irish Catholics. They had a dual grievance: the Emancipation Proclamation and a conscription which discriminated against the poor and the foreign-born.

Although the Irish had gone to war in great numbers, they had done so to preserve the Union, not to end slavery. They were fiercely antiabolitionist, not only because of their mistaken belief that the Negro slave was their economic enemy, but because of their foaming contempt for the Abolitionists, whom they knew to be the sons of New England slave traders, the grandsons of those very New England politicians who first spoke of secession in the War of 1812. Thus, it is hard to say whom the Irish hated most: the Negro or the Negro's friend, the Abolitionist. But they did love the Union. Completely detached and unsentimental, they saw that its preservation was the true objective, just as Lincoln did. Then came the Emancipation Proclamation, which Lincoln had devised as a military measure, in order to gain the sympathy of the people of Europe and so prevent their governments from supporting the Confederacy. In this, Lincoln was successful; but in this also, he alienated the Irish. So he was "for the Nigger," after all, they thought. So this was "Honest Abe's" thanks for Irish cannon fodder.

Next, Northern conscription was notoriously unjust. A man could buy a substitute for three hundred dollars, and among those who purchased their exemption thus was a promising young Buffalo lawyer named Grover Cleveland, as well as numerous Abolitionists, who, once the war was over, persuaded their state legislatures to reimburse them for this patriotic expenditure. Meanwhile, as immigrants who had come to America chiefly to escape military service were herded into the Federal Army against their will, many of the now-famous fortunes of America were being made. Among them were Armour in meat packing, Remington in guns, Marshall Field in merchandise, Borden in dairy products, Carnegie in iron and steel, Huntington in merchandise and railroads, Rockefeller in oil and Weyerhaeuser in lumber. Profiteering naturally contributed to inflation, and wages consequently fell far behind prices. Thus, it was not only the Irish who had come to believe that the Civil War was "a rich man's war and a poor man's fight." But it was chiefly the Irish who rioted against the draft. For three days they terrorized New York, raging through the streets with the cry of "Kill the Naggurs!" seizing innocent, defenseless freed black men and hanging them from lampposts. "To hell with the draft and the war!" they howled, battling police and soldiers and setting fire to homes, public buildings, churches, police stations, factories, saloons, even an orphanage, so that in the end the draft was suspended in New York and regiments from the Army of the Potomac had to be brought into the city to restore order. Much as the authorities themselves might have been responsible for this uprising—in which four hundred persons were killed or injured and five million dollars lost in property damage—the fact remains that it was the one great black mark on the otherwise shining record of the Catholic Irish in the Civil War.

Curiously enough, perhaps because so many of the poorer old stock who also could not afford to buy a substitute sympathized with the rioters, it was not made the pretext for a renewal of anti-Catholic feeling. This had to await the assassination of Abraham Lincoln. Although John Wilkes Booth was not a Catholic, some newspapers managed to discover that he was a Jesuit in disguise. One of Booth's accomplices, John Surratt, was a Catholic, however. So was his mother, Mrs. Mary Surratt, in whose boardinghouse the conspirators had met; and Doctor Samuel Mudd, who had treated Booth's wounds. Thus, some people found the assassination a popish plot, and Mrs. Surratt, who knew nothing of the conspiracy, went to the gallows to satisfy the shouting mobs, and Doctor Mudd went to prison. Actually, the death of Lincoln was almost as stunning a blow to Catholics as to the South. His passing left the country in the hands of men who hated the Church nearly as much as they hated slavery. Well might Theodore Maynard remark: "Reconstruction came very near to being, among other things, the destruction of the Church in the South."

Chapter XIII

A decade before the Civil War began, the problems of rapid expansion induced the American hierarchy to request the Holy See to convene a plenary council, that is, a gathering of all the bishops and archbishops in the country under the presidency of an apostolic nuncio. Accordingly, the Holy Father named Archbishop Francis Patrick Kenrick of Baltimore as his nuncio, and in 1852 the First Plenary Council assembled in that city.

Chiefly concerned with regularizing discipline and unifying the American Church, the Council was perhaps too successful in the second objective, provoking a mild warning from Rome that a too rigid uniformity might result in creation of a national church, one that would be more American than Catholic. The Council was also successful in its appeals to the laity for more vocations to end the shortage of priests, and in its efforts to establish more seminaries in the country. As a result of its emphasis on training more men for holy orders, an American College for young men was established at the great University of Louvain in Belgium in 1857, and in the following year the now-famous North American College was established in Rome. Both these schools were to have great influence on the American Church, especially the North American College, which became, in effect, the cradle of American bishops. Within a century of its founding, no less than 105 of its alumni received the miter, and 6 of them won the red hat of a cardinal. Thus, satisfied with its achievements in the field of organization, the First Plenary Council came to an end, its prelates hoping to meet again within another decade.

This, of course, was prevented by the Civil War. Nevertheless, in October of 1866, only a year and a half after that fraternal struggle had ended, the American hierarchy met again in the Second Plenary Council of Baltimore. The nation was astonished. Here was not only amity and unity in the midst of hatred and division, but here also was the Catholic Church showing unmistakable signs of health and growth. No less than seven archbishops, thirty-seven bishops and two mitered abbots, as well as an imposing array of minor dignitaries, marched in solemn procession into the Cathedral of the Assumption in Baltimore.

"Even the housetops of downtown Baltimore were crowded with observers," one Baltimore newspaper reported. "Shortly after nine o'clock on the day of the closing session, two carriages made their way with difficulty through the crowd, and, to the surprise of many, deposited His Excellency Andrew Johnson, the President of the United States, accompanied by the mayor of Washington and the President's private secretary, all of whom proceeded to seats in the pew of Francis Elder and remained during the entire service, which lasted until 2 P.M."

Such was the effect which Catholic unity had upon Baltimore and nearby Washington, at least, and according to Bishop John Lancaster Spalding, the nation at large felt the same way. "All [Americans] were ready to applaud any power that had been able to live through that frightful struggle unhurt and unharmed," Bishop Spalding wrote in 1873, "and when the Catholic Church walked forth before the eyes of the nation, clothed in the panoply of undiminished strength and of unbroken unity, thousands, who but a little while ago would have witnessed this manifestation of her power with jealous concern, now hailed it with delight as the harbinger of good omen."

Although it is likely that more Americans were disturbed than delighted at this display of Catholic strength, the fact remains that the bishops of both North and South were amazingly free of sectional rancor. They worked closely together to set up new dioceses to meet the continuing influx of Catholic immigrants and in formulating a moral code for the American Church. They also expressed their misgivings over the Reconstruction then taking place in the South, declaring: "We could have wished that in accordance with the action of the Catholic Church in past ages, in regard to the serfs of Europe, a more gradual system of emancipation could have been adopted, so that they might have been prepared to make a better use of their freedon than they are likely to do now."

As the bishops probably feared, Reconstruction very nearly meant the end of the Catholic Church in the South, or at least in the old Confederacy exclusive of Louisiana. A small but respected Catholic aristocracy, not quite so wealthy as the Protestant gentry, was simply unable to survive the shock of impoverishment resulting from the loss of its slaves. Its members either married rich Protestants or sank into the company of the poor Protestants. In a word, it vanished, and an embittered Protestant South, for some inexplicable reason forgetting the legacy of the Beauregards and Longstreets, the Taneys and the Gastons, began to equate the word "Catholic" with the image of an ignorant Irish laborer. Many of the Catholic Negroes also lost their faith, if only because their former masters no longer had the money for the support of the priests who had ministered to them. Moreover, a whole army of fundamentalist or revivalist Protestant ministers of their own race had sprung up after Emancipation, providing them with the kind of emotional religious service which they found more appealing than the measured ritual or the intellectual refinements of Catholicism. Although some writers have made much of the defection of these Catholic Negroes, the fact is that they were never really very numerous. Out of about 4,000,000 Negro slaves, no more than 100,000 were Catholics.

Actually, the Church was more concerned with the non-Catholic mass of black men. Before the Second Plenary Council convened, Archbishop Spalding of Baltimore had written to Archbishop Hughes: "Four million of these unfortunate beings are thrown on our charity, and they silently and eloquently appeal to us for help. We have a golden opportunity to reap a harvest of souls, which neglected may not return."

It was neglected. Even though the Council made a moving appeal to priests to "devote to this work their labors, their time, and, if this can be done, their whole life," few clergymen responded. The Catholic priests of America, both secular and religious, were still too busy caring for immigrants to minister to the newly freed, native-born Negroes. Moreover, the Council had only exhorted. It had not made any concrete provisions for the mission to the Negroes, preferring to leave specific action to the individual bishops.

Apparently, only the Southern prelates made any real attempt to care for the black people, and all of them failed. When the Archbishop of New Orleans returned to his see and appealed to religious orders within his jurisdiction to open schools for Negroes, he received stony silence for an answer. Southern sentiment against Black Reconstruction was so strong that many of the orders feared to provoke white reaction. Schools that were eventually opened were forced to close. The spirit of Jim Crowism was simply too much to overcome. Before the war, there had generally been a feeling of equality, or at least of commonality, between whites and blacks inside the Catholic churches of the South. Often master and slave knelt side by side at the altar rail to receive Communion. After Black Reconstruction and the white reaction as manifested by the Ku Klux Klan, however, bitterness brought segregation into the House of God. This made it that much more difficult for the Church to reach her strayed black children.

This bitterness also accounts for the fact that many Southern priests and nuns were infected with the white Southerner's superiority complex, or so Cardinal Vaughan of England thought when he came to America as a young priest to found St. Joseph's Missionary Society for work among colored people. After a trip to Memphis, Father Vaughan observed: "I visited the hospital where there were a number of Negroes. All said they had no religion. Never baptized. All said that they would like to be Catholics or something to show that they were not opposed to it. Neither the priest with me nor the Sisters in the hospital do anything to instruct them. They just smile at them as if they had no souls."

In addition to Vaughan's missionary society, the Mill Hill Fathers also came over from England to work among Negroes, as the Holy Ghost Fathers were to do later. Some churches and schools exclusively for Negroes were opened. Negro religious communities such as the Oblate Sisters of Providence founded in 1829 were expanded. Nevertheless, in contradistinction to its policy in Asia and Africa, where sincere efforts to establish a native clergy and even hierarchy were made and are still being made, the Church did not make any serious effort to recruit Negroes for the priesthood, and this was another reason for her signal failure to harvest the richest field which she had yet encountered in America.

Other reasons were the attitude of the Irish and the constantly spiraling immigration, a problem which seems to have dwarfed all others. Of the Irish, although it may be said that there exists not a stick of evidence suggesting that their antagonism to colored people sabotaged the Church's attempts to convert them, the fact remains that they contributed neither funds nor workers for the Negro apostolate. It was this lack of finances and manpower that in the end thwarted the efforts of the Southern bishops. In fairness to the Irish, however, it should be remembered that they still were mistakenly convinced that the freedman was their economic rival, and that the Abolitionists who had only lately been cheering them into battle were now saying openly, "The home-born Negro is far better entitled to his vote than the Romanist immigrant." Moreover, no ethnic group has ever contributed more to the American Church or sent more of its sons and daughters into her service.

In the end, the Negroes were neglected because the Church was compelled to choose between them and the immigrants. She chose the immigrant, or rather, elected to continue with the immigrant, if only because she was already "the Church of the Immigrant." It was a case of a bird in the hand being worth two in the bush. Unfortunately, at the very moment when the opportunities among the emancipated slaves became evident, the Church was inundated by a fresh flood of foreign-born, the so-called "New Immigration" which brought thousands of Italians, Poles, Hungarians, Lithuanians and various Slavic people from eastern and southern Europe. By 1870, there were 4,500,000 American Catholics, of whom 741,000 were new arrivals. Willy-nilly, the Church had to take care of these people, and to do so she created no less than fifty-five new dioceses and thousands of parishes and missions during the last half of the century. Such an effort, naturally enough, required every available priest and penny. It was also during this period, roughly the three decades succeeding the close of the Civil War, that the Church took on the strict urban cast which characterized her up until World War II.

Because the immigrants, especially the "new" ones, usually settled in the big industrial centers, causing the Protestant old stock to migrate to the suburbs, it was natural for the Church to be located there, too. As Arthur M. Schlesinger has said, the American Church "reared its edifices where humanity was densest, and thronged its pews three or four times each Sunday with worshippers whose hands and clothing plainly betrayed their humble station."

Thus, she was also the Church of the Worker, and because so many of these workers were foreigners who could not speak English, and because the Holy See constantly emphasized the need for providing priests who spoke the language of their congregations, she now had to minister to her new flock in their own tongues. Fortunately, the misfortune of the Church in Europe again came to the aid of the young Church across the seas. Just as the French Revolution had driven French clerics to America to establish John Carroll's first seminary and to evangelize the West, Otto von Bismarck's persecution of the Church in the new German Empire was to force a new stream of fugitive priests and nuns into the service of American Catholicism. The Iron Chancellor had begun what he called the *Kulturkampf*, that is, an attempt to unify Germany as a Protestant empire by destroying Catholicism. To do so he instituted the infamous May Laws aimed at crushing the Church by abolishing the clergy. Although exigencies of state eventually compelled Bismarck to drop his campaign, ten years of persecution had the effect of providing the American Church with many of those badly needed priests, sisters and brothers who could speak the various languages of Central and Eastern Europe. Meanwhile, many other orders and societies of dedicated men and women from the other nations of Europe continued to locate in America.

All were of great service in founding the vast system of hospitals, orphanages and homes for the aged which were still springing up across the country under the aegis of Catholic charity. They also served in the growing parochial school system, to which the American hierarchy, stung by the failure of the Church's prewar campaign against the Protestant influence in the public schools and its drive for public funds to support their own educational system, was now committed without reservation. In fact, the growing number of Catholic schools—and a Catholic population which was to reach 6,260,000 served by six thousand priests by the end of the seventies—had elicited from Rome the one mark of prestige which American churchmen dreaded most: the red hat of a Roman Catholic cardinal.

Almost without exception, the prelates of the American hierarchy believed that the presence of a cardinal, of a prince of the Church, in the United States would irritate democratic Americans. In 1864, after John McCloskey had been made Archbishop of New York, he wrote to Archbishop Martin Spalding of Baltimore: "I hope we shall have no cardinal's hat in this country. We are better without one. I will not answer, however, for what may be in store for you. For myself I have no fears." Twelve years later, to the utter amazement of the gentle, pious but generally undistinguished McCloskey, Pope Pius IX placed the red hat on his own head. Cardinal McCloskey was not the only prelate who was flabbergasted. When the Pope's intentions were made known to Cardinal Antonelli, the papal secretary of state, he gasped: "But His Holiness must be mad!"

To many Americans, His Holiness was more malevolent than mad, and his elevation of McCloskey seemed to revive and lend new force to the old fears of a papal plot to subdue the United States. Unfortunately, the Papacy was just then held in special scorn after the First Vatican Council in 1870 defined the dogma of papal infallibility. By this, the Universal Church declared that the Pope cannot err in matters of faith and morals. Such a doctrine shocked and infuriated most of America's Protestants. Believing as they did in the autonomous man who accepts dictation from no one, they considered any attempt to establish authority as an effort to turn back the clock of history. The eminent American historian George Bancroft put this conviction clearly when he said: "To carry out this system civilization must go back; the beams of the state must decay from dry rot; and the eyes of the people must be put out. I adhere to the protestant doctrine, the great teachings of Luther, that every man is his own priest; and this is but the statement in respect of religion of the principle which divides ancient civilization from modern . . ."

Not all the forty-five American prelates who attended the Council had been enthusiastic supporters of papal infallibility. Quite a few of them, such as Bishop Bernard McQuaid of Rochester, were convinced that the time was inopportune for such a pronouncement and that it would be "highly injurious to us in America from the handle it will give our enemies." From the short-range view, McQuaid was right; and when the despised and derided Papacy went on to create an American cardinalate, it only gave momentum to a new anti-Catholic movement induced by Catholic protests against the growing secularization of the public schools as well as the Church's stand against both divorce and birth control, practices which were not only becoming widespread among American Protestants but were also being given moral justification. Apparently the greatest cause of alarm and anxiety was the Church's great material "wealth," i.e., schools, convents, hospitals and orphanages. Thus, in 1875, the third-term-conscious Ulysses S. Grant proposed a tax on all church property and recommended a constitutional amendment forbidding distribution of public funds to sectarian schools. To President Grant and the Republican oligarchy then controlling Congress, the word *sectarian* was used in the customary sense that "nothing Protestant is sectarian and everything that is Catholic is." Fortunately, nothing came of Grant's plans.

Nevertheless, the feeling of prejudice continued. Bismarck's *Kulturkampf* was widely acclaimed in America, and in 1876 the Union Republican Congressional Executive Committee circulated a pamphlet entitled *Vaticanism in Germany and the United States* in which it was maintained that "if knowledge of what has been done in Germany through priestism will awaken our people to the depths of the same power in the United States, the firm stand of Bismarck has not been taken an hour too soon." Congress also heard James A. Garfield, the future President, castigate the "combined power of rebellion, Catholicism, and whiskey," a cry which James G. Blaine was to make notorious a dozen years later when he apparently lost the White House with his description of the Democrats as the party of "rum, Romanism and rebellion."

Although Blaine was an Easterner, he was looking for support in the rural Midwest, where this newest resurrection of the old

No-Popery spirit was centered. Many of these people were descendants of old-line Yankees who had moved west from New England under the pressure of the immigrant invasion. There were few Catholics living among them—proof again that the wolf-cry is loudest where there are no wolves—but they had been trained from childhood in all the literature and mythology of this apparently deathless American prejudice. Thus, in 1887, the American Protective Association was organized at Clinton, Iowa, by a man named Henry F. Bowers. Its purpose, identical with that of another A.P.A.—the American Protestant Association—was made clear in the following secret oath which members were obliged to take:

I do most solemnly promise and swear that I will always, to the utmost of my ability, labor, plead and wage a continuous warfare against ignorance and fanaticism; that I will use my utmost power to strike the shackles and chains of blind obedience to the Roman Catholic church from the hampered and bound consciences of a priest-ridden and church-oppressed people; that I will never allow any one, a member of the Roman Catholic church, to become a member of this order, I knowing him to be such; that I will use my influence to promote the interest of all Protestants everywhere in the world that I may be; that I will not employ a Roman Catholic in any capacity if I can procure the services of a Protestant.

I furthermore promise and swear that I will not aid in building or maintaining, by my resources, any Roman Catholic church or institution of their sect or creed whatsoever, but will do all in my power to retard and break down the power of the Pope, in this country or any other; that I will not enter into any controversy with a Roman Catholic upon the subject of this order, nor will I enter into any agreement with a Roman Catholic to strike or create a disturbance whereby the Catholic employes may undermine and substitute their Protestant co-workers; that in all grievances I will seek only Protestants and counsel with them to the exclusion of all Roman Catholics, and will not make known to them anything of any nature matured at such conferences.

I furthermore promise and swear that I will not countenance the nomination, in any caucus or convention, of a Roman Catholic for any office in the gift of the American people, and that I will not vote for, or counsel others to vote for, any Roman Catholic, but will vote only for a Protestant, so far as may lie in my power. Should there be two Roman Catholics on opposite tickets, I will erase the name on the ticket I vote; that I will at all times endeavor to place the political positions of this government in the hands of Protestants, to the entire exclusion of the Roman Catholic church, of the members thereof, and the mandate of the Pope.

To all of which I do most solemnly promise and swear, so help me God. Amen.

Under the aegis of the A.P.A., all the old apparatus of earlier anti-Catholic campaigns was reassembled and sent shrieking around the country. "Escaped" nuns and "saved" priests warned a gullible public of the Pope's plans to enslave them all, this time pointing to the presence of the growing number of Catholics in business and government as proof of the alleged conspiracy. Unfortunately, they were believed. The A.P.A. was even believed when it published the so-called "encyclical" of Pope Leo XIII calling upon all Catholics to slaughter the Protestant population of America, or claimed that Catholic Irishmen were secret soldiers in the Papal Army. In Chicago in September of 1893, the place and time appointed for the "American Massacre" to begin, some of the surrounding villages were in a state of terror, with some people arming and others fleeing. And it was not only the ordinary folk who believed these horror stories. No less a personage than George Bancroft, perhaps the outstanding American historian of his time, once told a friend: "No band of conspirators was ever more closely welded together. The one will of the Pope rules the creed, the politics, the conduct of all. The selfsame malign influence is at work in Spain, in France . . . and in Austria. Nay, it extends to England . . . and the United States." With this from the learned and reflective American Minister to Berlin, it was no wonder that by 1894 the A.P.A. numbered one million members and had made itself a political power. Fortunately, the organization died the death of Know-Nothingism, torn apart by internal dissension over the issues of Free Silver and William Jennings Bryan. It had also been snubbed by both political parties and been openly opposed by prominent Americans such as Grover Cleveland and Theodore Roosevelt. Finally, American Catholics themselves, having become accustomed to this kind of petty persecution, wisely refrained from actions which might have aggravated the prejudices of their fellow citizens, becoming preoccupied instead with an internal dispute of their own which has entered American Church history under the name of "Americanism."

Chapter XIV

Much as the history of the American Church has been a narrative of the attacks made upon her and her children, it would nonetheless be a mistake to conclude that she spent her time engaged solely in defending herself. On the contrary, even as she continued to protect herself with one hand, she was using the other to build a solid organization that was at once the marvel of European Catholicism, and the despairing envy of some portions of American Protestantism.

Like primitive Christianity in the Roman Empire, she had prospered during persecution: not by converting the hostile mass around her, as the Church of Augustine and Athanasius did with Rome, but rather by making herself a haven and a mother for the oppressed and desperate peoples of Europe. Thus, even though she was despised and oppressed herself, she not only continued to grow but actually outstripped the national growth. In 1870, Catholics numbered 4,504,000 out of a total U.S. population of 38,558,000;* in 1880 it was 6,259,000 out of 50,155,000; in 1890, 8,909,000 of 62,947,000; and in 1900 it was 12,041,000 of 75,994,000. During these last three decades of the nineteenth century, then, the American Church actually tripled in size while the national population itself was only doubling. This phenomenon, of course, in the very face of renewed hostility and formation of the A.P.A., was chiefly due to immigration. Thus, in the decade of the eighties immigration accounted for 1,250,000 of the total Catholic increase of 2,650,000; and in the decade of the nineties it was 1,225,000 of the total increase of 3,132,000. Judging from these figures, it would not be too much to suggest that

* To avoid the impression of exactitude which I believe to be impossible either in census-taking or casualty-counting, I have rounded the last three figures off to zero.

immigration had become the veritable Trojan Horse of the American Protestant Establishment. Nor is it very difficult to understand why anti-Catholics wanted an end to immigration.

Also, in these last decades of the 1800s the influx of immigrants into the Catholic Church shifted from the heavy Irish and German preponderance in favor of southern and eastern Europeans. Thus, in the eighties, the Germans had passed the Irish by 400,000 to 300,000, with another 134,000 coming from Austria-Hungary, 100,000 from Italy and 78,000 from Poland. But in the nineties, the figures were Italy, 390,000; Austria-Hungary, 232,000; Poland, 190,000; Canada (chiefly European immigrants using Canada as a steppingstone to the U.S.), 161,-000; Germany, 105,000; and Ireland, 40,000. In other words, the Catholic immigrant was now "more foreign" than ever, if only because he could not speak the language like the Irish and was not quite so akin to the old-line Yankees either in his customs or in the color of his skin, as were the Irish and the Germans. There was almost no immigration at all from England, the homeland of most American Protestants, and very little from such acceptable Protestant countries as Holland or Scandinavia. To use the language of the racist, the people coming in now were "Hunkies" and "Polacks" and "Wops," and they were beneath contempt. Yet, the American Church cared for them. As Henry Steele Commager has observed of the years after 1880:

It might, indeed, be maintained that the Catholic church was, during this period, one of the most effective of all agencies for democracy and Americanization. Representing as it did a vast cross section of the American people, it could ignore class, section, and race; peculiarly the church of the newcomers, of those who all too often were regarded as aliens, it could give them not only spiritual refuge but social security.

This the Church did do with an amazingly serene self-confidence. With the unruffled calm of a master mason, she erected her nationwide establishment diocese by diocese, church by church and school by school. Gone were all her self-doubts about her ability to survive in the United States. If, like the rest of the nation, she had failed with the Negroes, she put this mistake out of mind and congratulated herself instead upon her undoubted success with the immigrant. In a word, the American

Church in the closing decades of the last century had become infected with something of the optimism which was characteristic of the entire country. America at this time was embarked upon the program of expansion and improvement which was to make her the world's industrial giant, and her people not only implicitly believed in the gospel of material progress but were also supremely confident that the entire globe would eventually and of necessity adopt "the American way of life." This also, to some extent, was the conviction of a group of Catholic prelates whose attempts to "Americanize" the Church provoked a reaction from their more cautious colleagues both in the United States and Europe.

In essence, the "Americanist" controversy was a conflict between those who believed that the Church should plunge into American life and embrace American institutions and those who preferred to remain aloof and separate. There were, of course, many Americanizing priests and prelates, but the most famous and influential of them seem to have been James Cardinal Gibbons of Baltimore, Archbishop John Ireland of St. Paul, Bishop John Lancaster Spalding of Peoria and Bishop John Keane, the first president of Catholic University in Washington. Of these, Gibbons was by far the most powerful. Indeed, the thirty-four years during which the cardinal of Baltimore was the effective if not the official ruler of the American Church have been called "the Age of Gibbons."

Although born in Baltimore in 1834, Gibbons moved to Ireland with his family three years later and did not return to his native land until 1853. He was ordained in 1860, and in 1868, at the age of thirty-four, he was made vicar apostolic for North Carolina and as such became the youngest bishop in the world to attend the Vatican Council. In 1877, Gibbons became the Archbishop of Baltimore, and after he had presided over the Third Plenary Council of Baltimore in 1886, he was made a cardinal. During the rest of his life he became identified in the minds of most Americans—Catholic or non-Catholic—as *the* cardinal. Although the American Church has never had a primate, that is, a prelate who exercises jurisdiction over all the other prelates in his country or region, whenever James Cardinal Gibbons made a statement from Baltimore, the country regarded his voice as the voice of American Catholicism. Moreover, he became one of the first citizens of the country. This slight, gentle, amiable man was the friend and confidant of the American Presidents of three decades, as well as of prominent Americans in or outside his own faith. Tactful yet firm, friendly but dignified, Cardinal Gibbons enjoyed an admiration and esteem bestowed upon no other American prelate since John Carroll, or, for that matter, after himself.

As such, he seemed a strange man to be in the storm center of the Americanist controversy. Actually, he was not the chief Americanizer, a distinction which probably belongs to the tempestuous John Ireland, if only because his position as the acknowledged leader of the American Church precluded his taking sides. It was Gibbons's job to hold the Church together, not to tear it apart; and so he could not be quite so open in his Americanism as his more flamboyant colleagues. Actually, because of his desire to preserve unity in the hierarchy, and not to offend such conservative prelates as Archbishop Corrigan of New York or Bishop McQuaid of Rochester, he has been accused of timidity in defending Keane or the others when they were under fire, both in the United States and in Rome. Nevertheless, Gibbons's love of America and his devotion to American republican values was sincere, and it has been said that his three outstanding characteristics were his patriotism, his belief in the American principle of separation of church and state and his unfailing courtesy to those outside his faith.

When he was the youngest bishop at the First Vatican Council, Gibbons wrote: "There is this striking analogy between the Republic of the Church and the Republic of the United States, that the son of a peasant is eligible to the highest ecclesiastical preferment, including the Papacy, just as the humblest citizen of our country may aspire to the Presidency." His wide travels abroad also taught him to prize the American system. "The oftener I go to Europe," he wrote, "the longer I remain there, and the more I study the political situation of the people, the more profoundly gratified I am to be an American citizen." Gibbons also had a profound distrust of established churches, of states or princes who sought to "protect" this or that religion, and he never forgot an incident in Savoy, when, on brief vacation from the Vatican Council, he visited St. Francis de Sales's episcopal palace at Annecy. Standing awestruck amid carpeted and gilded opulence, he was mentally comparing this splendor to his own "palace" in Wilmington—four bare rooms beside a wooden church—when the bishop beside him read his thoughts and remarked sadly: "Ah, Monsignor, all is not gold that glitters. I cannot build even a sacristy without the permission of the government." Perhaps he had this in mind when he consecrated his cathedral in Baltimore with a warning against "the erroneous impression that the crowned heads of Europe have been the unvarying bulwark of the Church and that she could not subsist without them. The truth is, her worst enemies have been, with some honorable exceptions, so-called Christian princes." Perhaps the best exposition of Gibbons's devotion to the separation principle came from Denis O'Connell, the young Americanist cleric who had become rector of the North American College through Gibbons's influence and who served as the cardinal's agent in Rome. Father O'Connell wrote: "Americans never suppressed a religious order, never confiscated a sou of church property, never suppressed the salary of a bishop, never sent a seminarian to the army, never refused permission to open a Catholic university, never forbade a Catholic school, never required a bishop to ask permission to go to Rome, never forbade anyone to become a religious, never forbade a meeting of bishops nor claimed a voice in naming them." All these restrictions, as Gibbons well knew, had been hung around the neck of the Church by the governments or princes of the so-called "Catholic" countries of Europe, as they are now fastened upon her by the Communist states behind the Iron Curtain. But in the United States, where the Church had truly enough been subjected to constant harassment, there was no policy of persecution, no official hostility. A misinformed populace, or one acting on genuine but exaggerated fears, might have attacked American Catholicism, but the government had not. The First Amendment still meant what it said, and as Father O'Connell concluded: "In the United States the government of the Church is not carried on by the state over the heads of the bishops."

Such was the credo of the Americanists, and none held it more passionately than the passionate, single-minded and bellicose

Archbishop John Ireland of St. Paul. Here was the most controversial, if not, like the milder Gibbons, the most influential figure
in American Catholic life. With his powerful physique and his
leonine mane of white hair, his hawkish nose, belligerent lower
lip and his flaming style of oratory, he seemed to be a man built
more for the barricades than for the pulpit; and in fact his opponents actually did complain that he seemed more intent upon
their extermination than their illumination. It was also said of
Ireland, probably with much justice, that if he had been a little
less witty at the expense of his enemies, and a little more inclined to concede their sincerity, the dispute between the Americanizers and the conservatives might not have been so
acrimonious.

John Ireland was born in Kilkenny, Ireland, in 1838. A decade
later, at the height of the potato famine, his family migrated
to Chicago, and thence in 1852 to Minnesota. Deciding to become a priest, Ireland went to France to study, returning to the
United States to be ordained and in time to volunteer for his
chaplaincy with the Fifth Minnesota. After the war, he returned
to St. Paul, serving Bishop Thomas Grace with such distinction
that when the First Vatican Council opened, the bishop, who
was too ill to attend, sent Father Ireland to Rome as his representative. There, of course, he met and befriended his colleague
and future ally, the youthful Bishop Gibbons. In 1884, when
Bishop Grace died, Ireland became his successor; and four years
later, when St. Paul was raised to an archdiocese, he was named
its first archbishop.

John Ireland's Americanist convictions were best summed up
in the remark: "The Church in America must be, of course, as
Catholic as in Jerusalem or Rome; but so far as her garments
may be colored to suit environment, she must be American."
Throughout his career, Ireland did all within his power to draw
the American Church out of the intellectual ghetto into which
she had retreated. Convinced that the Church was the religion
of the future for America, he repeatedly entreated Catholic laymen to take up the cudgels of social action like their Protestant
countrymen. "Into the arena!" he would cry. "Priests and laymen, seek out social evils and lead in movements that try to
rectify them . . ." Or else, in the purple rhetoric of the day, he

would implore them to make their presence felt in America with the words:

. . . whisper in tender accents to liberty that religion cherishes it, go down in sympathy to the suffering multitude, bring to them charity and what is more rarely given, justice. Let them know what religion will ward off the oppression of capital and will teach capital that its rights are dependent upon its fulfillment of duties . . . Laymen need not wait for priests nor priests for bishops nor bishops for Pope. The timid move in crowds, the brave in single file, the Church must regain the sceptre of science which she wielded for ages. To sing lovely anthems in cathedral stalls, wear coats of embroidered gold . . . while the world outside is dying of spiritual and moral starvation, that is not the religion we need today.

Such appeals annoyed Ireland's conservative brothers, who usually regarded the "world" as a source of contamination, counseling their flocks to withdraw from it rather than to enter and convert it. When the flamboyant Ireland's ardor for social justice led him to insist upon equal rights for Negroes, he found himself more unpopular. Hostility, however, seemed to be the climate which John Ireland liked best, and criticism apparently only hardened his self-confidence. "Untimely today," he said, "my words will be timely tomorrow. My fault, if there be a fault, would be that I'm ahead of my day."

My fault, if there be a fault . . . No phrase could more aptly suggest the messianic certitude which possessed this "consecrated blizzard from St. Paul," and when John Ireland interested himself in politics, he became characteristically convinced that one of his many missions in life was to lead his coreligionists out of the Democratic Party and into the Republican Party. He campaigned openly for Republican presidential candidates, and he also did not scruple to heap public abuse upon brother bishops who refused to vote in national elections for fear that they would be criticized for "meddling" in public affairs. To Ireland, who constantly preached what he called "the unity of Church and age," such an attitude was the *ultima thule* of timidity, the supreme misconception of separation of church and state, and he declared that any man who refused to vote should be defranchised or exiled.

Above all, John Ireland was an American. He had studied in

France and traveled abroad, and although he remained a lifelong admirer of French culture, he was passionately convinced that the American political system was the hope of both mankind and the Catholic Church. Thus, again in the florid style of his time, he offered this encomium to his native land:

Republic of America, receive from me the tribute of my love and of my loyalty. With my whole soul I do thee homage. I pray from my heart that thy glory be never dimmed. *Esto perpetua.* Thou bearest in thy hands the hopes of the human race, thy mission from God is to show to nations that men are capable of highest civil and political liberty. Be thou ever free and prosperous. Through thee may liberty triumph over the earth from the rising to the setting sun. *Esto perpetua.* Believe me, no hearts love thee more ardently than Catholic hearts, no tongues speak more honestly thy praises than Catholic tongues, and no hands will be lifted up stronger and more willing to defend, in war and peace, thy laws and thy institutions than Catholic hands. *Esto perpetua.*

Not content with merely saluting his homeland, Ireland ardently desired to convert it, and he constantly exhorted his brother bishops to come out of their isolation and mingle in the market place. "We desire to win the age," he told them. "Let us not, then, stand isolated from it. Our place is in the world as well as in the sanctuary; in the world, wherever we can prove our love for it or render it a service. We cannot influence men at long range; close contact is needed. Let us be with them in the things that are theirs—material interests, social welfare, civil weal—so that they may be with us in the things that are ours, the interests of religion. Let us be with them because their interests are ours, and ours theirs, because nature and grace must not be separated."

With these remarks, however, Ireland only irritated conservative prelates the more, and they passed such declarations along to their allies in the Vatican as proof that Ireland and the rest of the Americanizers were becoming too dangerously nationalistic. They also reported the speeches and public statements of Bishop John J. Keane, the rector of Catholic University and another Americanist who, though not quite so distasteful to American conservatives, was probably more irritating than Ireland to the bishops of Europe and some Vatican bureaucrats.

To most Europeans of the nineteenth century the Catholic

Church in America was still a church of immigrants living in a huge mission country still peopled by savages. Moreover, it lived in separation from the native government, neither protected nor persecuted by it. Now, protection or persecution had been the alternating rhythm of the Church's long life of nineteen hundred years. No one had yet questioned the principle of unity of church and state, of establishment, or had drawn from history the obvious lesson that governments which protected the Church were always being overturned by governments which persecuted her. Separation of church and state was novel, even in Protestant countries, and it was profoundly distrusted both in Europe and in Rome. Thus, when the Americanists began to sing the praises of separation and freedom, and to disparage the ancient tradition, they made episcopal hackles bristle from Paris to Rome. Bishop Keane was particularly adept at Europe-baiting, and because he made his attacks from his position as the rector of Catholic University, the American hierarchy's official institution of higher learning, what he said was that much more effective.

Born in Ireland a year later than his brother from St. Paul, John Keane was an earlier fugitive from the potato famine. In 1845, his family migrated to Canada, moving south to Baltimore three years later. Ordained there in 1866, Keane was assigned to St. Patrick's Church in Washington, which was then still part of the enormous metropolitan see of Baltimore, and where he eventually came into association with the young Bishop Gibbons. In 1878, a year after Gibbons became Archbishop of Baltimore, John Keane was made Bishop of Richmond. Nine years later, again through the influence of his powerful friend in Baltimore, Keane was appointed the first rector of Catholic University.

It was in this capacity that Keane joined the vanguard of the Americanists. Milder by nature and more diplomatic than Ireland, he was nevertheless just as indomitably American and he hoisted his colors to the masthead with lectures in which he would frequently maintain that the Church was at home only in America, whereas in the Old World she had been "fettered and hindered and treated shamefully . . . both by open enemies and by false-hearted self-seeking believers." As rector of Catholic University, Keane also accepted an invitation from President Eliot of Harvard to preach at Appleton Chapel there, and he horrified conservatives by requesting that Protestant hymns be sung at the opening and close of his appearance. On another occasion, he laid the cornerstone of a Washington church with the declaration: "We will not come here to abuse Episcopalians, Presbyterians, or Methodists, but will worship God according to our faith, minding our own business and expecting our neighbors to do the same. The Church is one of universal charity, and instead of abusing the neighbors that do not agree with us in matters of faith we can but say, 'Brothers, though you do not serve God in our way, serve Him the best you know how in your own way.'" Again, anticipating the modern ecumenical spirit, Keane was the chief mover in the American Church's participation in the World Parliament of Religion held as part of the Columbian Exposition in Chicago in 1893. Rome solemnly disapproved of the spectacle of Ireland, Keane and Cardinal Gibbons surrounded by Protestant churchmen, but then, Rome was already frowning on "Americanism" and especially on Keane.

As often as the irrepressible rector might suggest that although Protestants might be in error, they erred in good faith, or that the European tradition of unity was actually a kind of silken bondage, his remarks would be forthwith reported to Rome by conservative prelates. Usually, this was done by Archbishop Michael Corrigan of New York or his more aggressive and acerbic suffragan in Rochester, Bishop Bernard McQuaid.

Corrigan's agent in the Holy City was a converted American newspaperwoman named Ella B. Edes. Variously known among the Americanists as "the antique spinster" or the "garrulous old maid" or "the Signorina," Miss Edes exercised a strange influence in Vatican City, and seemed to be always capable of laying Archbishop Corrigan's latest complaint at the feet of the correct cardinal. As a result, Keane was forever defending himself against charges of nationalism. But he never backed away from his position. When Pope Leo XIII suggested to him that he was too loud in his praise for America, Keane is supposed to have replied: "Please God, I will never be less loud." Inevitably, however the activities of what Keane called "the mischief bureau" in New York and the innate conservatism of the Roman Curia conspired to bring him down. Cardinal Gibbons might have saved him, but once again it appears that the "Prince of Democracy" was willing to sacrifice an ally in the interests of unity in the American Church, and so, in 1897, Pope Leo dismissed Keane as rector of Catholic University, much to the open delight of Corrigan and McQuaid. More to the credit of Keane, he took the demotion with exemplary humility and obedience, saying: "I welcome the act of the Pope without the slightest desire to ask why it was taken or how it was brought about." Remaining in Rome for a period of about four years, during which he was the victim of some rather nasty bureaucratic bullying, Keane was finally appointed Archbishop of Dubuque in 1900.

These three, then, Gibbons, Ireland and Keane, were the chief Americanists, sometimes but not always joined by a fourth, John Lancaster Spalding, the Bishop of Peoria. Here was a true American. Unlike the three others, who spent their childhood in Ireland, Spalding was the descendant of a family which had been in America since before the Revolutionary War. Born in Kentucky in 1840, he studied at Louvain. His uncle, Martin John Spalding, was the Archbishop of Baltimore, a fact which undoubtedly helped to make Spalding the Bishop of Peoria in 1876.

An aristocrat, then, Spalding was also more gifted than the other three Americanists: as an intellectual, as an original thinker, and as a poet. Nevertheless, John Lancaster Spalding was a gloomy, introspective man whose behavior was often erratic or incomprehensible. He repeatedly and inexplicably refused promotions to more important sees. He could have easily been archbishop of Milwaukee or San Francisco, or bishop of Newark, but he preferred to remain in Peoria ruminating and writing poetry. Moreover, his character appears to have been flawed by some mysterious faults or mistakes, which, as Father Andrew Greeley has observed, his biographers seem to have deliberately obscured. Thus, when he did aspire to the powerful see of Chicago in 1900, "serious" but probably never-to-be-known charges against him prevented his promotion.

At any rate, Spalding was not always to be found shoulder to shoulder with Gibbons, Ireland and Keane. Indeed, he often opposed them or derided them. Unimpressed by Bishop Keane's docile acceptance of his dismissal from Catholic University, he said: "If the Pope had him down on all fours kicking him each time, the enthusiastic bishop would shout, 'See how the Holy

Father honors me.'" Of John Ireland he could say: "Archbishop Ireland, I think, is a voodoo. Whatever he touches seems to go wrong." Sometimes Spalding would suggest that Ireland was only an adolescent drum-beater eager to win a red hat from Rome with his noise. He also opposed the Archbishop of St. Paul on one of his favorite movements, temperance. His clear undeceived intelligence understood that frequently men cursed to live in an industrial slum simply had to drink, because: "The perfectly sober would die from mere loathing of life." But when he proposed his own solution, an attempt to induce Irish Catholics to leave the big Eastern cities to take up residence in the rural West, he found himself siding with the Archbishop of St. Paul, who believed until his dying day that the Church should settle its immigrants in rural communities of their own faith. These colonization schemes, of course, ultimately failed because they were nipped in the bud through the early opposition of John Hughes, and because the Irish, unlike the Germans, were not pastoral or agricultural people but villagers whose fondness for socializing made them eminently unfit for the loneliness of the farm.

Like Ireland and Gibbons, Spalding was devoted to the American principle of separation. However, his was not the "instant" patriotism which, after all, was only to be expected from men whose birth and blood made them so self-consciously "American." Spalding was old stock. He "belonged," and he could therefore criticize, as he did when he denounced the imperialism of the Spanish-American War with the remarkably prophetic remark: "Should we go to the ends of the earth to take forcible possession of islands lying on remote oceans under tropical skies, inhabited by barbarous or savage tribes where both race and climate preclude the hope of ever attaining to any high degree of culture? Why should we own Cuba? We do not need it, its population is undesirable, and to hold it we must increase our army and navy and gradually drift into a militarism which must threaten our most cherished institutions. What can imperialism bring us except the menace of ruin and military rule?"

With less rhetoric than Ireland but with more insight, Spalding also proclaimed the unity of church and age. "Whatever we may think of the past," he said, "whatever we may fear or hope for the future, if we would make an impression on the world around us, we must understand the thoughts, the purposes, and the methods of those with whom we live; and we must at the same time recognize that though the truth of religion be unchangeable, the mind of man is not so, and that the point of view varies not only from people to people, and from age to age, but from year to year in the growing thought of the individual and of the world." Most boldly of all, he attacked the Catholic Church's fascination for the Middle Ages, its morbid veneration of a dead past as manifested in its rigid adherence to Scholastic philosophy. "Aristotle is a great mind," Spalding said, "but his learning is crude and his ideas of Nature are frequently grotesque. Saint Thomas is a powerful intellect; but his point of view in all that concerns natural knowledge has long since vanished from sight." What? Disparage Aristotle and *Saint Thomas?* One might as well imagine an American liberal belittling Thomas Jefferson or Franklin Delano Roosevelt. No wonder, then, that the conservatives should shudder at the "novelties" of the Americanists and do all within their power to bring them into disfavor in Rome.

No one, of course, worked harder to do this than Archbishop Corrigan of New York. Here was the apotheosis of conservatism. The sheltered son of a wealthy family, a privileged product of the North American College in Rome, this corpulent, cautious, shy and frequently sly churchman was the antithesis of rivals such as John Ireland. His was the siege mentality that has characterized so many Catholic bishops since the Council of Trent. Thus, he distrusted progress. American society was suspect. Indeed, he rarely exposed himself to it, both by inclination and because his enormous influence with Tammany Hall usually got him what he wanted without the necessity of having to work with non-Catholic elements.

Oddly enough, this supreme reactionary was not an outspoken or combative man. On the contrary, he was quiet and unobtrusive. Sometimes, at gatherings of bishops, he would by his silence appear to give consent to propositions he actually opposed. Corrigan's technique was to sow suspicion, either by planted newspaper stories, or by secret accusations made in Rome by Miss Edes. Gradually, as the Americanist controversy rose in intensity from 1885 to 1900, his rivals, even the gentle and charitable Gibbons, came to dislike Michael Corrigan.

Bishop Bernard McQuaid, Corrigan's suffragan in Rochester, if not actually the archbishop's mentor in these matters, was quite a different man. He was more like Ireland. Indeed, this forthright and irascible prelate, who might well have inscribed his scorching indictments of the Americanists on asbestos paper, seemed to delight in controversy. Certainly, his running battle with the Americanists was like a personal vendetta. Thus, in 1894, when Ireland indiscreetly interfered in New York State politics by successfully campaigning against McQuaid's candidacy for the Board of Regents, the infuriated Bishop of Rochester ascended his cathedral pulpit to denounce his brother from St. Paul as a supporter of the A.P.A. and a recipient of political bribes whose conduct was "undignified, disgraceful to his episcopal office, and a scandal in the eyes of all right-minded Catholics." For this, McQuaid was rebuked by Rome; but two years later, after Keane was dismissed from Catholic University, His Excellency of Rochester again mounted the podium to chortle with public glee. "The news from Rome is astounding. . . . What collapses on every side! Gibbons! Ireland!—and Keane! They were the cock of the walk for a while and dictated to the country and thought to run our dioceses for us. They may change their policy and repent, but they can never repair the harm done in the past."

It was with this doughty ally, then, and sometimes with the support of the fence-straddling Archbishop Ryan of Philadelphia, or the German prelates of the Midwest, that Michael Corrigan sought to block and undo the work of the Americanists. Ironically enough, the first real battle between these two camps was over a project which both had supported in the beginning: the proposed Catholic University.

Chapter XV

A central seminary for the entire United States had often been proposed, particularly in earlier days when the little diocesan seminaries were not only unequal to the task of turning out educated priests but also tended to dissipate the Church's supply of trained teachers. The opening of the American colleges in Rome and Louvain had made higher education available to only a few picked candidates, and the idea of a national university persisted until it was openly discussed at the Second Plenary Council of 1866.

It remained for John Lancaster Spalding, however, to give the proposal any real driving force. Remembering his own days at Louvain, Spalding always held before him the idea of a national university at which priests might go beyond their seminary education to do graduate work. In the years prior to the Third Council of Baltimore in 1884, Spalding began to campaign for the institution, suggesting that the impoverished Mount St. Mary's Seminary in Cincinnati might be taken over by the national hierarchy. Response was lukewarm, but when the Council did convene, Mary Gwendolyn Caldwell, a prominent Catholic laywoman and a close friend of Spalding,* offered $300,000 to get the project started. Later, Miss Caldwell's sister Lina donated an additional $80,000. This was an enormous amount of money in those days, and the bishops were impressed. They became enthusiastic a few days later when Bishop Spalding made a stirring appeal from the pulpit of the Baltimore cathedral.

"Let there be, then," he concluded, "an American Catholic

* And later his enemy. It was she and her sister who preferred the "serious" charges against Bishop Spalding.

university, where our young men, in the atmosphere of faith and purity, of high thinking and plain living, shall become more intimately conscious of the truth of their religion and of the genius of their country, where they shall learn repose and dignity which belong to their ancient Catholic descent, and yet not lose the fire which flows in the blood of a new people; to which from every part of the land our eyes may turn for guidance and encouragement, seeking light and self-confidence from men in whom intellectual power is not separate from moral purpose; who look to God and his universe from bending knees of prayer."

With this, a committee composed of Spalding, Corrigan of New York, Ryan of Philadelphia, Kenrick of St. Louis and Alemany of San Francisco was formed to study the proposition, finally recommending that the Council adopt the idea. As is customary after the delegates go home, there ensued a period of inactivity, during which Miss Caldwell astutely refused all attempts to persuade her to turn over the money to the hierarchy with no strings attached. She also held out for a site somewhere in the national capital, turning down the suggestion that Seton Hall College in South Orange, New Jersey, be converted for the purpose. Here she was seconded by Cardinal Gibbons, who warned his brothers of "the terrible Jersey mosquitoes." Finally, it was agreed that the university would be erected in Washington, a decision which was not applauded by the Jesuits, who had their own university at Georgetown, and who henceforth became effective enemies of Catholic University.

Now, with the university approved in principle in Rome, it was unanimously agreed that Bishop Spalding should be its first rector. With characteristic contrariness, Spalding refused the appointment, and Keane was named in his place. It could be, of course, that Spalding was not just being obstinate, but that he foresaw that growing opposition to the project would prevent the institution from fulfilling his high hopes for it. At any rate, the anti-Americanists had begun to intrigue against the university. Archbishop Corrigan, who apparently had decided that he would rather have a Jesuit university located in New York than a national one in Washington, had played upon the German bishops' distrust of Keane to enroll them on his side. As a result, Archbishop Michael Heiss of Milwaukee resigned from the university committee, thus bringing the entire project under suspicion in Rome. Corrigan added to Roman fears when he planted the impression there that many of the American bishops who had signed the petition for the university had done so against their will. Gradually, the opposition snowballed, until even Keane and Gibbons had become so discouraged that they were willing to drop the project, placing the blame squarely on the shoulders of Corrigan and McQuaid. Archbishop Ireland, however, refused to join them in "cowardly surrender to so unworthy an opposition." Regaining his enthusiasm, Gibbons wrote a long letter to the Pope. In 1887, the same year in which Gibbons received his red hat, Leo XIII issued the papal brief formally establishing Catholic University.

So the Americanists had won, but at the cost of hardening the opposition. Corrigan became so set against the new institution that he banned all collectors of funds for it from the Archdiocese of New York, and even after Cardinal Gibbons had laid the university's cornerstone in the presence of President Grover Cleveland and the United States Marine Band, Bishop McQuaid issued a blistering pastoral letter denouncing it.

Nevertheless, it began its unique career under the dual control of the American hierarchy and the Holy See, and it immediately ran into difficulties. In addition to the obstructionism of the conservatives, Catholic University suffered from a chronic shortage of funds, a situation which continued into the twentieth century, when Denis O'Connell, the third rector, unhappily discovered that his trusted financial adviser had misappropriated one million dollars. Moreover, Bishop Keane, warmhearted and sincere Americanist that he might have been, apparently was not a gifted educator. Even John Ireland joked about his recruiting tactics, saying that he "descends like a benevolent angel on Washington society and chooses a professor whenever he goes out to dinner." Maurice F. Egan, the former Minister to Denmark, and one of the university's earliest faculty members, has left a description of Catholic University's early years.

The school of philosophy began to take shape. The departments of physics and chemistry were manned by men who knew just what they wanted. Latin and Greek philosophy were looked on as important.

Profane history was regarded as of no real importance and English
literature hung on to an insecure edifice by its thumbs. There was no
Teutonic philologist, no chance of getting one. The kindly cardinal
said to me on several occasions, "Just wait, my dear Egan, a few more
deaths will set us all right." I do not think His Eminence prayed for
the death of anybody, yet I am sure he made a point of praying for
the happy death of those who had left donations to the university. But
one of the surest means of obtaining longevity seemed to be for a man
to write a gift to the Catholic University of America into his will.

Of the inner discord, Egan wrote:

There was probably no ecclesiastical institution, Protestant or Catholic, in the world, where laymen in the faculty were given as much
freedom of action and opinion as at the Catholic University; but the
discord of opinions or convictions among the ecclesiastics themselves
was a constant source of embarrassment and difficulty. Cardinal Gibbons, making no reference whatever to the laity, often declared that it
was harder to govern the university than the whole of his diocese; and
I always thought that the "War March of the Priests" from *Aïda,* which
the organist played for the opening procession at the beginning of
the year, was singularly appropriate.

Nevertheless, the university endured and eventually prospered,
and in the meantime the running Americanist fight shifted to
other battlegrounds.

Two movements—one innocuous and even trivial, the other
serious and important—helped to bring conservative and progressive prelates into conflict again during the last two decades
of the nineteenth century. These were the proliferation of secret
societies and the rise of organized labor. To some extent they
were intertwined, or at least the American fondness for secret
societies was made manifest in the organization of the controversial Knights of Labor.

From its infancy, the American Church had been puzzled by
the American male's predilection for membership in secret organizations. Traditionally, the Church has opposed secret societies
because they are usually religious sects and are frequently
anti-Catholic. Thus, no Catholic can be a Mason. In America,
however, most of the secret societies were harmless fraternal organizations. Among them were the Knights of Pythias, the Odd

Fellows, the Ancient Order of Hibernians, the Grand Army of the Republic, the Sons of Temperance, Clan-na-Gael, the Fenians, the Modern Woodmen, the Improved Order of Redmen and the Knights of the Maccabees. Many Catholics were joining these groups, and the bishops were concerned. Their position was made clear at the Third Plenary Council when they declared:

But if any society's obligation be such as to bind its members to secrecy, even when rightly questioned by competent authority, then such a society puts itself outside the limits of approval; and no one can be a member of it and at the same time be admitted to the sacraments of the Catholic Church. The same is true of any organization that binds its members to a promise of blind obedience—to accept in advance and to obey whatsoever orders, lawful or unlawful, that may emanate from its chief authorities; because such a promise is contrary both to reason and conscience. And if a society works or plots, either openly or in secret, against the Church, or against lawful authorities, then to be a member of it is to be excluded from the membership of the Catholic Church.

Unfortunately, the bishops never could agree on just what societies fulfilled this definition and should be condemned. Most of them were against any specific condemnation at all, especially during the nineties when it was feared that to do so would only give organizations such as the A.P.A. another stick with which to beat the Church. They maintained that there was no certainty of any positive evil in the societies and therefore no reason for a general condemnation, especially one that would be offensive to many non-Catholics in America. So Cardinal Gibbons avoided the issue, until 1894, when the Holy Office took matters into its own hands and condemned the Odd Fellows, the Knights of Pythias and the Sons of Temperance, directing the American bishops to warn their people against these three organizations. Any Catholic who persisted in membership after being warned was to be deprived of the sacraments.

For once, the usually obedient Gibbons set his face against Rome, neglecting to publish the condemnation in his own archdiocese and persuading the other archbishops to suppress it. Eventually, however, the arch-conservative Corrigan promulgated the decree, and after the diocese of Brooklyn followed suit and the Holy Office brought pressure to bear, Gibbons and the others reluctantly obeyed.

As Gibbons had anticipated, the condemnation had the effect of helping to fan anti-Catholic fires then being carefully stoked by the A.P.A., and it also made it that much more difficult for him to defend the Knights of Labor. This organization, the forerunner of the American Federation of Labor, was the cruelly exploited American workingman's answer to the bloated "robber barons" of the age. Since the Civil War, labor had been desperately struggling to organize against the iron and inhuman power of the monopolies. Grown men with families worked as long as eighteen hours a day for as little as six dollars a week, and any attempt to improve their condition either by collective bargaining or strikes was attacked by the vested interests as the work of "socialists" or "anarchists." Thus, driven beyond endurance by sweatshops and starvation wages, inflamed by unscrupulous agitators, the workingmen sometimes rose in violent wrath. Among the results were the infamous Haymarket Square Riot in Chicago, and the murderous career of the "Molly Maguires," for the most part discontented Irish miners (some of whom belonged to the Ancient Order of Hibernians) who attempted to gain a bloody redress from the coal-mine operators of Pennsylvania. These lawless events and movements often were unfairly blamed on organized labor, and in particular on the Knights of Labor.

The Knights had been founded in 1869 by Uriah Stephens, a Mason and an Odd Fellow. One of the first big trade unions, it included unskilled as well as skilled workers, and by 1886 it claimed 700,000 members. Of necessity, the Knights of Labor was a secret organization. Any worker known to be a member was immediately dismissed, and management actually employed a corps of spies charged with discovering the identity of members. Thus, its founder, Stephens, drew upon his experience with the Masons in drafting an initiation ritual, handshake and secret password.

To the Knights themselves, two-thirds of whom were Catholics, and to Grand Master Workman Terence V. Powderly, also a Catholic, the need for secrecy was obvious. To some of the American bishops, however, the secrecy was too much like the

Masons or the openly anarchistic Carbonari of Italy. Conservatives such as James Roosevelt Bayley, Gibbons's predecessor in Baltimore, had openly condemned the Knights and other labor groups with the words: "These miserable associations called labor organizations are subversive of government and communistic. No Catholic with any idea of the spirit of his religion will encourage them." Pontificating from the head of the well-laid table in his episcopal palace, Bayley could say: "God permits poverty as the most efficient means of practicing some of the most necessary Christian virtues of charity and almsgiving on the part of the rich and patience and resignation to His holy will on the part of the poor." In this, Bayley was no different from Protestant preachers such as Channing with his message of "trust in God," or Henry Ward Beecher's famous "Bread and Water" sermon in which he declared that a dollar a day was pay enough for any workingman. Bayley, however, was an aristocrat, and far from representative of the American hierarchy, most of whom were the sons of workingmen. Moreover, the American Church had actually been more in sympathy with the position of Orestes Brownson, who said: "The mass of workers are virtually slaves—slaves in all except name—as much as are the Negroes on our Southern plantations." In 1872, Bayley's predecessor, the gentle Martin Spalding, had said: "In our country capital is a tyrant and labor is its slave. I have no desire to interfere with the poor in their efforts to protect themselves unless it is proved that these societies are plotting against the state or the Church." This was the attitude of Gibbons, whose father had ruined his health working to support six children, and who had himself worked for three dollars a week as a grocery clerk in New Orleans.

Unfortunately, much as the majority of the bishops might sympathize with the working people, they really had no answer to the question: "Can a Catholic belong to the Knights of Labor?" True enough, Terence Powderly had succeeded in eliminating the secret oath and ritual which the bishops found so offensive, but the Knights still found it necessary to convene in secret. Worse, the hierarchy of Canada had begun to importune the Holy Office for outright condemnation of the organization. Dismayed by the strikes and disturbances which seemed to follow in the wake of Knights of Labor organizational drives, Archbishop Elzéar Taschereau of Quebec forwarded a copy of the organization's constitution to Rome, following this up with repeated queries on what should be done about the society. Finally, the Holy Office replied: "These societies ought to be among those prohibited." Triumphant, Taschereau informed his clergy that all Catholic workingmen who remained in the Knights of Labor faced excommunication or exclusion from the sacraments. Inasmuch as it would be most difficult to find a workingman in Quebec who was not a Catholic, this was tantamount to a threat of wholesale interdiction of the working class of the province. Such draconic measures, however, apparently suited the temperament of His Lordship of Quebec. So also, ironically enough, did it appeal to Bishop James Healy of Portland, Maine. This first Negro prelate in America, a man born in slavery, published the prohibition against the Knights of Labor in his own diocese.

Bishop Healy's action threw the American hierarchy into a turmoil. Some bishops supported him; others, the majority, did not. Pressed on all sides to declare themselves, Archbishop Corrigan delivered the conservative viewpoint when he said, "The Knights are undoubtedly forbidden," but Gibbons counseled his fellow progressives to adopt a policy of "masterly inactivity" in hopes that the ban would be forgotten. Events, however, were making Gibbons's favorite tactic of procrastination impossible. In his own see city the Knights paraded twenty-five thousand strong, demanding social justice. Even President Grover Cleveland was showing a growing concern for the rights of labor, and when Gibbons called upon his friend in the White House he was told that the Knights of Labor were not considered a threat to the government. Next the cardinal called in Terence Powderly, the Grand Master Workman of the Knights, to determine whether or not the society was truly a secret one. Satisfied that it was not, he next asked Powderly to appear before the nation's twelve archbishops who were meeting in Baltimore to discuss the problem of secret societies. Actually only nine convened, three of the others absenting themselves after sending Gibbons their vote against condemning the Knights.

Standing before these nine solemn, scarlet judges, this neat small sparrow of a man—whose slight figure and modest demeanor concealed the fierce, burning zeal of a crusader for social justice—gave a remarkable performance. In this, he was assisted by Gibbons, who used all his diplomatic skill in an attempt to persuade the balky conservatives to drop their opposition to the Knights. "Labor has rights as well as capital," Gibbons said. "We should not condemn labor and let capital go free. I would regard the condemnation of the Knights of Labor as disastrous to the Church. We should send the documents to Rome, and if the objectionable features are eliminated, the Knights of Labor should be tolerated and not condemned. We have a controlling influence over them. But if they are condemned, a secret organization will follow in their wake and over that we will have no control."

In the end, however, the combined efforts of Powderly and Gibbons failed to obtain the unanimous vote necessary under rules laid down by the Third Plenary Council. Two archbishops remained adamantly opposed to the Knights, and although their names are not known, it is not difficult to guess the identity of at least one. Clearly, the only alternative left to Gibbons was to take the path to Rome. Even as he came to that conclusion, he received a remarkable letter from Bishop Keane, who was then in Rome with Archbishop Ireland attempting to obtain approval for Catholic University. The candor of Keane's letter was amazing, considering the fact that even today an archbishop rarely hears criticism from the crowd of self-seeking or timid clerics who often try their hardest to get between His Excellency and the truth. Keane wrote:

"I find to my intense regret that an impression has taken shape in Rome to the effect that Your Eminence is changeable in views, weak and vacillating in purpose, anxious to conciliate both parties on nearly every question; that it is hard to know, therefore, on which side you stand concerning any important question. Hence I find a growing inclination to look elsewhere than to Your Eminence for reliable information and judgment, a tendency, not only here, but among the bishops of the United States, to look to New York rather than to Baltimore for the representative and leader of our Hierarchy."

Although Keane sweetened the bitter pill of his reproach by maintaining that if Gibbons actually was vacillating it was because of "your kindness of heart, your anxiety to be gracious and yielding to everyone," there could have been no more stinging indictment of the cardinal-elect's policy of "masterly inactivity." Keane also hit home with his suggestion that the hierarchy might be turning away from Gibbons to Corrigan in New York. In truth, the fact that the American cardinalate was going to Baltimore rather than remaining in New York was at the heart of the Americanist controversy. Bishop McQuaid particularly resented Gibbons's pre-eminence, and he repeatedly taunted "the little man at Baltimore." Keane's letter, then, had the desired effect, and to Gibbons's great credit, it did not turn him against his friend but rather redoubled his determination to have the ban on the Knights of Labor lifted.

Ironically enough, when Gibbons sailed for Rome in January of 1887 to receive his red hat, one of his fellow passengers was Archbishop Taschereau, the enemy of the Knights who was also being elevated to cardinal. Described by Gibbons as "a very persistent man who was working hard to have the Knights condemned in the United States to save himself from the odium of undue severity," Taschereau could be expected to do his utmost to wreck the American churchman's plans. In this, he was assisted by a powerful ally, Giovanni Cardinal Simeoni, Prefect of the Congregation of the Propaganda, "the Red Pope" who exercised such enormous power over missionary areas. To Bishop Keane, Cardinal Simeoni was "the embodiment of timid and suspicious conservatism." It was to Simeoni, as well as to the inflexible Vincenzo Sallua, the Commissary of the Holy Office, that Gibbons had to take his appeal. At first, he encountered a stone wall of opposition. His anger aroused, he confronted Sallua in a stormy interview and warned him that he would hold him responsible for the loss of thousands of souls in the United States if the organization was condemned. Next, he sent Simeoni his famous memorial on the Knights of Labor. A document that has since been hailed as "one of the great charters of the labor movement," its language was frank, even blunt, considering the place where it was uttered. Of the alleged secrecy, Gibbons said: "There is no oath, no promise of blind obedience, no secrecy." Moreover, Powderly had agreed to remove everything that the Church might find objectionable. Going over the charges against the Knights point by point, he refuted them all and pointed out that only five out of the seventy-five bishops in America desired the organization's condemnation. Warning of the dangers of losing the allegiance of the workingman, he said: "It is evidently of supreme importance that the Church should always be found on the side of humanity. To lose the heart of the people would be a misfortune for which the friendship of the few rich and powerful would be no compensation." And again of the workingmen: "They love the Church and they wish to save their souls, *but they must also earn their living*, and labor is now so organized that, without belonging to the organization, it is almost impossible to earn one's living." Finally, with an astute allusion to American sensitivity to "foreign interference": "To speak with the most profound respect but with the frankness which duty requires of me, it seems to me that prudence suggests and that even the divinity of the Church demands that we should not offer to America an ecclesiastical protection for which she does not ask and of which she believes she has no need."

With this masterful defense of the workingmen's right to organize, the onetime exponent of "masterly inactivity" carried the day. Ultimately, Rome decided not to condemn the Knights of Labor, and when Gibbons returned to the United States the details of his memorial were leaked to the press, and his popularity with the labor unions soared. He was hailed as a hero. The *New York Times*, however, thought otherwise, describing the new cardinal as "a man of weak judgment,* and the Church would make a terrible blunder if it permits him to persuade [it] into taking the side of an organization which was trying to substitute brute force, intimidation, for law, reason, equity and the precepts of the Christian religion." Indeed, the Knights at that particular moment did not look too respectable, being in trouble because of unsuccessful strikes and the apparent misuse of funds. Up in Rochester, Bernard McQuaid was chortling: "How does His Eminence feel now about his pets, the Knights of Labor? They are evidently breaking to pieces and are getting many more kicks than kisses."

Eventually, as Cardinal Gibbons had foreseen, the unstable Knights did vanish from American life. But they had prepared

* When Gibbons died, the *Times* said: "He was one of the wisest men in the world."

the way for the American Federation of Labor and had given the entire labor movement a powerful and unstoppable impetus. In this, James Cardinal Gibbons had been a powerful ally. Four years later, his stand was justified when Leo XIII published his encyclical, *Rerum Novarum* (Of New Things), defending the right of workingmen to form trade unions. This, too, was to become a great charter for the rights of labor, not only in America but in the world; and *Rerum Novarum* had been influenced by the thinking of the Baltimore cardinal. It is true that the attitude of Corrigan and McQuaid, who regarded labor unions as dangerous socialist organizations, was far from being vanquished in the Church, and that another half century would pass before the laity would become fully aware of the social doctrine laid down in Leo's encyclical. Nevertheless, Gibbons had made it possible for Catholic workingmen to join labor unions, and it is not too much to suggest that the strong Catholic influence in the labor movement, as well as the enormous number of Catholic labor leaders—from Terence Powderly at the outset through "Black John" Mitchell to George Meany at the present—may also be attributed to the firmness and eloquence of "the little man at Baltimore." Thus, the Communist take-over of labor which so many bloated "Christian men of property" feared with good cause was in great part prevented by a Catholic cardinal.

The Knights of Labor struggle, then, had ended in another victory for the Americanists. Unfortunately, this one also proved to be costly, if only because the intervention of Gibbons in a related controversy was to make Archbishop Michael Corrigan his implacable enemy.

The rising clamor for social reform which had called forth organizations such as the Knights of Labor had also created numerous crusaders against the injustices of capitalism, among them a self-educated printer named Henry George. By turns a foremast boy at sea, a prospector, a typesetter and finally a printer and a newspaperman, George elaborated a single-tax theory which became wildly popular with social reformers. Basically, George said that there should be but one tax—an impost on the rent derived from land—and that this single tax, by eliminating all others, would enable the economy to operate without hindrance or inequity. George's theories were advanced in his book *Progress and Poverty,* and they were immediately attacked as "socialistic," a word which then carried the same ugly connotation as today's epithet "communistic." Some of the more conservative prelates wanted *Progress and Poverty* placed on the Prohibitory Index, the index of forbidden books. Cardinal Gibbons, however, again taking the long view, regarded the single-tax proposal as a harmless and transitory fashion in social thinking. To condemn George's theories, he argued, would only give them a dangerous celebrity and make a martyr of Henry George.

In 1886, George ran for mayor of New York on the Labor Party ticket. His opponents were the young Theodore Roosevelt, the Republican, and Abram S. Hewitt, the Democrat. Because of the wide attention given to George's teaching, the campaign attracted national attention. It also attracted the Reverend Dr. Edward McGlynn, pastor of St. Stephen's Church, to George's standard. A fearless and eloquent fighter for social justice, Mc-Glynn had been a president of the Anti-Poverty League and was among the most popular leaders in America. Long before George ran for mayor, he had espoused his single-tax theory with such public zeal that the mild-mannered John Cardinal McCloskey had teasingly warned him against his plans "to cut up Manhattan into little pieces and give us all equal parts of it."

Dr. McGlynn's present ordinary, however, the irascible and inflexible Michael Corrigan, was not inclined toward little jokes. Having been a classmate of McGlynn's at the North American College, he was well aware of his "dangerous" views and he ordered the priest not to attend a public rally for Henry George. McGlynn refused. He declared that his rights as a citizen "were not surrendered when I became a priest." At once, Archbishop Corrigan suspended him, and the single-tax dispute was back in national headlines again. Labor periodicals denounced Corrigan as "a fat rascal" and praised McGlynn as "the best-known priest in America, the friend of the poor and the eloquent defender of the Church," while the conservative press praised the archbishop and attacked "this disobedient and cranky priest" for his "radical badness." In an effort to bring McGlynn "back to his senses," the *Chicago Tribune* printed the following verse:

Dr. Mac! Dr. Mac!
Are you on the right track?
In clinging to George
Do you not "Progress Back"
Backward to anarchy
Backward to Sin
Dr. McGlynn?

Dr. Mac! Dr. Mac!
You are on the wrong track
In fighting your Mother
In snubbing His Grace.
Are you helping your brother
To win in this race?
A desperate struggle
Life's race he is in
You are tripping, not helping him
Dr. McGlynn.

Unmoved even by rhymed exhortation, Dr. McGlynn remained
a staunch supporter of Henry George, continuing to preach the
single-tax gospel after George was defeated, so that in 1887 Archbishop Corrigan removed him from St. Stephen's Church. In
this same year, Gibbons was in Rome to receive his red hat and
to make his successful plea for the Knights of Labor. In his first
private audience with Pope Leo XIII, the frail old pontiff told
the cardinal designate that he had sent a cablegram to Dr. Mc-
Glynn, inviting him to come to Rome to discuss the situation.
The suspended priest refused, however, and Leo, solicitous as
ever for strayed sheep, now asked Gibbons if he could do something to bring the balky McGlynn to the Vatican. Gibbons
reluctantly agreed, knowing full well that the autocratic Archbishop of New York would regard his intervention as unwarranted poaching upon his own ecclesiastical preserve. He was
right. Corrigan was furious. Even though the Pope himself had
requested the favor, Corrigan was a stickler for protocol. Nothing
could mitigate his conviction that Gibbons's letter to McGlynn
was another instance of presumption on the part of "the little
man at Baltimore," and he never forgave him.

Actually, Corrigan became so incensed that he redoubled his
efforts to have Henry George's book *Progress and Poverty*

condemned. He had already denounced George's theories as "advanced socialism" and had warned from the pulpit that circulation of it would not be tolerated in the archdiocese. Now, he put pressure on Rome to place the book on the Index. Gibbons, of course, had been constantly struggling to prevent just that. He had put his position clearly: "To condemn the works of George would give them an importance they would not otherwise have had and would excite an appetite of curiosity that would make them sell by the thousands of copies and would thus extend immensely the influences that the condemnation sought to restrain and prevent." For two years the struggle over George's book continued between Gibbons and the progressives on one side and Corrigan and the conservatives on the other. The outcome was of enormous importance to both prelates, so much so that John Ireland wrote to Denis O'Connell: "If George is put on the Index, there will be a vacancy at Baltimore from a broken heart."

Eventually, the book was condemned. But with the subtlety characteristic of Rome, the American hierarchy was advised that the condemnation need not be published. Corrigan and McQuaid were dismayed. "What is the use of it if you can't publish it?" McQuaid complained. Dr. McGlynn, meanwhile, was excommunicated, but the ban was lifted in 1892 and the doughty doctor went to Florida to serve, returning to New York in 1895 to accept Corrigan's grudging appointment to the pastorate of St. Mary's Church. Two years later, McGlynn preached the funeral eulogy for his friend Henry George, and it was thus the affair ended.

Once again, the Americanists had won. By blocking at least publication of the condemnation, Cardinal Gibbons had prevented the unwise martyrdom of a social theory that was no threat to American Catholicism, but once again at the cost of enmity from Corrigan and brother conservatives. For the moment, however, the running battle between the two camps was suspended in the interests of a division of a different order: the final eruption of the century-old Irish versus German conflict under the name of "Cahenslyism."

Chapter XVI

The antagonism between the Irish and German populations in the American Church was as old as immigration itself. It had been there since the Revolution, smoldering beneath a surface unity, but sometimes flickering briefly into flame as in the early days at St. Mary's Church in Philadelphia, when the Germans complained that the Irish were shorting them on cemetery and pew allotments.

There was nothing doctrinal in the dispute. Basically it was racial and cultural. The Germans simply wanted to remain as German as possible while the Irish insisted that they become rapidly Americanized. At the heart of the matter, however, was the predominantly Irish hierarchy's fear that the separatism of the Germans might seem to confirm the ancient charge that the Catholic Church in America was a foreign institution. In the early part of the century, the presence of numerous French clergymen had suggested this "alien" quality, in its middle the nativists had invented it, and here, at its end, the German Catholics were unconsciously giving it new life. No wonder that the Irish bishops, even the conservatives among them, were so determined to reaffirm the American character of the Church in the United States.

For their part, the Germans regarded Americanization as secularization carried out at the spiritual neglect of the immigrants. Protestants as well as Catholics, they regarded America as a "New Europe" in which they might carve out cultural enclaves of their own free of the poverty or persecutions of the Old World. Their attitude was probably best expressed by King Ludwig I of Bavaria, saying farewell to the first group of German teaching sisters sailing for the New World in 1847. "I shall never forget you," he said, "but stay German—German! Do not become English." Three years later, when he forwarded ten thousand gulden for the new Ursuline convent in St. Louis, he wrote: "I am very, very anxious that only Germans enter the convent as sisters, and that the instruction should be only in German, both to be perpetual." Doubtless Ludwig's warnings were aimed against the "contaminations" of Protestant America. To him, to "become English" was synonymous with "turning Protestant," and he feared for the faith of thousands of his subjects even then fleeing the poverty of his kingdom.

In Bavaria [a contemporary observer wrote] whole village communities sell their property for whatever they can get, and set out, with their clergymen at their head. "It is a lamentable sight," says a French writer, "when you are traveling in the spring or autumn on the Strassburg road, to see the long files of carts that meet you every mile, carrying the whole property of the poor wretches, who are about to cross the Atlantic on the faith of a lying prospectus. There they go slowly along; their miserable tumbrils—drawn by such starved, drooping beasts that your only wonder is, how can they possibly hope to reach Havre alive —piled with the scanty boxes containing their few effects, and on the top of all, the women and children, the sick and bedridden, and all who are too exhausted with the journey to walk. One might take it for a convoy of wounded, the relics of a battlefield, but for the rows of little white heads peeping from beneath the ragged hood."

For all the hundreds of thousands of Germans who migrated to the United States, however, they were still outnumbered by the Irish and found themselves compelled to set up their national parishes as mere adjuncts of the Irish territorial parishes. Although they were the second largest ethnic group in the American Church, their influence in proportion to their numbers was far less. But then, after the Civil War, German migration overtook and passed the Irish. American industrial and commercial expansion and the completion of the transcontinental railroad drew the Germans here. They were also driven from their homeland by the Prussian spirit of militarism which Otto von Bismarck had made the soul of the new German Empire he had built and, for Catholic Germans, the fear of his *Kulturkampf*. Many thousands of them, unable to endure Bismarck's persecution of their religious leaders or the vilification of their faith, turned their eyes toward the New World. In 1883, a Catholic from the Rhineland explained why he was leaving the country:

My landlord gave us free lodging and 23–30 pfennig a day for wages. For this my whole family had to labor on Sundays as well as weekdays. We were obliged to do our own chores during free hours and on Sunday afternoon. If we asked permission to go to Church on Sunday, then the man abused us . . . every time and said: "You won't always need to be running after the priest if you find yourselves in the alms house." And so I am going to America. My acquaintances write from there that they have such good conditions, and on Sundays as many as wish to may go to Church. My children shall not imitate my slavery.

In all, about 700,000 Catholic Germans came to the United States between 1865 and 1900. Like their predecessors, they were farmers or independent craftsmen and they tended to settle in the rich agricultural regions of middle America—in Pennsylvania, Ohio, Indiana, Illinois, Iowa, Missouri and Kansas, and north into Wisconsin, Nebraska and the Dakotas—an area which came to be known as "the German belt." In the triangle formed by Cincinnati, Milwaukee and St. Louis the German population was especially dense.

Whether on the homestead or in the city, the German immigrants were truly solid citizens: industrious, thrifty, moral and dependable. Nevertheless, they kept clannishly to themselves, resisting every attempt to induce them to adopt the English language. There was, of course, more than mere Teutonic mulishness in this attitude. To the Catholic Germans, the love of God and the love of Fatherland were mystically united. They believed that their culture was the highest in the world and their Catholicism the finest expression of the universal faith. Thus, they insisted on practicing their faith in the German way and clinging to the customs of the Fatherland, all of which could only be done in the mother tongue. The German language, then, was the cement of this mystical union. To ask them to change it was to ask them to cease being German, and this they simply would not do. Moreover, their priests insisted that loss of language was tantamount to loss of faith. If a German Catholic could not practice his religion in a Germanic atmosphere, then

he would be tempted toward either German liberalism or Protestantism, both of which operated in a German milieu. As Father
Colman Barry, the historian of German Catholicism in America,
has observed:

During the nineteenth century the German spiritual leaders in the
United States were insistent upon these special provisions because they
had witnessed immigrants turning to non-Catholic churches, especially
Lutheran, where they felt more at home because they could hear their
mother tongue spoken. Editors of the German-American press, liberals
and freethinkers of the *Achtundvierziger* type, as well as influential
German societies were all leading a concerted campaign to preserve
the German language and German culture in the new world. German
Catholics, both in Germany and the United States who were judged to
be hyphenated Germans because of their allegiance to Rome, realized
they would be open to cynical attack if they should diminish their efforts to preserve *das Deutschtum* in the new world. And many of the
common people among the German Catholics, timid and homesick in
a new environment, would be easy prey to such charges.

Thus, in the face of the Irish insistence that the Germans adopt
the language of their new homeland, the German spiritual
leaders countered with the slogan: "Language Saves Faith." German continued to be taught in their schools, spoken in their
homes, preached from their pulpits and printed in their newspapers. And this, of course, was only inexplicable and maddening
to the pugnacious Irish, who believed that the English language
was the single, ineluctable *sine qua non* of Americanization. Indeed, they inquired, how could any national language save a
universal faith? and with this seemingly obtuse attitude they
only hardened the German resentment of them. German displeasure with the Irish "domination" of the American Church
also grew apace with the growth of Irish influence in the hierarchy. Despite the fact that the Germans were now challenging
Irish numerical supremacy, the fact was that Irish bishops outnumbered the Germans two to one. Worse, they were not above
intriguing in Rome to have traditionally German sees filled with
ordinaries of their own blood, and thus, Bishop John Henni of
the German stronghold of Milwaukee once thundered: "No Irish
bishop will ever sit on my throne!"
Actually, the Church more than once tried to come to grips

with the problem of separate German (and later Polish) cultural enclaves within its midst. The Third Plenary Council of 1884, over which Gibbons presided, provided many churches for foreign-language groups together with priests who spoke their language. Nevertheless, the conflict continued to grow, nourished by both misunderstanding and the acrimonious rhetoric of the protagonists of both sides. On the Americanizing side, John Ireland was especially detestable to the Germans. For one thing, "the anti-Christ of the North," as they called him, was a temperance crusader, an unpardonable crime in the eyes of the beer-drinking, beer-making Germans; for another, he had publicly defended the American public school system, which most German Catholics regarded as an invention of the Devil. Although the Archbishop of St. Paul honestly opposed any manifestation of foreignness (he once asked the Irish Benevolent Society to drop the racial prefix), he was uncommonly harsh on those who resisted Americanization. To him, any immigrant "who does not thank God that he is an American should in simple consistency take his foreign soul to foreign shores and crouch in misery and abjection beneath tyranny's sceptre." To this, Father Anton Walburg of Cincinnati replied: "A foreigner who loses his nationality is in danger of losing his faith and his character. When the German immigrant, arriving in this country, seeks to throw aside his nationality and to become 'quite English, you know,' the first word he learns is generally a curse and the rowdy element is generally his preference to the sterling qualities of the Puritan. A German aping American customs and manners is, in his walk, talk, and appearance an object of ridicule and contempt." Father Walburg also believed that America was a "hotbed of fanaticism, intolerance and radical ultra views on matters of politics and religion. All the vagaries of spiritualism, Mormonism, free-loveism, prohibition, infidelity, and materialism, generally breed in the American nationality."

Not all the German clergy accepted Walburg's judgment of American society, and many of the younger ones were anxious to become Americanized. This divergence was made plain in an interview which James Gibbons gave to a correspondent of *Frankfurter Zeitung* in Baltimore. Gibbons said: "Some people in America and elsewhere seem not to understand that the Americans are striving for developing into one great nationality. Just as Germany has developed into one national union by a struggle of many years' duration, so we are striving in the States for a common homogeneity, whose outward expression consists in the possession of one common language, the English language. . . . The Germans in America are handicapped without the knowledge of English, they are socially at a disadvantage. . . . For some time I have been in possession of petitions from German clergymen desiring the introduction of the English language."

These priests, however, were few and ineffectual, and the true German position was expressed by Archbishop Michael Heiss, the successor of the indomitable Henni in Milwaukee and Michael Corrigan's ally in the war on the Catholic University; the German bishops themselves; most of the Jesuits, as well as a few Irish conservatives such as Corrigan, ever eager to do his enemy in Baltimore a disservice; and sometimes, but not always, McQuaid. It was Heiss who apparently conspired in the opening of a campaign to have German separation approved in Rome. At least he permitted his personal theologian, Father Peter Abbelen of Milwaukee, to approach Gibbons for a letter of recommendation to the Vatican. Unaware of Abbelen's true intentions, the cardinal designate complied, only to find to his dismay that Abbelen had presented a memorial to Cardinal Simeoni complaining of "unjust treatment" of German Catholics in the United States. Abbelen declared that there was a tendency on the part of many Irish priests to regard German parishes as subordinate to theirs, to deprive German priests of their rights and to work for the elimination of German-language parishes. He said:

All direct and violent efforts to deprive the Germans of their language and customs, to "americanize" them in a quiet way, are nothing but fatal means of leading them away from the Church. Let us leave this "americanization" to its natural course, to a gradual amalgamation. It will come of itself, especially when and where immigration ceases. Self-interest is its more potent, irresistible factor. But let no one force it, and least of all, a Catholic bishop and priest. The German is tenacious; the German Catholic is proud of his country, especially since the glorious *Kulturkampf;* the German Catholic—unlike the Irish—is surrounded by countrymen, who, as Protestants, Infidels, Secret-Society men, do everything in their power to allure him away from his church. If they could taunt him with being considered, here in America, only as a second-rate Catholic, etc.—the consequences, Your Eminence would be too sad to think of.

Father Abbelen's memorial burst among the Americanist bishops like "a keg of ecclesiastical gunpowder." Bishop Keane thundered: "A more villainous tissue of misstatements I have seldom read." With Ireland, who was still with him in Rome, Keane presented a counter memorial which went over Abbelen's charges point by point, insisting that the basic dispute was not between German and Irish Catholics but between "the English language, the language of the United States, and the German tongue." Their memorial concluded:

The Church will never be strong in America; she will never be sure of keeping within her fold the descendants of immigrants until she has gained a decided ascendancy among the Americans themselves. She must be presented in a form attractive to Americans. The great objection which they have until now urged against her—an objection which at certain periods of her history they have entertained so strongly as even to raise persecutions—is, that the Catholic Church is composed of foreigners, that it exists in America as an alien institution, and that it is consequently, a menace to the existence of the Republic.

Even the mild Cardinal Gibbons was incensed by Abbelen's appeal, considering the Milwaukee theologian's approach as secretive, underhanded and productive of disunity among American prelates. Publicly, he went straight to the heart of the matter by informing Rome: "The only way to correct the evil at the beginning is to refuse absolutely to recognize any distinction in our government of the Church, for if any one nationality is accorded special privileges, other nationalists will thereafter demand the same." This, he predicted, would only lead to "a war of races, and the charges of our enemies that we are a religion of foreigners would be vindicated." In his counterattack, Gibbons had a strange ally in Bernard McQuaid, whose Irish indignation was apparently more than a match for his conservatism. Apparently, however, McQuaid could never quite down his dislike of Gibbons, for he derided the cardinal's controlled reply to Rome with the remark: "Alas, the cardinal is weak in the face of those above him." But McQuaid was wrong. The Abbelen Memorial's divisive clauses were bluntly rejected with the declaration: ". . . the Sacred Congregation of the Propaganda will never consider these petitions." Even His Excellency of Rochester was delighted with the outcome, celebrating the victory with typical relish: "The dirty, mean, underhand business of these schemers has come to naught!"

As Gibbons unhappily suspected, McQuaid's vaunt was premature. The German bishops were far from being finished. Indeed, their repulse only deepened their conviction of the justness of their cause, and they resented the charge of having been "underhanded" or of having operated outside the national hierarchy, maintaining, with much justice, that because they were so badly underrepresented in that hierarchy they had been compelled to state their case through irregular channels. Thus, when Archbishop Heiss died and Gibbons and the Americanists sought to fill the vacant see at Milwaukee with a prelate of their own convictions, they were able to thwart them and secure the appointment of another German, Frederick X. Katzer, a priest whom John Ireland had once described as a man who "knew less about America than any Huron!" Then, on the death of Gibbons's close friend, Bishop Gilmour of Cleveland, another German, Ignatius Horstmann, took his place. The Germans were elated, and then infuriated when Ireland expressed the Americanist dismay by calling Katzer "thoroughly unfit to be an archbishop." Matters worsened when the fiercely patriotic Ireland delivered an address before the American Education Association, crying: ". . . the Free School of America—withered be the hand that is raised in sign of its destruction." To the Germans, it appeared that the "anti-Christ of the North" was preparing to support the "godless" public schools while scuttling their own parochial schools. And thus, the argument began to develop to the effect that both Americanization and alleged discrimination against them was causing the loss of millions of Catholics. The German-language newspaper *Herald des Glaubens* said: "Many American priests in this country would rather see several million Germans go to hell than forgo the opportunity to convert a few hundred Yankees." Thus both sides were becoming embittered, setting the stage for the appearance of Peter Paul Cahensly.

Peter Paul Cahensly was born in Limburg in the Rhine province of Nassau on October 28, 1838, the son of a prosperous merchant. Upon his mother's death in 1868, Cahensly inherited the family business. Because he had been trained for commerce since childhood, traveling widely and serving as a journeyman in Le Havre in order to study shipping and freight techniques, Cahensly became an excellent businessman. He increased the firm's lucrative trade in coffee, developing his own roasting process for Java and Ceylon coffee, and expanded sales in petroleum and imports. Cahensly was also an ardent and devout Catholic, having interested himself in the mission activities of the St. Vincent de Paul Society. This association, it appears, led to his concern for the welfare of German immigrants to the United States.

As a young man in Le Havre, he had become aware that thousands of his countrymen, many of them of the impoverished classes already described, were taking ship for the New World. He saw how these poor people came pouring into a strange and foreign city, exhausted from their travels, frightened, unable to speak French and therefore the prey of dishonest innkeepers and agents. Cahensly did what he could to assist these poor wretches materially, but was even more concerned with their spiritual problems. He put signs in lodging houses directing Catholic Germans to the single missionary chapel that existed for them in Le Havre, and also boarded ships to inspect their quarters.

Cahensly was horrified by what he saw. Most of the immigrants were traveling steerage, that is, in the empty holds of vessels sailing to Philadelphia, New Orleans and New York to pick up cargoes of cotton or tobacco. It was as though every available inch of space had been utilized. Boards were placed in double rows to be used as beds, with two and sometimes three persons assigned to a "bed." Cahensly has described these squalid quarters:

A person could climb only with the greatest difficulty to the upper and rear places because of the small amount of free space which was usually barricaded with boxes and trunks. Besides, there was almost total darkness, and I became frightened when I thought that in these small rooms of indescribable disorder and darkness hundreds of people should spend weeks and months. By dividing the sleeping places, difference of sex was almost absolutely neglected, and it is not surprising that under such circumstances immoral situations developed which defy description.

Cahensly's impressions were verified by Father John Albrinck, a German pastor from the Archdiocese of Cincinnati, who witnessed similar scenes aboard the *Deutschland:*

There was not the least interest shown in the separation of the sexes in the steerage, and all lay across one another like cabbage and turnips. Sexual intercourse was unlimited. The common people not only acted in this way with depraved women, but more than once I saw the women's room of the steerage become around eleven o'clock the sleeping quarters for women with the higher officers. It was a real Sodoma.

In August of 1868 Leopold Kist sailed aboard the *Saxonia*, and found: "The steerage is a pig stall, a robber's den, a cut-throat and poisonous abyss. Truly, I wonder that this swimming hell is not regularly swallowed up by the deep."

Because the memory of such squalor had been indelibly impressed in his mind, Cahensly could not forget it, not even after he had taken over the family business and was deeply immersed in commercial affairs. Eventually, and with the encouragement of the St. Vincent de Paul Society of Paris, Brussels and Antwerp, he brought the plight of the immigrants to the attention of the Catholic societies of Germany. In 1871, chiefly through the efforts of Cahensly, the General Assembly of the German Catholic Societies created the St. Raphael Society especially charged with the care of German Catholic emigrants. Named for St. Raphael, the patron saint of travelers, the Society was to care for the emigrant before he sailed, during his voyage and at the ports of debarkation. Peter Paul Cahensly was named as its first secretary, a post which he held for years, and which ultimately led to his making transatlantic voyages himself. In doing so, he learned that immigrants arriving in the New World were exposed to the same swindling and robbery which they had met in Le Havre, and, far worse in the mind of the devout Herr Cahensly, a searing trial of faith. At Castle Garden in New York in 1883, Cahensly was appalled to find twelve Protestant ministers but not a single Catholic priest. Arriving immigrants were met by these ministers, who gave them Protestant Bibles, tracts and calendars. Cahensly himself had these objects pressed into his hands. Moreover, he saw thousands of Catholic immigrants taken to large Lutheran lodging houses where new arrivals were accommodated free of charge. As he was to write later: "What will it avail our Catholic emigrants if, after we have conducted them safely to the ship, they run into the danger on the other side of the ocean of losing the greatest treasure they have, their holy Catholic faith."

Unfortunately, Cahensly seems to have exaggerated the number of Catholics who lost their faith in America. He accepted without question the Jesuit Father Richard Clark's unwarranted claim that the number of Catholics in the country then should have been 12,000,000 rather than 7,500,000,* and blamed this imagined loss of 4,500,000 on "the peculiar, extremely independent, and unrestrained American conditions." In his tour of America, Herr Cahensly saw only one non-German archbishop, Corrigan, the implacable enemy of Gibbons and all things Americanist, and it seems that as sincere and noble as Peter Paul Cahensly undoubtedly was, he was also extremely gullible. He was far too willing to believe everything the German clergy told him about the dangers of Americanization, and he asked no one outside the German Catholic community to verify their charges.

Thus, in 1890, when Peter Paul Cahensly and other members of the St. Raphael Society journeyed to Lucerne, Switzerland, for a congress on immigrant problems, the result was the notorious Lucerne Memorial calling for separate ethnic churches in the United States. Fifty-one Catholics from seven nations signed the memorial, but because it was presented to Pope Leo XIII by Cahensly, and because the thinking behind it manifested his fears for his Catholic countrymen in America, authorship has been charged to Peter Paul Cahensly alone.

If the Abbelen Memorial had been a powder keg, then the Lucerne Memorial was an earthquake. Beginning with the incredible assertion that sixteen million Catholics in the United States had been lost to the faith, when in fact there were in 1890 only a total of twelve million Catholics in the United States, the memorial laid down an eight-point proposal. The Holy See was asked to set up separate parishes for each nationality, staffing them with priests of the same national origin. If there were not

---

* Actually the number of Catholics in 1883 was closer to 10,000,000.

enough faithful for a national parish, then it was urged that the parish to which they belonged should provide priests who spoke their mother tongue. Priests of every nationality were to have equal rights with native-born priests. Parochial schools were to be maintained in all parishes, and as far as possible should be separate for all nationalities, with the curriculum to include their national language as well as the language of the land of their adoption. All Catholics, meanwhile, were to be organized into societies and mutual-aid unions which would pre-empt any desire to join the Freemasons or similar organizations. Cahensly also asked the Holy See to sponsor mission seminaries to train priests for the United States, and then came the temblor, the earthquake at its shocking peak: "It seems very desirable that the Catholics of each nationality, wherever it is deemed possible, have in the episcopate of the country where they immigrate, several bishops who are of the same origin. It seems that in this way the organization of the Church would be perfect, for in the assemblies of the bishops, every immigrant race would be represented, and its interests and needs would be protected."

There it was: nationalist bishops, ethnic dioceses. The American Church was to become a conflicting congeries of races, each teaching and praying in its own mother tongue, each governed by bishops of its own nationality, and each, in any so-called assembly of the "American" Church, arguing its own causes and pursuing its own purposes. In effect, the Lucerne Memorial proposed to make the American Church into a Tower of Babel, confirming every charge of "foreignness" leveled against it since the Puritans of Maryland reversed George Calvert's Toleration Act in the name of allegiance to the English crown. Although some historians have maintained that the suggestions were all relatively harmless, the fact is that they raised a furious outcry among the country's non-German prelates.

Bishop John Kain of Wheeling, West Virginia, said: "Satan himself could not invent a means more capable of rendering the Church odious to Americans." John Ireland cried, "We are American bishops, and an effort is made to dethrone us and to foreignize our country in the name of religion," going on to denounce "the impudence of the men in undertaking to meddle under any pretext in the Catholic affairs of America. This is simply un-

pardonable and all American Catholics will treasure up the af-
front for future action . . ." Bishop Foley of Detroit implored
Cardinal Gibbons: "We need you more than ever. For to Your
Eminence we must look for salvation from the wicked wretch
Cahensly, who is striving to undo the work of the Church in our
Country."

Gibbons himself was furious. Though outwardly calm and silent, he wrote to his friend Archbishop William Elder of Cincinnati to decry "the Americo-European conspiracy which has inflicted so deep an insult on the episcopate and Catholics of the
United States, and seems to regard the sees of America as fit
to be filled by the first greedy ecclesiastical adventurer that
comes to our country. An American bishop, in view of the important position which he has as a property holder and a citizen,
should be a man possessed of a deep love, not only for his
Church, but also for this country, and a thorough acquaintance
and sympathy with our political institutions."

From all over the country messages poured into Baltimore from
prelates beseeching Gibbons to make a fierce protest or call an
indignation meeting of all the country's archbishops, but the
cardinal refused to be moved from his public stance of monu-
mental silence. He was waiting for the opportune moment before he made his move. Meanwhile, with or without Cardinal
Gibbons's knowledge or encouragement, it is not known, the
forceful John Ireland in St. Paul had joined forces with the
equally aggressive Denis O'Connell in Rome in an effort to discredit what was now being called "Cahenslyism." Ireland had already won wide acclaim in the secular press through his public
denunciation of the movement. In praising Ireland and condemning Cahensly, the Philadelphia Press had stated that
Cahenslyism confirmed those fears of foreign influence which had
"found a place in the platform of the Native American party
and the Constitution of the Know-Nothing order."

Neither Ireland nor O'Connell, nor, for that matter, Gibbons
himself, actually feared Cahenslyism. They were confident in
their own ability to block foreign interference, and they were
aware that Rome's policy has traditionally been one of trusting
in the hierarchy of each country. What Ireland and O'Connell, at
least, perceived in Cahenslyism was the opportunity to destroy

foreign influence utterly. So the two men got to work manufacturing and disseminating misinformation about Cahensly and the Lucerne Memorial, hoping, in this way, to stir up American non-Catholic as well as Catholic opinion. They were highly successful, so much so that Ireland wrote to O'Connell congratulating him on dispatches filed by the Associated Press: "They are so cleverly put, and always hit the nail on the head. . . . They are creating a tremendous sensation, and affecting more than aught else could have done Catholic public opinion." Later, Ireland got off two gleeful cables to his colleague in Rome: "SEND MORE. SEND ALL. MIRACLES OF GOOD DONE" and "GREAT DISTURBANCE, DANGER OF SCHISM AND PERSECUTION UNLESS ROME DENOUNCE CAHENSLY, AND DENOUNCE ONCE FOR ALL, AND FOR TIME BEING NAME NO GERMAN BISHOPS." Evidently delighted with the results of his rabble-rousing, the Archbishop of St. Paul wrote O'Connell again: "I think we have the country well worked up now and we will be able to begin reaping the harvest. I sent an 'alarming' cable to you yesterday. You may be able to show it around. As a matter of fact, Americans are most angry and I am sure that in the next Congress Cahensly will get an airing."

Much as Ireland and O'Connell did arouse the country, they also angered German Catholics. The German-language division of the Catholic press launched a thundering counter charge, claiming, among other things, that the truth of the Lucerne Memorial would prevail over the misrepresentations of "the Irish," that the accusations against Cahensly were "wicked and false," that Ireland and his cohorts were making the Church a laughing-stock, that they were robbing immigrants of their right to preserve their faith and that anyway German priests were better than Irish priests because they could speak a second language. From Ireland and his associates came the uncharitable reply that Cahenslyism was "a pan-German plot, dividing the Church in the U.S. into little foreign kingdoms" or "an attempt to found a religious and political Prussia here." At the height of this unedifying exchange of invective, Archbishop Katzer of Milwaukee, hoping to calm the storm, wrote to Gibbons to say that he knew nothing about "the deplorable Cahensly affair," and beseeching the cardinal to come to Milwaukee to bestow the pallium on him. Gibbons consented, judging that the time for him to make his move had come.

Throughout the furor, Gibbons had clung to his stance of statesmanlike calm, refusing to allow other bishops to importune him into making a false step. Being a cardinal, he understood the political situation at Rome better than most bishops. For one thing, O'Connell had informed him and Ireland that the Germans were being represented in Rome as the only reliable Catholics in America. The Americanizers, i.e., the Irish, were described as being far too liberal and therefore dangerous. Furthermore, because of the American principle of separation of church and state, the Americans had no one to represent them before the Vatican's secretariat of state. The Germans, however, had the support of a German government very well represented in Rome, and the Vatican at that time was most anxious to relieve the pressure of Bismarck's *Kulturkampf* on Catholicism in Germany. This is not to suggest that any this-for-that deal between Berlin and the Vatican was being arranged in the interests of German Catholics in America, but it must have seemed a possibility in the eyes of the astute cardinal in Baltimore. Moreover, Denis O'Connell had already informed him of how he had thrown the dust of an *American Kulturkampf* into the eyes of Cardinal Rampolla, the Vatican foreign secretary. O'Connell wrote:

Now the apprehension of the American government must be your protection. When I spoke to Cardinal Rampolla of the indignation the Amer. Bps. would feel if the Cahensly plan were approved, I made no impression on him. They were Irish, they were interested and their opposition and indignation were only a matter of course. But when I said that the American Government would settle the matter for itself without Mr. Cahensly, the Cardinal changed his manner. It was an idea they never contemplated, and I said a Culturkamp [sic] was as possible in America as in Germany. So I verily believe this is the only grounds on which to settle the question. They thought they had it all their own way to settle according to their views or interests between "German and Irish" without even being required to take into account the feelings of the American people. This element must figure in all future considerations of the question and then the solution will be easy and practical. The indignation of the "Irish" counts for nothing. They are after all like the Irish in Ireland, they will obey anyhow and the influence of the Government in Germany need not be sacrificed for their sakes.

Such considerations were never out of Gibbons's mind. He was also aware, with Ireland, Keane and O'Connell, that the Germans were in fundamental error. They simply did not understand the American character and could not grasp the fact that the United States was in process of melting all its disparate races into a homogeneous mass, of producing a distinct American nationality. Since the 1880s, under the renewed spell of the "Manifest Destiny" that had led an American army into Mexico in the middle of the century, a deep sense of national purpose had gripped the American people. The imperialist theories of the great exponent of sea power, Alfred Thayer Mahan, had captivated the imagination of American leaders, and the country had begun to look outward for the colonies and naval stations that would support the powerful navy proposed by Mahan. Annexation of Samoa and Hawaii, the war with Spain in 1898, seizure of the Philippines, the big-stick diplomacy of Theodore Roosevelt, one of Mahan's most devoted disciples, by which the Republic of Panama was quite literally torn from the body of Colombia so that the Panama Canal might be dug—all these were manifestations of the new American nationalism. Denis O'Connell's close friend, Senator Albert Beveridge of Indiana, was perhaps the most flamboyant evangelizer of Manifest Destiny, rising again and again in the Senate to maintain that God had singled out the "American people as His chosen nation to finally lead in the regeneration of the world." Today, under the ominous Sign of the Mushroom cloud, Beveridge's declarations may sound childishly chauvinist and even mawkish; but at the end of the nineteenth century they were taken seriously. They were real, they were earnest, and no one understood this more clearly or was more in sympathy with American aspirations than the Americanist bishops.

The Germans did not share this vision. Unlike the Irish, who had immigrated earlier, who were thoroughgoing, English-speaking democrats who had become almost instantly attached to American institutions, the Germans had for the most part remained aloof in racial enclaves. Many of them were still deeply attached to the Fatherland, which was then experiencing a similar thrust toward nationalist imperialism. Kaiser Wilhelm II had also read Mahan, had come under his spell, and opted for a powerful navy. Otto von Bismarck had never been quite able to conceal his contempt for America. He had called the Monroe Doctrine "a species of arrogance peculiarly American." He had sneered, "There is a special Providence for fools, drunks and the United States of America." The German Reich had opposed the American war with Spain; and Germany's colonial and naval expansion into the Pacific, the ocean which Beveridge had piously proclaimed an American lake, had also angered the American people. Thus, with many Americans considering Germany as one of their country's most consistent enemies, it was not difficult for them to regard the Lucerne Memorial as an attempt to make a colonial thrust into American soil under cover of the Catholic Church. True enough, the immigrant societies of seven nations had signed the document, but in the American mind there was only one signer—Herr Peter Paul Cahensly—and Ireland and O'Donnell had been so successful in describing the memorial in guttural Teutonic accents that the entire Cahensly affair began to take shape as a conscious German attempt to gain influence in the United States. For the American Church to have appeared as the agency through which this insidious invasion was to be effected would have been to provide the A.P.A. with a Gunpowder Plot of its own.

Perhaps even worse was the certainty in the mind of Gibbons that nationalist political parties would follow nationalist churches, and that Cahenslyism was therefore not only a divisive force in religion but in American political life as well. Therefore, it was not only as Catholic cardinal but also as a loyal democratic American that he waited for the moment to launch his counterstrike. On June 28, 1891, at the dedication of St. Mary's Church for Germans in Washington, aware from O'Connell's reports that Cahenslyism was being looked upon with disfavor in Rome, he made his first public statement on the subject. Reminding everyone present that the Catholic Church was a family of many peoples, he pointed to the great number of ethnic churches throughout America. No other country in the world, he claimed, had a hierarchy so concerned for the spiritual needs of the foreign-born, observing that hardly a Sunday passed in America without some church being dedicated for the use of Germans, Poles, Italians, Bohemians or Lithuanians. Abroad, he said, in Paris, Vienna, Berlin and Rio de Janeiro, where there were large foreign Catholic populations, no such provisions were made. Therefore, he concluded angrily: "With these facts before us we cannot view without astonishment and indignation a number of self-constituted critics and officious gentlemen in Europe complaining of the alleged inattention which is paid to the spiritual wants of the foreign population and to the means of redress which they have thought proper to submit to the Holy See."

Gibbons's remarks, which stunned the Germans, could not have been better timed. On the very Sunday on which they were uttered, Cardinal Rampolla, under orders from Pope Leo XIII, addressed a letter to the Baltimore cardinal. Alluding to the German St. Raphael Society's "proposal to give to each group of emigrants according to their nationality their own representatives in the American episcopate," Rampolla said: "The Apostolic See, however, after careful examination, finds that plan neither opportune nor necessary."

Cardinal Gibbons was elated, especially after he learned that the day before the Papal Secretary of State wrote to him, Cardinal Simeoni informed Cahensly in a personal interview that his proposal was impossible. Thus, Cahenslyism had been utterly rejected: by the Holy Father himself and by the Propaganda. Moreover, the repulse had been dealt at Rome, where the appeal had been made, and not by the American bishops themselves. Now it remained for the American Church to make some assurance to the American government over an affair which was still causing such a commotion. On July 11, a few days after the letter arrived, the opportunity arose. With one of those strokes of good fortune which by then were common in the Cardinal's career, Gibbons was vacationing at Cape May, New Jersey, and was strolling along the boardwalk when he encountered President Benjamin Harrison, who also was on holiday in the Jersey resort city.

"He greeted me most cordially and invited me to walk with him," Gibbons later told Denis O'Connell. "We went together for some time, chatting pleasantly till we approached his cottage.

When I was in the act of saying 'good-bye' to him and continuing my walk, he kindly asked me to accompany him to his cottage. I cheerfully complied, of course."

Walking side by side toward the cottage, the slight, clean-shaven little Prince of the Church and the bulky, white-bearded Chief Executive doubtless made a vivid impression on passers-by. Once the two men were indoors, Harrison brought up the question of Cahenslyism with the remark: "I have followed the question with profound interest. And I regard it as a subject of deep interest to our country at large, one in which the American people are much concerned. I have also conversed on the subject with Mr. Tracy, a member of my cabinet. Foreign and un-authorized interference with American affairs cannot be viewed with indifference." Harrison then said: "I was very much pleased with the opinion you expressed publicly in the matter. I had thought several times of writing to you and offering my congratulations on the remarks you made, but I refrained from doing so lest I should be interfering in church matters. But I am glad to have the opportunity of expressing my satisfaction . . . This is no longer a missionary country like others which need missionaries from abroad. It has an authorized hierarchy and well-established congregations. Of all men bishops of the Church should be in full harmony with the political institutions and sentiments of the country."

Delighted, Cardinal Gibbons at once told President Harrison of his message from Rome. "The President seemed much pleased," Gibbons wrote. Realizing that Harrison's concern for Cahenslyism was just the right "apprehension" prescribed by O'Connell, the astute little prelate from Baltimore pressed the American Chief Executive to write a letter to the Pope on the subject. Harrison, however, demurred, fearing "to burn his fingers" by meddling in Church affairs. Instead, he suggested that Gibbons pass his views along to Rome, and the jubilant cardinal at once agreed. Later, after he had released the story of his meeting with Harrison to the newspapers, and sent a full account to Rampolla in Rome, Gibbons felt satisfied that Cahenslyism had been mortally wounded. Harrison's words, he felt, were worth more than the combined protests of the American hierarchy. With both Pope and President at his back, it now remained to give the stricken movement its death blow—and to do it right in the German bishops' stronghold.

Milwaukee, of course, was the very place, and so, when Cardinal Gibbons came to St. John's Cathedral there, bearing the pallium or white wool band which every archbishop needs to exercise his metropolitan powers, he mounted the pulpit to deliver a tribute to the many nationalities which had formed the American Church into a single harmonious mosaic. Then, his voice vibrant, he cried:

Woe to him, my brethren, who would destroy or impair this blessed harmony that reigns among us! Woe to him who would sow tares of discord among the fair fields of the Church in America! Woe to him who would breed dissension among the leaders of Israel by introducing a spirit of nationalism into the camps of the Lord! Brothers we are, whatever may be our nationality, and brothers we shall remain. Loyalty to God's Church and to our country—this our religious and political faith. Next to love for God should be love for our country. The Author of our being has stamped in the human breast a love for one's country and therefore patriotism is a sentiment commended by Almighty God Himself. Let us glory in our title of American citizen. We owe our allegiance to one country and that country is America. We must be in harmony with our political institutions. It matters not whether this is the land of our birth or our adoption. It is the land of our destiny!

With these stirring words, Gibbons would have seemed to have spoken the funeral eulogy for Cahenslyism. Certainly he received a torrent of praise from the American press, secular as well as Catholic. But the movement—rather, the idea—was not completely destroyed. It remained to be denounced on the floor of the U. S. Senate as an "infamous attempt to prostitute religious powers to political purposes," and for the deeply injured Peter Paul Cahensly to reply that the whole affair had been maliciously and deliberately misrepresented by American prelates and politicians and to deny that he had concocted any pan-Germanic plot. Eventually, the furor over Cahenslyism died down, and John Ireland and Peter Paul Cahensly even became good friends, once they had met each other. But the problem of nationalities was to plague the Catholic Church in America even after World War I seemed to have eliminated the problem with the Germans.

But after the Germans came the Poles, Italians and the various Slavic nationalities of eastern Europe, all of them, like the Germans, deeply resenting Irish domination of the Church and Irish insistence that they put aside their national tongues and customs and do as Americans do. The problem of ethnic pluralism, then, still exists in the American Church and probably will continue to exist as long as America remains a haven for the world's "huddled masses yearning to breathe free." Thus, even on the dark side, the American Church is again a faithful mirror of American society.

From another viewpoint, however, it may be said that the nationalities problem does not still exist to the same degree of intensity which called forth Cahenslyism. Although it is true that, again excepting the old German strongholds in the Midwest, the American hierarchy still consists mostly of Irish bishops, the fact is that entrance to an American seminary is no longer dependent upon a candidate's being one of "the micks and the O's." There are now many priests, as well as a few bishops, with Slavic and Italian names. Furthermore, the Irish-Americans are now two and three generations removed from their immigrant forebears and no longer think of themselves as being hyphenated. With the exception of the Puerto Ricans, the latest ethnic group speaking a foreign language to tax the resources of the American Church, immigrant nationality has also changed. New laws have closed the gates to the old nations of Europe, and today the influx is from primarily non-Catholic countries of Asia and the Middle East. Thus, ethnic pluralism is not the problem that it was in the 1890s, and the Church may at last have a chance to employ elsewhere all those energies which were consumed in Americanizing the immigrant.

So Cahenslyism, probably the most serious threat to the unity of American Catholicism throughout its long history, was decisively repulsed. Much as Cahensly and the German bishops in America might have protested that the movement was not an outgrowth of pan-Germanism, it is difficult to escape the conclusion that, consciously or unconsciously, the German Catholic's attachment for the Fatherland was too deep for the good of his patriotism. If successful, Cahenslyism would have been destructive of the national unity required for American participation in the first of the world wars. As the *New York Times* wrote in 1917: "The Cahensly movement was a direct outgrowth of pan-Germanism. Many who recall the struggle in the eighties and nineties do not hesitate to say that it was due to Gibbons and Ireland more than any others in the U.S. that the country went to war with so great a degree of solidarity against the government of one of the great peoples from which the American nation sprang."

If, however, it should be argued that the idea of separate nationalist churches had nothing to do with politics but was only a sincere attempt to preserve the Catholicism of immigrants set down in a Protestant milieu, then the answer is that Cahenslyism would have set up religious enclaves based upon a fixed European mold cast by the dictums of the Council of Trent. They would have been not only non-American but also antimodern. They would have been ossified fossils of the Counter-Reformation and would have resembled the European churches from which they had sprung—churches now in full flux and ferment under the stimulus of the *aggiornamento*—about as much as a Swiss Guard looks like a United States Marine.

Cahenslyism, then, deserves no mourners. It died the death it should have died, and its epitaph, fittingly enough, was written by the colorful Archbishop of St. Paul. Hearing that his two new suffragan sees of Duluth and Winona were to be filled with Irish prelates, John Ireland is said to have struck the table with his fist, roaring:

"Thank God, we've dished the Dutch!"

Chapter XVII

The struggle over Cahenslyism had been bitter, far too bitter, and one reason for the acrimony and lack of charity was that the battle erupted just as another long-smoldering issue burst into flame. This was the public versus parochial schools controversy, and once again the flamboyant figure of John Ireland was at the heart of the dispute.

In its essence, the disagreement arose over Ireland's apparent —but not actual—abandonment of the Church's treasured parochial school system in favor of the state or public school. Catholics were very proud of their schools. They had begun building them since the 1840s, after John Hughes failed in his fight to remove the Protestant influence from public schools. As that influence gradually died away, being replaced by a secular or openly irreligious atmosphere, the Catholics redoubled their efforts to preserve the faith of their children by seeing to it that they had religious instruction. In 1884, the Third Plenary Council of Baltimore decreed that every pastor in the country should erect a parochial school within the next two years.

This object of a school at every church was, of course, quite impossible. Without public funds, dependent upon the pennies of the poor, who were also taxed for the support of the public schools, the Church had taken upon herself the labors of Sisyphus. By 1890, out of 2,200,000 Catholic children only 725,000 were in Catholic schools. In New York City alone, out of 150,000 Catholic children only 42,000 were receiving Catholic education. Many of the members of the hierarchy had become convinced that the faithful, most of them working-class people, had not the financial means to erect a widespread parochial school system, and they were also indignant over the injustice of these same people paying what was in effect a double tax. As might be expected, one of these practical prelates was John Ireland, and in 1890, when he was invited to speak at the National Education Association's annual convention in his see city of St. Paul, he gave the entire question a public airing.

For any Catholic prelate to be asked to address the nation's predominantly Protestant schoolteachers was in itself an indication of the esteem in which "the consecrated blizzard from St. Paul" was held in America, and Ireland at once justified this faith in his open-mindedness by launching into a perhaps overblown tribute to the public schools.

Beginning by saying that the state school existed not only by right but by necessity as well, he said: "The child must have instruction and in no mean degree, if the man is to earn for himself an honest competence and acquit himself of the duties which, for its own life and prosperity, society exacts from all its members." Although Ireland insisted on the fundamental Catholic teaching that the care of the child's mind as well as its body was committed to parents by divine appointment, he also declared that many thousands of children would remain uneducated if the task of instruction rested solely with the parents. Therefore, state action was necessary, and universal education would be impossible without the public schools. "Free schools!" Ireland exclaimed. "Blest indeed is the nation whose vales and hillsides they adorn, and blest the generations upon whose souls are poured their treasures." Warming to his theme, Ireland even defended compulsory education, declaring that "instruction is so necessary for the sake of the individual and society that the parent who neglects to provide it sins against the child and against society and should be punished by the State." Proceeding next to praise the public schools of America, he spoke the words that were to bring down upon his head a torrent of rebuke.

"The free school in America!" he cried. "Withered be the hand raised in sign of its destruction."

But then, having saluted the public school system, he turned to indict it for its failure to provide religious instruction. Multitudes of children were growing up with no knowledge of religion and no instruction in morals, he said, maintaining that "the State school crowds out the Church." He insisted that religion should be included in the curriculum of the state school. "It is manifest that dissatisfaction exists with the State school because of its exclusion of religion. This dissatisfaction, founded on conscience, will continue until the cause of it is removed."

At this point, the archbishop denounced the injustices to which Catholics of America were subjected. He said that ten million people were compelled by law to pay taxes in support of schools which they could not approve in conscience, and then were forced to build and maintain schools of their own. The situation was, in effect, double taxation. To remove this inequity, he proposed two solutions.

One was the so-called "Poughkeepsie Plan," which had originated in that city in 1876 and was also in effect in Savannah, Hartford, Boston and Cleveland. Under this scheme, the local board of education leased the parochial school for one dollar a year, supervising the standard of teaching while paying the salaries of the nuns, who taught secular subjects during the day and religion after school hours. "This is not paying for religious instruction," Ireland said, "but for the secular instruction demanded by the state and given to the pupil as thoroughly as he could have received it in the state school." Of the other solution, Ireland declared: "I would permeate the regular state school with the religion of the majority of the children, be this religion as Protestant as Protestantism can be, and I would, as in England, pay for the secular instruction given in denominational schools according to results."

Ireland's speech, printed in the nation's press, was electrifying, not because of his proposals, which, after all, were far from being new, but because of the boldness with which he had advanced them. At once, he found himself shot at from both sides. Non-Catholics accused him of trying to take over the public schools, and conservative Catholics, especially the Germans, charged that "the anti-Christ of the North" was planning to wreck the parochial school system they had built through years of patient sacrifice in the interests of the "godless" public schools. The outcry from the Catholic conservatives, naturally enough, was the loudest of all. Ireland realized how serious it was when he received a letter from Denis O'Connell, who said: "Now you have a little case yourself before the Propaganda—a little case of doctrine, your last speech. It was sent from America to the Congregation of the Council, and thence to the Propaganda, and Sbarretti is translating it '*per un po di esercizio pure di lingua inglese*' into Italian for the priests that make up the Congresso or maybe for the *Padri Cardinali*." O'Connell also wrote later that "baskets of papers" were arriving in Rome accusing him of disobeying the decrees of the Third Plenary Council. The alert Americanist agent in Rome also communicated his fears to Cardinal Gibbons, who at once wrote him an eloquent defense of the accused archbishop, one which, as both men knew, Monsignor O'Connell would know where to circulate.

"He is really a power here," Gibbons wrote, "and has more public influence than half a dozen of his neighbors. Such a man should not be under a cloud. There is no prelate in the United States who has done more to elevate and advance the Catholic religion. Protestants and Catholics alike almost idolize him. . . . Had he been a dumb dog, no whelps would have barked at him here."

Archbishop Ireland was most grateful to Cardinal Gibbons for "extending over him at the first sign of danger the shield of his powerful influence." But then, unable to overlook any opportunity for a counterattack, he said he regretted the fact that "some of our own men are so ready to slay the bishops." Irrepressible as ever, he added: "I rather enjoy the predicament into which I have got."

For his part, Gibbons did not enjoy the squabble at all, especially after Cardinal Rampolla wrote to him asking his opinion of Ireland's speech. With this Gibbons persuaded the Archbishop of St. Paul to translate the entire address into French himself, and to append his own explanation of the allegedly offensive passages. In essence, Ireland explained to Rampolla that glowing tributes to "Free schools!" were to free schools in the abstract, to the idea of universal free education. When he spoke of his regret for the necessity of parochial schools, it was not in the sense that he deplored religious education—he had a network of schools for twelve thousand Catholic children in his own archdiocese—but that the public school, in failing to provide religious instruction, had made the parish school necessary. Finally, his seeming espousal of Protestantism in the public schools was only to say that he preferred any kind of Christianity to godless materialism, a position advanced by theologians such as Newman and Manning.

When Gibbons forwarded Ireland's explanation, he also sent the Holy Father a ten-page letter of his own. In it, he explained the educational system which was—and is—peculiar to America. He wrote: "It is true that in the public schools there is no religious education given, but, Most Holy Father, this is not, as in France, Italy, and elsewhere, out of opposition to religion. Thank God, the public spirit in this country is fundamentally religious and there is everywhere a great respect for liberty of conscience well understood and in the legitimate sense of the word. Consequently, the religious question is set aside in the schools in order not to offend the sentiments of the children who attend them and the parents who send them there. The care of providing the religious education of the children is left to the Church and to the Protestant sects."

With these communications, the campaign against Ireland in Rome came to naught, much to the Minnesota prelate's joy. The school squabble might have been forgotten, had not the audacious archbishop subsequently put his own theories on combining Catholic and secular education into practice. In August of 1891, Ireland made an arrangement with the school boards of Faribault and Stillwater, Minnesota. For the nominal sum of one dollar a year, he leased the school building to them. In turn, the boards agreed to pay the salaries of the nuns as teachers. During school hours, they taught nothing but secular knowledge, giving religious instruction only after classes were over.

Here was a sincere attempt to remove the financial burdens of a double school tax from the shoulders of the Catholic laity, and also to free struggling pastors of one of the most severe drains on their energy. Generous in the sense that use of the parochial school saved the entire community the expense of having to build one itself, the plan also tried to reconcile religious and secular instruction. But the "Faribault Plan," as it came to be known, brought few hosannas upon Ireland's white-maned head. Instead, he heard once again—but much louder—the same hue and cry that had succeeded his address to the teachers' association. Once again, Ireland was like a man standing against a glass wall to be shot at from both sides. From Protestant ministers and the infuriated A.P.A. came the charge that the Catholic archbishop was plotting to secure state subsidies for sectarian schools, and from many Catholics came the protest that the plan would wreck the parochial school system. Catholic opposition to Ireland's educational theories hardened and grew almost hysterical after Dr. Thomas Bouquillon, Professor of Moral Theology at Catholic University, defended the state's right to educate children, in the first of three pamphlets entitled *Education, to Whom Does It Belong?*

Dr. Bouquillon's pamphlet, closely reasoned and liberally buttressed with quotations from such great Catholic theologians as Thomas Aquinas and Suárez, did not depart from the Catholic tradition that the parent has the prior right to educate his child. But it did introduce what many Catholic writers considered a novelty by upholding the state's right to enter the field of education and even to make it compulsory. Although the Church, he said, has received her mandate to teach supernatural truths from her Divine Founder, she imparts merely human knowledge indirectly, as a work of charity when it is insufficiently taught by others, as a work of necessity when it is opposed to supernatural truth and morality. He declared: "Education belongs to the individual, physical and moral, to the family, to the State, to the Church, but to all four combined in harmonious working, for the reason that man is not an isolated but a social being."

At once, Dr. Bouquillon's pamphlet provoked a storm of reaction. If, by drawing on the thought of the Jesuit theorist Suárez, he had hoped to preclude the Jesuit counterattack he must have anticipated, he failed utterly. Again and again, Bouquillon's theories were attacked by Jesuit writers. In Rome, the highly influential Jesuit publication *Civilta Cattolica* showed itself among Ireland's most bitter and unscrupulous opponents. Only a few months ago, *Civilta Cattolica* had been unstinting in its praise of Bouquillon's *Theologia Moralis*, hailing him with the title of *"sommo maestro,"* but now it condemned him utterly as an advocate of state control of the schools. The Jesuits (not all of them, of course, opposed Ireland) were supported by Monsignor Joseph Schroder of Catholic University, an ardent Cahenslyist as well as an eloquent German whose imperfect English flawed his arguments, while seeming to suggest the wisdom of the Americanists' conviction that Germans should learn to speak English.

Once again the American hierarchy found itself divided, with Archbishop Corrigan leading the conservative-German coalition and Gibbons and Ireland at the head of the progressives. To Corrigan's forces, the Faribault Plan was compliance in the encroachment of the state upon religion, to Ireland and Gibbons it was an attempt to solve a heretofore insoluble problem by compromise with the state. Neither side budged, and as the controversy became even more heated than the earlier Cahenslyism struggle, Father Thomas Shahan, professor of church history at the Catholic University, lamented: "Such bad faith, secret tyranny, double-dealing, and distortion of the plain truth was seldom witnessed in the Church, never in our American church history. I trust the right views will prevail at Rome. The Catholics of the English-speaking race have toiled for three centuries to break down the accusations of disloyalty to government, intolerance, and slavish submission to Rome. Though a minority, we have worked wonders and now here come the German medieval priest and members of an order whose powers for harm are great, to upset the whole. May they reap confusion!"

Hoping to calm the turbulence, Cardinal Gibbons invited Archbishop Ireland to explain his position at a meeting in St. Louis of all the archbishops of the thirteen American provinces. Ireland accepted the invitation, advising his brothers that he would discontinue the plan if they so advised him. None objected, and some congratulated the prelate from St. Paul, Archbishop John Williams of Boston wishing aloud that he could put the Faribault Plan into practice in his own see. Nevertheless, the acrimony continued, infecting even the laity. As might have been expected, the A.P.A. seized upon the Church's apparent disunity as the opportunity to attack Gibbons's friendship with Grover Cleveland. It declared: "When Cleveland became President, he had installed in the White House a wire to the cardinal's palace and he placed a Roman Catholic at the head of every division of the 1500 employees in the public departments." Cleveland replied: "I know Cardinal Gibbons and know him to be a good citizen and first-rate American and that his kindness of heart and toleration are in striking contrast to the fierce intolerance and vicious

malignity which disgrace some who claim to be Protestants. . . .
I know a number of members of the Catholic Church who were
employed in the public service during my administration and I
suppose there were many so employed. I should be ashamed of
my Presbyterianism if these declarations gave ground for offense."

Still gleeful at the spectacle of Catholic bishops exchanging
public insult, the A.P.A. maintained its attacks, and it was at this
time that they invented the "encyclical" in which Pope Leo XIII
was supposed to have ordered the massacre of all non-Catholics
in America. When this widely advertised bloodbath did not appear, the A.P.A. blamed the "encyclical" on the Jesuits!

Meanwhile, Monsignor O'Connell in Rome had advised Archbishop Ireland that attacks on him were multiplying throughout
Europe and that he had better come in person to the Eternal City
to defend himself. Ireland did go, and there he found the Jesuits
standing against him in a solid phalanx. He wrote: "They say all
round that in the memory of man no bishop has come to Rome
who was able to triumph against such fearful odds." In a more
playful mood, he also wrote: "All the papers owned or controlled
by Jesuits in Italy are writing against Dr. Bouquillon and myself. Miss Edes watches, and whenever she finds a number
steeped in gall, she puts it into Propaganda." Eventually, Ireland
submitted his own memorial to the Pope. He repeated all his old
arguments, but also advanced the contention that much of the opposition came from foreign Catholics seeking to cling to their
native tongue. "They thought it my intention to have [English]
applied everywhere to the detriment of their language, and they
sought an opportunity of ruining me at Rome." That chance, however, was ultimately missed. In April, 1892, Pope Leo spoke two
words about the Faribault Plan: *"Tolerari potest. It may be
tolerated."*

Jubilant, Ireland issued a characteristically indiscreet victory
statement: "The so-called Faribault Plan is now formally allowed
in spite of Germans and Jesuits." Stung, Corrigan and his supporters replied that the Pope had not approved the plan but had
condemned it. Weary of the contention, but still reluctant to
make a public statement, Cardinal Gibbons wrote to a friend: "It
neither condemns nor approves but tolerates; it enjoins a cessa-
tion of controversy and urges that children not attending paro-

chial schools be cared for." Nevertheless, the controversy did continue, and the dispute was not settled until Archbishop Francesco Satolli, the Papacy's first representative in the United States, arrived in this country.

The question of whether or not the Pope should have a personal emissary in the United States was one of the few issues on which the members of the American hierarchy were almost solidly agreed. They did not want one. From John Carroll to James Gibbons, with very few exceptions the Catholic prelates of this country feared that the presence of a Roman curial official on American soil would antagonize the non-Catholics of America, and perhaps also curtail their own freedom of action. For the United States to send a diplomatic representative to the Vatican, as was done in 1797 under John Adams, when John Sartori was named the first American consul to the Papal States, and as was continued until 1870 when the Papal States were absorbed in the new Kingdom of Italy, was always acceptable and even desirable to the American bishops. But for the Vatican to reciprocate, to enter into direct diplomatic relations with Washington, was always abhorrent to them. They thought that Protestants would regard a papal delegate as a violation of the American principle of separation of Church and State. Furthermore, they were against the presence of a Roman official whose office would become a sort of national grievance center. Being so readily available, disgruntled Catholics could easily lay before him trivial complaints which might hamper administration of their sees. Without a delegate, malcontents would have to take or send their cases to faraway Rome, where the mills of the Curia ground slowly and where the single tactic of delay had been refined into a science.

Actually, some of the American bishops did not even like the authority being exercised by Cardinal Gibbons. Although he was indeed a prince of the Church with the power to advise and elect Popes, he was actually no more than Metropolitan of Baltimore, the equal of his brother archbishops. He was not a primate, with jurisdiction over all metropolitans and bishops of the country. Yet, some bishops such as the acid Bernard McQuaid thought that Gibbons was acting like a primate. "Baltimore wants to set up as the American Vatican with its Curia under the management of the Sulpitians," McQuaid wrote to Bishop Gilmour in 1887. "Here in the North we don't propose to be tied to the chariot wheels of Baltimore." Or, to Corrigan: "This everlasting talk about the *head* of the *American Church* annoys me. The good little man can't see that he is making himself ridiculous."

Despite such protests, someone had to preside over the hierarchy whenever it assembled in council, and so, the Popes had usually delegated this jurisdiction to the occupant of the See of Baltimore acting as the Papal Delegate. However, this arrangement had never been satisfactory to either side, if only because Baltimore was not a primatial see and because the Papacy, naturally enough, wanted its own representative in the country. Thus, at the Third Plenary Council of 1884, Leo XIII questioned the bishops on the advisability of sending his own delegate. With the one notable exception of John Ireland, the bishops expressed themselves as being against it. Nevertheless, Leo persisted in his conviction, especially during the Cahenslyism controversy. At the time, he was much saddened by the dispute, and said so to Denis O'Connell, who reported him as saying: "The whole evil is in this, that they do not want to have a representative of me there. If they had one of my representatives there now who could speak to them of the sentiments of the Pope, this trouble would never have happened. But for some reason of jealousy among themselves they do not want to have my representative there, though I would only name someone acceptable to them all. Why don't they want the Pope there? If Christ were to return again to earth, you would all rejoice to give Him a welcome. Why not, then, receive His vicar? No, if I had my nuncio there, all would go better and you would be rendered independent at once of Propaganda and made dependent immediately on the Department of State."

O'Connell's reply skirted the real objection, the everdreaded imputation of "foreignness," and spoke only of the bishops' fear of a curtailment of their authority. "On the contrary," the Pope replied, and then, in a tone of sorrow and regret: "However, I respect their sentiments in the matter and I don't love them the less for it. Let us talk of something else."

After Cahenslyism came the schools squabble, deepening Leo's desire to have his own man in the United States. In 1892—the four-hundredth anniversary of Columbus's discovery of America —the World's Columbian Exposition was held in Chicago, and Leo seized this opportunity to send Satolli there as papal representative. When it was learned that Satolli had special faculties empowering him to settle disputes between priests and bishops, the suspicion grew that the delegation was to be permanent, and so, all of the American archbishops sent a letter to Rome opposing such an appointment. Meanwhile, Bishop John Lancaster Spalding made his own opposition public in unusually blunt terms, declaring:

There is, and has been for years, in the Catholic Church of the United States a deep feeling of opposition to the appointment of a permanent Delegate for this country. This opposition arises in part from a fixed and strongly-rooted desire, which exists throughout the whole English-speaking world, to manage as far as possible one's own affairs. The firm determination of the American people to permit no needless foreign interference is shown in the Monroe Doctrine, and it was more practically demonstrated by the overthrow and death of Maximillian. Catholics who live here, and who, wherever they were born, are true American citizens, feel the impulse of this desire and wish to manage as far as possible their own affairs. They are devoted to the Church; they recognize in the Pope Christ's Vicar, and gladly receive from him the doctrines of faith and morals; but for the rest, they ask him to interfere as little as may be.

Despite such protests, the Pope had made up his mind, and in May of 1893, he appointed Archbishop Satolli as the first Apostolic Delegate to the United States. Satolli had no diplomatic status, and his successors have had none to this day, but he had full authority to act as the Pope's intermediary in any further disputes among the hierarchy, and his decision would be final. Thus, he addressed himself immediately to the schools controversy, issuing a series of fourteen propositions which were generally favorable to Ireland's cause. Public education was not to be condemned, Catholics were to be permitted to go to public schools if there were no parochial schools available, sacraments were not to be forbidden to parents who sent their children to public schools and experiments such as the Faribault Plan were to be allowed. So the schools dispute ended in another Americanist victory, one signaled by Bishop McQuaid when he growled: "We are all in a nice pickle thanks to Leo XIII and his delegate. Just as our arduous work of forty-five years was beginning to bear fruit, they arbitrarily upset the whole. If an enemy had done this!"

McQuaid's fears were greatly exaggerated, however, if only because Archbishop Ireland's school scheme met but brief success. In 1892, the arrangement in both Minnesota towns fell through. In Stillwater, the board of education rejected the application of five nuns as teachers, and thus precluded the signing of a new contract. In Faribault, a new and unfriendly school board assigned two Protestant teachers to the former parochial school, an action which the pastor, Father James Conry, found unacceptable. Moreover, Father Conry apparently aggravated rising Protestant opposition to the plan when he ran for the board in place of a Catholic layman. Thus, the Faribault Plan, the one arrangement by which secular and religious education might have become reconciled, thus relieving Catholics from the burden of dual taxation while removing from American life the bitter and divisive feelings which the presence of the two systems continues to inspire, was wrecked on the reefs of Protestant suspicion and Catholic clumsiness.

For this hollow Americanist victory, John Ireland was to pay a prohibitive price. He had supported the Satolli mission to America, probably because he considered the archbishop a progressive and was confident of his support. Within two years of his arrival, however, the Apostolic Delegate's sympathy with the Americanists turned into hostility, probably after he learned "in pained surprise" that Gibbons had refused to publish the papal condemnation of the three American secret societies. For this, Satolli denounced Gibbons to Rome for "insubordination," and thereafter grew so disenchanted with the progressives that in 1895 he came out publicly against them and in support of the German-conservatives. When Satolli returned to Rome in 1896, after having already thrown his weight into the successful campaign to have O'Connell and Keane removed from their respective rectorships at the North American College and Catholic University, it appears that he also blocked Ireland's elevation to the College of Cardinals. Finally, Francesco Satolli was also suspected by the Americanists of having been instrumental in securing the condemnation of the so-called heresy of "Americanism"—the final round in the American Church's long internal struggle between progressives and conservatives.

Chapter XVIII

During the early years of the nineties it appeared that the future of the American Church belonged to the progressives. They had been everywhere successful, having triumphed on the issue of a Catholic University, in the Knights of Labor dispute, on Cahenslyism and, apparently, on the schools controversy.

When Archbishop Satolli lifted the excommunication against Dr. McGlynn, it seemed that the Americanist ascendancy was to be guaranteed by the powerful support of the Apostolic Delegate. In the McGlynn case, Satolli acted with admirable circumspection. Having studied the excommunicated priest's economic theories, he submitted them to a committee of professors at Catholic University, and after they had pronounced them harmless, he at once restored Dr. McGlynn to his priestly duties.

The decision delighted Cardinal Gibbons and so elated John Ireland that he could not refrain from gleefully predicting that when Archbishop Corrigan heard of it, "It will break the poor man's heart." At this time, Ireland was probably at the height of his success. Immensely popular in America, he was all but idolized by the Republicans of France, who were then, like the Archbishop of St. Paul, basking in papal approval. In 1892, Pope Leo had addressed an encyclical to the French hierarchy calling for the *Ralliement* or rallying of French Catholics to the standard of the Third Republic. Leo's letter had been a stunning blow to the Royalists, and they particularly resented it when Ireland, fluent in French and boastful in manner, came to Paris to lecture the French on the beauties of the American system of separation. "If the Pope in the future is to have any world-wide prestige," Ireland said, "he must deal as never before with America." Other

Americanizing bishops, equally bumptious, took up the theme that the eldest daughter of the Church, and all of Europe for that matter, must now "learn" from American Catholicism. Even the Apostolic Delegate appeared to have become infatuated with Americanism, declaring to a great gathering of lay Catholics: "Go forward, in one hand bearing the book of Christian truth and in the other the Constitution of the United States! Christian truth and American liberty will make you free, happy, and prosperous."

Ultimately, Satolli soured on Gibbons, Ireland, Keane and their associates, and as he did—not, of course, entirely because he did—the Americanist cause went into decline. They had made too many enemies: first, Corrigan, backed up by the irascible Mc-Quaid, supported by the indefatigable Miss Edes, flooding Rome with letters of grave warnings; next, the German bishops of America, still smarting over the Cahenslyism defeat; then, the Jesuits, also brooding and now studying Archbishop Ireland's unflattering remarks about religious orders; after them, the French Royalists and many European Catholics, enraged by the insolence of the upstart Americans, convinced that democracy was heresy; behind them, the Redemptorists, remembering that Father Isaac Hecker had been expelled from their order for an act of disobedience, and that the Paulist Society which he had founded was not only peculiarly American, but also, unlike most religious orders, required no solemn vows from its members; and, finally, Francesco Satolli. The array was impressive, and although Ireland and Keane were not alarmed, the watchful and perceptive Gibbons had begun to shake his head.

The first hint of danger was the condemnation in 1893 of the three secret societies, followed by the disaffection of the Apostolic Delegate. In the fall of the same year, Gibbons, Ireland and Keane participated in the World Parliament of Religions in Chicago, thus sharpening the suspicions of critics who thought that they were guilty of irenicism or indifferentism, the belief that one religion is as good as another and that there are many roads leading to heaven. During the following year, Ireland infuriated Corrigan and McQuaid by openly campaigning for Republican candidates for Congress, even "invading" New York City to attend political rallies. Corrigan's rage was choleric, and McQuaid ascended his cathedral pulpit in full episcopal regalia, brandishing his crozier as he denounced the St. Paul prelate for political activity, after which he proudly announced that he had personally found political entanglement so abhorrent in a clergyman that he had refrained from voting for the past twenty-seven years. Ireland, naturally enough, pounced on this indiscreet confession with the shout: "Any American who refuses to vote deserves disfranchisement or exile!"

Thus, the anti-Americanist fires were being constantly refueled, until, in 1895, another setback was experienced with the arrival in America of the long-awaited papal encyclical *Longinqua oceani*.* Leo had been long unhappy that the American Church continued to be attacked from without by nativist or bigoted organizations such as the A.P.A., and divided from within by feuding bishops, and in this letter he attempted to restore unity and harmony by analyzing both the strengths and weaknesses of American society. Generally, the tone was favorable to the Americanists, but one passage explicitly stated that it was wrong to think that the American principle of separation of Church and State was "the most desirable status of the Church or that it would be universally lawful or expedient for state and church to be, as in America, dissevered and divorced." As Cardinal Gibbons gloomily predicted, "That clause will of course be assailed by the Protestant press." It was, and it was also indicative of the rising suspicion in which the progressives were being held in the Vatican.

Four months later Gibbons again sailed for Rome to reverse the stand against the secret societies, only to find that his cherished friend and protégé, Monsignor Denis O'Connell, had been compelled to resign as rector of the North American College. In the following year, the Holy See peremptorily demanded the resignation of Bishop Keane as the rector of Catholic University. Both dismissals, for that, in effect, is what they were, were the cause of jubilation for the conservatives and gloom for the progressives. Keane's demotion, and subsequent planned humiliations in Rome, was particularly galling and even the sec-

* Encyclicals are known by their first two words, but *Longinqua oceani* is impossible to make meaningful in English. Literally, it means "wide expanse of ocean." Because of the peculiarity of Latin syntax, the phrase forms the first two words of a sentence which begins: "We traverse in spirit and thought the wide expanse of ocean. . . ."

ular press castigated this "high-handed interference in American affairs." Stories appeared suggesting that Gibbons, Ireland and Keane were to be condemned as "heretics" and Rome had to make a formal denial of the charges. In the meantime, the bishops continued their vendetta, exchanging their accusations and unpleasantries in a manner described by Cardinal Gibbons.

"Though more rare than other causes of enmity," the cardinal wrote in his book *The Ambassador of Christ,*

Religious hatred is proverbially intense and implacable. The contestants in the controversy confine themselves for a while to the subjects under consideration. After hotly arguing the question for a time, they gradually glide into personalities and impugn each other's motives. While both were probably within the line of orthodoxy, one took a conservative, the other a liberal view of the subject. The one leaned to the side of authority, the other contended for freedom. The conservative begins to call his liberal opponent a radical; the liberal stamps the conservative a reactionary. The conservative goes a step further and throws out thinly veiled hints about his antagonist's heterodoxy—a method of controversy which is aptly called "poisoning the wells." The liberal retaliates by calling his opponent a fossil. The respective allies of the two combatants take up the dispute and fan the flame. The arena of this war of words is still more widened when the newspapers plunge into the debate and sometimes, without caring to ascertain the original basis of the discussion, decide the dispute with oracular dogmatism according to their individual prejudices. Once the subject of discussion has drifted into the open sea of promiscuous controversy, it is as hard to lead it back to its first moorings as to gather up feathers scattered by the winds.

Unwittingly, Gibbons had set down what may be called "ground rules" for the transatlantic religious hostilities that were soon to be loosed within the Universal Church. Even as he wrote, in France a young professor, Abbé Felix Klein, was also writing, retranslating an American biography of Father Isaac Hecker. Written by Father Walter Elliott, *The Life of Father Isaac Thomas Hecker* had been a dull, overlong book, but in the hands of Abbé Klein it came alive. It was, in fact, a little too lively, especially the thirty-five-page preface in which Klein summed up Hecker's teachings and techniques. Published in 1897 as *La Vie de Père Hecker*, it was an immediate success, rapidly passing through seven printings.

In effect, Abbé Klein had out-Heckered Hecker. In his preface he had argued that if Catholicism were to adjust to the changing modern world, it must look to the dynamic democratic virtues preached by the founder of the Paulists. Delighted, the French Republicans seized upon the book as a charter for the Third Republic's new approach to the Church. Chagrined, the Royalists denounced it as a new and false theological doctrine, a heresy, to which they gave the name of "Americanism." They accused Father Hecker of a form of Protestant "private judgment," and as proof they quoted his remark that "there is too much waiting upon the actions of others; the layman waits for the priest, the priest for the bishop, and the bishop for the Pope, while the Holy Ghost sends down to all the reproof that He is prompting each one and no one moves for Him." This, the enemies of so-called Americanism charged, was an overreliance of the individual soul upon private guidance from the Holy Spirit.

Hecker, or Americanism, also professed a faith in dynamism, they said, a preference for the active over the passive virtues, for the doer over the thinker, the active over the contemplative —and this was also unorthodox. After all, had not Jesus Christ said: "Martha, Martha, thou art careful, and art troubled about many things," thus reproving the "activist" in favor of Mary, the passive contemplative, who "hath chosen the best part." It was also remembered of Hecker that his Paulists took no vows, and any reply that this was in the interests of greater freedom in their work, only brought the countercharge that Hecker's cry for "new methods" and "newly-equipped men" was proof that Americanism believed in altering Church doctrine and discipline in order to gain converts.

This, then, was "Americanism," a phantom heresy held or preached by no one in the United States, one which had nothing to do with the United States but which was rather a distinctly French controversy—indeed, a political rather than a religious dispute—over the exaggerations in Abbé Klein's preface. Nevertheless, the heresy-hunters were making the charge stick throughout Europe. Even Cardinal Gibbons was under attack there. In France, the newspaper *L'Éclair* claimed that the "Americanizer

party" was plotting to make Gibbons the next Pope, and the
cardinal at Baltimore wryly observed to a friend: "I am told that
a Paris newspaper, *La Vérité* [save the mark] says that I am
favoring Freemasonry, and the article is copied in a Canadian
paper." Ridiculous as Americanism may now appear, it was to
become worse after Abbé Charles Maignen, a rabid Royalist,
published a book called *Studies on Americanism: Father Hecker,
Is He a Saint?* Maignen's book was a vicious, slashing attack on
Klein, Hecker and the American republic itself. He did not quote
Father Elliott's life of Hecker but from Klein's exaggerated preface, and he used every opportunity to distort or misrepresent
even this. Worse, his book carried an imprimatur granted by the
Pope's official censor. Unable to obtain approval from the cardinal of Paris, he had secured it from the unsuspecting Alberto
Lepidi, master of the Sacred Palace at the Vatican, and this seeming papal approbation disturbed the Americanists even more
than the book's malevolent contents. Gibbons wrote to O'Connell, still in Rome: "I regard the attacks of Protestants as mild
compared with the unprincipled course of these so-called
Catholics."

Now the controversy had gone to Rome, where Satolli had
been busily planting distrust of the American hierarchy, and
where the Spanish-American War just begun had aggravated
anti-American sentiment. Most of the older countries of Europe
had been angered when the upstart American republic disman-
tled the ancient Spanish Empire, and Rome was particularly unhappy to see this brash young Protestant nation enriching
herself at the expense of one of her oldest and most loyal daughters. Some Vatican officials thought the American bishops had
not lifted a finger to prevent it. In fact, John Ireland had vainly
believed he could stop it, and Gibbons had preached against it
in his cathedral. Nevertheless, the war had erupted, and it was
just one more round to fire at Americanism.

This animosity shook the Americanists as much as the out-
cries of the professional heresy-hunters, and many of them
thought they could perceive a kind of Old World petulance behind the headlines which, in France, Italy, Germany, Switzerland
and the Low Countries, were heralding the impending condemnation of Gibbons, Ireland, Keane and the Paulist Fathers.

This was also at the back of Cardinal Gibbons's mind when he wrote a long and impassioned letter of protest to his friend, Cardinal Rampolla, the Vatican Secretary of State. After denouncing Maignen's book for its "perverse insinuations" against the American hierarchy and insisting that "you have not in the whole world an episcopate, a clergy, and believers more fundamentally Catholics" than in the United States, he deplored the imprimatur given to the work as making it seem that it was the Pope, not Maignen, who was bringing the charge of a heretical "Americanism" against the Catholics of this country. "And I fear," he declared, "that among our political men and others the one meaning given to it will be a more or less hidden attack against the United States and a kind of revenge for Spain beaten in war by us."

It was fortunate that the cardinal's letter arrived in Vatican City when it did, and that John Ireland, with characteristic directness, had set sail for Rome to defend himself and his brother bishops, for Leo XIII had already formed a commission of cardinals to draft an encyclical on the subject. Heading this body were Cardinal Mazzella, a Jesuit and the implacable enemy of things American, and Francesco Satolli, now a cardinal and as anti-American as ever. Even as Gibbons's letter arrived, the Congregation of the Index laid a condemnation of the French translation of Hecker's life on the Pope's desk. With this, Leo drew back. To put Abbé Klein's book on the Index would be, in effect, to put the American bishops to the ban. "No," the Pope was reported as saying, "I can do no more against these Americans. Now I reserve the entire affair to myself. I permit no more examinations of the book or anything else. I will arrange all myself with an encyclical."

Apparently, Leo rewrote the letter prepared for him by the Mazzella-Satolli commission, softening it, toning it down. It was a strange encyclical, one of the most unusual in the long history of the papacy, and certainly the most ambiguous written by Leo in his twenty-five years as Pope, the longest reign ever. Signed January 22, 1899, called *Testem Benevolentiae* (Proof of Our Love), it was addressed to "Our Beloved Son, James Cardinal Gibbons, Cardinal Priest of the Title Sancta Maria Beyond the Tiber, Archbishop of Baltimore." In it, the only allusion to the

Abbé Klein's book was that a controversy had arisen over it. Thereafter, Leo went on to censure the belief that Christian doctrine must be softened in order to gain converts, that the natural and active virtues were superior to the supernatural and passive, that spiritual direction was not necessary, that vows were not relevant to the modern world and that the Church's authority and discipline must be adapted to modern living.

Throughout the letter, the Pope was careful to point out that the term "Americanism" was not to reflect upon the honor of the people of the United States or the laws and customs that prevailed there, using it only to describe the beliefs previously outlined. Furthermore, he said that he was sure the American bishops would reject and condemn this "Americanism."

Nowhere in his encyclical did the Pope claim that these errors were held by anyone in the United States, that they were held by Hecker or even attributed to him by the Abbé Klein. Thus, *Testem Benevolentiae* was an ecclesiastical thunderbolt hurled at a shadow. Historians still find it difficult to understand why it was written at all, unless Leo did actually fear that American Catholics might eventually come to entertain convictions which conservative French Catholics were now accusing them of holding. Here, indeed, was a phantom heresy; here was a real novelty in Catholic history: a heresy without a heresiarch. Arianism had had its Arius, Nestorianism its Nestor, Protestantism its Luther and Calvin and Knox and a host of others, but Americanism had who?

No one, it appears, but its accusers. And yet, until his dying day in 1903 at the age of ninety-three, Leo XIII, one of the most eminent statesmen and scholars to sit in the Chair of Peter, still appears to have believed that Hecker *might* have held it. In 1900, when Bishop John Lancaster Spalding met Leo in an audience, the Pope questioned him about Americanism. Spalding at once replied that no such heresy had ever been taught in the United States.

"That is what many American bishops have written to me," Leo was quoted as saying, "but there was that poor Hecker. He taught the guidance of the Holy Spirit without the Sacraments."

"Holy Father," Spalding remonstrated, "I knew Father Hecker well and immediately, and he was a holy, disinterested, zealous and enlightened priest. I am certain he never believed or taught what they accused him of."

Still apparently unconvinced, Pope Leo continued to criticize Hecker, until Spalding burst out bluntly:

"Holy Father, did you know Hecker?"

"No, I did not know him."

"Well then, I did," Spalding said, "and a better Catholic we've never had."

Still, the Americanism charge had been made and it seemed to stick, much to the indignation of Archbishop Ireland, who was one of those who wrote to Pope Leo to disclaim knowledge of any such beliefs in America. Gibbons also wrote, saying: "This extravagant and absurd doctrine as I would willingly call it, this Americanism as they have chosen to call it, has nothing in common with the views, the aspirations, the doctrines and conduct of Americans. I do not think that in the whole country could be found a single priest or bishop or even a well-instructed layman who has ever put forward such an extravagance. No, this is not and never has been and never will be our Americanism. I am deeply grateful to your Holiness for having yourself made this distinction in your apostolic letter."

Such disclaimers, however, were at least offset by letters from conservatives. Archbishop Corrigan wrote to congratulate both himself and the Holy Father for having saved the American Church from the dangers of Americanism and to imply that the phantom heresy had indeed been held by many Catholics. Apparently, Corrigan went so far as to sign the names of his suffragan bishops to the epistle, thus giving it a sham aspect of solidarity. The German bishops of the Province of Milwaukee also saluted Leo for his "condemnation" and maintained that those who denied having held the heresy were dishonest.

Thus, the tiresome war of words continued, until Cardinal Gibbons put an end to it at the archbishops meeting in October, 1899, when he cast the tie-breaking vote to defeat a resolution offered by Ireland and Archbishop John Kain of St. Louis. This was to ask the entire hierarchy two questions: Were the errors held in their dioceses, and if so, where and by whom? Gibbons's motive in rejecting the proposition was to allow the entire "Americanism" affair to die the death it deserved.

Eventually, it did. Most of the furor seemed to have taken place in episcopal palaces. The secular press gave *Testem Benevolentiae* the scantiest coverage, while only the conservative wing of the Catholic press treated it as important, hailing the encyclical as a defeat for the Americanists and an actual condemnation of Archbishop Ireland. The Catholic laity hardly knew of it, either through lack of understanding or sheer indifference to what seemed at best a boring subject. Nevertheless, the American Church had been humiliated. Try as they might, the Americanists could not efface a stigma that has remained to this day. As affectionate and conciliatory as Leo's language may have been, his letter forced the progressives among the American clergy to take refuge in a kind of intellectual underground from which they are only now emerging. Moreover, "Americanism" was taken as a forerunner of the true heresy of Modernism, a belief condemned in 1907 by Pius X. Modernism, which apparently had been infiltrating the universal Church since the Reformation, denied dogma, the efficacy of the sacraments and the authority of Scripture. Although it was never a problem in the United States, the intellectual reign of terror which succeeded its condemnation spread to this country and deepened the caution of bishops already made timid by publication of *Testem Benevolentiae.*

In the end, then, it may be said that, if the Americanists were never personally defeated in theological or ecclesiastical battle, the cause for which they struggled did not succeed. Instead, the conservatism and caution characteristic of American prelates up to the present day seems to have prevailed. Yet, they were magnificent churchmen, whose like has never been seen since, and Father Andrew Greeley has given them a stirring epitaph:

There have been great bishops in the twentieth century, many of them more democratic in their personal behavior and in the governance of their dioceses than was John Ireland, who for all his democratic beliefs was quite a bit of an autocrat within the boundaries of St. Paul. There have also been some bishops whose intellectual and scholarly capacities certainly excelled those of all the Americanists save perhaps Lancaster Spalding. There have been bishops who have been far better informed on social questions and at least as concerned about social problems as were the Americanists. What the twentieth century has failed to produce in church leadership is not democratic inclinations, social concern, or intellectual competence. All of these have existed and at least on occasion in abundance. What is missing is the style, the flair, the charismatic enthusiasm which could move the minds and hearts of men as they have not seemed to have been moved in the years since 1900. It can be argued that the Americanists were ahead of their time, that they would have been giants of the Second Vatican Council if they had lived to attend it. This argument is probably quite correct, but where the American Church might be today if their intuitions, which antedated the Vatican Council by seven decades, had been given an opportunity to develop and flourish is a question that points up one of the great tragedies of ecclesiastical history. It isn't wise to lament too long about those things that might have been; but a great Catholic University, a *modus vivendi* with the public schools, a solution to the ethnic problem, a more intense commitment to questions of social justice, and more vigorous experimentation with implications of American democracy for the life of the Church could have given to the vigorous American Church a depth, a richness which it does not have and which lack is increasingly becoming a serious defect.

The odds, however, were against the Americanists. They had strong and at times unscrupulous opponents within the American Church. The Roman officials did not understand the Church in the United States and were growing more deeply suspicious of it. The church universal was still in an era when problems were to be treated by condemning evil rather than by attempting to understand its occasions and change evil to error. The American Protestants were not yet ready to accept Catholics as full-fledged partners in a national enterprise. The enthusiasm and the optimism of the Americanists must in that respect be judged as a mistake. Yet one cannot help but wish that they had been right.

Chapter XIX

The decade 1900–1910 which succeeded the final failure of the Americanist attempt to harmonize Catholicism with American life appears to have been one of retrenchment significant of the spirit of conservatism which had emerged from the struggle victorious.

True enough, John Keane had been elevated to the rank of archbishop, and Denis O'Connell was made the rector of Catholic University, but John Ireland was never to wear the cardinal's red hat which he desired with such unbecoming ardor, and in American public life Catholics were to hold positions of influence or authority which, in proportion to their numbers, could hardly have been fewer and farther between. Intellectually, Catholics also were remiss, compelling the British observer D. W. Brogan to remark: "In no Western society is the intellectual prestige of Catholicism lower than in the country where, in such respects as wealth, numbers, and strength of organization it is so powerful."

The Catholic laity was an anonymous, amorphous mass. Ireland and Gibbons might sing the praises of the American way of life from sunup to sundown, but the fact is that it was the conservative prelates who had the layman's ear. They had convinced them of the "contaminations" of "pagan" America, and had virtually herded them into a mental ghetto from which they emerged only for football games and the Fourth of July. Politically, Catholics were extremely active in the cities, and sometimes active on a state level in those regions where they were numerous, but they seldom entered the national arena. In the field of social justice they were a cipher. And this, again, is because the layman had almost no standing. Having been indoctrinated with the siege mentality characteristic of the Council of Trent, they regarded themselves, to extend the military metaphor, as the ordinary soldiery, while the priests were the captains, the bishops were the colonels and the archbishops were generals. Generally speaking, for a layman actually to *do* anything without orders was not only unthinkable but perhaps even insubordinate. And this habit of mind, it seems, is directly attributable to the fact that the bishops actually did not trust the laymen.

Even before the Civil War, Orestes Brownson had been urging that the Catholic laity be given a larger role in the life of the Church, calling for a Congress of Catholic Laymen which would "unite Catholics, giving them an opportunity to see and know one another, of proclaiming to the world that the laity are not priest-ridden . . ." Following the war, a handful of prominent Catholic laymen pursued the idea, gaining the support of John Ireland and a few other bishops. Eventually, Cardinal Gibbons was persuaded to give his reluctant approval to the proposal, and the first Catholic Lay Congress was scheduled for Baltimore on November 11-12, 1889.

Before it convened, however, the bishops took steps to disarm it of any explosive potential. First, an episcopal commission created to "work with the laymen" accepted the recommendation of Bishop Foley of Detroit that all papers to be read at the gathering be submitted beforehand to a commission. Ostensibly, this was to facilitate the printing and distribution of the speeches, but as Bishop Foley himself said: "That was the reason I assigned but in my own mind was the idea that we should get hold of all the papers and have a committee of bishops to be here at that time and pass upon the character of the papers." A second defusing device came from Archbishop Ryan of Philadelphia, who wrote to Gibbons: "Only the safest men should be selected to write, and they had better be left entirely free, after some preliminary advice." Finally, invitations to the Congress were issued by the bishops only, and thus, "protected from the unexpected or unacceptable," the gathering was held.

It attracted fifteen hundred lay delegates, including Negroes and Indians, and was productive of some of the most advanced Catholic social thinking of the day—particularly on the rights of labor and the evils of capitalism—but it was also the high-water mark of enthusiasm for lay activity. A second convention of laymen was held at the Columbian Catholic Congress of 1893, during which Leo's great encyclical *Rerum Novarum* was hailed as a blueprint for Catholic social action, but by then the movement had lost its vigor. What has been called the lay renaissance was an ephemeral reawakening indeed. By the end of the century the Catholic laity was once again an intellectual hewer of wood and drawer of water, so much so that the attempt to organize all lay societies and sodalities into a single omnibus Federation of Catholic Societies ended up with the bishops at the controls and the priests patrolling the aisles as conductors. Once again, the layman was only a passenger, and with the exception of Ireland and perhaps a few others, it is difficult to avoid the conclusion that the hierarchy—including Cardinal Gibbons—wished no other status for him.

Meanwhile, the Spanish-American War and the annexation of the Philippines had presented the American Church with a set of new problems. From the outset of the agitation for war with Spain, the American hierarchy had been against such a policy and some had worked actively to prevent it. Rome had requested Archbishop Ireland to do what he could with President McKinley, while it made its own behind-the-scenes effort to discourage the war party in Spain. Because of diplomatic blunders, the shameless war-mongering of the Hearst and Pulitzer newspapers, the romantic imperialism of influential Americans such as Theodore Roosevelt, captivated by the imperialist theories of Alfred Thayer Mahan, all attempts to head off the struggle failed—and the United States went ahead with what one angry French writer called "this atrocious American filibuster against a valiant people exhausted by centuries of glory." Whatever her motives, America did humble Spain, win independence for Cuba, and, most significant step of all, annex the Philippines. This act, together with the proclamation of the Open Door policy in China, led directly to Pearl Harbor and American participation in World War II. It made the United States an imperialist nation and a Far Eastern power, a fact which Cardinal Gibbons understood clearly enough when, in response to President McKinley's request for his opinion on holding the Philippines, he replied: "Mr. President, it would be a good thing for the Catholic Church but, I fear, a bad one for the United States."

The Spanish-American War and the so-called Philippine Insurrection which succeeded it were not, as might have been expected, the occasion of a resurrection of the anti-Catholic spirit in America. Even though both enemies were Catholics, and many Americans believed that the Spaniard was as effete as they imagined him to be because of his enervating faith, the instant loyalty of Catholics rallying to the colors once again obviated all such charges. If most of the hierarchy had not approved the war, they took no open stand against it, and Cardinal Gibbons was successful in raising the number of Catholic chaplaincies in the armed forces. Gibbons was also instrumental in solving the vexatious problem of the "Friar Lands" in the Philippines.

The Filipinos, of course, were Catholics, having been evangelized by Spanish friars—Augustinian, Dominican and Franciscan —since the early days of "discovery" of the islands. As early as 1585—220 years before Baltimore became a province—Manila was elevated to the rank of an archdiocese. Throughout the centuries, the friars acquired great holdings in land, all of which were seized by Filipino revolutionaries during the rising of 1896. When Theodore Roosevelt entered the White House upon the assassination of McKinley, he recognized at once that settlement of the friars' claim to their lands was essential to peace in the islands. So he sent William Howard Taft to Rome to negotiate terms of compensation for the dispossessed friars. Throughout this delicate affair, the Pope acted as mediator while Cardinal Gibbons acted as a liaison between Roosevelt and Taft and the Holy See. In the end, the United States paid seven million dollars for the Friar Lands, which it then sold to Filipinos on easy terms.

Annexation of the Philippines brought another problem to the American Church. With the departure of Spanish priests (Spain apparently had not trained up a native clergy), most of the Catholic Filipinos were left without clerical care and at the mercy of a swarm of proselytizing Protestant ministers following in the track of the victorious American Army. Indeed, one of the reasons advanced for annexing the Philippines had been the "conversion" of the Filipinos to "Christianity."

Thus, the Holy See was eager for the American Church to take up the labor abandoned by the Spanish Church. At first, the response to this appeal was hardly spectacular, as may be judged by this excerpt from the *American Ecclesiastical Review:* "There was a demand for the American priests to go to the Philippines to take the place of the Spanish friars who were withdrawn. The bishops made a quest everywhere, in the religious orders as well as among the diocesan priests, for some American priests to replace the Spaniards. A few were found in Philadelphia to accompany Bishop Dougherty, and with these the list begins and ends." Eventually, missionaries from both Europe and the United States established themselves in the islands, and the Filipinos themselves were encouraged to become priests and nuns. Gradually, the ancient faith was restored and strengthened, so that on July 4, 1946, when the Philippines received their independence, about 90 per cent of the population was again Catholic.

Similar missions went to Puerto Rico and Guam, also ceded to the United States by Spain, as well as to the Hawaiian Islands, which had been annexed in 1898 through American diplomatic intrigue backed up by the threat of naval power. Thus, the imperialist thrust which had brought the United States out of its long history of isolation and into the world arena had been weighted with significance and responsibility for American Catholicism as with no other religion in the country. Meanwhile, the American Church had to cope with the continuing problem of Americanizing the immigrants, this time with the Italians and the Slavs. Once again, the language barrier was the greatest problem, and the ordinaries in whose sees these people concentrated were compelled to invite priests who spoke Italian or any of the various Slavic languages to come to these shores to minister to them. Although the Italians seemed to adapt very rapidly to American Catholicism, becoming assimilated with what may be described as only a minimal protest against Irish domination, some of the Slavs were not so malleable. Like the Germans before them, they appealed to Rome for ethnic dioceses and bishops, and after this request was denied, a few of them formed their own schismatic Polish or Lithuanian national churches which exist to this day. Actually, the attachment of the Poles to the Polish language was even more difficult to discourage than the Germans' preference for German, and as late as 1947 Bishop (later Cardinal) John O'Hara of Buffalo had to caution some of the teaching nuns of his heavily Polish diocese against giving instructions in that language.

Another problem posed by the "new" immigration was that of the Eastern or Oriental Catholics. These are the Byzantine Catholics or the Ukrainian Greek Catholics who are also known as the "Uniate" churches because of their union with Rome. Most of them resent the "Uniate" term, however, as a derisive nickname pinned upon them by their opponents of the Russian or Greek Orthodox Churches who sought to impose their religion upon them. In language and in ritual, the Eastern Catholics are different from the Roman Catholics. Doctrinally, there is no difference, and on the great question of allegiance to the Pope—the stumbling block which caused the Orthodox Church to break away into schism—the Eastern Catholics accept papal supremacy. Some of their priests, however, are allowed to marry *prior* to ordination, and for a time the existence of this married clergy was a source of scandal to the Catholics of America. This problem was apparently solved when the Holy See forbade more married clergymen to migrate to the United States. No attempt was made, nor has any been made since, to compel them to accept the Latin Rite of the dominant Roman Catholicism. In 1913, the diocese of the Byzantine Catholic rite was established in Philadelphia, and in 1924 a similar see for Ukrainian Greek Catholics was set up at Pittsburgh. Since then, one more Byzantine diocese was created at Passaic, New Jersey, and two more Ukrainian Greek sees at Chicago and Stamford, Connecticut. In all, in 1968 there were more than 600,000 Byzantine and Ukrainian Greek Catholics in the United States.

With these provisions, with more and more new dioceses being created throughout the country, and with total Catholic population for 1900 standing at 10,774,000, it was obvious that the American Church was approaching maturity. In 1903, upon the death of Pope Leo XIII, she moved closer to world recognition because of the influential part played by Cardinal Gibbons at the conclave to elect Leo's successor.

Gibbons was not himself a *papabile* or candidate, even though pre-conclave speculation had mentioned him. Although this in itself was a tribute to the young American Church, Gibbons was practical enough to realize that any talk of an American Pope was absurdity, and he was wise enough to entertain no ambitions to succeed Leo as "the lonely prisoner of the Vatican." Cardinal Rampolla was the leading choice. The late Pope's secretary of state, Rampolla has been described as "a giant in physique and intellect, a holy man with the saddest face that one could look upon." On the first ballot, Rampolla received 24 votes and all others 38. On the second, he picked up more and his election on the next vote seemed so certain that Gibbons, who was seated on his right, turned to congratulate him. Then, to the consternation of the entire conclave, Cardinal Puzyna of Cracow arose to pronounce the solemn veto of Emperor Franz Josef of Austria against the election of Rampolla. Franz Josef found the former secretary of state *persona non grata* because of his friendship for his enemy, France.

Outraged by what they considered unwarranted state interference in church affairs, Rampolla and the other red-robed cardinals assembled in the Sistine Chapel protested vigorously. But the Austrian emperor refused to withdraw his veto, an ancient right held by custom by Austria, France and Spain. It was the last time such a right was to be exercised, but Franz Josef nevertheless ruined Rampolla's chances. Now the tide began to swing toward Giuseppe Sarto, the humble postman's son who had risen to the rank of Patriarch of Venice. Well known for his charities, and for the invincible modesty which had led him to purchase a round-trip ticket to the conclave, Sarto had already received five votes on the first ballot. "The cardinals are amusing themselves at my expense," he had said nervously, but now, as his undesired candidacy began to gather momentum, Giuseppe Sarto began to weep. "I beseech you to forget my name," he pleaded, and when the haughty Cardinal Lecot of France discovered that he did not speak French and remarked, "Your Eminence will never be Pope if you do not speak French," Sarto exclaimed: "Thank God!"

With Rampolla out of the running and Sarto still adamant, the cardinals were confused. They were also getting restive at being so long confined to the uncomfortable little cells in which they were compelled to live until they named a new Pope. At this juncture, Gibbons made his influence felt. He alone among the cardinals still believed that Sarto could be elected. Convinced that the humble patriarch was the choice of the Holy Spirit, Gibbons consulted with Cardinal Satolli, the former Apostolic Delegate to the United States. Satolli was convinced that it was useless to expostulate with Sarto. Gibbons did not agree. "Cardinal Sarto must be *made* to accept," he said, and persuaded Satolli to speak to the reluctant candidate again. "Impress upon him," he said, "with all the force of the eloquence which you possess that he is the choice of his colleagues, that God's will is being manifest through them, that he must accept the sacrifice, take up the burden, and God will give him the necessary strength to guide the bark of Peter."

Satolli did persuade Sarto to accept, and when he was elected on the seventh ballot and all of the red velvet canopies but the one over Sarto's throne were lowered in his honor, he turned pale and nearly fainted. Thus, through the determination of the lone American cardinal at the conclave, Giuseppe Sarto began his eventful reign as Pope Pius X.

Pius's admiration for the American hierarchy never flagged, and in 1908, in the apostolic constitution called *Sapienti consilio* by which he reorganized the Roman Curia, he removed the American Church from the jurisdiction of the Sacred Congregation of Propaganda and placed it under the general jurisdiction of the Church. With this, the United States ceased to be a mission country. The American Church had reached full maturity. One year later, a second manifestation of maturity, a sufficiency of priests so large that some of them could be spared for the foreign missions, was made evident when St. Mary's Mission House in Techny, Illinois, began training young men for this purpose. In 1911, the archbishops of the United States at their annual meeting established the Catholic Foreign Mission Society of America, which was approved that same year by Pius X. Called Maryknoll after the hilltop in Ossining, New York, where the seminary is located, the society sent out its first missioners in 1918 when four young priests departed for China, and now has close to a thousand in the field, together with more than sixteen hundred Maryknoll nuns. Joined by foreign missioners from the other orders and societies, the American Church, which once depended on France, Ireland and Germany for its priests and upon Europe in general for some of its finances, now sends close to ten thousand priests and perhaps twice as many sisters and brothers to other lands and has become the chief supplier of funds for the Universal Church.

Meanwhile, missionary work at home also was pursued. On October 18, 1905, Father Francis Clement Kelley, later Bishop of Oklahoma City and Tulsa, founded the Catholic Church Extension Society, an agency devoted to help Catholics in isolated areas, particularly in the Southwest. Through the years, the society helped to build many little churches for those Catholics stranded in a Protestant sea, even constructing railroad chapels and later automotive chapels so that the Mass and the Sacraments might be brought to them. Concurrently, missionary work was continued among the American Indians, especially by the religious orders, so that at this writing more than a third of the Indians are Catholic. Missions to the black people of America, however, showed no corresponding prosperity, and the Catholic rate among Negroes remained less than 1 per cent.

Nevertheless, the first decade of the new century ended with a mature and vigorous church claiming 14,618,000 baptized Catholics and 17,000 priests. During the decade no less than three thousand new churches had been built. Once the tiniest fraction of the population, the Catholics now numbered about 16 per cent of the total. Moreover, the Church once again had grown faster than the country. In 1900 there had been 10,774,000 out of a total U.S. population of 75,994,000, or one Catholic for roughly every 7.5 Americans, but in 1910 there were 14,618,000 out of a total of 91,972,000, or one Catholic for every 6.5 Americans. Vigorous, numerous, seemingly powerful because of her exaggerated political influence, apparently wealthy because of her vast network of churches, schools, hospitals, orphanages, convents, monasteries and other institutional buildings, the American Church was still not quite acceptably "American" to some of her critics. In 1909 two large synods of both the Lutheran and Baptist faiths publicly declared that no Catholic should be trusted to hold public office. Once again the American hierarchy found itself obliged to defend the loyalty of Catholics, and Cardinal Gibbons had to make public allusion to the constitutional declaration which says: "No religious test shall ever be required as a qualification to any office of public trust under the United States." The two synods, he said, apparently wished to amend this with a clause which would read: "Provided, of course, that this provision be not understood to apply to Roman Catholics."

After nearly three centuries, No-Popery apparently was still alive in American life. It would remain for the decade which witnessed America's entry into World War I and into international life for a few more scales to be sent flying from the hide of that apparently imperishable monster.

Chapter XX

Three years after Pope Pius X had certified the maturity of the Catholic Church in America, he gave further recognition to it by raising three American citizens to the rank of cardinal.

The new princes of the Church were Archbishop William O'Connell of Boston, Archbishop John Farley of New York and Archbishop Diomede Falconio, an Italian-born Franciscan who had been ordained in Buffalo and became a naturalized American citizen while serving as president of St. Bonaventure College in Olean, New York. Falconio had also been Apostolic Delegate to America. To his death, he continued to cherish his American citizenship. Thus, with the aging but still vigorous Gibbons, the United States now boasted four cardinals, a total exceeded only by Italy and France.

Indeed, at the beginning of the second decade of the twentieth century, it appeared that continuing immigration together with a prolific birth rate among the laity would send the Catholic population soaring well over the twenty-million mark, thus rivaling some of the older European nations which had been Catholic since the days of the Roman Empire. But then the military catastrophe now known as World War I erupted, shutting off the flow of immigration and even inducing many of those already here to return to their homeland for war duty. As a result, Catholic population in 1920 stood at 17,885,000, with some 21,600 priests. In the meantime, the World War shocked the American people as had no event since the firing on Fort Sumter which triggered the Civil War. Stunned and horrified, the Americans were also nevertheless determined to stay strictly neutral, an attitude for which President Woodrow Wilson appealed when he told the nation: "We must be impartial in thought as well as in action, must put a curb upon our sentiments."

Inevitably, such a counsel of perfection turned out to be impossible. Old-line Yankees remembered their British blood and sympathized openly with England, those of German origin insisted that Germany must have her place in the sun, and the Irish, aware that Albion's distress is Erin's opportunity, prayed to see Britain humbled. In this, the Catholics were no different from their Protestant countrymen, with the exception that most of the anti-British Irish were Catholics. Eventually, the sinking of the *Lusitania*, unrestricted German submarine warfare and the clear superiority of the British propaganda effort in the United States would combine to make the pro-German attitude unpopular. And in the meantime, the American Church itself, or at least some members of the hierarchy, was distracted by the anti-Catholic persecution begun in Mexico.

Since 1857, the Mexican government had placed severe restrictions on the Catholic Church. Even though two priests had led the revolt which overthrew the Spanish, Mexican governments had been consistently anticlerical. In 1914, during a cycle of revolution and counterrevolution, President Wilson intervened in Mexican affairs by temporarily seizing the port of Vera Cruz. By this action, he effectively insured the triumph of the rebel Venustiano Carranza, who turned to active persecution of the Church. Religious orders were suppressed, religious property confiscated, religious demonstrations forbidden and priests and bishops driven from the country. With all seminaries seized and all seminarians impressed into the army, the exiled bishops became alarmed for the future of the Mexican clergy, and they appealed to their American brethren for help. Accordingly, the Americans set up a seminary in a building in Castroville, Texas. It remained open for about three years, training a hundred priests to keep the faith alive south of the border. In the meantime, attempts were made to arouse American public opinion against the brutalities, which sometimes included the rape and murder of nuns, regularly occurring in Mexico.

The Spanish-speaking Archbishop James Blenk of New Orleans, together with Father Francis Kelley, the founder of the Extension Society, persuaded Theodore Roosevelt to write a syndi-

cated column based upon affidavits which they had taken from
exiled Mexican priests and bishops in Cuba. Next, Father Kelley
called upon President Wilson in the White House, asking him,
not for intervention, but to direct a few words of restraint toward
Mexico City. According to Kelley, Wilson replied: "I have no
doubt but that the terrible things you mention have happened
during the Mexican revolution. But terrible things happened
also during the French revolution, perhaps more terrible things
than have happened in Mexico. Nevertheless, out of that French
revolution came the liberal ideas which have since dominated in
so many countries, including our own. I hope that out of the
bloodletting in Mexico some such good yet may come."

Having thus instructed his caller in the benefits which must
perforce accrue to mankind out of the systematic robbery, murder, torture and rape of people holding a proscribed religious
conviction, the professor in politics suggested that Father Kelley
visit Secretary of State William Jennings Bryan, who expressed
his deepest sympathy. Obviously, the Wilson administration was
committed to supporting the revolutionaries. All efforts of Catholic Americans to succor their coreligionists across the border
were to prove fruitless, as they were to prove once again in
1924, when the fiercest persecution of all was begun by President
Plutarco Calles. In this systematic pogrom, all public worship
came to an end in Mexico and priests were methodically hunted
down and executed like outlaws. It was of this travail which
Graham Greene wrote in his famous novel *The Power and the
Glory*. Generally, however, the world press ignored the Calles
persecution in a "conspiracy of silence" which the American
hierarchy and Pope after Pope were powerless to break. Finally,
in 1937, under President Cárdenas, the persecution was relaxed,
and the Mexican Church has so far regained its liberty that a
practicing Catholic was elected president in 1964. Moreover,
the Mexican clergy which the generosity of the American Church
helped to preserve is now vigorous enough to send its own missionaries to the Far East.

In the meantime, in 1916, while the American Church pressed
its efforts to succor its persecuted sister south of the Rio Grande,
it was momentarily stunned by perhaps the most bizarre—and
sinister—event in its history: the "poisoned banquet" for George

William Mundelein, the new Archbishop of Chicago. Actually, the banquet was a welcome for the new archbishop, who had been the auxiliary bishop of Brooklyn. In all three hundred dignitaries—the governor of Illinois, members of the legislature, more than thirty bishops, the presidents of three universities, executives from forty railroads, judges, civic leaders and the heads of all the great corporations of Chicago—attended the affair, held in the Cathedral Hall of the University Club. No more distinguished gathering had ever assembled in America's second city. After the soup, while the second course was being served, it became evident that many of the diners were acutely ill. Men with pale faces contorted with pain were hurrying or staggering to the door. Some sank to their knees. Physicians present at the banquet hastened to their side, helping them to bedrooms. One of the doctors rushed a vial of the soup to a laboratory asking for an immediate test. When the report came back, it stated that the soup had been poisoned with arsenic.

Fortunately for the guests, the dose had not been quite as lethal as the poisoner intended. That morning, the chief steward of the club had inspected the soup. Although he did not suspect poison, he had not liked the liquid's color and had ordered the contents of four of five kettles thrown away and new soup prepared. Thus, the poisoned soup was only one-fifth as deadly as the poisoner intended, and all the affected guests recovered. Although thwarted, the culprit nevertheless exulted over his deed, bombarding the police with letters from New York and Chicago in which he described himself as an anarchist who had sought to do the world a favor by relieving Chicago and the state of Illinois of many of its leaders. Unfortunately, he was never caught, and the episode of the "poison banquet" remains a mystery both for the American Church and the Chicago police force.

A year later, with the entry of the United States into World War I, the event was forgotten. Immediately, as in all previous wars, the American hierarchy proclaimed unreserved loyalty to the country's cause. At the annual meeting of the archbishops at Catholic University, a resolution was adopted which declared in part: "Our people, as ever, will rise as one man to serve the nation. Our priests and consecrated women will once again, as in every former trial of their country, win by their heroism and their service new admiration and approval. We are all true Americans, ready as our age, our ability and our condition permits, to do whatever is in us to do for the preservation, the progress and the triumph of our beloved country."

Once again, in this freshest manifestation of Catholic "instant loyalty," it is possible to detect a faint plaintive note, as though the American Church shyly felt herself constrained to plead her patriotism. But this, once more, also sprang from the hierarchy's very genuine gratitude for the freedom of religion granted here. Eventually, the Church might also be grateful for the unity which the war effort conferred on her. The Great War, as it was originally called, killed Cahenslyism. Catholics of German origin put aside their old allegiance to the Fatherland and the Irish shelved their hatred of the English, all remembering that they were Americans first. The war also presented the Church the long-sought opportunity to set up a single coordinating agency such as the lay Federation of Catholic Societies never quite became. This was the National Catholic War Council, conceived by Father John J. Burke, an able Paulist who had already founded the Chaplains' Aid Association. With the approval of the hierarchy, Father Burke called a meeting at Catholic University in August, 1917. On that occasion, 115 delegates from sixty-eight dioceses, together with representatives of twenty-seven national Catholic societies, set up the N.C.W.C. Throughout the war, the council functioned as a highly effective agency, either by providing assistance to chaplains serving with the troops or by raising funds with the official approbation of President Wilson.

Using the parish as the basic unit, the N.C.W.C. was able to organize the entire Catholic population in support of the war effort. In its first fund drive, it raised five million dollars, no small sum in those days. Next, it participated in the greater all-agency drive aimed at raising $170,500,000, of which the Council was to be allotted $30,000,000. As Cardinal Gibbons expressed it: "The President, in recognizing the National Catholic War Council, recognized the Hierarchy. The honor of the whole Hierarchy is pledged to this undertaking."

The Catholic War Council also provided funds for Knights of Columbus huts which ministered to the social as well as spiritual needs of Catholic servicemen at home and abroad, and it provided mass kits and other material assistance to chaplains. The problem of providing chaplains for the armed forces, of course, was one of the most trying that the Church had to meet. In the main, American commanders thought of chaplains as being Protestant ministers, and many of them also regarded a chaplain as a kind of recreation officer, the sort of supernumerary who would provide entertainment in the rear areas and perhaps also pass out contraceptives to soldiers going on leave.

If the Church's first difficulty was to get Catholic chaplains assigned in proportion to the number of Catholics in the services, the next was for the chaplain himself to convince some hard-bitten colonel that he really was interested in saving souls. Once these obstacles were hurdled, however, the Catholic chaplains usually became highly popular officers. Their bravery was legendary. Men who sincerely believed that they had the power to forgive the sins of stricken men—in effect, to confer salvation on them—or to put the Body of Christ into their mouths, obviously were not frightened by specters of their own death. Their cheerfulness and understanding also impressed the troops. One incident is typical. At Camp Sivier, South Carolina, there were only six hundred Catholics among thirty-two thousand men, but by some mistake five Catholic chaplains had been assigned there. When the Chaplain-Bishop attempted to have them transferred to camps where they were more badly needed, the commanding general not only insisted that they remain there but also that they accompany his division overseas.

Meanwhile, World War I also forced the Church to create the Military Ordinariate to care for all Catholics in the armed forces of the United States. Patrick Hayes, auxiliary bishop of New York and later its archbishop and a cardinal, was the first ordinary of the Military Ordinariate, and it was a post which he held until his death in 1938, when he was succeeded by Francis Cardinal Spellman. When the Armistice ended the war, there were one thousand chaplains serving under Hayes and with the armed forces, with another five hundred waiting to be commissioned.

The huge, disproportionate number of Catholics in uniform had called forth this army of chaplains. Although there are no definite statistics on the subject, a letter written by Secretary of War Newton D. Baker spoke of Catholic soldiers who "will constitute perhaps 35 per cent of the Army," while the Navy and the Marines were estimated to be as high as 50 per cent Catholic. This, from a minority representing only one-sixth of the population.

There are various explanations for the Catholic spirit of sacrifice. First, the hierarchy was behind the war with solid enthusiasm. Second, Catholicism was until recently completely free of doctrinaire pacifist thought, and its doctrine of the "just war" evolved by St. Augustine and improved upon by St. Thomas Aquinas and others makes military service in wartime almost mandatory. Third, a surprisingly large number of men from the Protestant South were found to be suffering from pellagra, a diet-deficiency disease of the skin and nervous system which was then mistakenly thought to be contagious, and the rejection of these men caused an abnormal drain on areas of the country where Catholics were concentrated. Fourth, even more astonishing, many war-eligible Americans were discovered to be suffering from syphilis. The Catholic emphasis on sexual purity had apparently preserved more of its men for the services. Although these and other reasons partially account for the Catholic preponderance among men in uniform, they certainly do not mitigate the high degree of patriotism characteristic of Americans of that faith.

As had happened in all of America's wars, the Irish distinguished themselves in battle, particularly the predominantly Irish 165th Infantry, better known under its old name of "the Fighting Sixty-ninth." Only General John J. Pershing, chief of the American Expeditionary Force, was more famous than the 165th's commander, Colonel William ("Wild Bill") Donovan. The regiment's chaplain was the celebrated Francis Patrick Duffy, "Fighting Father Duffy," while its poet was the laureate of the entire A.E.F., the gay and devout Joyce Kilmer, who fell near Ourcq on July 30, 1918, with a German bullet through his brain. Like the great French poet, Charles Péguy, Kilmer had believed passionately in the Allied cause, and he, too, laid down his life for it.

And so had thousands upon thousands of other Catholic men among the 126,000 Americans who had died "far from the customary skies."

Chapter XXI

One of the striking characteristics of the Catholic Church in America has been its tendency to emerge from an American war stronger and in higher esteem than when it entered, and in no struggle was this trait better shown than in the World War just ended.

As in former conflicts, the devotion of Catholic chaplains and nursing nuns had excited the admiration and gratitude of their fellow countrymen; but more than this, the war effort had mixed Americans of all creeds and races in a way that could never have been possible in peacetime. Many Americans from the South and other rural areas, trained from childhood to expect cloven hooves and tails, were slightly astonished to find that their Catholic comrades were neither Belial nor Beelzebub. On the other hand, the Catholics were able to come out of the mental ghettos into which they had been herded by conservative bishops, and to learn that the so-called "contamination" of American life was at the least exaggerated. Catholic ethnic groups such as the Germans or Poles profited especially from this chance to shed Old World attachments and customs and to become more American. Thus, there was an exchange on both sides, a give-and-take which was all to the country's good, and because it was to mean, for a time, at least, diminution of religious suspicion, it was of particular benefit to American Catholicism.

Another powerful force operating to the profit of the American Church was the habit of bold and vigorous action which the war had instilled in the hierarchy, and the National Catholic War Council which had been created to coordinate Catholic war effort proved to be so successful that the bishops decided to continue it in peacetime as the church's major coordinating agency. Thus, in 1919, at the first postwar meeting of the hierarchy, 92 of the 101 prelates present voted to establish the National Catholic Welfare Council. Some conservatives such as Bishop Charles McDonnell of Brooklyn opposed the council on the ground that it would be an invasion of his jurisdiction, an objection which attracted other protestors who carried their complaints to the Holy See. They succeeded in persuading Pope Benedict XV to withdraw his tentative approval of the idea, but Benedict's successor, the farsighted Pius XI, eventually gave it his approval. The only change resulting from the opposition to the agency was that the name was changed from "Council" to "Conference," the word "council" having a definite canonical connotation suggestive of an invasion of episcopal authority.

The war, then, had given birth to the National Catholic Welfare Conference, a coordinating agency which proved itself so efficient and successful that the Holy See took the lead in proposing it as a model for the hierarchies of all other countries. And it was adopted. The Second Vatican Council in 1967 specifically endorsed episcopal conferences, defining them as "a council in which the bishops of a given nation or territory jointly exercise their pastoral office to promote the greater good which the Church offers mankind, especially through the forms and methods of the apostolate fittingly adapted to the circumstances of the age."

In the United States, the N.C.W.C. was ruled by an administrative board of ten bishops, but the actual work was carried out by a kind of secretariat, comprising nine departments ranging from Education through Press to Lay Organizations. In addition there are the various bishops' committees interested in special problems such as emergency or war relief, missions or motion pictures. In 1966, the N.C.W.C. changed its name to the United States Catholic Conference, actually a dual organization which also includes the National Conference of Catholic Bishops. As it now stands, the U.S.C.C. consists of a national conference of bishops and the secretariat which does its work. But it now also has the hitherto unprecedented power of making its decisions binding on all bishops. Thus, when the laws of fast and abstinence for American Catholics were changed in 1967, the vote of well over the required two-thirds majority changed the rules for every diocese in the country.

In the beginning, however, the suspect N.C.W.C. was a comparatively modest organization, operating only five departments: Education, Lay Activities, Press, Social Action and Missions. Of these, none was more successful or more influential in American life than Social Action. Under the direction of Monsignor John A. Ryan, who directed the department from its inception until his death in 1945, the American Church made itself one of the leaders in evolving a new social philosophy for the United States.

Raised on the Minnesota prairies south of Minneapolis in the heart of the American Populist country, John Augustine Ryan was born and bred to social reform. His father was a member of the National Farmers Alliance, a Populist group which fought big business and the railroads. As a youth he had listened to the theorizing of the Populist leader Ignatius Donnelly, a congressman from his own district. Deciding to become a priest, Ryan entered St. Paul's Seminary, and there, at the age of twenty-five, he discovered Leo XIII's *Rerum Novarum*, written three years earlier but by then generally forgotten. The event was decisive in Ryan's life. The reforms recommended by Leo were to become his life's work, and thus, after his ordination, he pursued studies in sociology and economics to give his essentially moralist views on social reform a sound, practical foundation. Some of his ideas, advanced as early as 1909, would be considered arrant socialism even today, including proposals for public ownership of utilities, public ownership of mines and forests, control of monopolies either by breaking them up or fixing their prices, progressive income and inheritance taxes, taxation on the future increase in land values and prohibition of speculation on the stock and commodity exchanges. In these, with the exception of death and income taxes, Ryan was undoubtedly proposing to substitute bureaucratic socialism for the American capitalist system, and in most of these recommendations he appears not to have understood human nature, or to have anticipated the rise of a "new class" of oppressors such as the Communist commissars who are the new tormentors of the Russian people.

In his proposals for labor legislation, however, Ryan was a social apostle indeed. It was he who wrote the so-called "Bishops'

Program of Social Reconstruction," which was adopted by the prelates of the Administrative Committee of the N.C.W.C. In it were twelve recommendations dealing with a legal minimum wage, an eight-hour day, protective laws for women and children, protection for peaceful picketing and boycotting, unemployment insurance and employment bureaus, provision against accident, illness, and old age, municipal housing and the rights of labor to a share in management. All these, excepting labor's right to participate in management, have since been enacted into law, into legislation so just and compassionate that there is hardly an American alive today who would wish to repeal any of them. Then, however, they provoked a storm of protest. Stephen C. Mason, president of the National Association of Manufacturers, wrote to Cardinal Gibbons to protest the "Bishops' Program" as "a covert effort to disseminate partisan, pro–labor union, socialistic propaganda under the official insignia of the Roman Catholic Church in America." Some prelates joined the protests, among them the arch-conservative Archbishop William O'Connell of Boston, but in the main the Church stood solidly behind Ryan's program. To this day, it remains a monument to the Church's leadership in social reform, given at a time when steelworkers were still working twelve hours a day seven days a week, when state minimum wage laws once sanctioned by the Supreme Court were outlawed by the same court, and when the greed and corruption of big business was in the ascendancy and three successive Republican administrations seemed more interested in reducing taxes or in demonstrating that Calvin Coolidge was perfectly correct when he made his inane remark: "The business of America is business."

Ryan was personally attacked, within and without his faith. O'Connell was one of his particularly savage enemies, who repeatedly castigated him for his "nefarious and false views." The label of "socialist" was pasted on him repeatedly, but he made no attempt to deny it. There can be no doubt that some of his theories were as socialist as anything proposed by Karl Marx, and equally unworkable, but these were seldom the ones for which he fought hardest. It was in the field of labor legislation that he worked the most diligently and was the most successful, and here, as his biographer has said, "He was about as radical as Leo XIII."

While thus applying the principles of justice and common sense to the rapid industrialization of American society during the postwar decade, the Church of that period was also distinguished by a remarkable expansion of educational facilities on every level. Although the ideal of "every Catholic child in a Catholic school" as enunciated by the various councils of Baltimore was not and probably never will be attained, Catholics continued to make heroic financial sacrifices to achieve it. Thus, the number of parochial elementary schools rose from 3,812 with 903,908 pupils in 1900 to 7,387 such schools with 2,283,084 in 1930. Even more outstanding was the Catholic emphasis on secondary education.

This, of course, was only because so many states had begun to demand that children be educated beyond the elementary grades; yet, in accommodating itself to the growing trend toward universal high school education, the Church once again was demonstrating how thoroughly American she was. Thus, by 1930, the number of Catholic high schools had risen to 2,123 with 241,869 students. The number of Catholic colleges and universities exclusive of religious seminaries was also growing, so that now the Church counted them in the hundreds rather than the tens.

Together with this growth in educational facilities there came the long-awaited intellectual awakening. Actually, it was not so much an awakening as a questioning. More and more Catholics, especially laymen, were asking the question: Where are our Catholic intellectuals? In 1921, the Brooklyn *Tablet* declared openly, "Although we are one-fifth of the population, we do not furnish one-fiftieth of the higher intellectual life of the country," and in 1926, *The Commonweal* complained that "we have no John Dewey, no Elihu Root, no Ralph Adams Cram, no H. L. Mencken, no Edwin Arlington Robinson—and we have not seemed particularly to care about having them."

The answer to the question, of course, was that most Catholic scholars were priests, men dedicated to the creation of the religious colossus that the Catholic Church in America was in fact becoming, and therefore men too preoccupied to make any sort of impact upon American intellectual life. Moreover, the Catholic system of higher education was at the time devoted to educating as many people as possible in their overcrowded and underendowed schools, not to turning out intellectual leaders. Perhaps most pernicious of all, there was, and to a lesser degree there still is, an emphasis in Catholic theology which tends to discourage ambition of any kind. This is the "traveler" complex, the notion of *homo viator,* man the traveler, a creature who is in this world but not of it. It derives from St. Augustine's concept of the "two cities": the City of God and the City of Man. The first is Heaven and the second the World, and Catholics are taught to cultivate celestial rather than terrestial values. They are travelers in this world, wayfarers en route to Heaven. If a man suffers defeat or disappointment, he is encouraged to "offer it up" as a sacrifice to Christ, to resign himself to "the will of God" rather than to defy fate and fight back. Fight back? For what? Some "worldly" success, which is as nothing in the sight of the Savior? The words of Jesus Christ are constantly quoted: "For what doth it profit a man, if he gain the whole world, and suffer the loss of his own soul?" The struggle, then, is primarily for salvation; not for success. Thus, out of the gigantic intellect of Augustine has come the building blocks for construction of an intellectual ghetto.

Happily, in the twenties, all such walls were beginning to crumble. The very fact that there was a publication such as *The Commonweal* was proof of the new spirit of criticism and self-analysis which had seized the minds of American Catholics. With other scholarly periodicals such as *Thought* and *New Scholasticism, The Commonweal* had come into being in the twenties, joining Father Hecker's well-established *Catholic World* as a stimulus to creating a higher Catholic intellectual standard in America. For the next four decades these magazines and a growing number of quarterlies and other intellectual publications, together with a proliferating Catholic book publishing industry, were to bring Catholics in America the thought of all the outstanding minds of the Universal Church, thus preparing the way for American participation in the *aggiornamento* or "updating" of modern Catholicism begun by Pope John XXIII, as well as the intellectual ferment which is still in process.

Another explanation of the changed attitude toward intellectualism which appeared during the twenties was that the Church herself was then undergoing a major transformation. She had ceased to be the Church of the Immigrant. The restrictive immigration laws enacted by Congress from 1921 to 1924 had reduced the foreign flood to a trickle, thus freeing the Church of the enormous burden which she had borne so unselfishly for a century and more. The end of immigration also freed her, as Daniel Callahan observes, "to find some genuinely American sense of Catholic self-identity. This was the task the Americanist bishops had set themselves in the 1880s and 1890s; but it required World War I and the end of immigration to establish the necessary base to re-open more successfully their passionate case."

As the American Church ceased to be the spiritual mother of immigrants and became the mentor of the sons and grandsons of immigrants, she also lost her character as the Church of the lower classes. Universal education and the Church's own parochial school system had given the immigrant offspring the opportunity to climb up the social and economic ladders into the ranks of the new and numerous middle-class America being created by the industrial expansion and mobility of the postwar period. Now affluent and educated, middle-class Catholics began to become dissatisfied with the layman's traditional lowly estate. They wished to become more deeply involved in the life of the Church, both as a spiritual and a social institution, and this new commitment from the laity was also partially responsible for the intellectual revival in the Church.

On the adverse side, the end of immigration also slowed the growth of the Church, so that by the end of the decade the increase was from 17,885,000 to 20,000,000, a distinct decrease in the rate. This modest rise was also attributable to the fact that Catholics were not reproducing themselves as prolifically as their ancestors had. Another explanation is that more and more young men and women were being drawn to the celibacy of a religious life, thus effectively curbing Catholic reproduction. Between 1920 and 1930 the number of priests had shot up from 21,600 to 27,900, an increase of roughly one-third in comparison to the total Catholic population increase of about one-eighth.

Although the postwar period was producing a new sense of American awareness in the Church, Catholics once more found themselves in opposition to a great number of their countrymen. This was during the dispute over prohibition, backed by many Protestant churches, notably the Baptist and Methodist, among other temperance groups. Almost to a member, the Catholic Church in America opposed the Eighteenth Amendment, if only because it was still able to distinguish between the use and abuse of an object. Catholics certainly agreed that drunkenness was wrong and even sinful, but they could not agree that there was anything wrong with drink in itself. From her ancient wisdom and unrivaled experience, the Church has learned to distrust all forms of absolutism, and she could not approve any attempt to make a public crime out of a private vice. Thus, to outlaw drink was only another form of confusing the means with the end. Although the hierarchy made no official pronouncement against Prohibition, this was and always has been the Catholic Church's attitude toward drink and drunkenness. At one point, however, Cardinal Gibbons did find it necessary to make public his own personal convictions.

"I am a temperate, not a temperance man," he said. "I have never been able to convince myself that what we call total abstinence is essential to morality." Again, he said: "I should regard the passage of a federal prohibition law as a national catastrophe, little short of a crime against the spiritual and physical well-being of the American people." Gibbons also predicted that Prohibition would lead to the proliferation of illicit stills turning out cheap whisky injurious to health as well as a general refusal to comply which would end, as it did end, in contempt for the law. For this stand, the cardinal at Baltimore was savagely attacked by the New York Anti-Saloon League, which accused him of opposing the amendment because the distillers and tavern-keepers of Maryland were heavy contributors to his Church.

Gibbons's protest against Prohibition was among the last public acts of his long and remarkable career. He had lived through three wars and seen the transformation of the United States from a comparatively simple agricultural society into a complex and complicated industrial giant, beset by all those racial, religious and social problems, which, in microcosm, are actually the basic woes of the civilized world itself. For forty-three years, Gibbons had been the archbishop of Baltimore and for thirty-four years he had possessed the power and prestige of a prince of the Roman Catholic Church. His effect upon the American Church had been enormous, probably only less decisive than the organizing influence of John Carroll, and he had also helped to shape the America he lived in. In 1920, however, at the age of eighty-six, both his health and his influence had begun to decline.

Gibbons had already been rejected at the White House. The valued friend of Harrison, Cleveland, McKinley, Theodore Roosevelt and Taft, he had called on Woodrow Wilson during the war and been dismissed in a few minutes without being asked to sit down. The coolness of Wilson's reception had shocked the cardinal, and he had also been shaken after the war by the revival of anti-Catholic bigotry under the aegis of the Ku Klux Klan and the personal slurs of the prohibition lobby. At the end of 1920, aware that he was failing, Gibbons left Baltimore for Union Mills and a rest at the home of his beloved friends, the Shrivers of Maryland, among the oldest Catholic families in the United States. While there, he became aware that the end was near and asked to be carried back to his cathedral. There, he gave an interview typical of his unflagging faith in God and America. To the young journalist, Bruce Barton, later a congressman, he said: "Young man, *expect* great things. Expect great things of God; great things of your fellow men and of yourself. Expect great things of America. For great opportunities lie ahead; greater than any that have come before. But only those who have the courage and the vision to *expect* them will profit when they come."

Soon afterward, the cardinal sank into a coma. On Wednesday of Holy Week in 1921, he spoke his last words: "I have had a good day." He died the next day, Holy Thursday, and so also ended the long good day of the Age of Gibbons.

Shortly after the death of "the American cardinal," the fury of the last organized sally of bigotry burst upon the head of the American Church. This was the campaign of the Ku Klux Klan. Actually, this was the second Klan, a resurrection of the first secret society created in the South after the Civil War as a terroristic means of hobbling Reconstruction. Disbanded in 1869 on the orders of General Nathan Bedford Forrest, its first chief, the Klan was revived in 1915 at Stone Mountain, Georgia, by William J. Simmons, a Protestant preacher who also made a fortune out of selling regalia to the fraternal orders he promoted.

Called "the Invisible Empire," this "high-class, social, patriotic" society was actually only a continuation of the anti-Catholic, anti-Jewish, anti-foreign bias which has appeared and reappeared in American history like the recurrent notes of an evil fugue. Having borrowed its ritual and regalia from the first Klan, as well as its anti-Negro prejudice, the second organization announced itself as dedicated to the protection of womanhood and the maintenance of white Protestant ascendancy in America. It was also "against" evolution, birth control, internationalism and the repeal of Prohibition. Most bitterly of all, it was against the Catholics, and by 1924, having grown in membership to a total estimated at from three to five million followers, it was able to block the nomination of the Catholic, Alfred E. Smith, at the Democratic Convention. By then, the Klan held political power in Indiana, Oklahoma and Texas, and was reaching for it in such supposedly "sophisticated" states as New Jersey.* By then also, the Klan had secured the alliance of the Scottish rite Masons in its campaign against Catholicism.

The target this time was the parental right to educate children in other than public schools. Choosing Oregon as a testing ground, the Ku Kluxers and the Masons in 1922 introduced a statewide referendum to compel all parents to send their children to public schools. Here was an unvarnished attack upon religious freedom, and no attempt was made to conceal it. Anti-Catholic feeling was deliberately whipped up, and the Klan, calling upon tactics in use in the South, burned fiery crosses opposite Catholic churches in town after town. As a result, the referendum won. By a vote of 115,000 to 103,000, parents in Oregon were to be forced to send their children to public schools.

Immediately, there was an outraged reaction in the American press. The *St. Louis Post-Dispatch* said: "This Oregon Law is

---

* As a boy growing up in Rutherford, New Jersey, every Memorial Day I would gaze in horror and dread at the large floral wreath marked "K.K.K." lying in the place of honor at the foot of the borough war memorial.

above all else . . . an un-American attempt to take away the constitutional right to liberty of conscience under the guise of zeal for education." And the Portland *Oregonian* branded the law as "a forthright declaration that the state, not the parent, controls the child. It is nothing else, and it is not pretended that it is anything else." Happily, Oregon's highest court declared the law unconstitutional. Oregon appealed, ostensibly in the name of the governor, but actually in the interest of the Masons. Wallace McCamant, the attorney supposedly appearing for the state, began his argument with the declaration: "I appear here primarily as the representative and at the instance of the Scottish rite Masonic bodies."

In a unanimous landmark decision, the United States Supreme Court struck down the law, issuing a broad declaration of parental rights, which held: "The fundamental theory of liberty upon which all governments in this Union repose excludes any general power of the state to standardize its children by forcing them to accept instruction from public teachers only. The child is not the mere creature of the state; those who nurture him and direct his destiny have the right, coupled with the high duty, to recognize and prepare him for additional obligations." Thus, the highest court in the land had upheld the *right* of parents to send children to the school of their selection, as well as the *right* of religious bodies to operate schools.

Defeated here, and in a similar attempt in Michigan, the Klan shortly afterward began to go into decline. Eventually, newspaper exposés of its tactics of murder and torture led to a national revulsion, and by 1926, Klan membership was on the decline. Nevertheless, it had called forth the old No-Popery demon which seems to dwell perpetually beneath the surface of the nativist character, and so did much to induce the wave of anti-Catholic bigotry which swept the United States in the national election of 1928.

In that year, for the first time in the history of the United States, a major political party nominated a Catholic for the office of President. Once before, in 1872, a group of independent Democrats withdrew their support of the regular Democratic candidate, Horace Greeley, and named Charles O'Connor, a New York lawyer and a Catholic. Although O'Connor declined, his name remained on the ballot, and he drew thirty thousand votes. Eight years later, the Catholic hero of the Civil War, General Philip Sheridan, was considered a candidate for the Republican nomination, but he declined the honor.

Thus, when the Democrats in 1928 named Alfred Emanuel Smith as their candidate, it was truly the first time that a Catholic was seriously seeking the nation's highest office. Born in Brooklyn, in the same neighborhood in which his mother and father and later his own children were born, "Al" Smith was truly a product of "the sidewalks of New York." Successively, he had been Sheriff of New York County, President of the city's Board of Aldermen, and Governor of New York, a position which he held four times. His record as an efficient administrator was rivaled only by his acute sense of social justice and keen insight into human nature. He had repeatedly carried his state for the Democrats in the face of Republican landslides, and it therefore came as no surprise when his party nominated him on the first ballot in 1928.

Yet, the "Happy Warrior," as he was called, went down to a resounding defeat, 444 electoral votes to 47, and for the first time since the Civil War the Republicans made inroads into the normally Solid South. One of the chief reasons for Al Smith's defeat was the vicious and sometimes obscene attacks made upon him by the Klan and similar nativist groups. Much of the old literature of No-Popery was reprinted and circulated, and it was charged, among other things, that after President Smith handed the United States over to the Pope, His Holiness would issue a decree bastardizing all non-Catholic children.* If this were not absurd enough, there were actually people who expressed their alarm that the tiny ceremonial cannon outside Georgetown University was pointed directly *at the Capitol.* Unfortunately, in minds disposed to think ill, nothing is too ridiculous to be believed, and much of this arrant if scurrilous nonsense was taken for truth. In fact, Governor Smith himself complained that the Republican party was not above issuing campaign literature "of a nature other than political." Smith's

* In Catholic folklore there is a probably spurious but nevertheless very funny anecdote which claims that after Smith was defeated he sent the Pope a one-word cablegram which said: "Unpack."

remark came during his celebrated speech in Oklahoma City. Aware that Southwestern states such as Arkansas and Oklahoma were particularly frenzied in their hostility to him, so much so that there "was real concern for Smith's personal safety" in Oklahoma City, he courageously decided to beard the lion in his den and bring the religious question into the open.

"I have been told," he said, "that politically it might be expedient for me to remain silent upon this subject, but so far as I am concerned no political expediency will keep me from speaking out in an endeavor to destroy these evil attacks."

The first myth which Smith demolished was the charge that as governor of New York he appointed practically no one but Catholics to office. "What are the facts?" he asked. "On investigation I find that in the cabinet of the Governor sit fourteen men. Three of the fourteen are Catholics, ten Protestants, and one of Jewish faith. In various bureaus and divisions of the Cabinet offices, the Governor appointed twenty-six people. Twelve of them are Catholics and fourteen of them are Protestants. Various other State officials, making up boards and commissions, and appointed by the Governor, make a total of 157 appointments, of which thirty-five were Catholics, 106 were Protestants, twelve were Jewish, and four I could not find out about." What Smith could but did not add was that in New York State was located the country's largest concentration of Catholics, and that his co-religionists had not fared quite so well under him as under non-Catholic governors. Having gone on to detail other examples of bigotry in his campaign, Smith concluded:

I here emphatically declare that I do not wish any member of my faith in any part of the United States to vote for me on any religious grounds. I want them to vote for me only when in their hearts and consciences they become convinced that my election will promote the best interests of our country. By the same token, I cannot refrain from saying that any person who votes against me simply because of my religion is not, to my way of thinking, a good citizen . . .

The constitutional guaranty that there should be no religious test for public office is not a mere form of words. It represents the most vital principle that ever was given to any people. I attack those who seek to undermine it, not only because I am a good Christian, but because I am a good American and a product of America and of American institutions. Everything I am, and everything I hope to be, I owe to these institutions.

Unhappily, Governor Smith was *not* believed. The slurs continued, and Herbert Hoover, a Quaker who was asked no questions about his faith—particularly about his doctrinal pacifism which in fact did cripple his administration and harm his country —won a resounding victory.

Doubtless, it would be a mistake to attribute Smith's defeat to his Catholicism alone. But the other explanations for it have an equally religious cast. Thus, Smith was a "wet" in favor of repealing Prohibition, and was therefore unacceptable to the "drys," most of whom were Protestants who had a religious abhorrence of alcoholic beverage. Prohibition, of course, was not solely a thrust of religious and temperance groups. It was solidly backed by some big business interests, and later, as Cardinal Gibbons had so wisely foreseen, by "bootleggers." Not all of these purveyors of illicit "booze" were gangsters of the Al Capone type. Many of them were old-stock Americans operating in those areas of the Southwest and Midwest, some of which are still "dry," where a religious abhorrence of liquor was almost a condition of social status, and they ruthlessly and cynically manipulated this loathing to their own profit. Thus, Al Smith the Catholic was also Al Smith the Drinker.

From the nativist-Protestant standpoint, Alfred E. Smith, for all his undoubted intelligence and capacities, was in appearance and personality almost a caricature of the traditional American concept of the foreign-born Catholic in politics. He wore a brown derby—his personal trademark—at a rakish angle, and a cigar was almost always jutting from his mouth. Sometimes, it seemed, he spoke out of the corner of that mouth in accents of the purest Brooklynese which were suggestive both of a lack of education and an unpardonably close association with the Tammany Hall political machine. All of this was apparent, not real, but it was sufficient to mark Al Smith the Catholic as Al Smith the Cheap Political Hack.

It was in all these ways, then, that the true image of Alfred E. Smith the Statesman was obscured. Nevertheless, it should be said that this latest outpouring of religious prejudice occasioned by the revival of the Klan and the campaign of 1928 was not quite as vicious or as sustained as it might have been a half-century earlier. Nor should it ever be forgotten that a major political party had actually risen above the long American tradition of bigotry to nominate a Catholic for the highest office in the land. This was very, very much indeed. Finally, the No-Popery of the twenties faded quickly, in part because of Smith's splendidly magnanimous post-election speech in which he thanked the fifteen million Americans who voted for him (twenty-one million voted for Hoover), and in greater part due to the distraction of the Great Depression.

Chapter XXII

Although the paralyzing and prolonged economic slump called the Depression naturally affected Catholics in the same degree as their countrymen of other beliefs, the mood of despair which had supplanted the cheerful confidence of the twenties did not prevent the American Church from continuing and all but completing its work of organization.

Diocesan development was characterized by a tendency to make each state an ecclesiastical province. Thus, New Jersey was made the Province of Newark comprising the new suffragan sees of Camden and Paterson and the old suffragan at Trenton; Michigan became the Province of Detroit with newly created suffragans at Lansing and Saginaw, and old ones at Grand Rapids and Marquette, which was separated from the province of Milwaukee; and Kentucky and Tennessee were united in the Province of Louisville with jurisdiction over the new diocese of Owensboro and the old one at Covington, both in Kentucky, and the diocese of Nashville, Tennessee. This confined the once-enormous Province of Cincinnati to the states of Ohio and Indiana. Another major change was creation of the Province of Los Angeles consisting of southern California and all of Arkansas.

Organizational progress was also outstanding in the field of "Catholic Action," the movement advocated by Pope Pius XI and defined by him as "the participation of the Catholic laity in the apostolate of the hierarchy." As in the days of early Christianity, he said, conditions in the postwar world required that the Catholic laity take a greater part in the work of the Church. Catholics were urged to give witness to Christ in their daily lives and to apply Christian principles to the societies in which they lived.

Although the appeal was made to laymen, it was to be organized under the guidance of bishops, an idea which was in harmony with the purposes of the National Catholic Welfare Conference.

In the thirties, then, the Social Action department of the N.C.W.C. promoted the work of such agencies as the Catholic Conference on Industrial Problems, the Family Life Bureau, the Rural Life Bureau, Parish Credit Unions, Peace and Post-War Reconstruction. The bishops themselves had special committees such as the National Legion of Decency, formed to fight against circulation of obscene literature or the showing of indecent motion pictures, and one to protect the Spanish-speaking people of the Southwest, mostly Mexicans, against the exploitation of the big growing interests. A second spur toward Catholic Action came from Pius XI in 1931, when he issued his encyclical *Quadragesimo Anno* (Fortieth Year) which commemorated the fortieth anniversary of Leo XIII's *Rerum Novarum.* Praising Leo's letter as the source of a true Catholic social science, Pius went on to condemn the injustices of capitalism as a kind of economic dictatorship. He called for the application of Leo's principles to the evils of society, but also warned that no real cure could ever be effected which was not based on justice and charity. In this, Pius made it plain that he wanted no reform based on the injustices inherent in atheistic Communism or in some forms of correction springing from a purely naturalist concept of mankind.

Quadragesimo Anno and *Rerum Novarum,* it would seem, had placed in the hands of the American Church a pair of blueprints for social reform; and yet, even to suggest that all the bishops actually guided themselves on them would be nonsense of the purest ray serene. In actual fact, most bishops seldom let the faithful know that their Church possessed a doctrine of social reform. As often as the Popes pronounced or reformers such as John Ryan exhorted, the hierarchy itself maintained a discreet silence.

Probably, the Catholic dread of socialism and Communism made most of the clergy and the hierarchy suspicious of any social reform movements. Foreign-born Catholics who had suffered at the hands of European liberals, as well as second- or even third-generation Irish with their dislike of wealthy Protestant "do-gooders" who were often the descendants of Know-Nothings and nativists, simply refused to trust reformers of any description; and that tradition of distrust for any form of doctrinaire social reform persists in the American Church to this day. The paternalism which was for so long one of the chief traits of American Catholicism also prevented papal social teaching from filtering down to the parish level. It was thought too dangerous, too radical. As long as Sunday attendance at mass remained high and the Sunday collections did not dwindle, everything was apparently "safe." After all, why should the "troops," i.e., the laity, be informed of the objective of the "officers"?

The Catholic press, dominated as most of it was by the hierarchy and the teaching orders, maintained its own "conspiracy of silence." Catholic education was also disinclined to jump on the papal bandwagon. In the thirties, it was almost certain that a youth in a Catholic high school would never hear of *Rerum Novarum* or John Ryan, and possible that if he went on to a Catholic college he would also not become acquainted with them. Of course, the same charge might be leveled against all other forms of religious and most of the secular educational systems in America, but neither of these were equipped with the splendid guidelines layed down by Leo and Pius. As Father Greeley, occasionally a too-tart critic of his Church, has remarked: "Sunday church attendance, loyalty to the Church, belief in the primacy of the Pope, and sexual morality were the principal areas in which Catholic education was affected. Social teachings were not completely ignored but they were not given very powerful emphasis either."

Nevertheless, in spite of official apathy there were some attempts to implement Catholic social doctrine, especially among Catholics in the labor movement. Many labor unions organized schools which taught the papal encyclicals and there were also classes held under Catholic auspices in such heavily industrialized cities as Buffalo, Chicago and Detroit. Meanwhile, many individual Catholics were deeply influenced by the appeal for Catholic Action, the most notable of them being Dorothy Day and Peter Maurin. Both Miss Day and Maurin were reformers in the tradition of Orestes Brownson. Everywhere around them they saw the evils of industrialized America, and they denounced them with an impassioned sense of social justice. Through lectures and articles published in *The Catholic Worker*, the periodical that they founded, they attacked the suffering of the unemployed and the homeless, the repression of minorities, the brutal dehumanizing of the factory worker and the cruel exploitation of migrant laborers. Taking to heart Pius's injunction to give witness to Christ in their daily lives, they opened thirty-three houses of hospitality across America, and in these sanctuaries they demonstrated that feeding the hungry, clothing the naked and sheltering the homeless were not exhausted and empty admonitions of an effete Christianity. Eventually, the Catholic Worker movement attracted many Catholic intellectuals dissatisfied with the pedestrian approach to social reform of parochial organizations such as the Knights of Columbus or the Holy Name Society. A living witness to Christ and the spirit of the Gospels was much more appealing, as were the fiery arguments published in *The Catholic Worker*, which, by the end of the decade, could claim a circulation of well over 100,000. In 1937, the Association of Catholic Trade Unionists was also formed as a result of the Catholic Worker movement.

Unfortunately, more in the tradition of William Lloyd Garrison than Brownson, Miss Day and Maurin were most emphatically "against" many things, and they, too, would not equivocate. Consequently, their loathing of the very real evils of industrialism led them to be anti-industrialist. Not content with attacking the new form of slavery which is the industrial servitude of the wage system, they wanted to destroy industrialism itself; in effect, to empty out the baby with the bath. Furthermore, their horror of war, an immemorial human institution which they, along with Karl Marx, naively considered to be another wicked consequence of capitalism alone, brought them to adopt a kind of confused doctrinal pacifism. The most striking manifestation of Miss Day's profession of nonviolence came after the Korean War, when she and other members of the Catholic Worker movement went to jail for refusing to obey orders to take cover during a Civil Defense air-raid drill in New York City. By then, Miss Day had such an unclear concept of Christian "charity" that she publicly reproached herself for having rebuked an inmate of her prison for having made indecent advances to a young woman in her company. Of the sincerity of Dorothy Day and Peter Maurin there can be no doubt, nor should it be forgotten that they *did* take the Church's social doctrine and Catholic Action seriously at a time when the vast majority of Catholics either ignored or did not know of it. Chiefly because of them, during the thirties many Catholic intellectuals and reformers became separated and even alienated from traditional Catholic culture in America.

From the thirties also came the liturgical reform movement which bound young priests and lay intellectuals closer together around the triple pillars of social thought, the lay apostolate and the liturgy. The attempt to bring the Catholic faithful out of the forms of worship and devotion in which the liturgy had been frozen since the late Middle Ages, or at least since the Council of Trent, was already a half-century old in Europe. In the United States, however, no such comparable movement had appeared. Here, the liturgy was in a strait jacket, and the sacramental life of the Church so desiccated that many pastors refused to open the tabernacle to administer Holy Eucharist (Communion) except at High Mass on Sunday. Much as there might have been a laic and intellectual revival in the Church, the bulk of the faithful was a supine mass; and there were clergymen who appeared to be motivated by a kind of elitism or priestly gnosis whereby the clerics were considered the "true" Catholics while the laymen were mere servitors or followers, like the "perfect" and the "believers" of the Albigensians. In this, they were hardly different from Melchor Cano, a famous Spanish theologian of the sixteenth century on whose evidence the Spanish Inquisition condemned the Archbishop of Toledo for writing a catechism explaining the faith to the laity. Cano declared "completely worthy of condemnation the temerity of giving to the faithful a religious instruction that was only proper for priests . . . He spoke out vigorously against the reading of the Holy Scriptures in the vernacular, and against those who make it their business to hear confessions all day long. He held highly suspect the zeal displayed by the 'spiritual' in inciting the faithful to go to confession and communion frequently, and he is reported to have said in a sermon that frequent and widespread reception of the sacraments was one of the signs of the coming of the Antichrist." Thus, an archreactionary of the Counter-Reformation, and four centuries later his spiritual heirs were acting as though Martin Luther were still pounding nails into the church door at Wittenberg.

With very few exceptions, the laity knew no Latin. Only the clergy did, and although the use of a universal dead language as the official tongue of the Universal Church certainly was and is defensible, it had become abused as the "inside" knowledge of the clergy. The entire liturgy, from the Mass, Catholicism's central rite offered as a re-enactment of the sacrifice of Jesus Christ on the cross, to the blessing of newlyweds' new homes, was in Latin. Except for the reading of the Gospel and preaching of the sermon, both in English, the laity sat at Mass in uncomprehending stupor—rising, kneeling or sitting according to the movements of the priest, just as they had been trained to do by the teaching sisters; or singing such Latin hymns as *Tantum Ergo* or *O Salutaris*, as the sisters had also taught them to do, without comprehending a single solitary word of what they sang —while the priest celebrating the Mass whispered the Latin words of the rite up against a wall. In the twentieth, just as in the eighteenth century, John Adams's derision of the Catholic laity's exclusion from participation in the ritual would still be justified.

As Father David Baier, a Franciscan, was to complain: "Catholic life for millions has become a passive thing—a having something done for one by somebody else. The priest offers the Mass, the priest says the Divine Office, the cloistered religious do the praying, the Saint Vincent de Paul Society performs the acts of charity; those in orders must be good, all others can be expected to be partially good. The religious are the elders, the lay people are the children who never reach maturity."

The purpose of the lay apostolate had been to revitalize a laity made apathetic socially by the petty despotism of the pastors, and now the aim of the liturgical reform was to involve laymen more intimately in the public worship which the Church pays to God the Father, the Son and the Holy Spirit. Apparently, the first attempts to do this were made in the twenties under the leadership of Father Martin Hellriegel of O'Fallon, Missouri, Father William Busch of St. Paul's Seminary and the Benedictine monks of St. John's Abbey in Collegeville, Minnesota. Probably the most outstanding contribution was made by Dom Virgil Michel, a Benedictine priest who in 1926 founded the periodical

Orate Fratres (now called *Worship*) as well as the Liturgical
Press. Through these outlets Dom Virgil was able to pump a
stream of information on the liturgy to his followers. Eventually
he also established a number of workshops and summer schools
on the liturgy. Through Dom Virgil and his colleagues the use
of a Latin-English missal, the liturgical book of the Latin Rite
containing the formulas and prayers used in the Mass, was encouraged and became popular. In 1926, there had been but one
English missal extant, and it was in very limited use, but in the
years following World War II there were at least nineteen editions available in millions of copies, and the practice of following
the priest's Latin in the English of the missal had become widespread. Thus, in the thirties, the seeds sown in the twenties had
begun to take root, and the movement to make the liturgy live
for the laity, as well as, if one may describe the language spoken
in the United States as "American," to Americanize all ritual from
the Mass on downward, began to spread. Those roots, of course,
were sunk in prairie sod. In the Americanizing tradition of John
Ireland of St. Paul and other prelates such as Keane and Spalding,
liturgical reform was a Midwestern growth which did not get
west of the Mississippi or east of Chicago until after World
War II.

Midwestern as well, made of the lakes and plains, was the
golden voice of Father Charles E. Coughlin, the famous "Radio
Priest" of the thirties and probably the most celebrated orator
produced by the Catholic Church in America. Born in Canada
and educated by the Basilian Fathers whose ranks he joined
temporarily, Coughlin became a priest of the Diocese of Detroit
in 1920. In 1926, as pastor of the Shrine of the Little Flower in
Royal Oak, Michigan, he began to make radio broadcasts to appeal for financial support. His fame grew. No one who heard
that rich, powerful, melodious voice, vibrant with the conviction
of his faith and faintly flecked with an Irish brogue, ever quite
forgot it. By 1931 he had a nationwide audience. A single broadcast brought him an avalanche of 350,000 letters. In that year,
he shifted from sermons on God and religion and took to politics
with a slashing attack on President Herbert Hoover and the international bankers on whom he blamed the Depression. Like
many spellbinders, Coughlin spoke a purple prose which listened

beautifully but read wretchedly. Thus, when he derided Hoover for his remark "Prosperity is just around the corner," he said: "It appears to have been a circular corner to which they referred, a corner which if we could turn, we would not be willing to negotiate if it foreshadows a repetition of those recent occurrences for the children a generation to come." However concealed in verbiage, the point was made, and there is no doubt that Father Coughlin helped Franklin Delano Roosevelt score a stunning victory over Hoover in 1932.

Unfortunately, the golden-voiced pastor of Royal Oak seems to have credited himself with a little more than an assist. He began to advance himself as a spokesman for the administration. Although Roosevelt frequently invited him to the White House, he never put much faith in Coughlin's advice, which appears to have been a hodgepodge of simplistic monetary reforms and random quotations from the papal encyclicals. Nor did the President make any public acknowledgment of his "debt" to the Radio Priest. Miffed, alarmed at the growing number of undoubted socialists with influence in Washington, Coughlin began to turn against Roosevelt. In 1935, he said: "The first two years of the New Deal shall be remembered as two years of compromise, two years of social planning, two years of endeavoring to mix bad with the good, two years of surrender, two years of matching the puerile, puny brains of idealists against the virile viciousness of business and finance." Obviously, when the Radio Priest was angry, his prose improved. By 1936, Coughlin came to a complete break with Roosevelt. In that year, he formed his own party, the National Union for Social Justice, and ran his own candidate for the presidency—Congressman William Lemke—against both Roosevelt and Alfred M. Landon, the Republican standard-bearer.

It was then that John Ryan, now a monsignor, entered the battle. Long an object of Coughlin's taunts of him as "the Right Reverend New Dealer," Ryan cited his own experience of forty-five years of study of social problems and said: "I say deliberately to the laboring men and women of America that Father Coughlin's explanation of our economic maladies is at least fifty per cent wrong and that his monetary remedies are at least ninety per cent wrong. If the latter were enacted into law, they would prove disastrous to the great majority of the American people, particularly to the wage earners. Moreover Father Coughlin's monetary theories and proposals find no support in the encyclicals of either Pope Leo XIII or Pius XI."

Unhappily, Ryan's wisdom was no match for Coughlin's rhetoric, and the Radio Priest built his National Union for Social Justice into a party of five million followers. High ecclesiastical criticism was equally impotent against him. Cardinal Hayes, Cardinal O'Connell and Cardinal Mundelein all chided Coughlin, and the Vatican newspaper *Osservatore Romano* rebuked him; nevertheless, the pastor of Royal Oak, secure in the powerful protection and enthusiastic support of his ordinary, Bishop Michael Gallagher of Detroit, remained undeterred. As Election Day came closer, the tempo and intemperance of Coughlin's attacks on Roosevelt rose higher. In July, at Cleveland, he said "Franklin Double-Crossing Roosevelt" was "a liar," and although he apologized the following month, he also called FDR "anti-God" and "a scab President." Soon, he was challenging Roosevelt to repudiate his alleged Communist support. Next, he charged that Roosevelt and many of his agency chiefs were Communists themselves, thundering: "As I was instrumental in removing Herbert Hoover from the White House, so help me God, I will be an instrument in taking a communist out of the chair once occupied by Washington."

Father Coughlin was not so naive as to think that he could defeat Roosevelt. His objective was to develop sufficient support at the polls in 1936 so that by 1940 he might be powerful enough to challenge the existing two-party system. Thus, growing confident, perhaps enchanted by the sound of his own propaganda, he predicted that his candidate Lemke would draw nine million votes. If he did not, Coughlin promised, he would go off the radio. In the event, the National Union for Social Justice received only one million votes, and the crushed Coughlin did, in fact, go off the air and dissolve his party. He did not, however, remain silent for long. Throughout Roosevelt's second term in office, the Reverend Charles E. Coughlin remained a very sharp thorn in his flesh.

Coughlin had gone back on the air shortly after the death of Bishop Gallagher in 1937, claiming that it had been the bishop's dying wish, a statement that was quite beyond anyone's power to disprove. He also began to publish the periodical *Social Justice* and resurrected the dead National Union for Social Justice under the name of the Christian Front. So armed with ink and airwaves, the golden doctor of Royal Oak resumed his attacks on FDR, and also, to the acute embarrassment of his Church, began to lash out at the Jews. Although Father Coughlin always denied being anti-Semitic, the fact is that *Social Justice* did publish the so-called *Protocols of the Elders of Zion*, a spurious document purporting to be the blueprint for Jewish domination of the world. And he did say of the *Protocols:* "Is it not true that some unseen force is taking Christ out of government, business, industry and, to a large degree, education? Is it not true that a force over which we Christians seem to have no control has gained control of journalism, motion pictures, theaters, and radio? Is it not true that some unseen force has woven the thread of international banking to the detriment of civilization, that a godless force is dominating industry, has monopolized controls of industrial activities, has used governments as their servants, and has been instrumental in flinging one nation against another's throat?" From here, Coughlin went on to accuse the New York Jewish banking firm of Kuhn, Loeb of having financed the Russian Revolution, an absurd charge which, incredibly enough, became dignified when not only Kuhn, Loeb but also Alexander Kerensky and Leon Trotsky denied it! Catholic reaction to Coughlin's anti-Semitism was almost solidly one of shock and shame, and his own diocesan newspaper rebuked him. Archbishop Edward Mooney, successor to Gallagher and later a cardinal, attempted to censor what Coughlin said on the radio, but backed off after an outpouring of mail in the priest's favor, apparently waiting for the pastor of Royal Oak to hang himself.

Unfortunately, this was to take a little time. From baiting the Jews, Coughlin turned to opposing American aid to Britain during World War II. He attacked Lend-Lease as a Communist plot and said: "The lend-lease bill will substitute Karl Marx for George Washington." After Pearl Harbor, he insinuated that the debacle there was a New Deal plot to involve America in the war. With this, Roosevelt found himself on the horns of a censorship dilemma. He did not wish to repeat Woodrow Wilson's harsh suppression of dissent during World War I; and yet, Coughlin and *Social Justice* were a threat to the war effort. Although *Social Justice* was banned from the mails under the Espionage Act, the silencing of Coughlin himself remained a problem. To bring the Radio Priest to trial might make a martyr of Coughlin and thus seriously hamper prosecution of the war. Fortunately, Roosevelt's dilemma was solved for him by two prominent Catholic laymen—Postmaster General Frank Walker and Leo T. Crowley, chairman of the Federal Deposit Insurance Corporation—who, without FDR's knowledge, approached Archbishop Mooney and persuaded him to silence Coughlin. This, Mooney was glad to do, much to Roosevelt's delight; and to the undying credit of Charles E. Coughlin he obeyed the orders of his ordinary. Without a word of complaint, the very model of a loyal priest, he went into obscurity; and from 1942 until his recent death he did not speak a word on the questions which had once made of him such an impassioned—and uncritical—pleader.

Many judgments have since been passed on Father Coughlin, ranging from a description of him as just another Populist from the Midwestern plains, differing "only" from John Ryan in that his was right-wing Populism as compared to the "Right Reverend New Dealer's" leftist brand, a distinction which seems about as small as the one between compulsion and persuasion; or that he was *ipso facto* a cynical, power-seeking demagogue, or worse, a congenital anti-Semite who, as a Catholic priest, was living proof of that faith's undying enmity toward Jews. Undoubtedly, Coughlin was in the Populist tradition, but it appears that his reforming zeal gave way to the anger and frustration which he felt when ignored by Roosevelt, and that his resentment turned him into a demagogue. It also seems likely that the naive and uncritical adulation of his followers turned his head. Any man who has received no more than a single fan letter may judge what may have happened to Charles E. Coughlin the week he received no less than 350,000 as the result of one broadcast. Furthermore, it is possible that this handsome, broad-shouldered man had in him the seeds of an incipient paranoia. He saw "conspiracy" everywhere, and he magnified what he saw. No honest man would deny that there are many Jews in international banking and in the American communications industry, facts which may easily be explained on economic or sociological grounds, or even the simple fact that Jews tend to congregate in the great cities which are also the communications and banking centers of the world. It might also be true that there is a certain conscious element of "pulling together" among Jews in these fields, which is only to say what may be said of any oppressed minority, but to see in this a deliberate, organized plot against the established order seems to be a mark of the paranoiac. Nevertheless, one thing must also be said of Charles E. Coughlin. He was unique among demagogues. When his superior ordered him to step out of the limelight, he did.

As he did, meanwhile, a new churchman rose into prominence in the American Church, and it is possible that Franklin Delano Roosevelt's very vexation with the Radio Priest of Royal Oak may have helped to be the "making" of Francis Joseph Spellman. Born in Whitman, Massachusetts, the son of a moderately prosperous grocer, Francis Spellman is in some ways one of the enigmas of Church history. During his long life and long career as the ordinary and then the Cardinal-Archbishop of the wealthy and enormous Archdiocese of New York, in effect the primatial see of America, he was the object of much hatred and much devotion. Perhaps only two things may be said of him without fear of contradiction: he had an amazing capacity for getting things done by the give and take of favors among powerful people, and he was as American as apple pie. His biographer, the Jesuit educator Robert I. Gannon, wrote of him: ". . . Francis Joseph, who was Frank by the time he could walk, lived the life typical of a lucky American boy at the turn of the century—small town, good schools, active parish, brothers and sisters, a store to tend, papers to sell, delivery wagon to drive, horses in the stable, with a pony for his little sister, enough prosperity to provide a comfortable home and the prospect of college—all brought to a happy focus by a good, hard-working father and a devoted mother." Here is wholesomeness par excellence, and it is likely that the word "wholesome" best describes Spellman. Certainly his boyish frankness and absolute refusal to be awed by rank or regalia charmed the Italian prelates whom he met at the North American College. Educated there in the days when, as he wryly observed later, the parental ability to pay was one of the chief qualifications, Spellman worked hard at his studies, especially at acquiring that fluency in Italian which was to help him make so many friends in Rome. Among them were Eugenio Cardinal Pacelli, Secretary of State for Pope Pius XI, and even Pius himself, who called him the "Benjamin" of the American hierarchy and his dearest friend. In 1932, the gruff and forthright Pius made Spellman an auxiliary bishop of Boston despite the unvoiced but nevertheless actual displeasure of Cardinal O'Connell. In fact, the irascible and autocratic O'Connell is supposed to have commented: "Francis epitomizes what happens when you teach a grocery clerk how to read and write." However apocryphal this remark may be, the fact is that O'Connell did assign the new bishop to an ordinary parish in Newton Center.

It was as the Pastor of Newton Center, then, that this plump and moonfaced prelate with the friendly smile and an iron will came into national prominence. That was in November, 1936, shortly after Roosevelt had won his landslide victory over Landon, and Eugenio Cardinal Pacelli had come to the United States on a visit. Bishop Spellman accompanied the cardinal on his tour, skillfully shielding him from the frequently sharp questions of American newsmen, especially from those queries suggesting that Pacelli had come to the United States to make a "deal" with President Roosevelt involving the silencing of Father Coughlin. Whatever the papal Secretary of State talked about with FDR is not exactly known, but he did confer with him at the Roosevelt family home in Hyde Park, a meeting which Spellman considered historic, and which he recorded in a letter to his brother John:

. . . I can see in my mind's eye as clearly as if it were yesterday, His Eminence and President Roosevelt talking alone near the fireplace at the far end of the great living room . . . President Roosevelt had been returned to office by the largest plurality of votes that any President of the United States has ever received. That had been the greatest day in the President's life, greater than the first election day because it meant the approval of his policies and actions.

This was a great day for America and a great day for Catholic America. I was so proud of the Cardinal on that day, and Mrs. Roosevelt, the President's mother, was proud too. I sat at her left at luncheon and she said to me, "What a joy to have His Eminence as our guest. He may be Pope some day."

Eugenio Pacelli did become Pope, being the overwhelming choice of his fellow cardinals to succeed Pius XI, who died in February of 1939; and not long after Pacelli began his reign as Pope Pius XII, the Pastor from Newton Center became the Archbishop of New York, much to the unhappiness of the consultors of that pre-eminent see, who, if they would accept any "outsider" at all, much preferred the brilliant Archbishop McNicholas of Cincinnati. But Pacelli's American tour had convinced him that Francis Spellman should be his principal channel of communication between the Vatican and the White House, and so the death of Cardinal Hayes of New York had given him the opportunity to place Spellman in exactly the right spot.

With the eruption of World War II, and President Roosevelt's mounting concern for the postwar flood of refugees he expected to come to America, as well as his desire to keep informed on European affairs, Spellman became the go-between in negotiations to send an American representative to the Vatican. Roosevelt had no qualms about opening relations with the Pope. An aristocrat who had none of the so-called "grass-roots" prejudice against Popery, proud of his blood relationship with Venerable Mother Seton and Archbishop James Roosevelt Bayley, he was also delighted that the cardinal he had met and befriended at Hyde Park was now Pius XII. Moreover, there was a precedent for his proposal. There had been consuls and consuls general at the Papal States from 1797 to 1847. In 1847 Congress raised the consulate to a legation, and Lewis Cass, Jr., of New York, who held the position, suggested to Franklin Pierce that he accept a nuncio. Unfortunately, the nation was then in the throes of Know-Nothingism and Pierce shied away from the idea. Nevertheless, he raised the Vatican post to the rank of minister, and relations with the Papacy thereafter grew so friendly that in 1866, when it was believed that the Pope would abandon Rome to the advancing Piedmontese army and seek sanctuary in the United States, Secretary of State Seward had two U.S. Navy vessels sent to Italy for that purpose. Aware of this, and of the need for a "listening post" in Europe, Secretary of State

Cordell Hull fell in with Roosevelt's project. In his *Memoirs*, Hull recalled: "In conversations with the President I cautioned that we could not send a regular Ambassador to the Vatican and should have to limit ourselves to a personal representative from himself to the Pope. I favored [Ambassador to Italy] Phillips's suggestion that this representative be a Protestant. Great Britain had followed the procedure of naming a Protestant as her Minister to the Vatican, with a Catholic as first secretary of the Legation. I also said that, if he took this step, he should simultaneously enlist the similar cooperation of the American leaders of other churches."

Hull's advice was followed, and after consulting with Protestant and Jewish leaders, Roosevelt named Myron C. Taylor as his personal representative to the Vatican. At first, there was no adverse reaction to the decision, and the secular press generally approved FDR's "statesmanlike" appointment. Gradually, however, some Protestant groups began to protest it as a "violation" of the principle of separation of church and state. Opposition grew more intense, with some of the more fundamentalist sects bitterly charging that the presence of an American representative in the Vatican would be an issue in the 1940 presidential election. If it was, however, it was only a minor one; and then, after Franklin Delano Roosevelt won his unprecedented third term in the White House, the Japanese attacked Pearl Harbor—and once again the distraction of a major war silenced all public criticism of the Catholic Church in America.

Chapter XXIII

In World War II, as in all previous struggles, the Catholics of America joined the Armed Forces in numbers beyond their proportion in the population, making up an estimated 25 to 35 per cent of the men in uniform. The number of Catholic chaplains was also high—some three thousand priests, of whom eighty-three were killed in action or died of other causes.

Once again also, the hierarchy rallied to the country's cause to a man, and the attitude of the bishops was probably best expressed by Archbishop Spellman, when, only hours after the attack on Pearl Harbor was made known, he issued this statement:

As Archbishop of New York, I place all our resources, hospitals, institutions and personnel at the disposition of the Government. As Bishop in charge of the Catholic priests in the Army and Navy I can state that there are five hundred chaplains on duty at the present time. They have been an important factor in the building of the morale of our soldiers and sailors. They will be with them wherever they go and whatever they do. As an American and one of twenty-five million Catholic Americans I follow the identically glorious traditions of my country and my religion.

Although such instant patriotism was by now to be expected of the American Church, especially in an America unified as never before by the Japanese sneak attack, what was undoubtedly new and encouraging was the lack of self-consciousness with which Catholics contributed to the war effort. In this war, it appeared, Catholics had become completely assimilated in American society. There was no replica of the National Catholic War Conference which directed the Catholic war effort in World War I, nor was there a trace of that self-conscious name-dropping or statistics-keeping by which it might be boasted that this general or that admiral was a Catholic. In World War II, Catholics were no longer almost exclusively enlisted men or junior officers but held commands of every rank, ranging from Fleet Admiral William D. Leahy, Chief of Staff to Presidents Roosevelt and Truman; to General J. Lawton ("Lightning Joe") Collins, a brilliant division and corps commander in Europe and later Army Chief of Staff; and General Alfred M. Gruenther, Eisenhower's successor as commander of NATO: down to a PT-boat commander named John F. Kennedy or Manila John Basilone, a gallant Marine sergeant who won a Medal of Honor on Guadalcanal and went back to war a second time to meet death on the sands of Iwo Jima. In a word, then, the Catholic record in World War II was once again one of unquestioning patriotism and unflinching loyalty, with the notable exception that there were now proportionately as many bars and stars on the shoulders of Catholics as there had formerly been stripes on their sleeves.

Probably the most startling result of the war, and one not generally known, was the birth of a solid contemplative movement in the American Church. It has often been said that one of the distinguishing marks of the Church in the United States has been its lack of an inner life. No less a church historian than the Protestant, Kenneth Scott Latourette, has alluded to this apparent defect by observing the "significant" fact that by the middle of the twentieth century only one American saint, Mother Frances Cabrini, had been canonized, and that she had been born and reared in Italy. This, said Latourette, together with the fact that many of Mother Cabrini's European contemporaries had also been raised to the altar, seems to suggest that "from the standpoint of Rome the Catholic Church in the United States was unpromising as a source of ideal Christian character."

Although Latourette's courteous and well-intended criticism seems to ignore the heroic sacrifices of the lowborn Catholic laity, millions of good and perhaps even some saintly people who struggled daily to keep Christ in their lives, while giving to His Church their hard-earned pennies and their children, there is no doubt that the history of the contemplative life in the American Church had been very slim indeed; and in Catholic teaching the presence of a flourishing contemplative movement is one of the surest signs of that holiness which is considered one of the four Marks of the Church.* Although it is possible for a layman such as the modern saint, Matt Talbot of Ireland, to attain the contemplative life, it is usually found only in the strictest religious orders. There, a man or woman may achieve the closest union with God, sometimes even an ecstatic one, through devoting themselves exclusively to prayer and worship, and by divorcing themselves from the material or dynamic life of "the world."

As early as 1790, there had been contemplatives in the United States, after a group of American-born Carmelite nuns who had trained in the English convent at Hoogstraet in Belgium founded their own house near Port Tobacco, Maryland. These tender shoots produced little growth, however, probably because of the American Catholic religious climate: activist and inclined to distrust the "foreign" concept of monasticism. Meanwhile, the travail of the French Revolution also provided this country with its first male contemplatives, a group of Reformed Cistercians, or Trappists, who came here in 1802 and for ten frustrating years attempted to establish themselves in various parts of the country. In 1814, with the return of religious freedom to France, these French monks also returned to their native land. Thirty years later a second band of French Trappists did strike roots in America, establishing a monastery about fifty miles southeast of Louisville, Kentucky. Other Trappist houses followed near Dubuque, Iowa, and Providence, Rhode Island. Nevertheless, these seemingly austere and difficult monasteries—with their vows of silence, simple food, manual labor and an incredibly regimented devotional life—had little appeal for the restless and impatient American temperament, and only a tiny stream of novices trickled inside the Trappist walls. American Catholics seemed so little disposed toward the contemplative life that in 1938 Jacques Maritain wrote, ". . . my Carthusian friends in Europe told me that the very idea of having a Charterhouse in America was ridiculous."

So it would seem, until the horror of World War II sent a flood of American Catholic servicemen flowing into the monasteries. Like great Dante before them, they sought "peace," and

* It is One, Holy, Catholic and Apostolic.

their desire to know God more intimately was celebrated in the famous, best-selling autobiography *The Seven Storey Mountain*, written by Thomas Merton, a Trappist of the Abbey of Our Lady of Gethsemani who had once sought to find fulfillment in the pseudo-intellectual circles of Greenwich Village, or, like Augustine before him, to drown his anguish in gaudy debauchery. Merton's book, together with his later works, gave to a surprised America a true and unvarnished account of the simplicity of monastic life, as well as the spiritual beauty of contemplation, and probably had much to do with giving further momentum to the monastic movement in this country. As a result, the Trappist monasteries in America are now thronged with novices, and in 1958 Maritain could gently reprove his doubting "Carthusian friends" with the remark: "Well, now Tom Merton's books are best-sellers, great classical works on spiritual life are published in abundance and are widely read in the most varied circles, the Trapp of Gethsemani alone has more novices than all European Trapps combined, and is obliged to multiply new foundations; the monasteries founded by various contemplative Orders are so crowded that they refuse candidates for lack of room; and there *is* a [Carthusian] Charterhouse in this country."

As might have been expected, these American contemplatives are perhaps a little more dynamic than their European counterparts. Spiritual and strictly disciplined, they are also as material and free-wheeling as any American "self-starter" or "go-getter." Thus, the Oblates of Mary in Washington, D.C., turn a tidy little profit by running their own golf course, while at St. Benedict's Abbey near Aspen, Colorado, mounted monks ride herd on five hundred head of cattle on a 3,800-acre ranch.

Thomas Merton's own Abbey of Our Lady of Gethsemani conducts a flourishing mail-order business in fruit cake, cheeses, ham, bacon and summer sausage. At the Abbey of the Genesee near Rochester, New York, the monks produce their famous "Monk's Bread," which is advertised in the New York subways. (To their credit, the Genesee monks turned down one adman's slogan: "Baked in Silence: Too Good for Words.") And from *Time* came this description of American monks "laboring in the fields:"

As they rushed to finish a 38,000-lb. order of jelly for shipment to

Chicago last week, the workers in the preserves factory outside Spencer, Mass., would have made any boss happy. They worked relentlessly, spoke not a word, took no coffee or cigarette breaks, smiled constantly. Occasionally, they glanced up at a sign that spurred them on even more: IT IS GOOD FOR US TO BE HERE. The contented workers were the Trappist monks of St. Joseph's Abbey, and their thriving jelly business (1,230,000 jars a year) is typical of a fascinating—and rapidly growing—phenomenon: the successful business set up and run by a religious community.

Not all of these monastic entrepreneurs were new, of course, the Western Province of the Christian Brothers having for years produced a nationally famous brand of wines in their Napa Valley vineyards. Three wineries turning out a total of more than a million cases of wine and brandy a year have become the virtual support of the entire province, and their seven-million-dollar stainless-steel grape-crushing machine was the first in the wine-growing industry. Fortunately, the brothers resisted the temptation to unfair competition offered by their tax-free religious status, and in 1957 they agreed to pay full federal taxes just like their secular competitors.

Meanwhile, the postwar years were also producing marked changes in the character of the Catholic laity. By the end of World War II, perhaps more than half the Catholics in America were still members of the lower classes. But the economic and educational opportunities provided by the postwar boom and the GI Bill changed that traditional status, and by the end of the decade —which saw the Catholic population rise to thirty million—great numbers of Catholics had climbed into the middle class and had joined the general flight of middle-class Americans from the city to the suburbs.

With this mass exodus to suburbia there came a host of new and complex problems for the Church. First, while better-educated and better-paid Americans of all beliefs were producing a suburban expansion which was to explode to sixty million in the quarter century between the end of World War II and 1970, the cities that they left behind were filling up with less fortunate Americans drawn to the metropolis either by the lure of welfare checks or the blandishments of manufacturers' recruiters sent into the countryside to find cheap labor. Where once the Irish, Germans, Poles, Scandinavians and Italians had been America's hewers of wood and drawers of water, now it was to be the Negroes, the Spanish-speaking Puerto Ricans and Mexicans and the so-called Country Folk, the poor whites and hillbillies of the South and Appalachia. These are the New Immigrants, the successors to the Old Immigrants; and, ironically, the American Church, having considered herself to have shed her old appellation as the Church of the Immigrants, found herself once more playing the role of mother and teacher to many of these unhappy, exploited people. With the blacks and the Spanish-speaking, her problems have been even more difficult, if only because they are the objects of a deeper racial prejudice, one that is shared, unfortunately, by many Catholics who were only recently the victims of the same kind of bigotry. With the Country Folk, of course, she has no problem, if only because these people are unapproachable. Fierce, proud and clannish, they not only resist all attempts at "acculturation," that is, to educate them and assimilate them into American urban society, they look upon the Roman Catholic Church with all the distrust of the Puritans from whom they are descended.

Nevertheless, an entire new mission field was opened up among the blacks and the Spanish-speaking peoples crowded into the urban ghettos. Where once it had been thought that nothing could be done with the large old parishes turned empty and silent by the flight to suburbia, the Church soon reorganized them as mission stations. Some progress was made among the blacks who had moved into these old neighborhoods, and perhaps more among the Spanish-speaking, who had at first been bewildered and resentful of the hostility they had encountered from the *Yanquis* of their own faith. Moreover, the universal plight of the cities in America caused some social-minded priests and bishops to consider urban planning as much a necessary component of Catholic Action as the labor-management theories of Monsignor John Ryan three and four decades earlier. Unfortunately, like their fellow countrymen of other faiths, most of the Catholics who fled city squalor for the "good life" of the suburbs show a spectacular lack of interest in the problems of the cities they evacuated.

In the field of race relations, however, it may be said that the Church's record has been outstanding, even if it may not satisfy those black militants or white liberals who feel that all the Christian churches are dragging their feet in the struggle to secure complete racial equality. The Church did not, of course, make the first breach in the wall of racial prejudice, an achievement which seems to belong to the black people themselves, if only because she has had a long tradition of respect for local customs. Thus, after the Civil War, Catholicism made no effort to alter the basic American pattern of segregation. But once the attitude toward this social evil began to change, the Church was in the forefront of those institutions moving to speed the process.

In 1934, the Catholic Inter-Racial Council was formed with the objective of seeking racial justice, publishing the *Inter-Racial Review* founded earlier at St. Louis by the Jesuits. Two years later, the Catholic University, which had had a colored graduate as early as 1896, reopened its doors to Negroes, the first white university of the federal district to do so. In 1938, Sacred Heart College in Manhattanville received a Negro girl student, and the Jesuits at St. Louis University shortly afterward adopted the same policy of integration, one which is now followed by all the Catholic colleges and universities in America.

During World War II, with the country absorbed in the national emergency to the detriment of all other problems, the Catholic bishops of the United States reminded their fellow Americans of the injustices still being done to Negroes, issuing in 1943 a statement which said in part: "In the Providence of God there are among us millions of fellow citizens of the Negro race. We owe to these fellow citizens, who have contributed so largely to the development of our country, and for whose welfare history imposes on us a special obligation of justice, to see that they have in fact the rights which are given to them in our Constitution." After the war, the Catholic bishops of the South and other integrated areas boldly put these words into practice in the face of what was frequently bitter opposition. In September, 1947, seven years before the Supreme Court's famous integration ruling of May, 1954, Archbishop Joseph Ritter of St. Louis ended segregation in the schools of his diocese. A year later, Archbishop Patrick O'Boyle of Washington began to integrate the Catholic classrooms of his archdiocese. In June, 1953, still a year ahead of the

Supreme Court decision, Bishop Vincent Waters of Raleigh, North Carolina, opened all the schools, churches and hospitals in his diocese to all Americans, keeping them open in spite of the vigorous protests of Catholics and non-Catholics alike. Even stronger opposition was raised in New Orleans, where Archbishop Joseph Rummel found it necessary to excommunicate some Catholics who defied his decision to integrate the archdiocese. Such obstructionism, meanwhile, compelled the bishops to speak once again on the racial question, and in 1958 they issued a statement setting forth the Church's doctrine on segregation, making it clear that anything less than complete equality for all races was incompatible with a Christian's duty toward his fellow men.

In its leadership, then, if not always among the bulk of the faithful, the American Church courageously attempted to be a part of the solution to the racial problem rather than part of the problem itself. Meanwhile, she also had to struggle with other postwar problems created by the flight to suburbia. Chief among these was the phenomenon of social mobility by which career-conscious, success-minded Americans were forever moving on from one kind of parish representing one level of the "good life" onto another wealthier one characteristic of the "better life" and from there, inevitably, onto the "best life." This difficult situation was made further complicated by the "religious revival" which swept the United States, or at least middle-class America, during the late forties and the fifties.

Much has been written about the "return to religion" of postwar America. On the one hand, it has been charged that it was a sham religious renaissance, born more of a sociological than a spiritual drive. Prone to identify, eager to "belong," Americans had now found it fashionable to be a member of some recognized faith. Moreover, most of those admonitions—"Go to Church on Sunday," "Find a Faith to Live By"—which came blaring out of the radio or were emblazoned on highway billboards appeared to be based on the idea that religion was "good for you," that it was part of the American Way of Life or the spiritual right arm of democracy. Thus, religion did not seem to be a dialogue between man and his Maker, or a means of spiritual experience or a formula for self-control or self-improvement, it was not Jesus Christ saying, "I am the Way, the Truth and the Life," and it was certainly not the Way of the Cross; rather it seemed to be a kind of sophisticated magic by which "Our Friend Upstairs" or "That Livin' Doll," i.e., Almighty God, might be impetrated for a promotion, a high College Boards or a low blood count. The religion of the revival, then, too often appeared to be nothing more than a social utility. People joined a church to make friends or to escape loneliness. But it was not God who was on the altar, but Man, deified and self-adulating. If religion was merely socially useful, it was also "good for democracy." Thus, perhaps the most famous exponent of this new and more subtle form of Caesaro-Papism was Dwight David Eisenhower, who, as president of Columbia University, told a reporter: "A democracy cannot exist without a religious base. I believe in democracy." In this, the City of Man supersedes the City of God and religion serves the state: it is the moral force by which the evil menace of Communism is to be overthrown.

Whether or not this subtle distortion of true religion—which puts God before man, religion above the state and conscience ahead of conformity—was actually characteristic of the revival is difficult to say. Some defenders of the movement insist that its critics were agnostics or atheistic humanists peeved by this unseemly resurrection of that very orthodoxy which they had pronounced dead. Such men would be upset by any religious renaissance tending to outdate their own ideas, and would be inclined to sneer at the authenticity of any kind of revival—especially among those dreadful Philistines of the middle class. Much as it may distress these fastidious traducers, however, it appears that the Holy Spirit has actually been to suburbia. On balance, the Catholic suburbanite is apparently an extremely generous and devout human being, one who contributes to all kinds of charities and spares no expense or sacrifice to see that his children are educated and morally responsible. He is probably more fervent and informed in his faith than his ancestors, and as Father Greeley observes: "In fact, he and his fellows have, it would seem, reached a level of *observable religious practice* seldom, if ever, surpassed by a large group of people in the history of the Church."

Whatever its motivations, the revival was real. In the 1950s well over 60 per cent of the American population belonged to an organized religion, an increase of 200 per cent in fifty years and of 300 per cent in one hundred years. That huge, sprawling, amorphous mass of Americans once known as "the unchurched," appeared to be taking on a religious cast. Not only church membership but also church attendance soared. Close to half a billion dollars a year was spent on new church construction, and in the Catholic Church alone it was estimated that four new churches were opened every week. Thus, even after the abatement of the religious revival which took place in the 1960s, by the end of 1968 there were no less than 18,146 parishes, to say nothing of another eighteen thousand missions, stations and chapels.

As far as the brick-and-mortar needs of the American Church were concerned, the religious revival was very real indeed. So was its middle-class character, and this, together with the flight to the suburbs, complicated the problems of the suburban pastor. Almost all of them are saddled with a big and what appears to be a never-ending debt. Suburban churches are not cheap, if only because motorized suburbia requires a huge parking lot, and because suburban Catholics, emulating their Protestant countrymen, demand a wide range of social services from their parish, making it mandatory to put in a hall or an auditorium replete with all kinds of gadgetry for lighting and recording, and, of course, a kitchen. Moreover, the suburban emphasis, not to say mania, on child care usually culminates in an irresistible drive for a new parochial school. Finally, it is likely that in some parishes the pastor will never get out of debt. These are the poorer suburbs to which the young, career-minded couples first move, where they have their children and where, because of their own exuberance and drive to "socialize," they demand so many parish activities. Mortgaged to the hilt, taxed to maintain the public school system, these young suburbanites rarely are able to make the barest contribution to the parochial complex which they so avidly desire; and yet, once the first good promotion comes, they move on to a better suburb, leaving the old pastor still staggering under a financial incubus perpetuated by the arrival of the new career-minded young couples who take their place. Social mobility, then, tends to make the rich parishes richer and the poor ones poorer.

A second problem springing from the flight to suburbia and

the emergence of a middle-class Catholicism was the growing change in the priest-laity relationship. Educated and prosperous, the layman now felt free to question the priest's role as the unchallenged ruler of the parish. On the spiritual level, of course, and in his mission to sanctify the laity, the priest still possesses all his old authority. But he can no longer expect the laity to accept any statement just because he or the Church says it is true. He must and he does expect to be questioned or even challenged by intelligent and informed laymen. Gone also is his role as the undisputed ruler—despot, even—of the parish. He is well aware that the parish may now contain men better educated than he or better equipped to lead or speak out on public questions touching on the Catholic faith. Thus, the Catholic priest of today is more like a coach than a commander.

Out of this new relationship, and the layman's growing refusal to submit to naked authority, there might probably arise the danger of a leveling tendency. The layman might come to think of himself as being as good as the priest "and maybe even a little better." The old ghost of Trusteeism might walk again in a Brooks Brothers suit. This, of course, is the risk which the postwar Church must run, as she attempts to adapt to the new kind of Catholic in her care. On questions of dogma and discipline, however, there seems to be no likelihood of lay intransigence. Only in the procedural or administrative areas do the priest and the people appear to be at times confronting one another, arrayed in the immemorial conflict between authority and liberty, which can only be, after all, a fruitful tension.

Meanwhile, the flight to the suburbs seems to have been through the crumbling walls of the ghetto. As in all previous wars, World War II demonstrated to many isolated or rural Americans who had been reared in bigotry that Catholic Americans were not really the sons of perdition. In the postwar years, the Catholic suburbanite looked, dressed, talked and usually thought no different than his Protestant neighbor. He was not completely accepted yet, if only because No-Popery appears likely to live as long as there are Popes living in Rome; and on such issues as birth control, abortion and divorce, it is likely that Catholics will still differ from Protestants. Otherwise, one appears to be as American as another.

Of vastly more importance, the walls of the intellectual ghetto in which American Catholic thought had long been imprisoned were also beginning to collapse. Since the birth of the American Church with the consecration of John Carroll as the first bishop in 1789, observer after observer had lamented the lack of Catholic influence in American cultural life. Brownson noted and decried it; so did Viscount Bryce, together with a horde of visiting prelates who came to these shores with or without a papal commission to study the American Catholic character. Almost to a man, however, these Cassandras of Catholic intellectualism were to some degree able to excuse its failures in the general economic disadvantages of the working-class Catholics, in the anti-Catholicism of the country or in the Church's preoccupation with the immigrants. As late as 1941, Professor D. W. Brogan of Cambridge could write: "One result of this preoccupation with the immigrants has been that the Catholic Church in America has counted for astonishingly little in the formation of the American intellectual climate." Others more openly apologetic claimed that "the best" of American Catholic youth were trained for the priesthood, and that the burden of priestly duties often precluded their going on to distinguish themselves intellectually. It was in these and similar warm snuggeries of self-excusing casuistry that most Catholics who were honest enough even to consider the defect were able to take refuge. Occasionally, some courageous outside critic such as President Robert M. Hutchins of Chicago might come along to remind American Catholic educators that they were not quite measuring up to the standards of "the longest intellectual tradition of any institution in the contemporary world," but generally Catholic education seemed content with turning out a proportionate replica of the Protestant businessman, quite a few doctors and lawyers, together with an astonishing number of demure and dense young ladies—the products of the teacup-balancing curricula at all those "little old nuns' schools"—while allowing the rest of America to carry off the palm of research and creation. When criticized for intellectual failures obvious to most outside students of the problem, as well as to a growing number of inside priests and laymen, the Church would usually respond by defending its record for improving the moral climate, or of fighting Communism. Undoubtedly, both these claims were true, but they were also both beside the point. In fact, the Church, or at least those in charge of education, appeared to be indifferent to encouraging a program of research or creativity, and it was this very insouciance which alienated such "born" Catholic writers as John O'Hara, F. Scott Fitzgerald and Eugene O'Neill, while horrifying converts like Ernest Hemingway and Allen Tate. It was as though the American Church were saying there was no need for free inquiry, at least not in such sensitive areas as theology, philosophy, biblical studies or social science. Matthew, Mark, Luke and John, apparently, had said it all—aided and abetted by Augustine and Aquinas. Thus, American Catholicism seemed to be echoing the ancient heretic Tertullian's obscurantist cry: "After Christ Jesus we desire no subtle theories, no acute inquiries after the gospel . . ."

Obviously, this was not and could never be the stated policy of American Catholicism. With the Universal Church she had always maintained that there was no conflict between faith and reason, that there is nothing in her teachings explicitly hostile to intellectualism. Yet, as any historian knows, between any given institution's policies and its practices one is often forced to walk a long, crooked mile. True enough, the Church did not frown upon research or free inquiry; and yet, the innovator was more often than not carefully watched and looked upon as a potential traitor. If he was not shunted aside or shanghaied to some lonely parochial outpost, then he might be denied promotion or reward or even delated to Rome. Among the laity, of course, this would not be possible; but then, most of the laymen educated in Catholic colleges and universities were usually thoroughly drenched in the "instant theology" courses which seemed dedicated to supplying them with a lifetime's supply of formulas, readymade "Catholic answers" to any "difficulties" which might be raised by their non-Catholic friends. Such indoctrination, of course, would not only dull the edge of most any inquiring mind, but also inculcate in the "educated" Catholic a kind of supercilious superiority toward the "confused" thinking of some genuinely puzzled non-Catholic intellectual trying to grope his way toward a better understanding of reality. As Professor Thomas F. O'Dea has maintained: "Unless it is possible for a Catholic youth to understand his faith, to know what faith really is, and maintain his faith, without having on the one hand to be spoon-fed when genuine difficulties are involved, and, on the other, having his head jammed with readymade formulae memorized in religion and philosophy classes, there is really no hope for the development of an intellectual life among Catholics. For to be an intellectual means to be engaged in a quest."

This, then, was the defensive attitude which made a mockery of Catholic intellectualism in America. Cut off from the European Church, where a new intellectual flowering had begun to bud and blossom, the Church in America was a kind of petrified growth. She was the Council of Trent set down in the twentieth century. Her cultural heritage had come from a European Catholicism besieged, first, by the Reformation, and then by the militant secularism born of the Enlightenment. But while the mental attitudes of this European Catholicism had begun to change after the First World War, they had not changed in the United States. Here, Catholicism still felt herself besieged, she still feared the "contamination" of secular society. If the American Church had been the descendant of a medieval stonemason, she would have still been building feudal keeps among the skyscrapers of Manhattan. Beyond doubt, this defensive mentality had served its purpose. It had kept the deposit of faith, the people had been sanctified, and the Gospel had been preached. Still, all this had also been done by early Christianity while it was in the process of converting Rome. Why could not American Catholicism do all this, too, the Catholic intellectuals argued, while attempting to inform the magnificent secular society surrounding it with its own moral purpose.

And so, in the 1950s, the Catholic intellectuals formed ranks and launched a counterattack. Indictment after indictment was leveled against their Church's defensive spirit, and probably the most effective charge of all came from the eminent church historian Monsignor John Tracy Ellis. In 1955 in an article published in the Jesuit quarterly *Thought*, Monsignor Ellis raised all the old accusations already catalogued here, but went on to deny that the Catholic intellectual failure had anything to do with economic privation, immigrant status or anti-Catholic prejudice. "The chief blame, I firmly believe," he said, "lies with Catholics themselves. It lies in their frequently self-imposed ghetto mentality which prevents them from mingling as they should with their non-Catholic colleagues, and in their lack of industry and the habits of work, to which Hutchins alluded in 1937. It lies in their failure to have measured up to their responsibilities to the incomparable tradition of Catholic learning of which they are the direct heirs, a failure which Peter Viereck noted, and which suggested to him the caustic question, 'Is the honorable adjective "Roman Catholic" truly merited by America's middle-class-Jansenist Catholicism, puritanized, Calvinized, and dehydrated . . . ?'"

Ellis's manifesto, as it came to be called, rocked the American Catholic community in an unprecedented earthquake of controversy. On the one hand, Ellis had defenders such as the distinguished theologian, Father Gustave Weigel, who put it bluntly, "The general Catholic community in America does not know what scholarship is," and Father John J. Cavanaugh, former president of Notre Dame, who, in an allusion to the great number of Jewish intellectuals in this country, asked: "Where are the Catholic Salks, Oppenheimers, Einsteins?" On the other hand, Father Robert I. Gannon, president of Fordham, criticized the critics in a speech with the self-explanatory title: "Enough Breast-Beating!"

Gradually, however, the critics gained the upper hand, especially after Professor O'Dea entered the battle with a penetrating sociological analysis entitled *American Catholic Dilemma.* O'Dea's book sought for the causes which inhibit American Catholic intellectual life, listing them as defensiveness, the strongly felt need to repel "attacks"; formalism, which replaces experience with ready-made "answers" and looks upon the world as "finished"; moralism, which regards the world almost exclusively as a place of moral danger; and a combination of authoritarianism whereby those in authority take over intellectual functions for which they are seldom qualified, and parochialism which looks inward and ignores secular realities. In a sense, O'Dea's criticism may be summarized in his quotation of Alfred North Whitehead's remark: "The worship of God is not a rule of safety—it is an adventure of the spirit. . . ."

American Catholic Dilemma had the effect of broadening the "new debate" on Catholic intellectualism. Where Ellis and his associates had successfully challenged American Catholic education to raise its standards, to concentrate on excellence and to seek for better faculties and higher endowments, O'Dea's questions ended in one large and still-unanswered question: What is the role of the Catholic in the modern world? Subordinate to this all-encompassing query came others: How independent is a Catholic's judgment in matters outside of faith and morals, indeed, even in faith and morals? How does a Catholic relate himself to secular values? What is the nature of authority and obedience in the Church? In other words, O'Dea opened up the problem which he actually wished to see explored: How does the Catholic Church in the United States make itself meaningful to the secular society around it? With this, of course, went a host of other questions relative to the relation between clergy and laity, questions which at this writing are still largely unanswered. But at least, in the decade of the fifties, the questions were being asked and what appeared to be a Catholic intellectual renaissance was in bloom.

A third happy development of the postwar years was the apparent end or at least diminution of "leakage" from the American Church. Since colonial days, Catholicism in America had had to contend with a Catholic immigrant's very human and understandable tendency to conform to the Protestant religion of the dominant majority. This inclination lessened somewhat after the restriction of immigration in the twenties. Still, there were the sons and daughters of Catholic immigrants who were ashamed to avow the socially attainted faith of their fathers. With the flight to the suburbs and the emergence of a middle-class Catholicism, however, this embarrassment was no longer such a powerful influence. Moreover, as sociologists have demonstrated, there is a tendency among third-generation Americans to seek to know more about their ancestral background. A second-generation American of Italian or Polish extraction might be ashamed to identify too strongly with his immigrant parents' culture. Even if he could speak Polish or Italian, he might in public pretend not to know it. But *his* children, the grandchildren of his father, feel no such compunction. They are inclined to be prouder of the Old Country heritage, and therefore disposed to drift back to the ancestral faith. This new attitude, reinforced by the obvious fact that a Catholic of the fifties or sixties would have very little to gain, either economically or socially, by changing his religion, seems to have made the problem of leakage at least a less serious one for the American Church.

Thus strengthened, already regarded by Rome as the financial bulwark of the Universal Church, the Catholic Church in the United States received special recognition in December, 1945, when Pope Pius XII created four new American cardinals. The new princes of the Church were John Cardinal Glennon of St. Louis, Edward Cardinal Mooney of Detroit, Samuel Cardinal Stritch of Chicago and Francis Cardinal Spellman of New York. With Cardinal Dougherty of Philadelphia, the American Church now possessed five red hats, the largest number ever. Even though this number was reduced the following year by the death of the aging Cardinal Glennon, the creation of four American cardinals at one time was a resounding endorsement of American Catholicism, as well as an indication that the United States might soon be challenging the prestige of France, the eldest daughter of the Church and the most heavily represented non-Italian nation in the College of Cardinals. Because all four of the new cardinals were not only American citizens but had all been born in this country, their elevation also suggested that the American Church had shed one of its most unmistakable marks of "foreignness": the foreign-born bishop. Equally significant at the time was the fact that some of the superiors of the oldest Catholic religious orders with headquarters in Europe were also American citizens.

It might even be argued that bestowal of the red hat on four conservative administrators such as Mooney, Glennon, Stritch and Spellman was evidence that the Catholic Church in the United States was perhaps a bit too "American." Certainly it seemed to confirm the financial or pragmatic character of American bishops as distinct from their more pastoral and intellectual brethren in Europe. From Archbishop John Carroll to Francis Cardinal Spellman, the American episcopate has failed to produce a single original thinker or theologian. Out of its ranks during 170 years of history as an established church there has come no prelate even approaching the status of a Cajetan or a Charles Borromeo or a John Henry Newman, and this includes the much-praised but apparently overrated John Lancaster Spalding. Instead, the American episcopate has been celebrated for producing a prelate distinguished for his caution, his almost incredibly defensive conservatism, his undoubted financial ability, his skill both at administration and his ability to rebuff any attempt to lessen or challenge his authority, his remoteness from the people and his lack of intellectual talent. In a word, he is a kindly, perhaps even saintly, chairman of the board; a banker-bureaucrat.

Unhappily, this same type of bishop has had a natural tendency to perpetuate himself, thus almost guaranteeing that his successor will be chosen from the ranks of the younger bureaucrats around him, the administrative monsignori whom he has hand-picked to run his diocese and function as the bishop's cabinet, rather than from experienced pastors in the field, i.e., out among the people. To use a military metaphor, it is the staff officer, not the leader of the line, who usually gets the promotion. Certainly it will almost never be a priest of any real talent, a man of "dangerous" ideas. Rather it will be the "practical" man, that is to say, some safe cleric with an outstanding record for carrying out His Excellency's wishes. As long ago as 1878, this American preference for the practical as opposed to the pastoral was observed by visitors to this country. Among them was Bishop George Conroy of Armagh, Ireland, who made a lengthy—and, according to Bishop Bernard McQuaid of Rochester, a "most damaging" —report to the Propaganda in which he declared: "In the selection of Bishops, priority is given to financial abilities, rather than to pastoral." Conroy also complained of "the introduction of a new and very false criterion in the selection of subjects recommended for vacant episcopal Sees. Whenever there is deliberation to choose a candidate for the episcopacy, the Bishops of a province feel constrained to seek, at all costs, a man skilled in financial administration. Indeed, it has too often happened that the most valued gifts in the candidate proposed to the Holy See were properly those of a banker, and not of a Pastor of souls." Appraising the general ability of the American episcopate, the visitor from Ireland was particularly scathing, observing that of the sixty-eight bishops then in the United States there were "hardly *ten* who are distinguished by talents of any kind. The others scarcely attain a decent mediocrity, and in theological knowledge they do not even reach mediocrity!" This, at the very moment when the great glories of the American Church—the Americanizers such as John Ireland, John Lancaster Spalding, John Keane and James Gibbons—were just beginning to make their presence felt.

Yet, if Bishop Conroy appears to be a little too acid, as late as 1959 an analysis made in the Archdiocese of New York seemed to suggest that in the American Church the accent was still on the practical. According to the survey, only 45 per cent of the pastors in the archdiocese were monsignori, compared to 80 per cent of those in administrative positions. And the report concluded:

There is then an indication of the existence of two types of clergymen evolving out of the two types of functions: 1. the less specialized, more priestly apostle or parish priest—less conducive to promotion to monsignor or more given to the consolation type of monsignor; 2. the more specialized, less priestly administrator or functionary—more conducive to promotion, more given to recognition and to the functional requirement type of promotion.

In their book *The De-Romanization of the American Catholic Church*, Edward Wakin and Father Joseph Scheuer relate an "illustrative though unconfirmable" story of the aging Midwestern bishop who sought to perpetuate his own type in his diocese. Thus, he chose two senior monsignori with excellent real-estate records and as an afterthought an intellectual. To the bishop's consternation, Rome approved the intellectual, who actually did succeed to the miter. The anecdote, however, appears to boomerang, if only because the new bishop now complains "that he is overwhelmed by his administrative duties."

Obviously, then, because of the dynamic, activist and highly social nature of the American Church, the bishop almost has to be a practical man. The reflective or thoughtful priest is by character and training unfit for the myriad "practical" problems which beset the ordinary bishop on an average day. Administration is his major concern and he relies heavily on administrative assistants who oversee the work of an appallingly large number of agencies and bureaus. Thus, taking the Archdiocese of Newark as an example, there are clerical administrators assigned to the following: Anti-Poverty Program, Apostleship of the Sea, Boy

Scouts, Building Commission, Catechetics, Catholic Students Mission Crusade, Catholic University, Catholic Youth Organization, Cemeteries, Censor, Charities, Choir Guild, Commission for Convent Visitation, Commission for Parish Visitation, Commission for Sacred Music, Confraternity of Christian Doctrine, Confraternity of the Blessed Sacrament, Cooperative Supply Services, Council of Catholic Men, Council of Catholic Women, Ecumenical Study Commission, Education and Economic Opportunity Programs, Family Life, Guilds (all manner of), Holy Name Society, Hospitals, Institute of Sacred Music, Interracial Justice Program, Lay Apostolate, Legion of Mary, Liturgical Commission, Mount Carmel Guild (a charitable organization chiefly concerned with collecting and distributing used clothing), Mount Carmel Guild Department of Special Services (for the deaf, disturbed, alcoholics, etc.), National Catholic Office for Motion Pictures, and National Office for Decent Literature, Newspaper, Nurses, Pope Pius XII Institute of Social Education, Priests Eucharistic League, Propagation of the Faith, Serra Clubs, School Board, School Commission, Schools, Sodalities, Vigilance for the Faith, Visitator General for Religious Communities and Vocations. This does not include, of course, the various archdiocesan courts or a large number of local guilds, orders and sodalities.

Just like the American society which it so faithfully reflects, then, the government of the Catholic Church in the United States had become a huge, finely structured, highly specialized bureaucracy, while the Church herself, in the postwar years of the late forties and the decade of the fifties, became more and more openly involved in the public life of that society.

Chapter XXIV

If, during the two decades between the end of World War II and the American military intervention in Vietnam, a foreign visitor had been observing the American scene, it is possible that he might have considered Catholicism to be either the established national religion or at least the faith of the dominant majority; and that would have been because Catholics of this period were consistently engaged in controversy: between themselves and their enemies, themselves and American practices, themselves and politicians and, finally, between each other. In a word, the religion that hit the headlines then was usually the Catholic one.

Doubtless, the Church would have preferred less publicity, but the fact was that a new and more subtle form of anti-Catholic prejudice had taken root in the minds of many American liberals and intellectuals. During the war, the mixing of so many Catholics with non-Catholics of all areas and creeds had done much to discredit the coarser myths of No-Popery. Since that conflict, however, a new, more sophisticated, perhaps even "educated" campaign against the Church began to develop. As Peter Viereck observed, "Catholic-baiting is the anti-Semitism of the liberals," a remark echoed by the distinguished Harvard historian, Arthur M. Schlesinger, when he told Monsignor John Tracy Ellis: "I regard the prejudice against your Church as the deepest bias in the history of the American people."

Like most prejudice, the new bias appeared to be a thick web of fear woven from the tiniest cocoon of real or apparent truth. It was a blend of resentment against American Catholicism's position on censorship of moving pictures, of its highly successful stand against that postwar Communism with which left-wing intellectuals had so frequently flirted, of her continuing fight to prevent the complete secularization of the public schools and of her own rapidly expanding school system in which some "liberals" professed to discern the chief menace to American democratic institutions. Probably the most celebrated of the latter class of critics was the writer Paul Blanshard, whose controversial book *American Freedom and Catholic Power* was published in 1949, immediately becoming a runaway best seller.

In this and other published articles, Blanshard made a sweeping indictment of the American Church as an insidious threat to the American state. His technique was to amass a wealth of pretended documentation, which, upon examination, usually turned out to be nothing more than Catholic self-criticism quoted out of context, or an array of ordinary harmless statistics quoting the number of pupils in Catholic schools and the value of school property, all set down in a sinister setting. As the Jewish sociologist Will Herberg declared: "Mr. Blanshard's book displays vulgar anti-Catholicism on almost every page."

Nevertheless, it was almost hysterically hailed by many non-Catholic religious leaders who should have known better as "the most penetrating analysis of the enormous power exercised by the Roman Catholic Church that has appeared in our time," or as "scrupulously fair" or "objective in spirit." Actually, it was rather more a recital of every pseudo-intellectual anti-Catholic shibboleth on which Blanshard could lay hands, joined to a collection of every misunderstanding or ignorant distortion of Catholic doctrine extant, all of which was fired by the author's deep distrust of *any* religion which refuses to recognize the supremacy of the state. Thus, among so many other charges, Blanshard attacked the Church's schools as being "divisive" or "harmfully separatist," misrepresented her teaching on the possibility of salvation for non-Catholics and repeated the old canard about the Church commanding that the mother must die to save the child. The first two accusations were refuted by Herberg, who said that if Blanshard had taken the trouble to consult the most rudimentary handbooks on Catholic teaching he would have found that "only those are condemned 'who are convinced of the truth of the Catholic Church but for some selfish reason fail to profess her faith in her.'" Speaking of "divisive" parochial schools, Herberg wrote: "However great may be the merits of the public school system, American democracy does not grant it a monopoly of education. On the contrary, American democracy recognizes the right of parents to send their children to private or parochial schools or even to educate them at home, provided the level of teaching meets certain standards. To deny this right would be totalitarian statism, and would justify defiance in the name of the 'higher law.' When Catholics say this, they are right, and when Blanshard attacks them for saying it, he simply reveals the totalitarian and statist strain in his own thinking."

Blanshard's undoubted statism, his perhaps unconscious worship of democracy, was also exposed by T. Robert Ingram, an Episcopalian theology student who wrote in the *Atlantic Monthly* of February, 1950: ". . . Blanshard takes issue with the Roman Catholic Church on the crucial point for all of us: he judges that church to be a sinister threat to the public weal because it 'refuses to admit that the Church in the social field is simply one agency within the state.' . . . All Christian profession, whether Protestant or Catholic, explicitly declares that the church derives its existence and its authority directly from God in Christ, and that it never can bow to the supremacy of the state and still be Christian."

The Catholic position on abortion, so often misrepresented or misunderstood, was patiently explained by the Jesuit, Father George H. Dunne, who, in discussing Norman Thomas's favorable review of Blanshard's book, declared:

The Church's position is not, as Mr. Thomas says it is, "that, if a choice must be made, the life of the unborn child, even the smallest embryo, should be preferred to that of the mother." On the contrary, the position of Catholic moralists is that, wherever a choice must be made, everything possible should be done to save the mother even though the measures taken indirectly result in the loss of the child. The measures which may be taken, however, do not include the right directly to kill the child in order to save the mother.

The Catholic position is based upon respect for the individual human life, any human life; upon the principle that the direct and voluntary killing of any innocent human being, by the state or an individual, is murder; and upon the principle that the end, however good and desirable in itself, does not justify the means. Once these values are repudiated there is no moral limit to the crimes that can be committed against the human person. A rigorously logical path leads from abortion to euthanasia and the gas chambers. A logically satisfying case can be made out for the extermination of all Jews. Without Jews there would be no Jewish problem (though other scapegoats could be found to take their places). The extermination of all Catholics would be a logically satisfying solution to the problem that haunts Paul Blanshard—the Catholic problem. Once we claim the right directly to kill one innocent person in the name of a greater good there is left no *moral* ground upon which to protest the killing of tens of thousands of innocent persons in the name of a greater good—unless morals is a mere matter of numbers.

Father Dunne's concluding phrase—"unless morals is a mere matter of numbers"—put the finger on the basis of Blanshard's moral philosophy, what Professor Brogan called "statistical morality." Whatever the majority wants is right, whether it be Auschwitz or abortion. Gradually, in the calm light of such discussion, the anti-Catholic furor which Blanshard's book and articles aroused died down, at least among fair-minded non-Catholics. Dog-eared and heavily annotated copies of *American Freedom and Catholic Power* which once had appeared to be on the verge of falling apart, were left to sag and gather dust on parsonage library shelves across the country. Nevertheless, it had had a reception too wide and too eagerly enthusiastic for Catholic complacency on the question of being finally accepted in American society, although it is possible that the American public had been prepared for it by other controversies preceding its publication.

Probably the most outstanding of these was the famous McCollum case in which the Supreme Court struck down released-time religious instruction in a landmark decision which gave an entirely new meaning to the First Amendment's prohibition of an established religion in this country. For a few brief years after the war, Protestant, Jewish and Catholic agencies had cooperated in creating a released-time program across the country. They had done so, however, only over the bitter opposition of the American Civil Liberties Union, and some Protestant and Jewish sects, all of whom opposed the program on secularist grounds. Looking for a test case, the secular opposition found one in Champaign, Illinois.

Here released-time activities had been approved by the state educational system and the local board of education, as well as the parents of 120 children involved in the program. One person objected. She was Vashti McCollum, the wife of a professor at the University of Illinois and the daughter of a militant atheist. Mrs. McCollum had a ten-year-old son at the public school where the program was in operation. She contended that having other children take the course embarrassed her son, and because the instruction was given within the confines of the tax-supported school, this violated the principle of "separation of Church and State" contained in the First Amendment.

In fact, the First Amendment contains no such clause. Nor does it appear *anywhere* in the entire U.S. Constitution. The phrase comes from a private courtesy letter from President Thomas Jefferson to the Baptists of Danbury, Connecticut. Jefferson wrote: "Believing with you that religion is a matter which lies solely between man and his God, that he owes account to none other for his faith or his worship, that the legislative powers of government reach actions only, and not opinions, I contemplate with sovereign reverence that act of the whole American people which declared that their legislature should 'make no law respecting an establishment of religion or prohibiting the free exercise thereof,' *thus building a wall of separation between church and state.*" (Italics added.) It has been on this last italicized phrase that the forces of secularism in America have hung all their weighty arguments designed to expel religion and the name of God from American public life. And yet, Jefferson's next sentence, *never quoted* by the secularists, went on to say: "Adhering to *this expression of the supreme will of the nation in behalf of the rights of conscience,* I shall see with sincere satisfaction the progress of those sentiments which tend to restore to man all his natural rights, convinced he has no natural right in opposition to his social duties." (Italics added.) What Jefferson was saying, then, was simply that there should be no established religion which would invade the *rights of conscience.* What he and Madison said, what they always said they said, was in Jefferson's own words, simply this: "I proposed the demolition of the church establishment, and the freedom of religion." Neither he nor Madison ever at any time proposed that religion should be excluded from public life; else, why, in the long history of the American nation, chaplains in the armed forces and in the Congress, chapels at the military academies, the *de facto* Protestantism of the public schools, the holy and ineffable name of God stamped on all its coinage and historic documents, or the GI Bill in which money for tuition followed the veteran to any school of his choice, regardless of religious affiliation. The list is much too long to bear recital, and yet, the Supreme Court by an 8 to 1 decision upheld Mrs. McCollum and outlawed the released-time program. It did so on the basis of the famous Rutledge Doctrine which gave an entirely new interpretation to Jefferson's words and those of the First Amendment.

The Rutledge Doctrine, as it came to be called, was advanced in a dissent by Justice Wiley B. Rutledge from a 5-to-4 Supreme Court decision upholding a New Jersey bus law providing transportation for children living at some distance from any private, nonprofit school in the state. In his dissent, Rutledge declared: "New Jersey's action therefore exactly fits the type of exaction and the kind of evil at which Madison and Jefferson struck." Discussing the First Amendment, he said: "It was to create a complete and permanent separation of the spheres of religious activity and civil authority by comprehensively forbidding every form of public aid or support for religion." This, in a Supreme Court which opens with a prayer! As Professor James M. O'Neill, student of the First Amendment and at one time Chairman of the American Civil Liberties Union's Committee on Academic Freedom was to write:

A glance at the language of the Amendment shows that its wording does not mention financial support or public funds. The record of history, legislative, executive, judicial, legal, from 1789 to 1947, is unanimously against the Rutledge Doctrine. Justice Rutledge gave no citation to any "consistent utterance" of the Supreme Court—for the best of all possible reasons: there never had been any. None of the well-known proponents of the second meaning [the Rutledge Doctrine] have ever cited a single example of any other meaning of this phrase than the *first* meaning given in the words of Jefferson, or Madison, or in the official acts of any President, or any Congress, or in any decision of the Supreme Court, except the McCollum decision. I have been looking for such citations for some years, and have been promised some, but have never received any.

Yet, when the Rutledge Doctrine was first advanced, it received the support of most law reviews and the entire Protestant press. Its use as a basis for the McCollum decision, however, horrified most of orthodox Protestantism, even though liberal Protestants and most Jewish agencies regarded it as a victory. A statement signed by thirty leading Protestant bishops, clergymen and theologians declared: "We contend that Jefferson's oft quoted words 'wall of separation' which are not in the Constitution but which are used by the Court in the interpretation of the Constitution, are a misleading metaphor. Cooperation entered into freely by the State and Church and involving no special privilege to any Church and no threat to the religious liberty of any citizen should be permitted. As Protestants we desire to affirm this interpretation of the American doctrine of the separation of Church and State, and to protest against the interpretation that has been formulated by the Supreme Court."

The Catholic Bishops of the United States issued a similar protest. However, this uncommon display of unanimity was to be short-lived, and the controversy over Rutledge's new interpretation of the principle of separation was now to shift from the abstract, and center around the bland, rotund figure of the outspoken Cardinal Archbishop of New York.

Spellman had already incurred the enmity of the secularists, as well as of many liberal Protestants and Jews, by his expression of satisfaction at the Supreme Court decision upholding the New Jersey bus law. In June of 1947, he provoked them further when, speaking at commencement exercises at Fordham University, his alma mater, he criticized what he contended had become an organized campaign against Catholic education, "which is claimed to be a constant threat against the supremacy of public education in the United States."

"Is it not clear," he asked, "that when a Catholic school child is denied the use of a public school bus an injustice is done not to the *Catholic* child, but to an American child who happens to be a Catholic? What is really involved is a violation not of religious liberty but of civic equality. In this land of freedom, of inalienable rights, can there be any excuse, even one based on religious considerations, for treating any children as second-class citizens and denying them their right to civil equality? . . ." Then, quoting Justice Hugo Black's contention that "it is not the purpose of the First Amendment to cut off church schools from those services which are separate and indisputably marked off from religious functions," the cardinal declared that the principle "is subject to criticism mainly by the intolerant, who in their failure to win a victory in the court of law seek recourse in the shady corners of bigotry."

The reaction to the cardinal's last remark was immediate and vehement. Once again, but in more sedate language, the Catholic hierarchy in America was accused of being "representatives of a foreign power," and the *Christian Century* declared in an editorial: "If Cardinal Spellman sees fit to consider that resistance to any program initiated by the hierarchy is equivalent to an attack upon the Roman Catholic Church, he is creating an anti-Catholic movement by definition, and he can easily bring on a real one." Unfortunately, the cardinal's intemperate rebuke had created such a storm of equally sharp replies that the real issue, the rights of American children who happen to be Catholics, was once again obscured.

One direct result of the controversy, however, was the creation of the organization called "Protestants and Other Americans United for the Separation of Church and State," familiarly known as the POAU. Although the identity of the "Others" has frequently changed during the history of this latest successor to the scepter of No-Popery, they usually have been either secularists of the American Civil Liberties Union stamp, or Jewish rabbis, all of whom have agreed with their "liberal" Protestant brethren that Justice Rutledge's interpretation of the First Amendment is the correct one. Thus, they dedicated themselves to the proposition that a wall of separation must be erected between Church and State, and that the slightest assistance given to any child in any school other than a public one—whether books or bus rides or cheap milk—was a violation of the constitutional principles set down by the Founding Fathers. In this, probably unwittingly, they enshrined the public school in a position of privilege for

which it has no constitutional basis, and thereby relegated all
other forms of primary and secondary education to a second-
class status. Not all Protestants, especially not the Lutherans,
who have built an extensive parochial school system of their own
in states such as Minnesota, were agreed with POAU, nor were
some of the Jewish sects which also conduct schools. Generally,
however, it may be said that most of non-Catholic America
agreed that any form of aid to nonpublic schools was unconstitutional, and that some operators of private or Protestant schools,
while perhaps not convinced of this on principle, were at least
willing to go without aid themselves if it would mean a kind of
financial starvation for "the true tiger": the Catholic school. Catholics themselves were just as bitterly certain that the POAU's
real position might be stated this way: "All churches must be
kept separate from the state, but the Catholic Church should be
more separate than others." At least, that was how the sharp-
tongued cardinal of Madison Avenue appeared to feel when he
lashed out at critics of the POAU conviction with these words:

These bigots, who strangely squeal and identify themselves when
one mentions unhooded Klansmen, have not yet insisted it is a violation of the American tradition of the separation of Church and State
for members of a fire department to extinguish a blaze in a parochial
school and to save children from burning to death, and we do hope
they will content themselves and satisfy their discriminatory thirsts
at seeing little children left standing in the snow as publicly-paid-for
buses transport other American children to and from school.

The POAU reply was to issue a manifesto which, reviving all
the old charges that the Catholic Church in the United States
sought to subvert the American government, specifically accused
it of "a policy plainly subversive of religious liberty," of intend-
ing "to breach the wall that sharply separates church and state
in this country," while warning of "the aggressive activities of
those who would subvert the Constitution to their sectarian interest." Thus, more than three hundred years after Lord Baltimore
founded his Catholic sanctuary in Maryland, the Catholic
Church in the United States found herself once again constrained
to defend her loyalty to American political ideas. This was done
at the annual meeting of the Catholic bishops in Washington in

November, 1948, and in a statement issued by Archbishop John T. McNicholas of Cincinnati, Chairman of the NCWC's Administration Board, who said:

No group in America is seeking union of church and state; and least of all are Catholics. We deny absolutely and without any qualification that the Catholic bishops of the United States are seeking a union of church and state by any endeavor whatsoever either approximate or remote. If tomorrow Catholics constituted a majority in our country, they would not seek a union of church and state. They would then, as now, uphold the Constitution and all its amendments, recognizing the moral obligations imposed on all Catholics to observe and defend the Constitution and its amendments. . . . The signers of the Manifesto assume that their attempt to have the Supreme Court reverse its decisions is a patriotic virtue, but that it is criminal for others to seek an interpretation of an amendment of the Constitution . . .

Probably, it would have been better for the American Church and for the country itself if McNicholas had not fired the parting shot of his last sentence. Certainly, it was the only remark remembered by a resentful POAU; and thus, into this sultry atmosphere of mounting mutual suspicion and recrimination, there came the final thunderclap of the Barden Bill. Introduced by Representative Graham Barden of North Carolina on May 11, 1949, this measure was to provide federal aid to the states in bearing certain costs of public elementary and secondary education. However, it also contained sections which would effectively prohibit the states from spending federal money to provide transportation for parochial school children. In this, the bill had the outspoken support of the same groups which backed Mrs. McCollum, along with the American Association for the Advancement of Atheism and the American Society of Freethinkers. A month later, speaking again at Fordham in an address entitled "Barden Bill— Brewer of Bigotry," Cardinal Spellman declared:

Catholics, themselves taxpayers, save others of the nation's taxpayers half a billion dollars yearly through the voluntary support of parochial schools in addition to the capital expense of the buildings. We Americans must not stand idly by and watch our government spend three hundred million dollars according to legislation that would be unjust and discriminatory against millions of our nation's children. A vote for the Barden Bill is a vote against parental rights, against constitutional rights, against American education as a whole, against America herself! Fearlessly, forcefully, we must unite to demand equal rights for all America's children, and in justice we must oppose unequivocally any bill that fails to guarantee at least non-religious textbooks, bus rides and health services for all the children of all Americans.

With this speech, the battle lines were drawn more sharply across America, and Bishop G. Bromley Oxnam, the Methodist prelate who had been among the foremost organizers of the POAU, defended the bill thus:

> Cardinal Spellman has used the term "bigot" freely of late. Now we know what he means by it. Anyone who disagrees with the Cardinal, or who objects to the hierarchy putting its hand in the public treasury, is a bigot. . . .
>
> Barden wants to preserve public education and to send federal aid to underprivileged areas for public schools. It is not "putting class against class" nor "vote against constitutional rights." It is the preservation of American public education and its protection from a prelate with a prehensile hand. . . .

Ultimately, the Barden Bill was defeated, especially after it became known that Barden's own state of North Carolina regularly contributed state funds for Protestant church schools there; but not until after the country—and the New York State Democratic Party—was rocked by a public quarrel over the bill between the Cardinal and Mrs. Eleanor Roosevelt. In three of her "My Day" syndicated newspaper columns, Mrs. Roosevelt came out, in effect, for the Barden Bill. Because of her inimitably vague style, this was not transparently clear; however, her unfortunate capacity for confusing the issue enabled her to say: ". . . we do not want to see public education connected with religious control of the schools," and again: "But neither do I want church groups controlling the schools of our country. They must remain free."

Thus, the Catholic request for relief in the form of funds for nonreligious textbooks, bus rides or health services was now being equated by Mrs. Roosevelt with a drive aimed at "controlling the schools of our country." With understandable but unfortunate human frailty, Francis Cardinal Spellman lost his temper, and he wrote Mrs. Roosevelt a letter which, distributed to the press, publicly accused her of inaccuracy and distortion and concluded with the explosive sentence: "For, whatever you may say in the future, your record of anti-Catholicism stands for all to see—a record which you yourself wrote on the pages of history which cannot be recalled—documents of discrimination unworthy of an American mother!" No one to sidestep an argument, Mrs. Roosevelt countered with a public letter of her own in which she protested that she did not support the Barden Bill but that "I think there is still a feeling that the public school is the school which is open to all children, and which is supported by all the people of the country, and that anything that is done for the public schools should be done for them alone." In conclusion, she said: "I assure you I have no sense of being 'an unworthy American mother.' The final judgment, my dear Cardinal Spellman, of the unworthiness of all human beings is in the hands of God."

Spellman, of course, had not called Mrs. Roosevelt "an unworthy American mother." Even though the words he used were certainly not charitable, he had only accused her of writing "documents of discrimination unworthy of an American mother." Mrs. Roosevelt's defenders, however, appeared to believe that there was no difference, and soon, according to the natural history of all such divisive squabbles, people were claiming that the cardinal had said the widow of the late president was "unfit to be a mother," and Bishop Oxnam had taken to the air to thunder: "It is not milk and medicine, books and buses. What he wants is the support of parochial schools by taxes levied on all the people. In a word, he seeks public funds for sectarian education. The Church not only wants public funds for private purposes, but must know that to drain off vast sums from public education is so to weaken it as eventually to destroy it."

So the quarrel continued, and as it did it helped to divide the Democrats of the Empire State. Although Bernard Baruch and Mayor William O'Dwyer professed admiration for both the cardinal and the former First Lady, Senator Herbert Lehman hastened to Mrs. Roosevelt's side, and James A. Farley, former Postmaster General and campaign manager for FDR, dryly suggested that Spellman might have been sorely pressed before he wrote his letter. Eventually, a reconciliation of a sort was effected between Cardinal Spellman and Mrs. Roosevelt, and the sultry atmosphere of acrimony in which the Barden Bill "debate" was being conducted was cleared considerably after the cardinal issued a statement clarifying exactly what the Church desired. This, he said, was only "incidental benefits" such as transportation, nonreligious textbooks and health services. Furthermore, he also declared that the Catholic Church in the United States was fully aware that, under most existing state constitutions and laws, as well as Supreme Court decisions, direct public aid to parochial schools was unconstitutional, and that it accepted that situation. With this, most of the Protestant opposition was satisfied, the Barden Bill furor died down and the measure itself was defeated.

At last, it appeared, the American Church was to be granted a respite, and would be able to continue the massive work of postwar adaptation without distraction. Not, so, however: on October 20, 1951, President Truman suddenly nominated General Mark W. Clark as America's first full-time ambassador to Vatican City. It had been eight months since Myron C. Taylor had resigned as the President's personal but unofficial representative in the Vatican, and it had seemed that Truman did not intend to name a successor. But here he was, going the entire distance in an unexpected announcement that exploded like a bomb in the Protestant community. Actually, the move was a transparent political ploy aimed at currying favor with the Catholic community on the eve of the election year of 1952, with no real danger of the appointment ever being confirmed.

General Clark appeared to be an excellent choice, being an Episcopalian, like Taylor, and a fairly young man with some diplomatic experience as well as some popularity in Italy, having commanded there during the occupation. A second glance, however, made it clear that Clark was really an impossible choice. In the first place, an old law of 1870 prohibited an Army officer from holding a civilian office, and Clark did not intend to resign from the service. Secondly, he was most unpopular in Texas because of the casualties suffered by Texas soldiers in his Rapido River campaign, and Senator Tom Connally of Texas was chairman of the Foreign Relations Committee which would have to report on his nomination. Thus, the old law precluded a recess appointment, and it would take many months for Congress to change the law and approve, if Connally actually ever let the nomination out of committee, and there would be plenty of time for the opposition to organize.

This it did. An example of opposition protest was furnished by five hundred ministers of the American Council of Christian Churches, who, assembled in Constitution Hall, informed Truman that "he had driven a sword deep into the heart of Protestant America," while approving such statements as this: "Communism is an enemy, we are all against it, but we have another enemy too, older, shrewder. It is Roman Catholicism and its bid for world power. In the United States it is Spellmanism."

In Rome himself at the time, Cardinal Spellman could only shake his head ruefully, while smiling wryly at the Communist report that he had a "hot line" to the White House. As he told an Italian reporter, he had not talked to the President on the telephone in at least two years. Meanwhile, the Vatican itself announced that it had not been consulted by President Truman. Eventually, probably a little shaken by the bitterness of the opposition to the appointment, President Truman withdrew Clark's name, and there has not been any attempt to name any form of representative since.

To most Catholics, the question of an ambassador to the Vatican was one of absolutely no importance as far as their faith was concerned. To the bishops, an American official with access to the Pope might have been tantamount to adding a papal halter to the bridle of the apostolic delegate already in Washington. The question should have been one of policy, whether an American ear in one of the world's great listening posts would be of value to the United States. It was of no religious significance whatever, a fact illustrated by an anecdote told to Monsignor Ellis by an Episcopalian rector.

He spoke of having attended a luncheon with many leading Protestant clergymen of the national capital where a visiting Anglican bishop was the guest of honor. The Taylor appointment came up for discussion and all the Americans, except the Episcopalian rector, were opposed to it. Meanwhile, the British bishop had sat in silence. Finally, one of the Americans asked his opinion, and the Anglican divine, recalling his own country's appointment of a minister to the Vatican in

1914, replied: "Why in England we have had a regular representative since World War I. We think it works very well, and we do not regard it as a religious issue at all."

Unhappily, it has remained to this day a "religious issue" for so many of the spiritual heirs of English Protestantism who still nourish in their hearts a hatred of Rome as old and outdated as the post-Reformation England which had bequeathed it to them. Even Communism, apparently, was to be preferred to Catholicism, and it seems a sorrowful commentary on how little the ancient prejudice has diminished to hear five hundred modern Protestant ministers echoing the No-Popery crusader of 110 years earlier, who declared: "I would rather be an infidel than a papist." Apparently also the specter of so-called "Spellmanism" could so unbalance minds that normally sincere and honest clergymen could offer this insult to a faith that had done so much to keep Communism at bay in this country. Undoubtedly, Communism was never the menace in the United States that it has been and still is in Europe and Asia, where it continues to regard the Roman Catholic Church as its chief enemy. Nevertheless, weak and ineffectual as the home-grown variety has turned out to be, it also has looked upon Catholicism as its mortal foe. A year before the Clark controversy erupted, the historian Henry Steele Commager published a study of the American character since 1880, in which he stated: "Whatever conclusions might be drawn from a scrutiny of Catholic doctrine, the fact was that Catholicism had flourished as a major religion for three quarters of a century without raising serious difficulties except in the imaginations of men and that democratic institutions seemed as sound when the church numbered twenty-four million members as they had been when it counted its communicants by the hundred thousand." As Professor Commager is undoubtedly aware, however, the "imaginations of men" do not often yield easily to facts or logic.

Concurrent, therefore, with the Clark and parochial schools controversy, there ran another public debate in which the American Church's attempt to improve the moral climate in America was represented as another form of "Spellmanism," an insidious movement to regulate the morals of all Americans. This was in the field of motion-picture censorship.

In the early 1930s, the still new medium of the motion picture had become what many Americans, Protestants as well as Catholics, regarded as a sink of moral corruption. If one judges by today's standards, when the public masturbation in "Oh, Calcutta!" is applauded as "art" and a film actor's ability is apparently measured by his skill in undressing on camera, such moral horror can only be regarded as quaint. Nevertheless, many Americans were distressed by the immorality of motion pictures, and so, in 1933, the Legion of Decency was formed under Catholic auspices but also with the support of many other religious bodies.

The Legion's attempt to "clean up the movies" was based on a simple economic boycott. Shrewdly judging that most Hollywood producers carried their convictions in their wallets, it brought pressure to bear simply by grading films according to their moral acceptability and asking its adherents to refuse to attend those found "objectionable," or to stay away from theaters which exhibited such pictures as a matter of policy. In the Catholic Church, everyone was asked to take the Legion of Decency "oath" once a year during Mass. Among the Protestants, it took different forms. Overall, the drive was amazingly successful—too successful, perhaps, if only because the emphasis on "decency" or "wholesomeness" tended to inhibit the making of mature and genuinely artistic films which might be able to treat such aspects of the contemporary human dilemma as alcoholism or infidelity without sensationalizing them. This, of course, might only have been a defect of the Legion's undoubted virtue of exercising a moral influence in the country. Nevertheless, many Americans, among them a growing number of Protestants, began to think that the Legion was perhaps too virtuous. It began to appear to them that the Catholic Church was attempting to impose a *de facto* censorship of the movies on all Americans, and only according to its own standards. Because of the growing number of Catholics in the country, it was argued, few producers were willing to run the financial risk of turning out a film which Catholics would shun en masse. Some less charitable critics insisted that this accidental form of censorship *in toto* was actually intentional, especially after Cardinal Spellman publicly warned Catholics against the film *Forever Amber*, and the producer, having at first declared that he would not "bowdlerize the film to placate the

Roman Catholic Church," later reversed himself and removed the "objectionable" material.

Gradually building up a head of pressure, this resentment at last exploded during the bitter debate in 1950 over the showing of the Italian picture *The Miracle*. The story is about an idiot village girl who is seduced by a stranger she believes to be St. Joseph. Giving birth in a church, miraculously, as she thinks, she is then mocked by the villagers who sing hymns in her honor to the Mother of God. Almost at once the National Legion of Decency attacked the film as "a sacrilegious and blasphemous mockery of Christian religious truth," and the New York State Board of Regents banned its exhibition on the same grounds. Immediately, the POAU sprang into action, followed by the American Civil Liberties Union, the Author's League and the American Jewish Congress. Protests against this latest "highhanded" instance of "Spellmanism" were raised throughout the state and New York City.

Unhappily, few if any of the agencies and authors who contended that "the Cardinal's command" was a breach of the First Amendment involving the freedom of the press appeared to consider Catholic sensitivities in the affair. To many Christians, not only Catholics, the film undoubtedly did seem to mock the sacred concept of the relationship between Jesus, the Third Person of the Holy Trinity, and his parents; and Catholics are especially sensitive on the subject of the Virgin Mary, whom they venerate above all other saints. From this standpoint, it may be asked what the Protestant reaction would have been if some Catholic had produced a play about Martin Luther based upon quotations from the Reformer's own *Table Talks*, or Jewish reception of a motion picture in which a demented Jew fancies he is Moses and leads himself and his followers to death by drowning in the Red Sea. Perhaps they too would have protested and picketed, even as the Catholics did, and they also would have been hurt and bewildered if charges of "Fascist" or "censorship" were hurled against them by defenders of the First Amendment; always providing, of course, that the American Civil Liberties Union or the left-wing press would have been upset by Protestant or Jewish attempts to defend their religion.

Ultimately, exhibition of *The Miracle* was upheld by the Supreme Court, which reversed the New York State Court of Appeals. An opinion delivered by Justice Tom C. Clark held: "It is not the business of government in our nation to suppress real or imagined attacks upon a particular religious doctrine, whether they appear in publications, speeches or motion pictures . . ." Whether or not the Court's decision was actually a "humiliating defeat" for Cardinal Spellman, as his opponents joyfully announced, it was certainly another victory for the forces of irreligion, and, as it turned out, the first breakthrough against the Hollywood Production Code Administration itself. Written by the Jesuit, Father Daniel Lord, the code had been respected for twenty-three years, but after *The Miracle* was afforded the protection of the First Amendment, it was followed by the openly salacious *The Moon Is Blue* and then, in 1956, by the much less "objectionable" *Baby Doll*. Ironically, the author of *Baby Doll*, the playwright Tennessee Williams, became a convert to Catholicism in 1968. Cardinal Spellman's objections to the film, however, were not based so much on its content as the advertising for it, a fact appreciated by the bitterly anti-Catholic clergyman, the late James Pike, a Catholic convert to Episcopalianism and later a bishop of that faith, who deliberately had himself photographed for the newspapers standing in a theater lobby under a suggestive picture of the principal character. After *Baby Doll*, the Legion of Decency's influence on Hollywood was almost negligible, and after the death of Father Daniel Lord, the Production Code was also dead.

The movies had been "liberated." They were free to produce as they pleased regardless of the effect on public morality, with the result that a fairly representative segment of the film industry shifted its emphasis from the old themes of cops-and-robbers or cowboys-and-Indians to the new formula of ogres-and-orgasms. How well did George Bernard Shaw observe that people from dull or tasteless backgrounds frequently find their only expression of art in sex; and so, with cold and conscious cynicism, this segment enriches itself by contributing to the general delusion that a man is "educated" or "enlightened" in so far as he will agree that nothing really happens after puberty. This, indeed, was exactly what the American Church had sought to prevent. She knew where it would end. Out of her ancient experience she knew, and she acted upon the wisdom of John Henry Newman's remark that it is not "a slight benefit to know what is needed for the proof of a point, what is wanting in a theory, how a theory hangs together, and what will follow if it is admitted." But the American Church failed. Having refused to join the rush to swim in the sewer, she sank trying to swim against the tide. It remains for historians of the future to say what effect this failure was to have on the public morality, or even if more has been gained in the interests of intellectual freedom than was to be realized in the cause of decency. That very word, of course, is now so openly derided and mocked that it may explain what may have been an inevitable reaction to the Legion of Decency. A stopgap measure at best, the Legion became so instantly successful that it may have ossified and tried to guide itself in the fifties and sixties by the solutions to problems of the thirties. Certainly, more could have been done—as is now being done—by moving away from the practice of rating films according to their morality toward a policy of the serious discussion of pictures in the Catholic press and schools. Admittedly, this would be hard on the kind of Catholic who reads only to find out what not to read; but then, it is this very kind of Catholicism—parochial, formal, facile and frequently arrogant—which too often characterizes the American Church in the minds of many non-Catholic Americans. This, too, was a legacy of the battle over "decency" in motion pictures. Yet, on balance, it must be said that if the Church erred, she sinned on the side of that puritanism which is sometimes the vice of the virtue of moral purpose.

Ironically enough, even as the Church was being castigated by her opponents for alleged intractability during her stand in defense of decent films or against abortion, she was also astonishing these same Americans with (to them) a highly uncharacteristic display of restraint and compassion. This was during the famous Father Feeney scandal in Boston, the first full-blown heresy in the history of American Catholicism.

Father Leonard Feeney was a Jesuit, one of three brothers who had become priests. He had distinguished himself within the Church as a writer and lecturer. In 1949 Boston College assigned him to the St. Benedict Center at Harvard, a facility similar to the Newman Clubs on many non-Catholic campuses, where lectures and discussions on Catholic subjects are offered. Under Father Feeney's guidance, however, the St. Benedict Center became almost a full-scale educational complex where students of all faiths might study Greek, philosophy, literature, church history and the lives of the saints. Here also Father Feeney became a favorite with his erudite lectures and his flair for mimicry, often impersonating a speech by Franklin Delano Roosevelt or the actress Katherine Hepburn broadcasting a prize fight. Eventually, the Center began to claim many converts, and it was also recognized as qualified for training under the GI Bill of Rights.

Gradually, however, Monsignor William L. Keleher, president of Boston College, became concerned over the "no-salvation-outside-the-Church" doctrine being taught at the center by four part-time instructors also assigned there. These men were Dr. Fakhri Maluf, an assistant professor of philosophy; James R. Walsh, an instructor in philosophy; Charles Ewaskio, an assistant professor of physics; and David R. Supple, a teacher of German at Boston College High School. All four were informed that they had better leave theology to those competent to teach it, or else leave the university. In reply, the four publicly "accused" Monsignor Keleher of heresy in holding that there might be salvation for those outside the Church, that a man might be saved without submitting to the authority of the Pope. This, of course, is exactly what the Church does teach. In its simplest form, it is stated in the Baltimore Catechism of 1884 which only says: "He who knows the church to be the true church and remains out of it cannot be saved." Nevertheless, the four continued to maintain that only Catholics can be saved. So they were dismissed. Two days after their dismissal, Father Feeney publicly came to their support, praising them and criticizing Keleher. Moreover, he took the case to the newspapers and began picketing churches with his followers. At last, Archbishop Richard J. Cushing broke his long silence on the subject. In a statement issued to press and radio on April 18, 1949, Archbishop Cushing withdrew all ecclesiastical approbation from St. Benedict's Center, forbade Catholics to frequent it under pain of forfeiture of the right to the sacraments and stripped Father Feeney of his priestly functions.

Feeney and the directors of the Center, nevertheless, defied Cushing and kept St. Benedict's open. They also maintained that the Pope would support them. In September, however, the Vatican's official censure of Feeney and the Center was made public. Archbishop Cushing declared: "As the shepherd of the Archdiocese of Boston, my heart goes out in love to Father Feeney and to those who have been misled by false ideas. It is my fervent hope that now, after the supreme authority of the Church has spoken, Father Feeney and his followers will prove themselves all to be loyal children of the Church and of our Holy Father, Pope Pius XII."

Father Feeney's effective reply was made in his visit to Archbishop Cushing, in which, by the Center's own account, he arose and said: "In the name of the Blessed Virgin Mary, I accuse you of heresy." In the following month, amid talk that Feeney and his flock faced excommunication, the wayward priest was dismissed from the Jesuit Society, and in the following year St. Benedict's lost its qualification for GI Bill money. Still adamant, Father Feeney formed his followers into an organization called "The Slaves of the Immaculate Heart of Mary." The men put on black suits and ties, similar to the dress worn by seminarians, and the women adopted a black "habit" similar to a nun's. For several years thereafter they made the Boston Common their Sunday afternoon headquarters, preaching sermons against Archbishop Cushing and against Jews and Protestants. Soon, in the inevitable way of the heresiarch, Father Feeney got out his own monthly called *The Point*, in which he again attacked Jews, Protestants and Masons, maintaining that they, together with all non-Catholics, were most irretrievably damned. Eventually, the "Slaves" tried to expand along the Eastern seaboard, but with very little success. In 1952, they invaded the office of Archbishop Amleto Giovanni Cicognani, Apostolic Delegate to the United States, in an effort to discover whether or not Feeney had been excommunicated. They reported that the delegate had said "No," but in February of 1953 Pius XII's reluctant excommunication of Leonard Feeney was made public.

Apparently, the decree only hardened the mistaken convictions of Feeney and his followers, and in July of 1953 six of them had to be escorted from the Notre Dame campus after pronouncing the dire condemnation: "The first sign of your approaching damnation is that Notre Dame has Protestants on its football team." Obviously, the Slaves were slightly unbalanced. Eventually, they came into conflict with Cambridge city officials over property which they owned near their Center, moving to another headquarters in the town of Harvard twenty miles away, where they remain to this writing, still consigning their non-Catholic brethren to the eternal fires of Hell. Although theirs was the first homebred heresy in the history of the American Church, it seems to have had a ludicrous if lamentable ending. Apparently, they sank beneath the surface with hardly a ripple, their only accomplishment, outside of deluding themselves and providing still another source of hatred and division for pluralist America, being the public airing of a dispute over dogma which catapulted Richard James Cushing into national prominence.

Indeed, it has been suggested that the unseemly publicity attending the Father Feeney controversy had so disturbed Pope Pius XII that it deprived Cushing of the red hat normally worn by the archbishop of Boston. Certainly, fourteen years had to elapse between the death of Cardinal O'Connell in 1944 and the elevation of Cardinal Cushing in 1958, and it was from the hands of Pope John XXIII, that this tall, lean, homey prelate with the rasping nasal voice was to receive the symbol of his princely rank. Thus, it was as Richard Cardinal Cushing that the archbishop entered the presidential election lists on the side of his young friend, Senator John Fitzgerald Kennedy of Massachusetts. Actually, Cushing did not openly campaign for Kennedy, conforming instead to the American hierarchy's policy of speaking neither for nor against any candidate, but he did help the Democratic nominee defend himself against the attacks upon his religion made during what was probably No-Popery's last organized effort to make Catholicism a test of holding office.

Again and again, Cushing denied that Kennedy would submit to clerical dictation or that any priest or bishop would dare attempt it. "Senator Kennedy would resent absolutely having a cardinal, a bishop or a priest telling him how to act," he said. "I don't know anyone who would try to tell him. I hope and pray that once and for all we'll be able to eliminate the religious issue from politics." Cushing also denied that there was any such thing as a "Catholic vote," declaring: "As far as I can make out, the only thing Catholics agree on is the dogma in the Apostles' Creed."

Nevertheless, Kennedy's Catholicism was an issue in the 1960 election, even though the attacks made on him and it were not nearly so scurrilous as the campaign launched against Al Smith in 1928. However, there was one startling similarity. Where Hoover had never been questioned about the Quaker pacifism which did in fact weaken his conduct of foreign policy, Richard Nixon, also a Quaker, was spared similar embarrassment. Undoubtedly, Nixon was not then and is not now a doctrinal pacifist, but the fact remains that no one asked him to deny it, while everyone but the Catholic press, it seemed, wanted to know how Kennedy stood on his Church's alleged "determination to breach the wall of separation between Church and State."

On September 7 a group was formed expressly for this purpose under the name of the National Conference of Citizens for Religious Freedom. Its chief organizer and driving force was Norman Vincent Peale of New York, a nationally famous Protestant clergyman. Peale, incidentally, was also a prominent Republican, and when asked why he had not questioned Nixon on his religion, he replied: "I didn't know that he ever let it bother him." Peale also told the group he organized: "Our American culture is at stake. I don't say it won't survive [Kennedy's election], but it won't be what it was." No Catholic, Jewish or liberal Protestant clergymen was invited to attend the conference, and its general attitude was probably best expressed by the Reverend Harold Ockenga of Boston, who compared Kennedy to Khrushchev and said the Democratic candidate was also "a captive of a system." Eventually, the great confrontation between Kennedy and the Protestant groups who opposed him came when he accepted an invitation to appear before the Ministerial Association of Houston, Texas. There, he made what was probably the most powerful and compelling speech of his campaign. He said:

I believe in an America where the separation of church and state is absolute—where no Catholic prelate would tell the President (should he be Catholic) how to act, and no Protestant minister would tell his parishioners for whom to vote—where no church or church school is granted any public funds or political preference . . . an America that is officially neither Catholic, Protestant nor Jewish—where no public

official either requests or accepts instructions on public policy from
. . . any . . . ecclesiastical source . . . where there is no Catholic vote,
no anti-Catholic vote, no bloc voting of any kind . . . and where
religious liberty is so indivisible that an act against one church is
treated as an act against all.

Kennedy concluded his speech by declaring that he would
resign his office rather than betray the national interest in order
to avoid violating his conscience. Afterward, he answered a bar-
rage of questions, most of them hostile, and few, if any, friendly.
Nevertheless, he fielded them all easily. In the words of Speaker
of the House Sam Rayburn: "As we say in my part of Texas, he
ate 'em blood raw." Perhaps, but the criticism of Kennedy's religion did not abate. Here and there, of course, there were
scattered "declarations of conscience" by an occasional Protestant or Jewish group. In the main, however, the attacks were
stepped up, as manifested by publication of more than three
hundred anti-Catholic tracts, together with radio and television
programs, anonymous telephone calls, flyers and chain letters,
all warning against the Catholic plot to take over America, and
some even going so far as to sound the tocsin against the Catholic-
Communist conspiracy. As in 1928, the gullible were told that
the Pope planned to rule the United States.* The Reverend Har-
vey Springer, the self-styled "cowboy evangelist of the Rockies,"
declared: "Let the Romanists move out of America. Did you see
the coronation of Big John [Pope John]? Let's hope we never
see the coronation of Little John. How many Catholics came
over on the Mayflower? Not one . . . The Constitution is a Protestant Constitution."

Some critics were more subtle. Dr. George L. Ford of the National Association of Evangelicals said that "religion definitely
should not be an issue in politics—and wouldn't be if the Catholic Church hadn't made it so." Ford's association made a spirited
but not very successful attempt to make Reformation Sunday—
October 30—the springboard for an outpouring of anti-Catholic
sermons and rallies which would defeat Senator Kennedy on

* John Cardinal Wright tells the story of talking with Pope John XXIII in 1959,
at a time when the Holy Father was trying to learn English. John asked Wright
about Kennedy's chances, and when the American prelate replied, "Very good,"
the Pope smiled and said jokingly: "Do not expect me to run a country with a
language as difficult as yours."

Election Day a few days later. In the event, of course, John Fitzgerald Kennedy was elected. To what extent the religious issue affected the campaign remains for sociologists and statisticians to say. Certainly, the issue worked both ways. It could have been that as many Catholics were eager to cast a vote for Kennedy which would be tantamount to ending religious prejudice in politics as there were anti-Catholics determined to keep the Whore of Babylon out of the White House. Indeed, John Kennedy himself attempted to persuade his party that his Catholicism might be the very remedy for the mass defection of conservative, middle-class Catholics from the political home of their fathers.

Nevertheless, the election of President Kennedy did end the prejudice against a Catholic Chief Executive. Thousands of Catholics present at his inauguration, as well as many millions more watching on television, wept openly when, as Richard Cardinal Cushing opened the invocation by crossing himself, the thirty-fourth President of the United States also made this once-abominated sign of the faith in which he was baptized. Now and forever more, it seemed, a man might be American and Catholic.

Chapter XXV

The decade following the election of John Fitzgerald Kennedy as President of the United States was one of the most momentous in the American Church's four centuries of history. It was a period full of growth, alteration and anguish, a time in which non-Catholic Americans were astonished to discover that Catholicism was not the cold, rigid, even ossified monolith which they had presumed it to be, and in which Catholics themselves were everywhere shocked—not to say shattered—by the hurricane winds of change which seemed to shake their "unchanging" church to its very foundations.

Among non-Catholics, especially the so-called Establishment "Wasps"—white, Anglo-Saxon Protestants—the election campaign had the effect of publicizing Catholic teaching on a wide variety of topics. Previously, there had been little serious discussion of Catholic doctrine. Criticism, even when it was conducted on a high level, had usually taken the form of polemics or "documented" exposés of the Blanshard variety. In 1960, however, the country learned of the Catholic position on such subjects as birth control, abortion, federal aid to private education, censorship, religious education and separation of church and state. Probably very few non-Catholics agreed with Catholic doctrine in some of these areas, but at least they understood it. For the first time they realized that there was a coherent and closely reasoned body of Catholic thought on these vexing questions, and this did much to dispel many of the older myths of No-Popery.

Kennedy's candidacy also showed, much to the greater surprise of many Protestants, that there was an enormous area of disagreement within the Catholic Church. Cardinal Cushing had expressed himself well when he said that the only things Catholics agreed on were the dozen or so dogmas set down in the Apostles' Creed. Otherwise, they seemed to disagree on almost everything, just like their Protestant countrymen. Between the conservative *National Review* and the liberal *Commonweal*, both periodicals edited by Catholic laymen, there was a spectrum of opinion on social, political and even religious matters that was truly poles apart.

Finally, the election ended a long-standing and long-cherished claim of Protestantism on the presidency itself. The White House, it may be said, had been the social citadel of the Wasp. Up until 1960, none but a Wasp had entered, and it had remained an apparently invincible status symbol which proclaimed the Protestant ascendancy in America. In fact, this may actually have been what Norman Vincent Peale was talking about when he predicted that America would not be the same after a Catholic President. Certainly, the election of a Catholic of Irish descent demolished that symbol for all time, and America was never the same thereafter. It was, in fact, a religiously neutral nation. The presence of a Catholic in the White House also destroyed the companion myth of papal or clerical dictation to a President of that faith. If, in his three years and more in office, John Fitzgerald Kennedy was an occasion of dismay to anyone, it was to those Catholic prelates such as Cardinal Spellman who were galled by his flat-out stand against public aid to parochial schools. To their unexpected glee, Protestants and others realized that the last person to be terrified by the specter of the so-called "Catholic vote" or to submit to any real or imagined pressure from the Catholic hierarchy was a Catholic. Thus, if it is too early to estimate the success or failure of John Kennedy as a President, it can be said now at least that he ended political prejudice against a Catholic as President, or even, for that matter, against any non-Protestant. Proof of this contention may be found in the struggle for the Democratic presidential nomination in 1968. In this, three Catholics—Senators Robert Kennedy, Eugene McCarthy and George McGovern—were prominent contenders, and none was asked a single question about his faith. Moreover, when the Eighty-ninth Congress convened in 1965, it was found that there were more Catholics in Congress than members of any other faith. Apparently, except for certain areas such as the South, whether or not a man was a Catholic no longer seemed of paramount importance in politics.

But if the campaign to keep Catholics out of high posts of leadership seems to be vanishing, it must be said that common or everyday prejudice still exists. It is not, of course, as blatant or as coarse as during the days of the Protestant Crusade or Al Smith's 1928 election campaign. But it is still there, especially in certain high circles of business, finance and—most covertly—in communications and education. Its presence is always denied, but any Catholic who has ever encountered it while aspiring to some higher position in his calling can testify to its existence. Writing in 1960, Gustave Weigel said of this persistent distrust: "The looming giant of Catholicism is always contemplated and always with suspicion. It seems to be by historical tradition the main foe —not communism, not nazism, not rationalism, not secularism, not naturalism, not neo-paganism. The Protestant naively believes that he can come to terms with these lesser threats. American Protestants often see great possibilities in Communist Russia."

John Kennedy's election victory, then, while surely proclaiming the end of Protestant political dominance in America, did not also end what is at the worst a petty prejudice against Catholics. It continues in the non-Catholic majority's irrational tendency to blame all Catholics for the actions of a few of their coreligionists or to hold the American Church accountable for the policies of the Spanish government or the Spanish hierarchy. With equally bad logic, Catholics might make all American Protestants responsible for the racist program of the Calvinist-based government of South Africa, or indict them for the activities of certain snake-charming Protestant sects in the hills of Tennessee. True enough, there are some Catholics who seem to act like self-appointed custodians of the public morals, and it is also true that they should conduct themselves with a little more charity in respect to their neighbors' rights and motivations. Yet, these people represent only private groups, and they certainly have no monopoly on bad manners in America.

More seriously, and certainly less excusably, Catholicism itself is resented because it continues to oppose such practices as euthanasia, abortion and artificial insemination. In the United States of the seventh decade of the twentieth century, what is convenient appears to supersede what is moral. Thus, in December of 1969, a U.S. District Court in Washington, D.C., upheld abortion on request on the ground that "a woman's liberty and right to privacy . . . may well include the right to remove an unwanted child, at least in the early stages of pregnancy." It was perhaps significant that the only voice raised in defense of the right of the unborn child to its own life was a Catholic one. Perhaps too simply, Patrick Cardinal O'Boyle declared: "Abortion is murder. That is the issue." For such forthrightness, then, for such refusal to conform to the relativism of modern America, it is likely that the American Church will continue to be distrusted. Catholics will be treated as equal by other Americans only for so long as they "get with the program," but once they refuse for reasons based on specifically Catholic precepts of morality, it will be remembered against them that they are Catholics. As far as the country itself is concerned, Catholic nonconformity will probably be a distinct benefit, if only because it is normally healthy for any people to have within their midst dissenters willing to risk unpopularity in the interests of serving a higher, transcendent truth. Nevertheless, it is still a mistake to continue to impute dishonorable motives to so large a religious body or to insist in the face of centuries of protestation and living proof to the contrary that the American Church is a sinister threat to American society or a force inimical to the principle of separation of church and state. To do so is only to create a reservoir of resentment among Catholics, one upon which some unscrupulous Catholic demagogue of the future might wish to draw; although in this regard it must be stated without fear of contradiction that no Catholic majority would ever even consider, still less attempt, altering any of these traditional American concepts. There were no Catholic penal laws in colonial Maryland, and it may be said of the United States in 1970 what Cardinal Manning said of Britain in 1875: "If Catholics were in power tomorrow in England, not a penal law would be proposed, not the shadow of a constraint put upon the faith of any man. We would that all men fully believed the truth; but a forced faith is a hypocrisy hateful to God and man."

Unhappily, it must be stated that as often as Catholics in America make similar statements they apparently are not believed. Therefore, it appears that none but a deluded Catholic in this country will be able to present himself as a "true" American until the day when the Church here ceases to be a minority and becomes instead the majority religion. Surprisingly enough, that day is not so distant as may be imagined. By the end of the 1960s, the Catholic Church in America was the third most numerous in the Universal Church and with ten cardinals was behind only France with eleven among the non-Italian nations represented on the College of Cardinals. In 1968, she had an enrollment of 47,873,000 out of a total American population of 199,342,000, and because many authorities maintain for a variety of reasons that these figures of the *Official Catholic Directory* are probably modest, it is likely that Church enrollment for 1970 would stand at well over 50,000,000 out of a total population of about 200,000,000. In other words, Catholicism in America has really ceased to be a minority. Certainly 25 per cent or one person out of every four is hardly to be so described, particularly after it is considered that all of the 250-odd non-Catholic Christian sects in the United States receiving the general designation of "Protestant" total only about 70,000,000.

Moreover, in her material possessions and myriad educational and charitable activities the Church also loomed as that menacing giant which haunts the dreams of so many non-Catholic clergymen. In 1968, the American Church was a colossus of 29 archdioceses and 121 dioceses including 18,146 parishes with another 18,000 missions, stations and chapels, all staffed by 59,640 priests, 11,758 brothers and 167,167 sisters. There are 137 diocesan seminaries and 407 religious seminaries in which 33,490 seminarians are enrolled, and in lay education the Church had built 297 colleges and universities for 435,716 students, 1,334 diocesan or parochial high schools caring for 693,270 students, 847 private high schools with 422,081 students, 10,050 parochial elementary schools with 3,845,694 students, 356 private elementary schools for 72,225 students, 105 "protective institutions" for slower children with 8,161 students, and was giving 1,462,741 high school and 3,995,692 elementary school students religious instruction on released time programs. *In toto*, the Church was giving some form of instruction to 10,969,483 American children and youths. In the field of charitable work, her record was equally distinguished. Here, she had 777 general hospitals with 155,544 beds which served a total of 20,425,267 patients, 134 special hospitals with 11,908 beds and 425,833 patients, 279 nursing schools for 28,415 student nurses, 221 orphan and infant asylums serving 19,160 resident children, a total of 22,325 children in foster homes plus 41,491 more dependent children and 429 homes for the aged with 39,897 guests.

Truly, the tiny grain of mustard seed planted by Lord Baltimore's Jesuits on the shores of the Chesapeake in 1634 had grown and become "a great tree." Moreover, it had changed considerably, at least in its externals, and especially during the quarter century which had succeeded the end of World War II. Once the city-centered Church of the immigrant and the working classes, she had shifted the weight of her operations to the suburbs and the middle class. Moreover, she was now established in some strength in practically all sections of the country, rather than concentrated in those areas north of the Ohio and east of the Mississippi as she had been prior to 1940. Furthermore, her sacramental life had been revitalized by the relaxation of the eucharistic fast and permission to hold evening masses, and the wide-ranging activities of the lay apostolate had given her a new vigor. None of these changes, however, was even comparable to the massive transformation which overtook the American Church after the Second Vatican Council.

Although the convening of this twenty-first general council in the Universal Church's more than nineteen centuries of existence is generally credited to Pope John XXIII, the fact is that Pius XII also had considerable influence in bringing it into being, either through his encouragement of biblical studies and his recognition of the necessity of revising canon law or his friendly attitude toward non-Catholics. Actually, Roman Catholicism's revolutionary decision to end its defensive posture and confront modernity face-to-face was the product of movements within the Church which were 150 years old. It may even be said that the so-called Americanizers—Ireland, Spalding, Keane, Gibbons, *et al.*—were a part of this campaign for the Church to abandon the siege mentality which had characterized her since the Counter-Reformation; and Leo XIII's very condemnation of the phantom heresy of Americanism was part of the intellectual reign of terror with which the Roman Curia sought to suppress the movement. Nevertheless, it persisted, gaining new life and irresistible momentum during the general reaction of horror toward the Europe created by the two world wars. It was a true Catholic renaissance—in philosophy, sociology, history, science and biblical studies—and it needed only the genius of Angelo Roncalli—John XXIII—the most lovable of popes, to give it the official blessing which it required.

It was John who gave the movement for renewal the name of *aggiornamento*, or "updating," and it was he who, in order to illustrate his purpose, opened a window in the Vatican with the remark: "I want to let some fresh air into the church." Thus, to the unconcealed horror of the Curia, he called an ecumenical council, a world-wide gathering of prelates—bishops, abbots, archbishops, cardinals—to discuss the condition of the Faith and to make decisions which are promulgated by the Holy Father. Usually, councils are internal Catholic affairs, but when the world press began to run headlines proclaiming "BISHOPS IN REVOLT," the Second Vatican Council ceased to be a private assembly and became the center of world interest. What was happening, of course, was that the Catholic Church was at last attempting to make Christianity relevant to the modern world with its science, technology, new and still-evolving social and political attitudes, as well as its vast expansion of knowledge resulting from the acceleration of communication techniques and its general disposition to reject older norms of living and morality. In a word, Catholicism was trying to reinterpret the historic faith so as to make it acceptable to the present age.

Actually, this was Christianity's second attempt to do so. As the perceptive Professor O'Dea has pointed out, the first attempt was made by liberal Protestantism at the end of the last century and just before World War I. Unfortunately, this confrontation with secularism apparently resulted in the vitiation of liberal Protestantism, with the consequence that it became more secular than religious. It became what it sought to convert. According to O'Dea, Catholicism may have a better chance, if only because of its unity and international character. To understand the present movement of renewal, then, together with the earlier work of the Council, it is well to quote O'Dea, writing in 1968:

. . . Catholicism stands as representative and surrogate for Christianity as a whole in its second great historic attempt to confront modernity. Can the Catholic Church succeed? Can the Catholic Church actually update Christianity? Can it adapt to the mentality of modernity, Christian ideas and values, Christian conceptions of God and man, Christian convictions of the reality and seriousness of the religious life? Can it accomplish this by giving to the challenging aspects of modernity the full valence they demand and at the same time not lose Christianity's deeper character and basic identity in the process? Can Catholicism confront the consequences, intellectual and spiritual, of modern developments in science and scholarship, and in political, social, and economic life and adapt to them and still preserve its own lively sense of God's reality and presence?

This, then, was what drew to Rome for a period of three years between 2,000 and 2,500 "Fathers of the Church"—that is, prelates who could vote—together with about 250 *periti*, or experts in the fields of theology, canon law, liturgy, sociology, history, Scripture and the many other subjects related to the work of the Council. The Americans were there in force, and although they were generally considered theological conservatives, especially in comparison to the Dutch, Belgian and German hierarchy, they did make one great contribution in the Council's historic declaration on religious liberty.

Known as "the American schema," this principle of the rights of conscience was chiefly the work of Father John Courtney Murray, an American Jesuit and an authority on church-state relations. Murray's work demolished the old Catholic notion that "error has no rights," demonstrating instead that rights do not belong to abstractions such as error but rather to people. Thus, a man has the right to his religious convictions, even though he may not agree that Catholicism is "the one true faith." While still insisting that hers was the one true faith, the Church was now upholding a non-Catholic's right to disagree. Moreover, his right of religious liberty was intrinsic. All governments must respect it, and none could give it or take it away. Simple as this may sound, it was revolutionary in Rome, like the declaration on the Jews absolving them of guilt in the execution of Jesus Christ, and both went a long way toward improving relations between Catholics and non-Catholics, especially in Father Murray's own country.

Apart from these contributions, however, the Americans were not particularly prominent in any of the other discussions, and their seemingly solid front of conservatism in the face of the new spirit of permissiveness blowing out of Europe—one characterized by the remark "The Rhone has flowed into the Tiber"—became both the embarrassment and despair of "liberal" Catholics at home. Thus, when the American hierarchy returned to the United States, a kind of "cold war" began between themselves and the self-styled New Breed, a group generally composed of younger priests, intellectuals and a growing number of laymen who edit periodicals or write columns for them. Very quickly, the battle between these two camps became open and bitter, and the prelates' position was probably most forcefully stated by John Cardinal Krol of Philadelphia. Speaking in May of 1966 at the installation of a new Bishop of Scranton, Krol denounced the New Breed with the remark: "Variously inspired by eagerness for novelty, exaggerated self-confidence or illusions of prophetic charism, they preach their own views with little concern for being united with the living and common *magisterium* [teaching authority] of the Church." There is no doubt that many members of the New Breed seem imbued with the same invincible faith in their own judgment which characterized many heresiarchs, and that the tone of their criticism of their own religious leaders is far from being charitable. They idolize public opinion, and they are fond of reiterating the slogan "The press is more powerful than the pulpit." In other words, might makes right, and here, it would seem, the New Breed is hardly different from the tyrannizing type of prelate with whom they are more justly in conflict.

Probably the most illustrative example of the priest-prelate confrontation occurred in Los Angeles in 1963 when Father William H. DuBay cabled the Pope and requested the removal of his archbishop, James Francis Cardinal McIntyre, for "gross malfeasance" and "abuses of authority." Specifically, DuBay accused McIntyre of conducting "a vicious program of intimidation and repression" against priests, seminarians or laymen who attempted to join the civil rights movement. According to *Commonweal:*

"Along with several other priests, most of them not long out of the seminary, he had become convinced that every possible approach to Cardinal McIntyre on the racial issue had been exhausted—repeated appeals for audiences, phone calls, proddings from outside bishops, even picketing of the chancery office by laymen—and that nothing else was left but open protest, even if it meant suspension or excommunication."

Cardinal McIntyre's treatment of Father DuBay was only too expressive of the medieval prince of the Church acting with bell, book and candle at his fingertips. DuBay was compelled to make a public submission. Before two hundred priests of the Los Angeles archdiocese on retreat at the seminary, he knelt before the cardinal, renewed his vow of obedience and kissed his ring. Then, one by one, the other priests filed by, also to kiss the episcopal ring, before marching into the dining room and there to give His Eminence a thundering ovation. Unhappily, the DuBay story had a sorrowful ending. Convinced that the ordinary priest had no right of appeal, that his supposed privilege of going directly to the Pope only meant, in practice, that this protest would be referred back to his bishop, he attempted to form a labor union for priests. On October 19, 1966, he announced the formation of the American Federation of Priests. As desperately unrealistic as his attempt to have the Pope remove his archbishop, the priest's union died a quick death and Father DuBay left the Church.

Nevertheless, he had dramatized the individual priest's rights vis-à-vis his ordinary. Even though the Los Angeles archdiocese probably represents the extreme in episcopal autocracy, with many gradations of liberty and authority lying in between itself and the traditionally permissive archdiocese of Chicago, the fact remains that the Church has little legislative provision for the rights of the junior clergy. Three weeks' vacation and one day off a week seems to summarize his "benefits." Since Vatican II, of course, this problem has been eased somewhat by the various priest senates which now convene regularly within the dioceses.

Yet, some Catholics have wondered why men dedicated to the spiritual life, whose mission on earth is to instruct and inspire the laity, should be so concerned with material pleasures and benefits; and it is exactly here that the New Breed and those who do not agree with them reach a crucial parting point. For many the question is: how far should a priest, or any Catholic for that matter, consider that his religion requires him to "make a commitment" to the various aspects of social justice: the civil rights movement, the war on poverty, urban renewal or even the problem, vaguely if ever understood by most Americans, of the morality of war. Here is the crux, the conflict between the so-called "social gospel" and the gospel of salvation. The question seems to be: Is religion a dialogue between God and man or is it a means of improving society? Will a man's faith commit him to the new sense of group action or will he continue to use it as a means of saving his individual soul? Traditionally, the Christian or at least the Catholic teaching on a man's duties toward society was expressed by Thomas More's remark that the world will be good when men are good, thus placing the emphasis on the individual, on the gospel of salvation. But now the American Church under the impetuous urging of the New Breed appears to be shifting toward the social gospel advocated by liberal Protestantism during its gallant but unsuccessful attempt to confront modernity. In effect, they are dividing the indivisible Christian recipe for salvation—faith and good works—and giving precedence to good works. Reversing Christ, they put Martha over Mary. And here, in this American Catholic cold war, there has entered on the side of authority, if not necessarily on the side of the hierarchy, a huge, unheard-from group of Catholics who are in some ways comparable to President Nixon's "great, silent majority."

These are the traditionalists. They are not conservative, they are not reactionary, and they are just as intelligent and informed as the intellectuals of the New Breed. Unhappily, few of them edit "impartial" journals of opinion or have columns to write. In the main, they are middle-aged or elderly Catholics, priests and laymen, who are afraid that the "fresh air" which Pope John wanted to let into the Church has turned into a tornado. They fear that "renewal" is actually the kind of reform that empties out the baby with the bath. It seems to them that the New Breed are trying to get Christ out of Christianity, and they are mindful of the Protestant theologian H. Richard Niebuhr's judgment on the "liberalization," i.e., watering-down, of his own faith: "A God without wrath brought men without sin into a kingdom without judgment through the ministrations of a Christ without a cross." To those innovators who appear so zealous to reform the work of Jesus Christ, they might quote the cynical Talleyrand's remark to the member of the Directory who wished to form his own faith based on reason: "To found his religion, Jesus Christ suffered and died. I suggest you do something of the same." The traditionalist view is that renewal is another word for accommodation. In Jacques Maritain's phrase it is "a genuflection to the world."

If religion is not a criticism, it is nothing; and when it ceases to criticize what is loosely called "the world," it ceases to be a religion. True enough, this concept may be open to the charge of being based on "old-fashioned morality," but the fact is that the American Church was until recently the last major repository of any reasoned or reasonable concept of morality in the United States, and that, if the Universal Church should decide to submit to the current moral fashion of permissiveness, she will have abandoned her position of authority at the one critical period in history when it was needed most. To say "authority," of course, is not to say the medieval or autocratic authority wielded by a prelate like Cardinal McIntyre. But neither is the solution to the abuse of authority a swing of the pendulum to the extreme of permissiveness. Furthermore, the world judges itself by its own standards, and these are as much a compound of sin, selfishness and blind materialism as of nobility, energy and efficiency. In truth, the world has only one standard: success. Is the Church founded by the Divine Failure to make the standard of success the norm to which it must adapt itself? Can it really "secularize" Christianity, as so many spokesmen for the New Breed are urging, without becoming secular—even as liberal Protestantism?

Again to quote Maritain, a thinker whose theories had much to do with the advent of *aggiornamento:* "Like Christ, the Church is of God, not of the world. And we have to choose to be friends of the world, or friends of God." This is a hard saying, but since when was Christianity a facile faith? From Jesus Christ himself came repeated warnings against the world. The Gospel of St. John is full of them. "The world cannot hate you, but me it hateth: because I give testimony of it, the works thereof are evil." "In the world you shall have distress: but have confidence, I have overcome the world." "My kingdom is not of this world." St. James, Christ's very kinsman, was even harsher. "Adulterers, know you not that the friendship of the world is the enemy of God? Whosoever therefore will be a friend of this world, becometh an enemy of God." "Love not the world or the things of the world."

It may well be argued by the New Breed that it would be cowardly for the Church not to confront modernity, that it would be a betrayal of the Holy Spirit for her not to divest herself of the spiritual strait jacket laced about her by the defensive strictures of the Council of Trent. To this, none but an ostrich could say other than "Amen!" Nevertheless, both rapport and rapprochement imply an exchange of views between parties meeting under their own standards. Anything else is submission. Thus, if the world's standard is success, then the Church should strive to understand it more clearly; she should belittle it less and also abandon her own emphasis on resignation or the traveler complex. But she must never forget that her own standard is the Cross, the crucified Christ, "unto the Jews indeed a stumbling block and unto the Gentiles foolishness." Is it possible that today's Gentiles, for which read secularism or modernity, are preparing to alter this attitude? Hardly. The religious revival of the late forties and the fifties is already on the wane, dying quickly down like a paper fire. The twentieth century no longer appears a particularly auspicious one for religion. In the Catholic Church, conversions have fallen off sharply and attendance and collections, under the impact of the defection of many of the older Catholics who feel that they have been turned out of their ancestral home by the innovations of the New Breed, are also down. Other religions report similar hard times. At an interfaith meeting in Istanbul in February of 1969, Protestant, Orthodox, Jewish, Buddhist, Hindu, Shinto and Zoroastrian representatives all testified to a reduction in growth.

The problem appears to be one of indifferentism, a kind of religious leveling which regards any faith as just as good as the next one, and all as the product of human speculation and regulation. No creed, says indifferentism, can speak with authority or certainty. The Catholic Church, of course, always did—claiming Christ as its invisible and the Pope as its visible head. But now, Christ and his Cross are glossed over and the Pope is ignored. To scrape the barnacles of the centuries from the Bark of Peter the New Breed appears willing to stove in the planking as well, and Christianity is to be cleansed by washing Christ away. This is no exaggeration. In many Catholic colleges and universities today the teaching authority of the Pope counts for so little that his decisions on such matters as birth control are not only discounted or defied but his very magisterium is made a debatable question.

As for Jesus Christ, one might well enter any of these institutions or one of the new Catholic churches and say, with Mary Magdalene: "They have taken away the Lord out of the sepulchre, and we know not where they have laid him." True enough, the colleges are ending an era when lay teachers were looked upon as clerical employees rather than associates, or when all scholarship had to be undertaken "under correction," and in the simplicity, grace and function of some contemporary church architecture one might well say that here are wood, stone and steel speaking with the very spirit of our times. Nevertheless, one must still ask: Where is Christ? Is he at Notre Dame, now under lay control, where one professor of theology attacks the resurrection and another the papal pronouncement on birth control, or at St. Peter's College, where a third teaches "Marxist Christianity," whatever that is? Is he on the Catholic campus at all? One must doubt it, if one judges from the poll of students at sixty-nine Catholic colleges which put Jesus Christ as the fifth most important man in history and John F. Kennedy and his brother Robert as Numbers One and Two. Here is Christianity not only cleansed of its Founder, here is testimony to the absolute failure of the history departments in Catholic education. If not Christ as first in history, then certainly Alexander or Augustus, Moses or Buddha, Socrates or Aristotle, Galileo or Columbus, Lenin or Luther, or any of those geniuses after whom mankind was never the same—but the Kennedy brothers? Is this the New Breed's triumph over parochialism?

To seek for Christ on many college campuses, then, appears to be a vain search indeed. If He is there at all, it is often as a simple man, a fanatic perhaps, who only gradually became conscious of His having issued from God, and whose virgin birth, miracles, resurrection, etc., all may be reduced to the natural order. To find Him in the writings of the New Breed, except as a perfunctory bow in some final or omnibus paragraph, is most difficult indeed. One may read chapter after chapter in a New Breed apostle such as Father Greeley (who offers John Kennedy as a Doctor of the Church!) and not see His name at all, nor that of God, His Almighty Father. One will find, however, frequent allusions to the Holy Spirit, which seems to suggest that the "renewed" American Church might be preparing to come down heavily on the third person of the Holy Trinity.

Although the Holy Spirit is frequently mentioned in the New Testament, He may actually be quite acceptable to the modern world. He has no virgin birth, no reincarnation, no hypostatic union, or resurrection, or miracles or ignominious death to be defended against the doubters of modernity. Nor is He a creator God like the Father Almighty, which removes all necessity to defend design against accident; or the Deity who made a compact with the Jews, thus making His uncomfortable entry into human history, His unseemly entry, even, if one remembers Him as "the God of Battles." But the Holy Spirit has never *appeared* on earth, like Jesus Christ who trod the soil and drank the wine of Judea; or the Father Almighty, who spoke to Abraham and Isaac, changed Jacob's name to Israel and appeared to Moses in the form of a burning bush. It is true that the Virgin Mary was conceived by the Holy Spirit, but inasmuch as the dogma of the virgin birth is already in question, this does not seem too great a difficulty in the way of reconciling Catholicism with the modern world. Otherwise, the Holy Spirit does not *do* anything. He merely "inspires" or "comes upon" people or is "received" by them, or else He is invoked. But He is not an actor in human history, and He is therefore a much more comfortable or convenient God than the other members of the Holy Trinity. Thus, one may expect to hear rather more about Him and less about Christ from the missionaries of the New Breed.

Whether or not this shift in emphasis is conscious or deliberate is difficult to say. In fairness, it should be suggested that many who embrace it are perhaps not aware of the consequences, any more than they perceive the destructiveness of the popular new theories advanced by the late French Jesuit, Father Pierre Teilhard de Chardin. They apparently are not disturbed by theories which turn Christianity upside-down. Teilhard has gotten rid of the Fall and Original Sin and the consequent need for a Redeemer. Catholic Christianity always held to the Incarnation, the proposition that God who made man became man to save what He had made. The story of Adam and Eve and the Fall shows that man was not equal to God's great gamble of free will. He preferred himself to God. This was the first sin, Original Sin, and after it man was unable to help himself. He had to have a Redeemer, and he was Christ the Savior. To Teilhard, however, the God-man is not Jesus the Savior but "the evolutory principle of a universe in motion." To simplify, and admittedly only a trained philosopher or theologian should attempt to simplify a writer as difficult as Teilhard, he has put perfection at the *end* of creation, not at the *start*, where it was lost and only to be regained through the merits of Christ the Redeemer. In short, there is really no need for Jesus Christ.

Again looking for Christ: is he in the churches? Certainly he is present in the Blessed Sacrament of the Altar, and some "old-fashioned" churches still represent him on their crucifixes or in their stained-glass windows. But there are many Catholic parishes in America where the crucifix has been taken down, along with those too-disturbing stations of the cross so crudely daubed with red paint, and a Catholic of another century entering some contemporary churches could be forgiven if he thought he had stumbled by accident into, say, a Quaker meetinghouse. Charming in a chaste and simple way, some of the new design seems to arrive at this quiet beauty by the simple expedient of excluding anything powerful, harsh or provocative—especially the crucifix—which might suggest a religion based on sacrifice and suffering. Once again, the baby has vanished with the bath; and so, the new design is not actually simple but only bland. Our God is no longer a Jealous God. He is the Permissive One, and we must not embarrass Him with anything but the most demure devotion. Yearning for the old atmosphere of the sacral and the reverent, the traditionalist had better get him to a bank or a brokerage house, where the Sons of Mammon, at least, still take their god seriously.

Even the sacrifice of the Mass has become a source of dismay to the traditionalist. For the liturgical reformers to have achieved their great objective of having Latin all but abolished from the Roman rite and the various vernaculars put in its place was truly an attainment of the highest order, and one on which they would deserve congratulation, had they not celebrated their success by introducing such indecencies as the "tom-tom mass," the so-called "folk mass" accompanied by guitars in the hands of youths who know ever so much more about Christianity than their elders. Apparently, to the New Breed, the acorn is worth more than the oak, and the adult is the ruination of the child. As a result, many older Catholics, devout people who suffered social ostracism or lost advancement or employment because of their courageous witness to their religion, men and women who sacrificed for years for the faith that they loved, have simply walked out of the American Church in disgust. For them, all the awe and reverence and mystery has gone out of the Mass. Chesterton said that all drama must be a foot above the ground, but the drama of the new Mass is now on everybody's level—and perhaps even a little lower.

The new liturgy, they feel, is soulless. It may be more accurate as a result of biblical scholarship, but it has no poetry in it. Thus, many older Catholics say, in effect, that if they were asked to swear on the new Bible they would not feel obliged to tell the truth, and that the new Mass seems hardly worth dying for. Traditionalist horror, however, only amuses some of the New Breed, especially the members of the so-called "Underground Church," who find any attachment to "old-fashioned" ritual or "archaic" parochialism a kind of quaint Neanderthalism. Underground churches or "floating parishes" are a phenomenon of the late sixties, and most of them function outside episcopal approval. Basically, the Undergrounders are against offices, leadership and fixed meeting places. They do not build churches or schools. Meetings and "Masses" based on unauthorized or avant-garde liturgies take place in the homes of members, and non-Catholics are not only invited to attend, but are sometimes allowed to receive "Communion," which often may be a piece of French bread torn from a loaf consecrated by an Underground priest. Usually, members of an Underground community are fairly mobile or rootless people with college educations, between the ages of twenty-five and forty-five. They are probably sincere in their discontent with the old authoritarian tribal parish, a form of organization which derives from the fourth century when the Church adopted Roman legal and political forms. The parish (which in Greek means "near the house") reflected the relationship between a tribe and its chieftain, and when the Church adapted to it, she substituted the pastor as the shepherd of his flock. It may be, as the Undergrounders maintain, that the parish is irrelevant to modern life. However, they have not offered any viable substitute. To be valid, their objections to a "brick-and-mortar" Church should be accompanied by recommendations for something better than churches, schools, hospitals and orphanages in which to carry out the missions of inspiration, instruction and charity. Actually, the Undergrounders seem romantic. They have got their centuries mixed. One only goes underground in times of persecution, when the tactic of dispersion is required as a defense against pogroms. In times and places of religious freedom such as ours, one concentrates openly because concentration is a much more effective means of organization than dispersion. But the word "underground" is really no more than a fanciful publicity tag, because as every reader of newspapers knows, the Underground Church is rather crowded with cameramen. As James P. Shannon, auxiliary Bishop of Minneapolis and St. Paul, has observed, the Underground Church "is divisive rather than cohesive; until it surfaces and integrates into the total Christian community, it will continue to be so."

These, then, are the areas in which the American Church is engaged in a kind of cold civil war. To the New Breed, the ferment is a crisis of growth; to the traditionalists, it is a crisis of growth in the wrong direction: away from the crucified Christ. And on no subject has this debate waxed fiercer than on the question of priestly celibacy.

Celibacy, of course, had always been praised by the Catholic Church, following the example of Christ and the urging of Scriptures. It was not exalted, however, because it was believed that there was anything evil in sexual union. Sex was not denounced but rather renounced. To be perfect, a man tried to abstain from this greatest of pleasures and offered the sacrifice to God. In early days, all monks and nuns were celibate, and in the sixth century Pope Gregory the Great introduced it for all priests as a matter of discipline. An unmarried man could do his work better unhampered by the distraction of a family to support. In this, the American Church had always vigorously concurred, regarding celibacy as so intimately associated with the character of a Catholic priest that in 1928 the American bishops had Rome extend the law to priests of the Eastern Rite, who had been allowed to marry before their ordination. At the Second Vatican Council and thereafter, however, it became clear that American priests, particularly the younger ones, were not so certain that celibacy should be mandatory. They preferred it to be optional. Although the problem was not discussed at Vatican II, Rome did agree to adopt new procedures under which priests upon request might be permitted to return to the lay state and marry. Some exceptions were also made for married Protestant clergymen who wished to become priests and continue to live with their wives.

Since then, more and more American priests have begun to argue that celibacy was beyond the strength of modern men, and that priests should be allowed to marry. When some of them find that permission will not be granted, they leave the Church and marry. Thus, the defection of trained priests has become a real problem for the Universal Church, and especially for the American Church, set down, as it is, in an environment which practically worships sexuality. Although no exact figures on defection are available, it has been estimated that in the decade 1958–1968 some ten thousand priests left the Church. In December of 1969, Pope Paul declared that the problem of priest defections was his "crown of thorns."

Although Paul has already closed the door on a married priesthood, some Churches, notably the Dutch one, appear to be defying him. What the American Church will do is difficult to say. It seems more likely that it will encourage married men who have raised their families, that is, ransomed their hostages to fortune, to enter the priesthood or at least take the lesser holy orders of deacon or subdeacon. At the Mass, of course, there are already lay readers. Perhaps even young men in the seminaries who feel that they must marry will be permitted to hold lesser orders.

Doubtless, some changes will have to be made, if only because, in a society as incredibly prosperous and luxurious as our own, vocations to the priesthood have been quite understandably sinking. To some New Breed advocates, the answer seems to be a Church without priests, a kind of belated confirmation of the Reformers' idea of a universal priesthood, every man his own minister. However, like all similar attempts to change the wine back into water, such a radical reversal does not seem likely. Nor does it appear that priests will be permitted to marry at will.

What seems more probable is that the shortage of priests will compel a reappraisal which will end with fewer men becoming ordained, but with the authority and prestige of a priest becoming greater. Moreover, priests will probably be less burdened by the material and financial cares of the parish (if this ancient system of tribal organization survives) and freer for the spiritual work which, after all, is the true mission of a priest.

Freeing the priest for his mission is one of the chief purposes of celibacy. Without wife or children, a celibate priest might take all mankind for his family. Responsible for no one, he could serve everyone; and in theory, at least, he was at the service of whomever might knock at his door. Raising a family, however, is a long, anxious and demanding process which is bound to interfere with a priest's ministry; his unique, arduous, twenty-four-hours-a-day calling. Moreover, a family will probably introduce him to that social whirl which he has so far avoided, exposing him to that familiarity which indubitably breeds contempt in exchange for the reverence and esteem in which the American faithful, at least, have generally held their clergy.

From the economic standpoint alone, a large, married priesthood does not seem feasible. It would deposit another financial incubus on the shoulders of Catholics already loaded with the double taxation of their school system. Priestly salaries would skyrocket. Young clergymen with growing families certainly would not be content with the present pittance of a curate. Nor would many parishioners of modest circumstances be delighted to see the pastor's wife in mink and his children in all the best colleges, while they, who contribute to his support, continue in cloth coats and trade schools. Obviously, if married priests attempt to supplement their scanty salaries by moonlighting on the job, they will be that much less priests. For priests to become engineers, doctors or airline pilots, just like the laity, will also have the same result. Therefore, it may be suggested that the rebellion against continence will not be successful. Indeed, it may well be over. In November, 1969, the Bishops of the United States formally endorsed compulsory celibacy for priests of the Latin Rite with the remark: "It is not only a legal requirement but a gift from Christ and a powerful aid to priestly service." Again, in early 1970, Pope Paul VI made what appears to be his final, flat refusal to soften the discipline, while John Cardinal Wright, prefect of the Congregation of the Clergy, ordered Roman Catholic priests throughout the world to make annual renewals of their vows of celibacy and obedience.

Meanwhile, the preoccupation with sex—not to say veneration of it—which seems to have been the movement's chief motivating force has become another mark of the American Church. Apparently, the old Catholic ideals of virginity in youth and chastity in marriage are one more pair of barnacles to be scraped away. Certainly, they are not in fashion, if one judges from the number of priests vowed to celibacy who busy themselves studying sexuality. In 1969, a pastoral of the American Bishops extolled "the value and necessity of wisely-planned education of children in human sexuality . . ." Immediately afterward, like a spring released and with a kind of eager gladness, the ladies and gentlemen of the Rosary and Altar Society or the Christian Family Movement began to organize classes in sex education. A decade earlier, the same people had been picketing theaters which showed "indecent" moving pictures or preparing "white lists" of bookstores which stocked only "wholesome" literature. In the sixties, however, they sat in solemn rapture while some psychiatrist with two or three ruined families of his own to his credit reverently unfolded to them the mysteries of the sex mechanism which would make theirs a happier marriage. To say this is not to mock or make light of truly unhappy people living marriages of despair or anguish or mutual hatred. For them the Church has begun to show a commendable compassion and concern, and to drop its old hostility to the teachings of Freud and Jung. What is objectionable, even comical, however, is to see the old Puritans turning to anti-Puritanism with all their unquenchable ardor, there to make a science or subject for instruction of something so natural as sex. Again, this is no bugle call to retreat to the sex-sad Jansenism of the old Catholic ghetto. One can only say good-bye and good riddance to a prudery grafted onto the American Church by an Irish priesthood trained in the Jansenist areas of France. But in getting rid of prudish modesty, it is not wise to eliminate modesty as well. Evidently, no one in the American Church seems to remember the Fathers' ancient warning that if man cannot obtain spiritual delectation he will seek sensual delectation, and too often under cover of a feigned "emancipation." Actually, the New Breed of Catholics would be more honest if they held a fertility rite. While the ladies are busy making sandwiches and identifying organs for the children, the men can go out and build a big phallus to erect over the church as a symbol of the new faith which only latterly seems to have replaced the cross they pulled down the day before.

And so, the problems of the Universal Church are reflected in the United States, where many Catholics are scandalized by the marriage of priests and nuns. Few of them realize that such unions are at least as old as Martin Luther and Kate von Bora, or that priestly defection and marriage in the American Church goes back to Doctor Wharton of post-Revolutionary days. If they are not new, however, they are certainly more numerous; and there is a perhaps more dangerous novelty in the general flight from the cloister. Since Vatican II so many monks and nuns have exchanged their habits for civilian clothes that the Official Catholic Directory for 1969 listed nine thousand less nuns than the 1968 edition. Meanwhile, such strongholds of discipline as the Society of Jesus have suffered collapses so spectacular that there are informed Catholics willing to suggest that in another decade there will be no more Jesuits in this country. Other rebellions have erupted among priests and nuns who joined the antiwar demonstrations of the late sixties. Some of them, of course, went rather too far, especially those priests whose pacifist theories induced young men to burn themselves alive in protest, or the ones who invaded federal property to burn draft records or deface them with duck's blood (which at first they had falsely maintained was their own). It is true that because of them the concept of the American Church of instant loyalty has finally been destroyed, and that Catholics are now in the mainstream of the American tradition of dissent. It may also be said of them, like their non-Catholic comrades, that they appear to know very little about war, foreign policy or good manners. Still, the sincerity of their anguish may provide a worthwhile stimulus toward rethinking the Catholic doctrine of a just war, especially with regard to the new era of war introduced by Communism's "national wars of liberation" or the morality of the tactics of guerrilla warfare.

Thus, in a state of constant flux and ferment, in a crisis of either growth or decay—only the future will know—an entirely new American Church turns toward the last three decades of the twentieth century. In the beginning, she had been the faith of the discoverers of this continent; and with the Spanish and French, she had been the Church of the missions to the Indians. Next she became in Maryland a sanctuary for the oppressed Catholics of England, as well as the first faith to grant religious toleration. There followed the post-Revolutionary period of a "quiet" Church with a distinct English base, a brief era of tranquillity which was shattered with the influx of Catholic immigrants from Europe. Thereafter, Catholicism in America was an urban Church of the Immigrant concentrated chiefly in what may be called the northeastern quarter of the country; and also, except for the short-lived ascendancy of priests from France, the spiritual preserve of an Irish hierarchy and priesthood. Now, she is apparently acceptably "American," a mainly suburban and middle-class Church established in all parts of the United States.

In the past, the American Church performed great services for the United States in the areas of education, Americanization of the immigrants, care of the poor and sick, service in wartime or defense of both democracy and public morality in the face of Communism and neo-paganism. All this she did while struggling against a deep and active prejudice which probably will persist until Catholicism ceases to be a minority.

As has already been suggested, that day may not be too distant. In 1970, Catholics represent 25 per cent of the population, they are one out of four, and they also make up about 40 per cent of the entire church enrollment in the country. Seldom in history has a steadily increasing group of that size failed to achieve dominance. If they have failed, it has usually been because of a successful persecution or military invasion, neither of which seems possible in the United States. Always, toward the end of a movement's struggle for supremacy—and *every* faith or creed seeks supremacy—there seems to have been a huge augmentation of "rice Christians," that is, people who feel that it will be to their profit to become converts, and inevitably, the bandwagon becomes a juggernaut. Whether or not this is a sign of health or corruption is beside the point. The fact is that this has happened repeatedly—in the Roman Empire of Constantine, in the once-Christian countries of the now-Islamic Middle East and in Reformation Europe and England—and it seems not only possible but probable that it will happen in the United States of the twenty-first century.

What Catholicism in the United States will have to pay for primacy cannot be stated with any hope of accuracy. It may, however, be remembered that Montesquieu once predicted that Protestantism would wither away, after which Catholicism would become Protestant. Bearing this in mind, recalling also how liberal Protestantism's attempt to Christianize secularism resulted in a secularization of Protestantism, it may be suggested that in its new emphasis on the social gospel, in its preoccupation with sex, its dissolving discipline, its abdication of moral authority and its own attempt to accommodate modernity, the American Church has already taken on much of the protective coloration of its environment. It is now thoroughly American, apparently riding the crest of the religious wave of the future, but whether or not it will still be Catholic remains to be seen.

Index